THE ORGANIZATION OF
BRITISH CENTRAL GOVERNMENT
1914 – 1956

THE ORGANIZATION
OF BRITISH
CENTRAL GOVERNMENT

1914–1956

*A Survey by a Study Group of
the Royal Institute
of Public Administration*

EDITED BY

D. N. CHESTER

WRITTEN BY

F. M. G. WILLSON

Ruskin House
GEORGE ALLEN & UNWIN LTD
MUSEUM STREET LONDON

FIRST PUBLISHED IN 1957

PRINTED IN GREAT BRITAIN
in 10 point Times Roman
BY SIMSON SHAND LTD
LONDON, HERTFORD AND HARLOW

In 1952 the Royal Institute of Public Administration embarked on a series of major research projects to be carried out by Study Groups. This book is the outcome of the first inquiry in the series.

The Executive Council of the Royal Institute wishes to record its thanks to the members of the Group who conducted the survey, and its appreciation of the contribution which they have made to the study of British Government.

PREFACE

THE Study Group which was responsible for this survey was composed of senior serving or former public officials, with two academic members. After Sir Henry Self, K.C.B., K.C.M.G., K.B.E., a Vice-President of the Royal Institute, had played a major part in getting the project started, Mr D. N. Chester, C.B.E., Warden of Nuffield College, Oxford, became Chairman. The other members of the Study Group were:

> Reginald W. Bell, Esq.
>
> Sir Robert Fraser, O.B.E.
>
> Sir Horace Hamilton, G.C.B.
>
> Sir Patrick Laird, K.B.E., C.B., F.R.S.E.
>
> Ernest Long, Esq.
>
> Dr A. H. Marshall, C.B.E.
>
> Sir John Maud, G.C.B., C.B.E.
>
> Professor W. A. Robson
>
> Dame Evelyn Sharp, D.B.E.
>
> Sir John R. Simpson, C.B.

Mr F. M. G. Willson was Secretary to the Group throughout, at first as a Research Officer of the Royal Institute and latterly while holding the Gwilym Gibbon Research Fellowship at Nuffield College. The late Sir Gwilym Gibbon was one of the most prominent early supporters of the Royal Institute and a benefactor of the study of public administration in Britain. It is very appropriate, therefore, that his name should be thus associated with this book.

The supervision of a project of this type is an onerous duty. The definition of purpose, the planning and shaping of the work – the grand strategy, if the phrase be preferred – has been the main responsibility of the Study Group as a whole. The execution – much of the detailed research and the bulk of the drafting – has been the primary task of the Secretary, Mr Willson. Inevitably both the Group and its Secretary have on occasion advanced into each other's territory, while the Chairman, Mr D. N. Chester, has played a leading part in both the basic thinking and the execution. The structure and scope of the survey are thus the results of a very real process of committee debate, and for them the members of the Group are ready to take their share of praise and blame. But the actual text of a work so much concerned with the details and lessons of history must in the end be the composition of one or two rather than of many contributors. The Chairman and Secretary have in fact taken responsibility for the precise wording of the text, and individual members of the Study Group are not necessarily in agreement with everything contained in it. The names of D. N. Chester and F. M. G. Willson appear on the title page because both the Royal Institute and the Study Group wish to give the fullest credit to them for the contributions they have made.

The reader may like to know something of how the work was undertaken. Each major government department contributed a memorandum on the changes which had taken place in its own field during the period since 1914. This information was supplemented by independent research, and first drafts of the various sections of the book were prepared. Those drafts were then discussed by the Study Group with 'witnesses', many of whom hold, or have held, high office in the Civil Service, or who have special knowledge of particular fields covered by the inquiry. The first drafts were then revised. Often the revised versions were sent for further comment to those who had already been consulted and to the departments, and on occasion to other knowledgeable persons. The sources of the Group's information are thus not merely documentary. In the course of some twenty meetings the Group culled much from the memories of people who have lived through the period and taken part in shaping the organization of the central government.

A great deal has therefore been done to ensure that the story is complete and accurate, but in dealing with such a multitude of detailed facts – and figures – it is too much to hope that there are no errors. There may, of course, also be some defects of interpretation, emphasis and general perspective to which the pioneer is prone. The Group regard this work, however, as a first attempt to bring together an enormous mass of information hitherto not systematically recorded: they trust that the inevitable shortcomings of the survey will be corrected in due course by students who will have access to sources which are still confidential and who will have the advantage of examining our period from the more detached standpoint of quarter or half a century hence.

The greater part of this book is a narrative of the growth and adaptation of institutions to meet changing political, social, economic and technical conditions. The Introduction is devoted to a description of the scope of the subject matter and to some problems of definition. Chapter I provides a general background with three 'panoramic' views of the central administration – at the beginning of the period (1914), in 1935, and at the end of 1956. Of the next eight chapters, seven deal with various fields of governmental activity and the eighth with the development of co-ordinative devices and institutions. Chapter X is neither part of the narrative nor an appraisal of administrative growth and organization over the last forty years: it is a discussion of the factors which influence the distribution of functions, together with reflections on the way in which problems of governmental organization can be handled. It is an analysis which draws to some extent on the earlier narrative but also introduces more general theoretical considerations.

To relieve the reader who is not concerned with the details of sources, etc., footnotes have been divided into two classes. Those which contain matter immediately relevant to the narrative are indicated by letters – *a*, *b*, etc. – and are printed at the foot of the pages: those which refer only to sources or which contain matter not so immediately relevant to the narrative, are indicated by numbers – [1], [2], etc. – and are printed together under chapter headings in Appendix A, beginning on page 367. A short Bibliographical Note, printed as Appendix B, supplements those references. There are no references in the text or footnotes to the statutory authorities under which many of the administrative changes have been made. These are recorded in Appendix C, where the changes made during the period are listed in chronological order.

Quotations from the various official publications mentioned in this book (other than House of Commons and House of Lords debates) are reproduced by permission of the Controller of H.M. Stationery Office.

The Study Group wish to thank a large number of people, particularly the 'witnesses' (whether they came to meetings or answered queries by correspondence). Among them were many Permanent Secretaries and other senior civil servants – serving or retired – and university teachers. The liaison officers appointed by each of the major departments gave invaluable aid – indeed the Group is most grateful to departments generally for much official help most willingly extended. The Group owe a special debt to Mr R. B. Moberly, until recently a member of the Machinery of Government Branch of the Treasury. He attended the majority of the Group's meetings, and his wide knowledge was of great benefit. In the earlier stages of the work, the Secretary had the assistance of Dr W. H. Oliver, now Lecturer in History at Canterbury University College, Christchurch, New Zealand.

The main burden of the clerical work was carried by the typing staff at Nuffield College, whose most efficient services were much appreciated by the Group.

The Group also wish to thank the Royal Institute of Public Administration for giving them the opportunity to conduct this survey, and in particular to thank its Director, Mr Raymond Nottage, for his ever-ready advice and help.

But the Group's greatest debt is to Mr F. M. G. Willson. He brought to the work the devotion and integrity of a scholar, and handled the Group's affairs and the large number of witnesses and officials with courtesy and unassuming efficiency. His indeed has been the major contribution.

CONTENTS

LIST OF TABLES AND DIAGRAMS

TABLES

DIAGRAMS

INTRODUCTION

THIS book is about the changes which have taken place in the broad organization of central government in Britain between the outbreak of the First World War in August, 1914, and the end of 1956. The years separating those dates comprise but a small part of the centuries over which the institutions of British Government have taken shape, though in the last four decades the rate of growth and change – in no small degree due to the impact of two World Wars – was perhaps unprecedented. Such long continuous historical development has ensured that our governmental institutions do not conform to a regular pattern but are involved and complicated, while their nomenclature is often baffling to the uninitiated. It is well nigh impossible to fit all our governmental institutions into a number of neat and unequivocal categories: there are always some which stand alone. Nor are students of those institutions ever likely to agree completely about either the scope of or even the titles to be given to any such categories. We have chosen to call the subject matter of our study the organization of central government: it is necessary, therefore, to discuss at the outset what we mean by 'central government' and by 'organization'.

We are not concerned here, except in passing, with the Crown, the two Houses of Parliament, or the work – as opposed to some aspects of the organization – of the Courts of Law. We are not concerned with local government or with the relations between central and local government. Nor do we deal with that large group of public authorities which are usually statutory and are sometimes called public boards or non-departmental bodies, whose rise to prominence – particularly in the form of huge industrial corporations – has been so marked a feature of the latter part of our period. These bodies are not wholly subject to ministerial and parliamentary control, and they are not staffed by members of the Civil Service. These characteristics put them outside the scope of this study. By 'central government' or 'central administration' (we use both terms in the text), we mean the government departments whose spiritual if not physical headquarters are to be found in Whitehall: for whose every action Ministers are directly and completely responsible to Parliament: and whose officers are, in all but a few exceptional cases, civil servants.

The basic pattern of the central administration is simple. First come the Ministers who form 'Her Majesty's Government'. The majority of them are 'departmental' Ministers, but there are a few whose titles – usually ancient, such as Lord Privy Seal – denote that they hold so-called sinecure posts carrying few or no departmental duties, though their parliamentary and other functions as members of the Government may be very important. The latter group are often called 'non-departmental' Ministers. For our purposes we are not including among Ministers the four Law Officers of the Crown – the Attorney General, the Lord Advocate, the Solicitor General and the Solicitor General for Scotland – nor do we include Ministers of State, Parliamentary Secretaries and Government Whips. The only junior Ministers who have come into our story are the Secretary for Mines and the Secretary for Overseas Trade, both of whom had definite statutory responsibilities.

The Ministers are assisted by departments. A departmental Minister is responsible for one or more departments: thus the Secretary of State for Commonwealth Relations has only the Commonwealth Relations Office, but the Chancellor of the Exchequer is responsible for several departments in addition to the Treasury. A department may have one of a variety of titles. If it is a large department established during the last half century it is quite likely to have the formal name 'Ministry', and the bigger departments are sometimes referred to collectively as 'Ministries'. There is no important constitutional distinction between the term 'Ministry' and the term 'Department', and as the latter has a wider application in practice it is usually preferred in this book.[a]

There are one or two complications which cannot be left as unexplained loose ends. In the first place there is a handful of departments which, for special reasons, have no ministerial chief. The Exchequer and Audit Department, of which the Comptroller and Auditor General is head, is one of these. This officer is independent of the Executive and responsible directly to Parliament for auditing, certifying and reporting on departmental accounts; and the Department works solely under his direction in assembling and examining the detailed material on which his audit and reports are based. There is also the Civil Service Commission, which selects each recruit to the Home and Foreign Services and in this task is independent of the

---

[a] The word 'Ministry' can also mean the Government of the day as a whole – i.e., all the Ministers together – though this usage is perhaps less common now than in the 19th century. 'Administration' is sometimes used in this sense, and both it and 'Ministry' are often employed by historians to describe Governments led by particular Prime Ministers – e.g., 'Gladstone's Second Ministry', 'Lord Rosebery's Administration'.

ministerial control which extends over general policy (e.g., over the determination of number and types of recruit), so that selection may be seen to be impartial and free from any hint of political patronage.

In the second place there is no single criterion by which to determine whether any given authority is a 'department' or not. There are a number of important organizations which have certain normal departmental characteristics and certain characteristics more usually found in the so-called non-departmental bodies. The National Assistance Board is the outstanding example of this at the present time: for establishment and financial purposes it is a department because it is staffed by civil servants and has its own parliamentary Vote for which the Permanent Secretary of the Board is Accounting Officer. It is at the same time non-departmental in so far as it is headed by a Board whose decisions on individual cases cannot be altered by a Minister. This Board is responsible for making recommendations as to the level and conditions of payment of national assistance. But responsibility for taking action on these recommendations rests with the Minister of Pensions and National Insurance, who has the power to reject the recommendations or to modify them, and who also speaks for the Board in Parliament.[b]

But despite the existence of a number of marginal cases, it is possible without too much equivocation to draw a line round about thirty major departments, together with some forty or fifty minor departments, and refer to them collectively as the central administration. (Lists of the departments are included in Chapter I.) However significant the non-departmental authorities may be or have been, the work of Ministers and the major departments has always been the core of British central government. The work of the various departments differs very much and their autonomy is real and important. But when taken together they form what is at any rate a far more homogeneous group than the non-departmental authorities. They share a number of common features of organization, they are nearly all staffed by the members of a unified Civil Service (who may pass from one department to another in the course of their careers), and they are bound by the collective responsibility of Ministers to co-ordinate their work so as to ensure that policies do not conflict. The extended scope of government has in recent years increased the amount of co-ordination which is necessary if collective responsibility is to be maintained, and departments are much more interdependent than they were in 1914. It is for these reasons that the

[b] The Unemployment Assistance Board and the Assistance Board—forerunners of the National Assistance Board—had a similar constitutional position.

broad departmental organization affords a notable and reasonably coherent theme for study.

By the 'organization' or 'structure' of central government (we use the terms interchangeably) we mean the number of departments and the distribution of functions between those departments. On the whole we do not deal with the internal organization and procedures of particular departments, although we have mentioned a number of major internal re-organizations and certain features of the organization of particular departments in order to clarify our account of the development of the main structure. The changes which mainly concern us are the creation and abolition of departments and the transfer of functions between departments. The word 'function' is of course commonly used very widely and loosely to mean anything from a whole field of governmental responsibility such as Defence to a relatively restricted section of work such as Factory Inspection or the payment of Children's Allowances. In this book, except when it is clear from the context that a wider meaning is intended, we use the word in its more limited sense.

I

THE CENTRAL ADMINISTRATION 1914-1956

THE POSITION IN 1914

AT the outbreak of the First World War the rôle of government in Britain was still widely regarded as embracing only the three classic activities – the maintenance of internal law and order, the defence of the realm, and the conduct of external relations. The widespread acceptance of free trade and economic *laisser faire* still cast central government, if not local government, in the character of referee rather than participant in commerce and industry. The social services existing in 1914 were largely the business of Local Authorities and the local Guardians of the Poor, though in the last few years the Liberals had introduced centrally administered Old Age Pensions, Unemployment Insurance and Health Insurance for a relatively small section of the community. But these innovations of the Liberal régime since 1905 had made no fundamental alteration to the late 19th century structure of central government. That structure was held together by a Cabinet which included practically all the departmental chiefs: by a Civil Service given shape by the vision of Northcote and Trevelyan and the dynamism of Gladstone: and by a highly developed system of financial control enforced by the Treasury, the Comptroller and Auditor General, and the Public Accounts Committee of the House of Commons.

There were twenty-one Ministers in 1914. Fifteen of them were clearly 'departmental' and four – the Prime Minister, the Lord Privy Seal, the Chancellor of the Duchy of Lancaster, and the Paymaster-General – were indisputably 'non-departmental'. The Lord President of the Council and the Lord Chancellor were, in a sense, borderline cases, but for the purposes of this study both are counted as departmental Ministers. The Lord President was in practice free enough of heavy administrative work in 1914 to be generally regarded as non-departmental, but he was responsible for a small department – the Privy Council Office – and we include him in the departmental group. The Lord Chancellor, too, had only a small personal Office at that time, but he is included in the departmental class because of the high importance of his extra-judicial duties.

TABLE I: THE CENTRAL GOVERNMENT IN 1914*

NON-DEPARTMENTAL MINISTERS

Prime Minister and First Lord of the Treasury   Lord Privy Seal   Chancellor of the Duchy of Lancaster   Paymaster General

DEPARTMENTAL MINISTERS AND THEIR DEPARTMENTS

FINANCE AND MISCELLANEOUS DOMESTIC ADMINISTRATION

Minister	Departments
Lord President of the Council	Privy Council Office
Chancellor of the Exchequer	Treasury
	Board of Customs and Excise
	Board of Inland Revenue
	County Courts Department
	Development Commission
	Exchequer Office (Scotland)
	Friendly Societies' Registry
	Government Chemist
	HM Stationery Office
	Insurance Commissions and Joint Committee
	National Debt Office
	Office of Parliamentary Counsel
	Paymaster General's Office
	Public Works Loan Board
	Remembrancer's Office (Ireland)
	Road Board
	Royal Mint
	Teachers' Pensions Office (Ireland)
	Treasury Solicitor

EXTERNAL AFFAIRS

Minister	Departments
Secretary of State for Foreign Affairs	Foreign Office
Secretary of State for the Colonies	Colonial Office
Secretary of State for India	India Office

DEFENCE

Minister	Departments
Secretary of State for War	War Office
First Lord of the Admiralty	Admiralty

SCOTLAND

Minister	Departments
Secretary for Scotland	Scottish Office
	Board of Agriculture for Scotland
	Fishery Board for Scotland
	Highlands and Islands Medical Services Board
	Local Government Board for Scotland

President of the Board of Education	Board of Education
President of the Local Government Board	Local Government Board Registrar General's Office
First Commissioner of Works	Office of Works

TRADE AND INDUSTRY

President of the Board of Agriculture and Fisheries	Board of Agriculture and Fisheries Office of Woods and Forests Ordnance Survey
Postmaster General	Post Office
President of the Board of Trade	Board of Trade

LAW, JUSTICE AND PUBLIC ORDER
(Mainly England and Wales)

Lord Chancellor	Lord Chancellor's Office Land Registry Public Trustee Supreme Court Offices
Secretary of State for the Home Department	Home Office Board of Control Prison Commission
Attorney General	Law Officers' Department Office of the Director of Public Prosecutions

Lord Advocate	Lunacy Commission and General Board of Control for Scotland Registrar General's Office (Scotland) Scottish Education Department Scottish Prison Commission Lord Advocate's Department

IRELAND

Chief Secretary to the Lord Lieutenant of Ireland	Irish Office Commissioners of National Education Congested Districts Board Department of Agriculture and Technical Instruction Endowed Schools Commission General Valuation Office Intermediate Education Board Land Commission Land Registry Local Government Board Office of Charitable Donations and Bequests Office of Public Works Prisons Board Registrar General's Office

* For a note on this table see following page.

The twenty-one Ministers controlled a non-industrial Civil Service some 270,000 strong.[a] The arrangement of the departments which employed these officials can best be seen from Table I. Here in the text we can indicate roughly the distribution of the Civil Service according to the major purposes of government. Already in 1914 the Post Office was a vast organization by any standards, employing a quarter of a million people, of whom about 209,000 were non-industrial civil servants. The rest of the departments at that time employed about 60,000 persons. No less than 20,000 of them were needed to collect taxes. Another 10,000 worked in the Service (i.e., defence) departments. Over 7,000, spread between London, Edin-

[a] Statistics of staff are quoted in this and the following chapters for the three years 1914, 1935 and 1956. There is no single set of figures which covers the whole of our period, but there is an official set for the years since 1935 which we have used and which differentiates between industrial and non-industrial civil servants on the basis of the classification used by the Treasury from 1946 onwards. This classification differs from the classification used in the 1930s, so that some of the figures quoted in this book for 1935 are not the same as the figures issued officially in that year. Thus the number of non-industrial civil servants employed by the Post Office on April 1, 1935, was given in the annual statement of *Staffs Employed in Government Departments* (Cmd. 4946/1935) as 199,350: but the figure given in Treasury statistics published since the Second World War and quoted here is 165,889. Over 30,000 employees in 1935 were thus classified at the time as non-industrial civil servants, whereas today they would be regarded as industrial civil servants. The departmental figures which are available for 1914 do not differentiate between industrial and non-industrial civil servants in every case. (The main source of the 1914 figures quoted here is a statement of *Staffs Employed in Government Departments* which was published as Cmd. 276 of 1919: the 1914 figures are for August 1 of that year.) Because of the changes in the bases of the statistics and because of occasional gaps, it has sometimes been necessary to interpolate freely, using figures given in the Annual *Estimates* of money required by the departments as a guide, in order that the totals for the three years quoted may be roughly comparable. The figures given in our tables are, therefore, not always exact, but they are sufficiently accurate to indicate the main distribution and movement of non-industrial staff.

NOTE TO TABLE I

Departments which cannot be placed unequivocally under particular Ministers have been omitted. For the constitutional positions of the Civil Service Commission and the Exchequer and Audit Department, see pages 16–17.

The Charity Commission was represented in the House of Commons by a non-ministerial Parliamentary Charity Commission, but the department came under Treasury control as regards its expenditure and establishment.

Though the Attorney General and the Lord Advocate are listed, they are not considered to be departmental Ministers for the purpose of this study. See page 16.

burgh and Dublin, were concerned with the maintenance of law and order and with legal services of various kinds. The departments whose main interests were economic, apart from the Post Office, employed about 9,000, most of them comprising the staff of the new Labour Exchanges administered by the Board of Trade. Of the remainder, the only substantial blocks which can be separated according to the major purposes of government were the 5,000-odd officials who belonged to departments mainly concerned with what are now called social services, and the handful – less than 1,000 – who dealt with external affairs.

As there was so little direct contact between the citizen and the central administration there were few departments which had any nation-wide network of local or regional offices. Again excluding the Post Office, only the offices of the Revenue Boards and the Board of Trade's new Labour Exchanges were to be found in every town, and it was the extent of these local organizations which made their parent authorities the largest employers of staff. Several other departments had outposts, but they were of a highly specialized nature, being mainly Inspectorates or other technical services, often concentrated in particular areas.

Much administration concerned the whole of the United Kingdom and was the business of authorities with a United Kingdom jurisdiction. Defence, external affairs and finance were dealt with from London, as were all economic matters concerning manufacturing and commerce, railways and shipping. Internal law and order, agriculture and fisheries, and those social services which were administered by Local Authorities, were the concern of separate departments in England and Wales, Scotland, and Ireland. There was a Scottish Office in London and an Irish Office divided between London and Dublin. Much of the domestic administration in Ireland and Scotland was carried on by departments which were located in the country concerned. Roughly 5,500 civil servants manned the departments in those countries, more than two-thirds of that number being stationed in Ireland (excluding the members of the Royal Irish Constabulary) and the rest in Scotland. There was no similar division of authority for Wales, which was regarded as part of a single unit with England for nearly all administrative purposes.[b]

---

[b] In the earlier part of the period covered by this study certain of the units of Irish and Scottish administration were in a rather peculiar constitutional position. Many of them were boards, and though for the sake of simplicity they have been treated here as being answerable to the Irish and Scottish Secretaries respectively, their exact relationship to the relevant Minister was in many cases somewhat equivocal.

THE IMPACT OF THE FIRST WORLD WAR 1914–1922

The period of upheaval which began in August, 1914, lasted well beyond the end of the fighting in November, 1918. In the administrative as in the political context the end of that period was marked by the fall of the Lloyd George Coalition in the autumn of 1922. The eight intervening years form the first of the three clear sections into which the recent administrative history of Britain divides itself. It was a time of rapid administrative change.

The main structural developments in central government during the years from 1914 to 1922 can be split into those which were clearly temporary and those which had a lasting significance. The temporary increase in the powers of the central government was enormous and spectacular: no less spectacular was the abandonment of most of the emergency powers, at high speed, in the years immediately following the Armistice. The huge demands of the armed forces for men and supplies were succeeded almost overnight in 1918 by a zealous policy of rapid demobilization, the cessation of armaments manufacture, and the hasty sale of surplus war material. These movements of expansion and contraction accounted for the temporary conversion of the War Office and Admiralty into departments with wide economic as well as military responsibilities: and for the short careers of an administrative colossus – the Ministry of Munitions – and of a less successful venture, the Ministry of National Service.[c] Under the stress of a siege economy the government took powers to ration food, to allocate raw materials, to control shipping and inland transport, to regulate external trade, and to stimulate agricultural production. For those purposes there were established Ministries of Blockade, Food, and Shipping, and a Food Production Department. In order to improve propaganda services there was for a short time a Ministry of Information, and for the purpose of planning the future a Ministry of Reconstruction made a brief appearance. All these temporary departments – and a host of other minor ones – set up to deal with temporary problems, were swept away within a year or two of the end of the war.

Needs which had their origin in war, and which led to the creation of new administrative departments, in some cases continued into peacetime, thus forcing the continuance of the departments. The Ministry of Pensions was set up to handle the enormous problem of dealing with the welfare of war-disabled servicemen and their

[c] The Minister of Munitions was the first Minister to be given the formal title 'Minister', and his department became the first 'Ministry'. See Table IV, p. 38, for the increase in the use of the title 'Minister' in later years.

dependants: a duty which required the attention of a separate department until well after a Second World War had added a similar but smaller social burden. The Air Ministry appeared when the Royal Air Force took its place alongside the two older Services, and the decision to retain the new Force as a separate Service ensured the Air Ministry's permanence.

It was not the immediate needs of war alone which accounted for the other changes which resulted in long-term administrative re-arrangements between 1914 and 1922, though the moods and circumstances of war and its aftermath certainly hastened some if not all of those re-arrangements. A long-felt anxiety about our need for scientific and technological progress lay behind the establishment of the Department of Scientific and Industrial Research under a Committee of the Privy Council in 1915–16. A perhaps inevitable break-away of the Board of Trade's big labour sections was given a wartime push which brought the Ministry of Labour into being. A long-standing inter-departmental dispute over responsibility for the promotion of external trade was settled in the midst of war by the creation of the Department of Overseas Trade, answerable jointly to the Foreign Secretary and the President of the Board of Trade. Pre-war ideas for the unification of central health administration came to fruition in 1919: the old Local Government Board gave place to the Ministry of Health which also swallowed up the two separate Insurance Commissions for England and Wales. A similar merger in Scotland followed. A Welsh Board of Health was set up and the Minister of Health was empowered to exercise such of his powers and duties through the Board as he though fit. Ideas of nationalization which came to nothing, financial troubles on the railways, and labour troubles in the mines, helped after the war to a further division of the Board of Trade's wide sphere of influence. In 1919 a Ministry of Transport was established, and in 1920 a Mines Department was set up, responsible to the President of the Board of Trade through a Secretary for Mines, but departmentally separate from the Board of Trade. By the end of 1922 practically all Irish administration had passed into the hands of the two new Irish Governments, though the Irish Office in London was not wound up until April, 1924.[d]

All these structural developments had been accompanied by heart-

---

[d] Since partition Northern Ireland has remained an integral part of the United Kingdom, but wide powers have been devolved on a local Parliament in Belfast. While some London departments have jurisdiction in Northern Ireland, most of the domestic administration of the area is handled by local departments responsible to the Northern Ireland Parliament. The history of that domestic administration does not come within the scope of this study.

searching about the work, status and internal organization of the Civil Service. As a result, the increased importance of establishment work was recognized, and in 1919 and 1920 a number of important changes in the organization and character of such work were made at the Treasury and throughout the departments. Another change of major significance was Lloyd George's decision on taking office in 1916 to fashion the Secretariat of the Committee of Imperial Defence into a War Cabinet Secretariat, and his later decision to continue the civil Secretariat in peacetime. Other administrative innovations symptomatic of the general spreading of the area of governmental influence were the establishment of the Government Actuary's Department, the University Grants Committee and the Forestry Commission.

INTER-WAR DEVELOPMENTS 1922–1939

The period of rapid change was followed by nearly two decades of comparative administrative stability. Only a few major structural alterations or innovations were made in the next seventeen years. In 1925 a Dominions Office was carved out of the Colonial Office – a diplomatic stroke bearing witness to the heightened international status of the senior partners in the British Commonwealth. In 1934 the Unemployment Assistance Board was set up to take over from the Ministry of Labour and from the Local Authorities responsibility for the care of able-bodied unemployed who had exhausted their insurance benefits. In 1936 a step towards a Ministry of Defence was taken with the appointment of a Minister for the Co-ordination of Defence.

Scottish administration was largely remodelled during the period. The Secretary for Scotland became a Secretary of State in 1926 and two years afterwards the Boards of Agriculture and Health for Scotland and the Scottish Prison Commission were reconstituted as Departments answerable to him. In 1939 the powers of these three departments and of the Scottish Education Department and the Fishery Board for Scotland were all vested in the Secretary of State, and henceforward exercised by him through four Departments – Home, Health, Agriculture and Education, with headquarters in Edinburgh. The term 'Scottish Office' until 1939 was usually meant to indicate the old office of the Secretary, most of whose duties were discharged after 1939 by the Scottish Home Department. Since 1939 'Scottish Office' has been used loosely to indicate either the whole organization controlled by the Secretary of State or his London headquarters.

A view of central government in 1935 might well be regarded as roughly typical of the period between 1922 and 1939. Nearly all the important inter-war changes had by then been made, while re-armament, which gradually increased the size of the Civil Service and made the distribution of staff by 1939 unrepresentative of the inter-war era as a whole, was just beginning.

THE CENTRAL ADMINISTRATION IN 1935

There were twenty-five Ministers in 1935, or twenty-six if a temporary post of Minister without Portfolio for League of Nations Affairs, which lasted from June to December of that year, is included. Apart from this special post there were four non-departmental Ministers, as in 1914, and twenty-one departmental Ministers, including the Lord Chancellor and the Lord President, whose administrative responsibilities had grown considerably since 1914. In addition there were the Secretaries for Overseas Trade and for Mines, who while being Parliamentary Secretaries none the less presided over small departments. The Secretary for Overseas Trade was responsible to the Secretary of State for Foreign Affairs and the President of the Board of Trade, jointly: the Secretary for Mines was responsible to the President of the Board of Trade. The number of departmental Ministers had thus increased by four since 1914, or by six if the two rather special Parliamentary Secretaries are included. The distribution of departments among the Ministers is shown in Table II.

The size of the Civil Service had undergone a proportionately much greater increase. There were over 303,000 non-industrial civil servants in 1935, and without the 166,000 employed by the Post Office this left 137,000 for the rest of the central administration as compared with about 60,000 in 1914 – an increase of some 225 per cent. The distribution of this official labour force reflected changes in the nature of governmental interests. The Revenue departments still had a large complement – over 36,000 – but that complement had not grown at the same rate as the complements of other sections of the administration. There were now more than 23,000 non-industrial officials in the Service departments, 34,000 in departments concerned with trade and industry, and at least 20,000 whose main job was to run social service departments. The number of civil servants concerned with law and order in Great Britain had risen to nearly 12,000. The external departments, though still employing only a tiny fraction of the total Civil Service, had more than doubled their staffs.

More contact was being made between the central administration and the individual citizen than had been the case in 1914. The social

TABLE II: THE CENTRAL GOVERNMENT IN 1935

NON-DEPARTMENTAL MINISTERS

Prime Minister and First Lord of the Treasury   Lord Privy Seal   Chancellor of the Duchy of Lancaster   Paymaster General
Minister without Portfolio for League of Nations Affairs (June to December, 1935)

DEPARTMENTAL MINISTERS AND THEIR DEPARTMENTS (a)

FINANCE, CENTRAL AND COMMON SERVICES AND MISCELLANEOUS DOMESTIC ADMINISTRATION

Lord President of the Council
Privy Council Office
Department of Scientific and Industrial Research
Medical Research Council
Agricultural Research Council

Chancellor of the Exchequer
Treasury
Board of Customs and Excise
Board of Inland Revenue
Development Commission
Exchequer Office (Scotland)
Friendly Societies' Registry
Forestry Commission (b)
Government Actuary
Government Chemist
HM Stationery Office
Import Duties Advisory Committee
National Debt Office
National Savings Committee
Office of Parliamentary Counsel
Paymaster General's Office
Public Works Loan Board
Royal Mint

LAW, JUSTICE AND PUBLIC ORDER (Continued)

Secretary of State for the Home Department
Home Office
Prison Commission

Attorney General (e)
Law Officers' Department
Office of the Director of Public Prosecutions

SOCIAL SERVICES

President of the Board of Education
Board of Education

Minister of Health
Ministry of Health
Registrar General's Office
Board of Control
Welsh Board of Health

Minister of Pensions
Ministry of Pensions

EXTERNAL AFFAIRS

Secretary of State for Foreign Affairs
Foreign Office

Secretary of State for the Colonies
Colonial Office

Minister	Department
	Scottish Savings Committee
	Treasury Solicitor
	University Grants Committee
First Commissioner of Works	Office of Works
TRADE AND INDUSTRY	
Minister of Agriculture and Fisheries	Ministry of Agriculture and Fisheries
	Crown Lands Commission
	Ordnance Survey
Minister of Labour	Ministry of Labour
Postmaster General	Post Office
President of the Board of Trade	Board of Trade
	Export Credits Guarantee Department
Secretary for Overseas Trade(c)	Department of Overseas Trade
Secretary for Mines(d)	Mines Department
Minister of Transport	Ministry of Transport
LAW, JUSTICE AND PUBLIC ORDER (Mainly England and Wales)	
Lord Chancellor	Lord Chancellor's Department
	County Courts
	Land Registry
	Pensions Appeal Tribunals
	Public Trustee
	Supreme Court Offices
Secretary of State for India	India Office
Secretary of State for Dominion Affairs	Dominions Office
DEFENCE	
Secretary of State for War	War Office
Secretary of State for Air	Air Ministry
First Lord of the Admiralty	Admiralty
SCOTLAND	
Secretary of State for Scotland	Scottish Office
	Department of Agriculture for Scotland
	Department of Health for Scotland
	Fishery Board for Scotland
	General Board of Control for Scotland
	Registrar General's Office (Scotland)
	Scottish Education Department
	Scottish Prisons Department
Lord Advocate(e)	Lord Advocate's Department

For notes to this table see following page.

services had been considerably extended: more people were eligible for the Unemployment and National Health Insurance Schemes and for contributory and non-contributory pensions: there was still a large number of war pensioners to look after and the great problem of mass unemployment had driven the Government to set up the new Unemployment Assistance Board. That Board and the Ministry of Pensions had country-wide organizations which took their place alongside the local Post Offices, Employment Exchanges and Tax Offices as outposts of Whitehall. Nearly 75,000 civil servants were employed by departments other than the Post Office which had extensive local organizations. There had been a notable increase since 1914 in the size of the total staffs of the Scottish departments.

MAJOR STRUCTURAL CHANGES 1939–1956

Unlike the war of 1914–18 and its immediate aftermath the years since 1939 have witnessed not merely the temporary dislocation caused by total war but also more fundamental change. In the first place, many special emergency powers taken by the State during the Second World War were retained for some years after the fighting stopped, in part because of the economic difficulties of the country and the disturbed condition of international relations, and in part because of the accession to power of a Labour Government dedicated to a close control of the national economy. In the second place the idea that the State should play a much more prominent and positive

---

NOTES TO TABLE II

(a) Departments which cannot be placed unequivocally under particular Ministers have been omitted. For the constitutional positions of the Civil Service Commission, the Exchequer and Audit Department and the Unemployment Assistance Board, see pages 16–17. The Charity Commission was represented in the House of Commons by a non-ministerial Parliamentary Charity Commissioner, but the department came under normal Treasury control as regards its expenditure and establishment. The Treasury Vote covered the expenditure of the Cabinet Office and the Office of the Parliamentary Secretary to the Treasury (the Chief Whip), but both offices were the particular concern of the Prime Minister.

(b) The Forestry Commission was represented in the House of Commons by a non-ministerial Parliamentary Forestry Commissioner, but ultimate ministerial control of the Commission rested with the Chancellor of the Exchequer.

(c) Responsible jointly to the Foreign Secretary and the President of the Board of Trade.

(d) Responsible to the President of the Board of Trade.

(e) The Attorney General and the Lord Advocate are not considered to be departmental Ministers for the purpose of this study. See page 16.

part in the economic and social life of the country than it had done before the war was accepted by all parties. To name the most striking aspects of this latter development, all Governments have since 1944 regarded the maintenance of a high and stable level of employment as one of their most essential duties and since 1948 they have administered a National Health Service and a scheme of social insurance far more comprehensive than any of the pre-1939 services. Central government since 1939 has, in short, come to exercise greatly extended powers, many of which are likely to remain for the foreseeable future.

The major structural changes which have occurred since 1939 have been so numerous and so closely related that it is impossible to treat the last sixteen years as comprising anything but a single period, and in any case we are too close to the events to be able to decide whether we have as yet reached or passed an administrative milestone comparable to the year 1922.

As we have seen, many of the structural changes in the central administration made during the First World War left little or no permanent trace. The same was not true of most of the innovations of 1939–45, partly perhaps because of the long continued difficulties of the post-war period and the application of those new ideas about the rôle of government which have been mentioned. Six major departments which were set up in or after 1939 did not survive after 1946 – the Ministries of Home Security, Economic Warfare, Information, Shipping, Aircraft Production, and Production. Of those six only the Ministry of Economic Warfare, like its 1914–18 counterpart the Ministry of Blockade, and the Ministry of Production, can be said to have contributed little to the departmental structure of post-war administration. The Home Office has taken over the civil defence work for which the Ministry of Home Security was responsible: the organization of governmental publicity has been continued by the Central Office of Information. The wartime Ministry of Shipping was merged early in the war with the Ministry of Transport, which then became the Ministry of War Transport before reverting to its more peaceful title in 1946. The Ministry of Aircraft Production was combined with another wartime creation, the Ministry of Supply, which as a military supply department seems destined to remain alongside the Service departments in the next period of administrative development.

Three other big new departments which were originally set up to meet the emergencies of war have remained in one form or other as permanent organizations. One of them is the Ministry of Supply. Another was the Ministry of Food, set up in 1939. It lasted as a separate department until 1955, when its continuing functions passed, in England and Wales, to a combined Ministry of Agriculture, Fisheries and Food, and in Scotland to the Secretary of State. The Ministry of Fuel and Power replaced the Mines Department in 1942. Its status has been enhanced since fuel problems have been so insistent and since the coal, gas and electricity industries passed into national ownership.[e]

The pressure for an extension of social services after the war led to several major administrative changes. In 1943 a Ministry of Town and Country Planning was established: eight years later it was combined with part of the Ministry of Health to form a Ministry of Local Government and Planning – a name changed to Housing and Local Government later in 1951. The Ministry of Health, which hitherto had performed most of its pre-1939 duties and also administered the new National Health Service, was left with the latter as its major duty. The comprehensive social security scheme envisaged in the Beveridge Report of 1942 needed a special department for its preparation and administration, and the wartime Government set up a Ministry of National Insurance in 1944. In 1953 that department took over the payments side of the old Ministry of Pensions, while the medical services provided by the latter were transferred to the Ministry of Health.

Military experience during the Second World War, with its stress on the increasing inter-dependence of the three Services, influenced the decision to create a Ministry of Defence in 1946. The need to give every assistance to the re-starting and extension of British civil flying was behind the establishment of the Ministry of Civil Aviation in 1945 – a department which was combined with the Ministry of Transport in 1953 to form the present Ministry of Transport and Civil Aviation. A crisis in the world supply of raw materials at the time of the Korean War will be remembered administratively by the short career of a Ministry of Materials which lasted from 1951 to 1954.

Apart from additions and mergers there were outright abolitions and some changes of status among the major departments. The independence granted to India, Pakistan and Burma made the India and Burma Offices superfluous as separate entities.[f] Similar developments led to the re-naming of the Dominions Office, which from 1947

[e] In January, 1957, the Ministry of Fuel and Power was re-named Ministry of Power. For details see footnote [o], p. 117.

[f] The Burma Office was set up as a separate department in 1937, but the same Minister – the Secretary of State for India and Burma – controlled it and the India Office.

became known as the Commonwealth Relations Office. Because of its new responsibilities in the manpower field the Ministry of Labour had been re-christened the Ministry of Labour and National Service in 1939. The Board of Education and the Office of Works were converted into Ministries of Education and Works respectively: the Unemployment Assistance Board became the Assistance Board in 1940 and the National Assistance Board in 1948. These changes of nomenclature marked real alterations in the scope of the departments.

THE CENTRAL ADMINISTRATION IN 1956

There are now twenty-nine Ministers, but this figure includes a Minister without Portfolio who was appointed in October, 1954, and whose post is unlikely to be permanent. The number of departmental Ministers, including the Lord Chancellor and the Lord President, is now twenty-four. The two Parliamentary Secretaries who between the wars had special departmental responsibilities for Overseas Trade and for Mines have disappeared. If those Secretaries were regarded as departmental Ministers, then the net increase since 1935 is only one: but if they are not considered of departmental status then there has been an increase of three departmental Ministers since 1935 and an increase of seven since 1914. Table III shows the present arrangement of Ministers and departments.

The departments other than the Post Office now employ over 385,000 non-industrial civil servants – nearly three times as many as the equivalent number in 1935 and over six times as many as the total staffs of these departments in 1914. Defence departments now employ 135,000. Departments concerned mainly with economic affairs other than the Post Office employ more than 60,000: roughly the same number is needed to administer the social services, and the same again to collect taxes. There has only been a small percentage increase since 1935 in the numbers concerned with the maintenance of law and order, etc., but the establishment of the external departments, though still less than 10,000, has grown by over three and a half times in the same period.

The growth of administration has not been confined to Whitehall, or indeed to London. It is broadly true to say that apart from the Treasury, the Ministry of Defence and the departments primarily concerned with external affairs, there is now scarcely a major central department without either a regional organization, or a local organization, or some other system of offices in the provinces. Some departments, like the Home Office, keep a regional organization going for the potential needs of civil defence, and this aspect of regional

B

TABLE III: THE CENTRAL GOVERNMENT IN 1956

NON-DEPARTMENTAL MINISTERS

Prime Minister and First Lord of the Treasury   Lord Privy Seal   Chancellor of the Duchy of Lancaster   Paymaster General

Minister without Portfolio (appointed October, 1954)

DEPARTMENTAL MINISTERS AND THEIR DEPARTMENTS (a)

FINANCE, CENTRAL AND COMMON SERVICES, AND MISCELLANEOUS DOMESTIC ADMINISTRATION

Lord President of the Council
- Privy Council Office
- Office of the Lord President
- Atomic Energy Office
- Department of Scientific and Industrial Research
- Medical Research Council
- Agricultural Research Council
- Nature Conservancy

Chancellor of the Exchequer
- Treasury
- Board of Customs and Excise
- Board of Inland Revenue
- Capital Issues Committee
- Central Land Board and War Damage Commission
- Central Office of Information
- Development Commission
- Exchequer Office (Scotland)

TRADE AND INDUSTRY (Continued)

Minister of Transport and Civil Aviation
- Ministry of Transport and Civil Aviation

LAW, JUSTICE AND PUBLIC ORDER (Mainly England and Wales)

Lord Chancellor
- Lord Chancellor's Department
- County Courts
- Judge Advocate General's Department
- Land Registry
- Lands Tribunal
- Pensions Appeal Tribunals
- Public Trustee
- Supreme Court Offices

Secretary of State for the Home Department and Minister for Welsh Affairs (d)
- Home Office
- Prison Commission

Minister of Works	Friendly Societies' Registry
	Government Actuary
	Government Chemist
	HM Stationery Office
	National Debt Office
	National Savings Committee
	Office of Parliamentary Counsel
	Paymaster General's Office
	Public Works Loan Board
	Royal Mint
	Scottish Savings Committee
	Treasury Solicitor
	University Grants Committee
	Ministry of Works

TRADE AND INDUSTRY

Minister of Agriculture, Fisheries and Food	Ministry of Agriculture, Fisheries and Food
	Crown Lands Commission (b)
	Forestry Commission
	Ordnance Survey
	Tithe Redemption Commission
Minister of Fuel and Power	Ministry of Fuel and Power (c)
Minister of Labour and National Service	Ministry of Labour and National Service
Postmaster General	Post Office
President of the Board of Trade	Board of Trade
	Export Credits Guarantee Department

Attorney General (e)	Law Officers' Department
	Office of the Director of Public Prosecutions

SOCIAL SERVICES

Minister of Education	Ministry of Education
Minister of Health	Ministry of Health
	Registrar General's Office
	Board of Control
	Welsh Board of Health
Minister of Housing and Local Government	Ministry of Housing and Local Government
	Welsh Office, Ministry of Housing and Local Government
	National Parks Commission
Minister of Pensions and National Insurance	Ministry of Pensions and National Insurance

EXTERNAL AFFAIRS

Secretary of State for Foreign Affairs	Foreign Office
Secretary of State for the Colonies	Colonial Office
Secretary of State for Commonwealth Relations	Commonwealth Relations Office

Continued overleaf

TABLE III (Continued)

DEFENCE	
Secretary of State for War	War Office
Secretary of State for Air	Air Ministry
First Lord of the Admiralty	Admiralty
Minister of Defence	Ministry of Defence
Minister of Supply	Ministry of Supply
SCOTLAND	
Secretary of State for Scotland	Scottish Home Department
	Department of Agriculture for Scotland
	Scottish Education Department
	Department of Health for Scotland
	General Board of Control (Scotland)
	Registrar General's Office (Scotland)
Lord Advocate (e)	Lord Advocate's Department

NOTES TO TABLE III

(a) Departments which cannot be placed unequivocally under particular Ministers have been omitted. For the constitutional positions of the Civil Service Commission, the Exchequer and Audit Department and the National Assistance Board, see pages 16–17.

The Charity Commission was represented in the House of Commons by a non-ministerial Parliamentary Charity Commissioner, but the department came under normal Treasury control as regards its expenditure and establishment. The Treasury Vote covered the expenditure of the Cabinet Office and the Office of the Parliamentary Secretary to the Treasury (the Chief Whip), but both offices were the particular concern of the Prime Minister.

(b) In December, 1956, the Crown Lands were renamed Crown Estate and placed under the control of a non-departmental authority, the Crown Estates Commissioners, who are subject to the direction of the Lord Privy Seal and the Secretary of State for Scotland on matters relating exclusively to England and Wales and Northern Ireland and to Scotland respectively, and to both of them jointly on other matters.

(c) Renamed Ministry of Power in January, 1957: for details see footnote o, page 117.

(d) For a change in ministerial responsibility for Welsh Affairs in January, 1957, see footnote g, page 37.

(e) The Attorney General and the Lord Advocate are not considered to be departmental Ministers for the purpose of this study. See p. 16.

organization is an inheritance from the Regional Commissioner system adopted during the Second World War. The trade and industry departments developed their regional offices when the war and post-war economic controls made it necessary to bring officials closer to the individual citizen or firm: while most of the controls have gone, part of the regional system remains. But the regional and local development most likely to be permanent – and which was probably inevitable, war or no war – is that which concerns the Social Services. To the Employment Exchanges of the Ministry of Labour and the offices of the National Assistance Board have now been added the offices of the Ministry of Pensions and National Insurance covering the country to provide a 'counter' service to the citizen. In addition to local and regional offices, several departments now have headquarters staff outside London. Altogether at the present time no less than 415,000 non-industrial civil servants – 65 per cent of the total – are based in the English provinces and in Scotland, Wales and Northern Ireland.

The re-arrangements in Scotland in 1939 have stood the test of time. A number of comparatively minor transfers of functions have taken place between United Kingdom and Scottish departments, while the emphasis all along has been on a greater delegation of authority to officials stationed in Scotland, whether answerable to the Secretary of State or to a Minister with a United Kingdom jurisdiction. The staffs of the Scottish departments now number well over 6,000 – more than double the 1935 figure. Various methods have been used to extend a degree of administrative devolution to Wales: a Welsh Office of the Ministry of Housing and Local Government has been established, and Wales is usually regarded as a single region for departmental purposes. The most publicized device in this context, however, was the decision of the Conservative Government in 1951 to make the Home Secretary also Minister for Welsh Affairs, and to give him a second Parliamentary Under Secretary who devotes his attention to Welsh interests.[g]

g When Mr Macmillan formed his Government in January, 1957, the general responsibility for Wales was transferred from the Home Secretary to the Minister of Housing and Local Government, who took the additional title Minister for Welsh Affairs and became personally responsible for matters affecting the Principality. A Parliamentary Secretary for Welsh Affairs was not appointed.

TABLE IV

USE OF THE TERM 'MINISTER' IN THE TITLES OF DEPARTMENTAL MINISTERS

1914	1935	1956
SECRETARIES OF STATE		
Home Department	Home Department	Home Department*
Foreign Affairs	Foreign Affairs	Foreign Affairs
Colonies	Colonies	Colonies
War	War	War
India	India	Air
	Air	Commonwealth
	Dominion Affairs	Relations
	Scotland	Scotland
OTHER TRADITIONAL TITLES		
Lord Chancellor	Lord Chancellor	Lord Chancellor
Lord President of the Council	Lord President of the Council	Lord President of the Council
Chancellor of the Exchequer	Chancellor of the Exchequer	Chancellor of the Exchequer
First Lord of the Admiralty	First Lord of the Admiralty	First Lord of the Admiralty
President of the Board of Agriculture and Fisheries	President of the Board of Education	Postmaster General
President of the Board of Education	Postmaster General	President of the Board of Trade
President of the Local Government Board	President of the Board of Trade	
Postmaster General	First Commissioner of Works	
President of the Board of Trade		
First Commissioner of Works		
Secretary for Scotland		
Chief Secretary to the Lord Lieutenant of Ireland		
MINISTERS		
None	Agriculture and Fisheries	Agriculture, Fisheries and Food
	Health	Defence
	Labour	Education
	Pensions	Fuel and Power†
	Transport	Health
		Housing and Local Government
		Labour and National Service
		Pensions and National Insurance
		Supply
		Transport and Civil Aviation
		Works

* Secretary of State for the Home Department and Minister for Welsh Affairs. For a change in ministerial responsibility for Welsh Affairs in January, 1957, see footnote g, page 37.
† Renamed 'Power' in January, 1957. See footnote o, page 117.

II

FINANCE, TRADE AND INDUSTRY

THE STATE AND THE NATIONAL ECONOMY
1914-1956

Laisser faire has never been fully acceptable to British Governments, but the view that the State should, as a general rule, have as little as possible to do with matters of finance and economics was for most of the 19th and early 20th centuries the orthodox ideal of at the very least a large and powerful minority. Though the first manifestations of what Dicey called 'collectivism' may be found not long after 1860, even in 1914 it remained largely true that the main work of government still only comprised the three classic functions – the maintenance of internal order, the defence of the realm, and the conduct of external relations. Nor had nearly a decade of Liberal administration after 1905 brought the organization of government into substantially closer contact with financial, commercial and industrial interests. The Liberals wanted social reform, and in pursuing that goal they introduced schemes for Old Age Pensions, for health and unemployment insurance, and for the provision of labour exchanges, which had direct, though before 1914 relatively small, effects on the economy and finances of the nation. But such effects were, so far as the Liberals were concerned, merely incidental to their main purpose of improving the lot of the poor and unemployed. Government did not subscribe to the idea that the State should help the business man, save by enforcing honest and orderly trade procedures, by providing some minor services such as collecting and distributing commercial intelligence from overseas, and by organizing a few trade exhibitions. The Liberals fought fiercely the movement to impose tariffs, and while one Radical wing wanted to nationalize the land, the party as a whole shared with their main political opponents a complete lack of interest in any proposals for the nationalization of industries. Apart from the Post Office, the Service departments with their ordnance and dockyard establishments, and a few other minor exceptions, the central government had no trading or industrial interests. At local level, where 'gas and water socialism' had made considerable headway, and where institutions such as the Port of London Authority heralded the later development of new forms of public ownership, the State was more heavily involved in industry and commerce. But in the main, the measurable increase of governmental participation in financial and economic affairs during the first fourteen years of the 20th century was not enough to alter the basic 19th century conception of what the State should and should not do in that context. And there was no suggestion in 1914 that the national economy could – let alone should – be 'managed' by the central government.

The development of governmental control over the national economy in time of total war has as its central theme the overriding need to concentrate production and imports on commodities urgently required for prosecuting the war and, complementary to this, to reduce the consumption of all other commodities to the minimum possible – or at least to the minimum which consumers will tolerate. There was such a development in 1914–18, but the circumstances were so unprecedented and unexpected that the development was of a piecemeal kind, never complete in its coverage of economic activity, and a high degree of efficiency was only achieved in the last year of the war. This spasmodic progress was mainly due to the early disbelief in a long war and the consequent desire to interfere with the existing order as little as possible. 'Business as Usual' was the slogan and aim in some quarters. As the speedy ending of the war became quickly more and more remote, and as the situation became more critical, a sense of extreme urgency supervened and promoted the adoption of all and any measures which seemed expedient. Controls were piled on controls: every trade and every citizen was affected. Government became not only a regulator of economic action but a director of economic effort and a giant practitioner in industry.

Under the terrible stress of the war – a war which to a generation brought up in a buoyant atmosphere of peace and progress had been almost unthinkable – this new rôle of government was accepted, and indeed, once the harsh realities of the situation had been revealed, was demanded. But the economic faith of at least two generations does not vanish overnight, nor even in four years of war. It was potent enough after the Armistice was signed to support a vast work of demolishing controls. This violent reversal was not, however, a result of weighing the advantages and disadvantages of governmental 'intervention' carefully in the balance and then rejecting the whole conception: nor was it the result of any very profound theoretical belief in the evils of such intervention. It was rather the reaction of a generation which thought of the pre-1914 system as perfectly normal, and which longed to return to normal and familiar ways of living. Moreover the retention of much of the control system introduced during the war was impracticable because of the institutional character of the controls themselves. In the desperate circumstances of the times, industrialists and traders had been invited to work for the Government and had been given practically *carte blanche* to make what internal administrative arrangements they liked. On the highly personal arrangements which often resulted nothing permanent could be based. A war machine had been created which was of no use for any other purpose. The need to clear it away and the desire of its businessmen leaders to get back to their own jobs were complementary.

The upsurge of enthusiasm for economic freedom after 1918 thus swept away restraining regulations and was too strong for most of the tendencies towards permanent control and public ownership of such activities as coal mining and the railway service, which had made some progress during the war years. It left the experience of the government in economic control in the First World War a rather isolated phenomenon, not very closely related to what came immediately afterwards, though the study of that experience and some of the contacts made between government, financial, industrial and commercial interests were to contribute towards the improved machinery of economic control in the Second World War. Nonetheless, the State came out of the period of decontrol with more functions in regard to financial and economic affairs than it had been endowed with in 1914, and henceforward, though the pace was rarely steady, the movement towards more and more contact between government on the one hand and financial and economic interests on the other hand was to continue unchecked for a quarter of a century.

A degree of protection and subsidy was introduced during the 1920s. The cause was threefold: a fear of shortages which might follow the outbreak of a further war, a desire to shelter new industries from foreign competition, and the hope of preventing unemployment. The Dyestuffs Act of 1920 prohibited the importation of dyes except under licence: under the Safeguarding of Industries Act, 1921, tariffs could be imposed in order to protect key industries and to counteract the practice of 'dumping': subsidies were paid to the domestic sugar beet industry and to civil air lines: the film industry was aided by the introduction of an Act of 1927 making it obligatory for a quota of British-made films to be exhibited every year. Among steps taken to counter and relieve heavy and persistent unemployment was the launching of small programmes of public works and the extension of unemployment insurance and assistance.

Alongside these mainly fiscal innovations came some new State trading ventures. A programme of afforestation and reafforestation, mainly with the strategic need of a reserve of timber in mind, was entrusted to a Forestry Commission established in 1919. In the same year the central government entered the field of commercial insurance when it established the Export Credits Scheme under which the government guaranteed bills drawn by traders in respect of exports to foreign countries. In 1926 a Central Electricity Board was set up to control the generation of electricity and to build and operate a national transmission grid. (An extended scheme for regulating the electricity industry had been entrusted to a semi-judicial Electricity Commission in 1919.)

In sum, however, the extent of actual intervention during the 1920s was quite small. Perhaps more important than the practical developments was the change in attitude towards the idea of governmental intervention in financial and economic affairs. By the end of the decade anxiety about the condition of the British economy and serious doubts as to the validity of long-accepted economic dogmas were growing among more moderate thinkers than those of the extreme Left. Representative of these new views is an extract from a publication of 1928, *Britain's Industrial Future*, by a group of prominent Liberals:

'The theory that private competition, unregulated and unaided, will work out, with certainty, to the greatest advantage of the community is found by experience to be far from the truth. The scope of useful intervention by the whole Society, whether by constructive action of its own, or by regulating or assisting private action, is seen to be much larger than was formerly supposed.'

Perhaps more powerful than shifts of intellectual opinion, however, were the pressures in favour of State intervention brought to bear by particular depressed interests, such as agriculture and the coal and cotton industries, for legislation which both the employers and employees concerned believed would improve their economic position.

All this was reinforced by the onset of the Great Depression, and the small advance of government into the commercial and industrial fields was not merely consolidated but considerably extended. The ineffectual attempts of Ramsay MacDonald's second Administration to cope with mass unemployment, the financial crisis of 1931, the abandonment of Free Trade and the decision to re-arm, all these were milestones on the road along which government progressed towards an increasingly close interest in economic affairs. Below the level of immediate concern for the vast and dominant problem of unemployment lay a widespread conviction that much could be achieved by a large-scale re-equipment of industry and by the adoption of modern production and distribution techniques. The new fiscal and economic policy of the early 1930s – a measure of protection and other financial assistance – was adopted in the hope that manufacturing industry would use the opportunities offered to modernize its plant and methods, while Parliament actually provided the legislative basis for a considerable internal reorganization of agricultural marketing.

Innovations in the early 1930s thus followed the lines sketched out tentatively in the previous decade. The Import Duties Act of 1932 imposed a general tariff of 10 per cent on all imports other than those scheduled in a free list (e.g., practically all the major food imports) and imports from the Dominions: it also provided for the imposition of additional duties in cases where particular industries could prove a real need, so long as such added protection did not result in monopolistic exploitation or gross inefficiency. The policy of financial assistance introduced for beet sugar and civil aviation in the 1920s was extended to industries which, it was feared, might easily collapse without some such help. The two most important ventures concerned shipping and agriculture. By the British Shipping (Assistance) Act of 1935 a sum of two million pounds was set aside for the payment of subsidies for tramp voyages on condition that internal competition was reduced by agreement, while a 'scrap and build' scheme was laid down in order to encourage shipowners to improve and modernize their fleets, the Government offering to make advances for such work.

Government aid to agriculture involved the creation of an extensive administrative structure within the industry itself. The background to the agricultural legislation of the 1930s is supplied by the inferior marketing of British products compared with foreign, and by the poor and highly individualistic marketing organization of British producers, among whom co-operative schemes had never made much progress. An Act of 1931 aimed at introducing some form of marketing organization which would prove tougher than voluntary schemes, which would prevent some producers from both avoiding the responsibilities and reaping the benefits of co-operation, which would redress the balance between the producers on the one hand and the distributors and processors on the other hand, and which would bring to producers the benefits of large-scale organization. Little or nothing was done to implement this legislation until 1933, when the Government agreed to protective regulation of imports. Producer marketing boards with a 'statutory and inviolable monopoly' were afterwards set up for a number of products and were joined later by three Commodity Commissions which disbursed grants and subsidies for wheat, sugar and livestock. In the years immediately prior to the Second World War 'there was hardly a major product of British agriculture that was not the subject of a subsidy'.[1]

It is unnecessary to make an exhaustive record of all the other aspects of governmental intervention in the 'civilian' economy of the 1930s. It is worth noting, perhaps, the deliberate attempt launched in 1936 to improve the position of the cotton spinning industry by a statutory scheme for eliminating redundant spindles. In another direction, the public ownership and control of transport undertakings were extended by the establishment of the London Passenger Transport Board in 1933 and British Overseas Airways Corporation in 1939.

The developments of the inter-war period outlined so far were almost all products of a conviction that the State should make itself responsible for relieving economic distress and for initiating a re-habilitation of the nation's commercial and industrial equipment. This new attitude was stimulated from 1934 onwards by the process of rearmament, even though that process was by no means given high priority until 1938. Planned, extensive re-equipment of the Air Force, the Navy and the Army, in that order, brought the military administrative machine into close contact with industry.

By 1939, therefore, the character of governmental functions in this context was very different from what it had been twenty-five years before. Nor was the change merely quantitative. The demands of certain business interests for State intervention on their behalf, the contacts made in 1914–18 between government and the business world, the changing public attitude towards the idea of governmental intervention in financial and economic affairs, the extension of public ownership and management and of public trading, and the widening knowledge of commercial affairs within the Civil Service, all combined to close what had been before 1914 an apparently unbridgeable gap between government and the business community. And behind all this was what was to prove to be, in the near future, an even more significant factor: the evolution of new economic theories which were to give to the State a far more prominent rôle than it had hitherto claimed.

The onset of another World War in 1939 marked the beginning of the second period of siege economy in thirty years. The problem was basically the same as in 1914–18, but the controls were much more comprehensive. The experience of the First World War, the substantial planning which had been done during the 1930s in preparation for war, and rearmament which had to some degree geared parts of the nation's industry to a war programme, facilitated the transition.

Many basic controls were enforced immediately war broke out, and though there was no small amount of confusion as more and more of the economy came under governmental supervision, the whole process was much more successful than it had been in 1914–18, perhaps to some extent because people were more aware of what total war would mean and therefore more willing to accept controls.

A detailed account of the wartime economy and the part which government played in it is not needed here. What is more important in our context is to see what happened during and as a result of the war to prevent government from 'reversing engines' as it did in 1918–21.

In May, 1944, the Coalition Government published a White Paper on *Employment Policy*.[2] This was a revolutionary document. The leaders of the three main political parties said that the maintenance of a high and stable level of employment was accepted as one of the primary aims and responsibilities of British Governments. The White Paper also stated that this aim was to be approached by way of maintaining total expenditure – public and private – by operating on its various components, e.g., investment and government expenditure. There was also an important reference to securing a rising standard of living.

The White Paper was a most important landmark in the relations between government and the national economy and has remained the background of domestic policy to the present day. The White Paper had, however, gone on to say that any Government during the transition from war to peace would have to take steps to guard against inflation, to secure the production and equitable distribution of essential supplies, and to avoid balance of payments difficulties. These three factors, rather than any immediate need to prevent unemployment (which has been negligible since 1945), have shaped most governmental activities in the economic field in the ten years after the war.

For six years after 1945, under a Labour Government, a considerable mass of physical controls similar in type to those established during the war was in operation, and through those controls government was able to keep closely in touch with the individual units of trade and industry and direct their efforts as much as possible to exports. The Bank of England and several basic industries were nationalized. Subsidies on foodstuffs were continued and a decentralized control of agricultural operations was established which provided farmers with guaranteed markets and assured prices. The social services were greatly expanded and new ones were launched which, together with the needs of defence, added heavy burdens of public expenditure. There was a notable extension of regulatory and consultative governmental functions in relation to trade and industry. The location of industry was subjected to closer control, primarily in the interests of the pre-war depressed areas: a special Commission was set up to investigate monopolies and restrictive practices: and industries were encouraged to consider their problems and measures for improving productivity through the establishment of Working Parties and Development Councils.

The continuation of many war-time restrictions and the establishment of new services of an economic nature was, however, accompanied after 1945 by some relaxation of controls which had reached their peak in the later stages of the war. As economic conditions improved the physical controls gradually decreased, and after the Conservatives came to power at the end of 1951 with a different political philosophy those controls mostly disappeared. The Conservatives also reversed the trend towards public ownership: denationalization of iron and steel was started, much of the long-distance road haulage business was returned to private hands, and the statutory monopoly of scheduled air services by the publicly owned airlines was relaxed. But the advent of a Government less addicted to intervention in economic and financial affairs did not mean a return to 1939, let alone to 1914. The Conservatives preferred to manage the economy by fiscal means and by allowing the price system to operate more freely rather than by a combination of fiscal measures with physical controls: what is more significant is that they still intended to manage it in so far as this was needed to maintain employment and balance the country's overseas trade.

At the end of 1956 the general position can be stated in this way. The country has not long emerged from an extended period of numerous governmental controls involving rationing, licensing of building, allocation of raw materials, price control, etc. The Conservative Government is against the renewal of these methods of controlling production and distribution and prefers either to let market forces take their course or to act through the more traditional fiscal and financial measures. The maintenance of a high and stable level of employment is a goal of public policy. Other goals which have so far been more difficult to achieve are the permanent satisfactory state of the country's balance of payments, and the maintenance of stable prices.

Before bringing this sketch of the changes in the relationship between government and the business world to a close, it is as well to consider certain developments within the sphere of industry and commerce which have helped in themselves towards a closer liaison.

During our period individual trade unions have become stronger, while the trade union movement as a whole has come to take a major part in economic affairs. The employers' side was less coordinated in the early years, but the growth of large-scale business and especially the development of trade associations have helped to establish national representation of commerce and industry through institutions which parallel the trade unions. It is in fact through the twin bureaucracies of employers' and employees' organizations that government keeps in touch with trade and industry, rather than through direct contact with individual units. No attempt has been made to develop a hierarchical structure of consultative and advisory organizations for bringing government, employers and unions together, but in recent years two very important representative bodies – the National Production Advisory Council on Industry, and the Minister of Labour's National Joint Advisory Council – have come to be regarded as major forums for informed discussion of government economic policy and industrial problems.

The rise of this representation of management and labour is symbolic of a deeper change which was given a great impetus by the Second World War and its economic effects. What evolved during that war and what, despite all political changes, has continued and is likely to continue, was a mutual realization of the benefits which might accrue to the nation by a partnership between government and commercial and industrial interests. While such a relationship cannot and should not be over-emphasized, the appreciation that government is closely concerned with the economy, and that it is in the general interest of commerce and industry that it should be so concerned, ensures that the atmosphere in which the financial and economic activities of government are carried on today is very different from what it was in the 1930s, and totally different from what it was in 1914.

If an attempt was made to present the changes in the extent of governmental intervention in financial and economic affairs graphically, the graph would show a sharp rise from the low level of 1914 to a peak in 1917–18, followed by an equally steep drop in 1919–21 to a level not very much higher than that of 1914: then a long, gradual but fairly steady climb to 1939 and subsequently a rapid ascent to a second peak which lasted from about 1941 to 1945 and reached a greater height than that attained in the First World War: the slope downwards from the second peak would be very gentle to the limit of the graph in 1956, the final level being considerably above that of 1939. With the shape of this imaginary graph in mind, we may turn to the corresponding developments in administrative structure.

SOME DEFINITIONS AND
INTRODUCTORY CONSIDERATIONS

If this chapter was to deal with every administrative development which has been in any way concerned with, or in any way a reflection of, the growing functions of government in relation to financial and economic affairs, then it would not be a chapter but a book in itself, and it would necessarily cover the work of many departments whose primary interests are not usually considered to be economic or financial. Departments concerned with defence and with the social services are the biggest spending departments of government, and their expenditure inevitably has a vital bearing on the national economy as a whole. But they are not departments which in an administrative context are generally referred to as being 'economic' or 'financial' in character. These latter headings are normally reserved for those departments whose primary business it is to regulate, to facilitate, and to advise on the processes of production and exchange – trade, industry, agriculture, fisheries, transport and communications, the exploitation of natural resources, and those aspects of finance which are of direct concern to the central government.

Finance in British central government spells the Treasury, the Revenue departments, and a group of small, specialized financial organs, all ultimately responsible to the Chancellor of the Exchequer, and henceforward this group of authorities is described by the term 'financial departments'. Each of the other departments dealt with in this chapter is (or was) concerned with either agriculture or with one or more industries, or with transport, or with some special aspects common to all economic activity, such as employment. These departments are henceforward referred to collectively as 'trade and industry departments'.

Vast changes have occurred since 1914 in both 'finance' and 'trade and industry', but while they have led to relatively little inter-departmental (as opposed to intra-departmental) change on the financial side, they have since 1914 forced radical alterations of the number, size and arrangement of the trade and industry departments. Because of this difference in the scale of inter-departmental change, and because of the different functions of the two sets of departments, each is best treated separately: 'finance' in a single short section dealing with the whole period since 1914, 'trade and industry' in four much longer sections describing developments in each of the three main chronological divisions – 1914 to 1922, 1922 to 1939, and since 1939 – with a concluding section on the position at the end of 1956.

Separate treatment of financial and trade and industry departments does, of course, ignore the supremely important developments since the Second World War whereby Governments have accepted responsibility for maintaining a high and stable level of employment and whereby the Budget has become a major instrument of economic as well as of fiscal policy. The major institutional manifestations of this development are, however, a few highly specialized organs of economic intelligence and advice, whose history can easily be treated quite separately from the history of the financial and trade and industry departments, though some of it is in the later stages part of the history of the Treasury. The arrangements for making economic policy are, moreover, in essence arrangements for co-ordinating several organs of advice and administration: as such they find a place in Chapter IX.

THE FINANCIAL DEPARTMENTS 1914–1956

Despite the importance of financial administration and the great increase in governmental revenue and expenditure, the general pattern of the administrative units concerned with financial affairs has remained largely unaltered during the past forty years. Stages of development have not been marked by the splitting up of one major department into two, or by the merging of a number of authorities into a single institution, or even by notable transfers and re-transfers of work. We cannot stray far into either a detailed examination of the growth of financial work, or of the internal changes within existing departments. Nor, as there has been relatively little structural change and few inter-departmental transfers, is there much point in telling the story in strict chronological sequence. Instead it may be sufficient for our purposes to describe the organization of financial administration in broad outline, indicating where necessary the main developments of the period.

Finance, as a field of administration, is not easy to define. It is as well, perhaps, to begin by dismissing briefly some marginal topics. The national implications of local finance naturally enough affect the central financial departments, but the handling of the general questions of local government finance has never been entrusted to a 'finance' department. In England and Wales the Local Government Board until 1919, the Ministry of Health from then until 1951, and since 1951 the Ministry of Housing and Local Government have made those questions their special responsibility – a responsibility which extends to the audit of Local Authority accounts. In Scotland the Scottish Office before 1939 and the Scottish Home Department since have had similar responsibilities. The only recognized 'financial' department which is entirely concerned with local government is the Public Works Loan Board, from which Local Authorities may borrow at rates fixed by the Treasury. The Board is a statutory body for which the Chancellor of the Exchequer has parliamentary responsibility.

The audit of the accounts of the central departments has rested throughout our period with the Exchequer and Audit Department and an independent Comptroller and Auditor General, reporting to the Public Accounts Committee of the House of Commons.

The main financial powers of the central government are entrusted to the Chancellor of the Exchequer. He does not, however, exercise his powers through a single department. His principal department is the Treasury, but the Treasury is at once more and less than a Ministry of Finance. Partly because the Prime Minister is the nominal head of the 'Treasury Board', partly because of a British conviction that the authority responsible for raising public funds should also have a say in how these funds are spent, and partly for other reasons of historical development, the Treasury has a unique constitutional position: it is, in the words of Sir Edward (now Lord) Bridges, 'in some sense the Department which is the headquarters of civil government or perhaps of all the government'.[3] Moreover it is not easy to say exactly what the Treasury comprises: because of its miscellaneous interests and its numerous subordinate departments, its boundaries may be drawn in a number of different places to suit different purposes. In this chapter we are not concerned with those parts of the Treasury or with those of its outlying subordinate departments which are totally divorced from financial work, like the Treasury Solicitor or the Office of the Parliamentary Secretary to the Treasury (the Chief Whip's Office). Consequently we cannot consider at this stage the position of the Treasury as the 'central' department: nor, as has already been explained, will this chapter deal with the new work of the Chancellor of the Exchequer in the field of economic policy.

Even with its subordinate departments, however, the Treasury is not a complete Ministry of Finance. It has no administrative machinery for raising funds, nor does it have officers stationed in every executive department to watch how money is spent. The tax machinery is provided by two separate establishments, the Boards of Customs and Excise and of Inland Revenue, which are responsible to the Chancellor of the Exchequer and work in close touch with the Treasury on Budget matters. The finance branches of departments have never been part of the Treasury, however close their relations with it may be or have been.

So far as financial administration means the work of government in connection with general fiscal policy and the regulation of national financial practices such as banking and currency, national debt, taxation, borrowing, etc., it was performed in 1914 by the Treasury, the Revenue Boards, the National Debt Office, the Public Works Loan Board and the Royal Mint. Since 1914 there have been few permanent additions to this list. The National Savings Organization, which was launched in 1916–17, is led by two Committees, one for England and Wales, the other for Scotland. The first Capital Issues Committee lasted from 1915 to 1919. The present Committee grew out of a Foreign Transactions Advisory Committee first set up in 1936. It advises the Treasury on applications for capital issues, which require consent under the Borrowing (Control and Guarantees) Act, 1946. This is a permanent statute, but questions are raised publicly from time to time whether the Committee should continue permanently.

The only other notable but temporary addition to the financial machinery was an independent body, in form advisory – the Import Duties Advisory Committee – whose establishment followed the adoption of protection. Its short career lasted from 1932 until 1939. In accordance with the terms of the Import Duties Act, 1932, the Committee had to consider applications for the imposition of duties on goods additional to the general duty of 10 per cent, or for the exemption of goods from the general duty. The Committee advised the Treasury, but the latter could not act without the Committee's recommendation or impose duties heavier than those recommended by the Committee. The Committee had, in fact, 'enormous powers' because it could 'insist upon conditions in return for the grant of protection'. Its constitutional status was due to a desire

'to remove the determination of the details of tariff policy away from political influence, by the device of referring the whole subject to an independent authority not responsible to a minister and Parliament. The Chairman and members of the Committee held salaried appointments, and they were assisted by a numerous staff of permanent Civil Servants. In fact in all respects except that of ministerial responsibility they were an ordinary, if small, Government Department.'[4]

It was the practice of the Bank of England after the First World War to act in close conjunction with the Treasury, and its nationalization in 1946 – at least in the form that it took – was a less spectacular change than the nationalization of the coal and iron and steel industries. The Bank since 1946 has in any case had a constitutional

position akin to that of a public corporation, and it is not regarded as an integral part of the central administration.

It is within the Treasury and the Revenue departments that the effects of the increased financial interests of government have been most marked. The growth of work has been phenomenal, as the mere size of the Budget shows. The major additions to the work of the Treasury have been in the field of overseas finance and exchange control. In 1914 there was very little overseas finance work. It grew temporarily in 1914–18 but the volume between the wars was again small. Now, however, because of the importance and difficulty of the problem of the balance of payments, the Treasury has a very large

TABLE V

FINANCIAL DEPARTMENTS
(With numbers of non-industrial staffs)

	1914	1935	1956
(a) DEPARTMENTS ANSWERABLE TO THE CHANCELLOR OF THE EXCHEQUER			
Treasury*	125	250	1,260
Board of Customs and Excise	10,260	13,940	15,060
Board of Inland Revenue	9,750	22,850	51,565
National Debt Office	45	55	50
Public Works Loan Board	35	65	70
Royal Mint	50	65	155
Paymaster General's Office†	70	300	630
Remembrancer's Office (Ireland)	15	—	—
Exchequer Office (Scotland)	15	25	40
National Savings Committee	—	200	635
Scottish Savings Committee	—	15	45
Capital Issues Committee	—	—	10
	20,365	37,765	69,520
(b) INDEPENDENT DEPARTMENTS			
Exchequer and Audit Department	250	330	530
Import Duties Advisory Committee	—	130	—
	20,615	38,225	70,050

*Treasury figures include a small number of staff not engaged on financial matters.

†The Paymaster General is a 'non-departmental' Minister, or Minister without Portfolio: his Office is under the supervision of a permanent Assistant Paymaster General who would regard the Chancellor of the Exchequer as his political chief.

Overseas Finance Division, and there is a permanent Treasury delegation in Washington. New taxes and new methods of collection have meant heavier burdens for the Revenue Boards, in particular the tariffs introduced in 1932, Purchase Tax in 1940 and the adoption and continuance of the Pay As You Earn scheme for Income Tax.

Central financial administration in Britain, however, includes more than the direction of fiscal policy, the collection of taxes and the other functions mentioned above. Financial administration also has a special internal significance for the departments of British central government. There is, of course, the internal banker – the Paymaster General's Office – but its work is routine and not controversial. The main internal 'financial' job is the control of departmental expenditure by the Treasury, a job which has two aspects. Insofar as the Treasury is controlling expenditure other than that concerned with the payment of personnel, it is said to control 'Supply'. (This, it should be noted, is a different, though related, use of the word 'Supply' from that common in a parliamentary context, where it means the discussion of the Estimates presented by the Government.) Insofar as the Treasury controls expenditure on personnel, its function might be defined as the supervision of establishments and administrative organization. Supply and Establishments are not, however, easily disentangled.

This is not the place to discuss 'Treasury Control'. It is obvious enough that the work involved in imposing such control has increased: indeed in a sense every new service provided by departments could be regarded as increasing the work of the Treasury, insofar as the new expenditure has to be controlled. Since 1914 there have been shifts of emphasis and extension of delegation to the departments in the practice and procedure of control, because of wars and new financial, economic and administrative ideas. But the basis of the system remains unaltered.

The changes in financial administration have thus been changes of degree rather than of kind, and changes within an existing framework rather than changes involving the establishment of new departments or the abolition of old departments. The Chancellor of the Exchequer has retained his comprehensive jurisdiction throughout: the Treasury, the Revenue Boards and the odd cluster of minor departments remain today not outwardly dissimilar to what they were in 1914. In few other areas of British central government have there been more determined or more successful efforts to cope with a tremendous change of scale without altering the shape of the departments concerned.

THE TRADE AND INDUSTRY DEPARTMENTS
1914–1922

THE POSITION IN 1914

Earlier in this chapter the trade and industry departments were loosely defined as those whose primary business it is to regulate, to facilitate and to advise on the processes of production – i.e., trade and industry, including transport and communications, agriculture and the exploitation of natural resources. It was also remarked that at certain times during the past forty years a number of other departments had exercised notable 'economic' responsibilities. The implication that there are several departments concerned primarily with trade and industry is in fact the first general point worth developing. Never during our period has there been any attempt or any apparent desire to have a single department to deal with the whole of that vast field. The story is, in the main, a story of the creation of new departments, though some abolitions occurred after each of the World Wars: it is, however, a study of expansion not from a single department but from a group of departments.

Before the First World War the departments which fell unequivocally into the trade and industry category were the Board of Trade, the Post Office, the Board of Agriculture and Fisheries for England and Wales, the Board of Agriculture for Scotland, the Irish Department of Agriculture and Technical Instruction, and the Fishery Board for Scotland. The Post Office was – and indeed to some extent still is – sometimes looked upon as a Revenue department, but its major work has always been the provision of various services which are generally described as posts and telecommunications. It formed in 1914, as it does largely today, a self-contained sphere of governmental administration which needs to be mentioned only rarely in this narrative.

The Board of Trade had become in the ten years prior to 1914 a giant among central departments. The causes of its growth – which had been steady from the 1870s onwards, though the great increase since 1905 tends to overshadow that fact – were the accumulation of regulatory work and the new governmental responsibilities for dealing with labour matters. The Board of Trade of 1914 was the nearest approach during our period to a comprehensive department of trade and industry. It performed, within the limits of the contemporary attitude to the relationship of government to economic matters, a general service of economic intelligence and advice aimed at helping commerce and industry: it was responsible for the administration of a wide range of regulatory legislation chiefly relating to companies, bankruptcy, patents, railways and shipping: and its labour or employment functions covered conciliation and arbitration in industrial disputes, the 'placing' service of bringing together employers in search of staff and workers in search of jobs, and the administration of the recently introduced scheme of Unemployment Insurance. Of the Board's staff of between 6,000 and 7,000 at the outbreak of war, over 4,000 dealt with employment.

Despite the comprehensive nature of its jurisdiction the Board of Trade was not concerned with the development of agriculture and fisheries. Not that government itself had until the previous quarter century shown any inclination to intervene far in either area, though in the past fiscal measures were often of vital importance to the farming community. The Board of Agriculture had been set up in 1889: fisheries had come to it from the Board of Trade in 1903. The Irish department appeared first in 1899 and the Scottish Board was established only in 1912. The Fishery Board for Scotland, founded in 1882, was the successor to various bodies which had long been concerned with an industry particularly important to that country. None of these authorities had far-reaching powers, however. They were concerned in the main with regulation and advice, land settlement, agricultural education, diseases of animals, and the collection of some statistics, etc. Another form of exploiting natural resources which attracted little attention was forestry, though the agricultural departments and the Office of Woods and Forests (which looked after Crown properties) had some responsibility for its encouragement. Since 1909 agriculture, fisheries, forestry and rural industries had been given limited financial assistance from a Development Fund disbursed by the Treasury on the advice of a statutory body of Development Commissioners.

TABLE VI

TRADE AND INDUSTRY DEPARTMENTS 1914
(with approximate numbers of non-industrial staffs)

Board of Agriculture and Fisheries (excluding Ordnance Survey)	635
Board of Trade	6,500
Board of Agriculture for Scotland	160
Fishery Board for Scotland	55
Irish Department of Agriculture and Technical Instruction	370
	7,720
Post Office	208,890

Even the very circumscribed governmental functions with regard to trade and industry were in 1914 scattered beyond the boundaries of those departments whose main business was economic in character. Functions relating to roads and road transport, then – in its mechanical aspect – in comparative infancy, were the concern of several central departments including the Local Government Board, the Home and Scottish Offices, the Local Government Board for Scotland, a number of Irish departments, the Office of Works and a semi-independent Road Board which could make grants to Local Authorities and had power to construct and maintain roads when it thought such action necessary to facilitate road traffic. This array of departments should not be taken as implying that the functions of the central government were extensive with regard to roads: in fact those functions were very limited. The Road Board, like the Development Commission, was a child of the Chancellor of the Exchequer in the Asquith Government – Lloyd George. While air transport was still only a possible future development, enough civil flying was being done for government to have imposed certain regulations on it in 1911, and those regulations were enforced by the Home Office. The Admiralty had a Transport Department which chartered ships for trooping and managed Admiralty-owned vessels such as colliers and tankers. The Admiralty was also responsible for the Coastguard Service.

Though the coal industry was entirely privately owned and managed it had, because of its size, its political importance and its concentration in a number of regions, and because of the dangers inherent in mining, attracted to itself in the 19th and early 20th centuries a comparatively high degree of State intervention for that period. While a small number of regulatory powers were exercised by the Board of Trade, the outstanding responsibility of government – the enforcement of safety regulations in the mines – was the concern of the Home Office. It was to the Home Office, too, that the mining industry tended to go for services of mediation when labour problems arose. Gas, water and electricity undertakings were already local monopolies, either private or municipal, in 1914, and were operated under stringent statutory control. But while the Board of Trade exercised the relevant powers over all electricity undertakings and over private gas and water companies, municipal gas and water works came under the supervision of the Local Government Board. The inspection of factories to ensure that proper safety precautions were observed was the business of the Home Office. The Board of Trade shared with the Foreign Office – none too harmoniously – the responsibility for an overseas trade intelligence service and for the protection of the interests of British traders in foreign countries.

GENERAL TRENDS AND INFLUENCES

In the course of the seven years which began in August, 1914, this arrangement of work, which despite its rough edges was quite compact and dominated by the Board of Trade with its wide jurisdiction, was to be radically disturbed temporarily and not much less notably modified for the long term. The changes that were made for purely war purposes inevitably reflected a spirit of emergency and improvisation. The pre-1914 work of the Committee of Imperial Defence did not include consideration of the changes which might have to be made in the structure of the civil administration.[a] Such changes were in fact made in response to desperate and unforeseen needs, and while detailed reasons may be found for each individual change, it would be quite wrong to suggest that there was, in the background, any conscious intention of building a 'rational' structure of departments or to look too far for complex motives. This lack of any carefully planned development did not, however, prevent a pattern of wartime administration emerging. The existing departments were, indeed, given tasks which were an abnormal extension of their peace-time functions, but the most novel emergency duties were not entrusted to them, being made instead the responsibilities of special wartime departments which could give undivided attention to those most vital matters. The permanent work of government which remained in greater or less degree was handled by the permanent departments. The creation of wartime organizations may well have been inevitable in the absence of any plans for rapid expansion and adaptation of the normal administrative units. But whatever the causes of this division of work, the use of temporary departments sometimes led to a peculiar double structure: two departments, one permanent the other temporary, dealing with the same general field, though the powers of each were usually so different that serious overlapping was avoided. The control of shipping under emergency powers was the business of a special Ministry of Shipping, but the Board of Trade continued to administer the Merchant Shipping Acts. The drive to increase agricultural output was organized in England and Wales by a Food Production Department independent of the Board of Agriculture though responsible to the same Minister. A similar distinction was made in the case of manpower. Even after a new permanent department, the Ministry of Labour, was set up to take over the employment functions of the Board of Trade, a temporary Ministry of

a For the Committee of Imperial Defence, *see* Chapter IX.

National Service was established to carry out recruitment and allocation of labour. This pattern, or semblance of a pattern, has perhaps no long-term significance, but it does underline the strength of the contemporary sense of emergency, and it affords an interesting contrast with the administrative arrangements of 1939–45. In the latter years a generation more used to the idea of total war had long been prepared to adapt peace-time departments to war purposes.

But there were administrative changes made during and immediately after the war which were intended as permanent alterations to the arrangement of the work of the central government. In some cases – notably the establishment of the Ministry of Labour – the changes were not basically due to the war at all, and would probably have come about in due course if there had not been a war, although perhaps not so soon. In other cases, however, the war helped more directly to produce such changes. Technological developments, e.g., the aeroplane and the motor car, meant extensions of permanent governmental work in connection with transport. The social upheaval and wartime regulation gave added strength to ideas of nationalization of the coal industry and the railways. The realization of how great was the disruption caused by the war, and of how much weakness in the national economy the war revealed, stimulated a wish that government should extend its activities after the war in order to protect and encourage national commercial interests when highly competitive international trade was re-started. In some respects many of these influences were remarkably transient. Nevertheless wartime thinking brought about changes which were to remain the basis of departmental arrangements for two decades.

1914–1916: MUNITIONS, LABOUR, FOOD, SHIPPING, BLOCKADE

The great turning point in the First World War from an administrative as well as from a political standpoint was the fall of the Asquith Government and the formation of the Lloyd George Coalition in December, 1916. Before that time the administrative developments had, with one major and a few minor exceptions, been kept largely within the traditional departmental framework and the traditional number of Ministers. With Lloyd George there came a rapid expansion of the number of big departments and the appointment of a number of new Ministers. The wartime narrative, therefore, can be properly divided into two sections.

The first great changes came not in the departments mainly concerned with trade and industry but in the War Office. Of the permanent departments it was the one whose work increased in the most spectacular fashion as it took the strain not merely of military direction but of massive recruitment and, most of all, of the problems of providing guns, equipment, etc. It was immediately involved in far more than the actual purchase and manufacture of munitions, and became the first department to attempt the control of raw materials. The story of how the job became too big for the War Office machinery and how the Ministry of Munitions was set up in the early summer of 1915 must be told in a later chapter. The formation of the Ministry of Munitions did not, however, denude the War Office of all its new-found functions. It retained a considerable proportion of them, and throughout the war was responsible for supplying the Army with food, clothing and a wide range of general stores. This responsibility extended in fact to general supervision of the woollen, flax and leather trades: supervision which was exercised through *ad hoc* bodies largely composed of persons drawn from the trades themselves – a method which was characteristic of a great deal of wartime economic control, whatever the department concerned.

TABLE VII

TRADE AND INDUSTRY DEPARTMENTS
Chronology of Major Changes 1915–1921

1915

June	Establishment of Ministry of Munitions
1916	
February	Establishment of Ministry of Blockade
December	Establishment of Ministries of Labour, Food and Shipping, and of Department of National Service
1917	
January	Establishment of Food Production Department
March	Department of National Service converted into a Ministry
Autumn	Establishment of Department of Overseas Trade
1919	
March/May	Ministries of Blockade and National Service and Food Production Department disbanded
September	Establishment of Ministry of Transport
1920	
December	Establishment of Mines Department: Mines and Quarries Inspectorate transferred to it from the Home Office
1921	
April	Ministries of Munitions, Food and Shipping disbanded

The Ministry of Munitions was the only really big administrative innovation of the first two years of the war. Together with the War Office and to a lesser extent the Admiralty it exercised the major pressure upon productive capacity and manpower. But the three departments did not form a harmonious group, largely because of the competition which developed between them for men. The allocation of manpower was, in fact, the administrative aspect of the war which has been the subject of most criticism. In part the failure of successive Governments to tackle the problem successfully was due to the absence of any prior study of the subject – nobody had envisaged a war so all-embracing in its effects that it would make recruitment and the distribution of labour a major question. But even after the problem had arrived – when the demands of the trenches and the ordnance factories proved to be well nigh insatiable – the idea that only comprehensive direction of labour administered by a single central authority could really meet the situation was never acceptable. A great fundamental aversion to conscription, even for military purposes alone, was not overcome until May, 1916: it was never overcome in the civil and industrial sphere. Moreover the relations between management and labour were dogged by suspicion and hostility which frequently flared up into damaging industrial disputes.

At the outset military recruitment was indiscriminate. This caused immense dislocation in industry, and there developed a number of administrative practices designed to strike a balance between military and civil needs – practices which merely reflected bitter rivalries between departments. Lack of co-ordination and of firm control nullified many of them. The Board of Trade, which had been most concerned with employment matters before the war, used its influence as much as possible to see that industry found the labour it needed. But the Board was not given full control of the situation, though it had in the Labour Exchanges the only machinery which could have formed the basis of a scheme of controlled allocation of manpower. Not only did the Service departments retain their recruiting responsibilities, but the Admiralty and the Ministry of Munitions also set up important Labour Departments. An ineffective Cabinet Committee on Exemptions was appointed in March, 1916, and was followed in the late summer by an almost equally ineffective Manpower Board. But it was not until December of that year that any major move was made to bring order into what had become an almost chaotic situation.

Just as the Board of Trade was not encouraged to develop its labour functions very far, so in other contexts it suffered neglect. This was no doubt partly due to the fact that many of the Board's

customary duties became, if not superfluous at least secondary for
the period of the war, and partly to the comparative lack of detailed
supervision of what can only be called civil industry and trade – i.e.,
industry and trade aimed at supplying the needs of the civilian consumer, foodstuffs apart. There was, for instance, no rationing of
clothing or furniture, and the controls on other trades were mostly
imposed by organizations of the trades themselves. The Board never
had to undertake so many narrowly executive duties in 1914–18 as it
did in the Second World War.

Even so one field of action – the control of food imports and distribution – was lost to the Board from the start, in large part because
of the Board's own short-sightedness. In the early part of the war it
adhered stubbornly to the orthodoxies of *laisser faire* economics and
to the view that from an economic standpoint its functions should be
essentially negative. This reluctance to face the economic facts of the
war led to the early controls on foodstuffs being placed elsewhere.
Executive Royal Commissions on Sugar and Wheat Supplies became
responsible for the bulk purchase of those commodities, which
before the war had comprised two-thirds of our food imports. The
Board of Trade did become a bulk purchaser of frozen meat before
the end of 1916, but by then other aspects of food supply had been
undertaken by various departments. The production of food at home
had not been controlled hitherto by government: here again the old
economic faith held strong in the early years of the war, and the
farmers were left alone. 'So long as food in abundance could be
purchased abroad, so long as we had money to buy without difficulty,
and ships to carry what was needed, it was held to be unnecessary to
interfere with the freedom of farmers in managing their land as
seemed best to them.'[5]

The most important part of the sentence just quoted is that referring to shipping. Of all the forms of transport it was on shipping that
the main interest of government was inevitably concentrated. Here,
too, the Board of Trade was brushed aside when the need for drastic
action became apparent. As soon as war broke out the Admiralty
was given power to requisition ships: its Transport Department was
entrusted with the emergency task and thus began its important war
career. During 1915, however, there was no single approach to shipping administration. The Admiralty was responsible for requisitioning most of the valuable cargo space, but the Board of Trade dealt
with insulated space for foreign meat supplies, and both departments
shared the management of captured vessels put to work in the coast-
ing trade. As the shipping position worsened a variety of new administrative devices were tried. There was a Board of Trade Ship

Licensing Committee, an Admiralty Requisitioning (Carriage of Foodstuffs) Committee, and a joint Admiralty/Board of Trade/War Office Port and Transit Executive Committee. Finally in January, 1916, an attempt to bring some unity into this diffused system of control was made by appointing a Shipping Control Committee. Lord Curzon was its Chairman, and he had direct access to the Cabinet. But the Committee could make little use of its wide powers, partly because it had no administrative staff. As 1916 advanced, the Admiralty's Transport Department emerged more and more as the principal shipping authority.

Meanwhile shipbuilding was under no sort of control and was greatly penalized on that account. The prospect of immediate requisition made shipowners loth to place orders, and the difficulty of finding labour and materials prevented shipbuilding firms from carrying out the orders they received. The industry indeed seemed likely to stop altogether unless it was placed in the care of a department strong enough to compete for men and materials with the Admiralty and the Ministry of Munitions.

In the course of 1915 and 1916 a service of economic intelligence about enemy countries and the enforcement of a policy of blockade were organized by the Foreign Office, by a Ministry of Blockade which grew out of the Contraband Department of the Foreign Office, and by a War Trade Department whose main work was to license exports.

By the end of November, 1916, therefore, the old and new administrative activity of government had together outgrown the existing departmental framework. There were areas in which power was so diffused that only concentration of authority would enable control to be effective. One new major department – the Ministry of Munitions – stood out amongst the tentative re-arrangements which characterized the rest of the central administration. Within a month the administrative position was to be radically changed.

1916–1918

Five big new departments appeared in December, 1916, and January, 1917: Ministries of Labour, Food, and Shipping, and Departments of Food Production and of National Service. Towards the end of 1917 a Department of Overseas Trade was established. These were the major structural alterations during the second half of the war, but in addition there were some important transfers of functions and internal re-arrangements, as well as a general expansion of the control functions of all the departments.

Manpower

At the end of 1916 there were two clear needs in connection with manpower: to establish an orderly and economic system of recruiting and distributing labour between the armed forces and civil occupations, and within those categories between the two Services and between the various occupations: and to strengthen the machinery for encouraging – or if necessary enforcing – industrial peace. There was, however, no conception of a combined 'Ministry of Labour and National Service': the distinction between dealing with 'labour matters' and with 'national service' was clear to contemporaries. The War Cabinet's Report for 1917 has one chapter headed 'Industrial Relations' with a sub-heading 'The Ministry of Labour', and a separate chapter dealing with 'National Service'.[6] The Report refers to the Ministry of Labour as 'an addition to the permanent machinery of Government'. It goes on:

'This reform had been pressed for by the Labour movement for many years, and the increasing difficulty and complexity of the industrial situation arising out of war conditions made it more than ever apparent that a Department was needed whose sole function should be to deal with Labour matters, not merely in the narrow or political sense of the word, but in its broader significance as covering the interests of industry at large.'

Apart from these general causes, the establishment of the Ministry of Labour in December, 1916, was part of the price Lloyd George paid for the political support of the Labour Party. He told the leaders of that Party on the eve of his acceptance of office as Prime Minister that there should be 'an absolutely new Department – a Ministry of Labour – that the Labour Department of the Board of Trade and the Labour Department of the Ministry of Munitions should be consolidated under one head'.[7] In addition, it must be remembered that the Board of Trade's Labour Departments were already very large in 1914, and that their detachment would relieve the Board of some of its enormously wide responsibilities.

In fact, only the Board of Trade's Labour Departments and the Exchanges were placed under the new Minister of Labour. The idea of transferring the Factory Inspectorate from the Home Office to the Ministry of Labour was considered but rejected. The Home Office was 'very reluctant to part', there was doubtless a wish to avoid any change which was not felt to be absolutely necessary for the better conduct of the war, and it may be assumed that there was as yet no general confidence that the new and untried department could manage the Inspectorate as well as the Home Office had done for over eighty years. The possibility of such a transfer at a later date was not ruled out by Government spokesmen, however.[8]

It was originally intended that the Department of National Service should be the means of putting into practice a compulsory system of service in both the armed forces and in industry. When this was mooted to the Labour movement, however, the reaction against industrial compulsion was so great that it had to be dropped. On top of this, the new department did not get control either of military recruiting or of the Labour Exchanges. The voluntary system of recruiting and distributing manpower for civil purposes was continued, the new department (which became a Ministry in March, 1917) only being empowered to guide volunteers into vacancies. It is not surprising, therefore, that the Ministry, constituted as it was during the first half of 1917, was an almost complete failure: it did not even become a useful co-ordinating authority. It did, however, afford some experience from which a reconstituted department could benefit.

Manpower administration was not substantially improved until August, 1917, when the first Director General of National Service – Neville Chamberlain – resigned and the Ministry was reconstituted under Auckland Geddes. The department was then given new powers and duties which came within calling distance of completeness. It was to advise the War Cabinet on the meaning of the plans of various departments in terms of manpower, to arrange the transfer of men to urgent national work from the Services and from less important civil occupations, to issue lists of reserved occupations, to provide substitutes for labour withdrawn from civil life, and to obtain the men required by the Services without dislocating civil life and industrial production. Though other departments retained their powers, something like a workmanlike arrangement was made with the Ministry of Labour:

'. . . the Employment Exchanges, while working in close co-operation with the Ministry of National Service, were to remain under the Minister of Labour and were to retain the executive functions of registering and enrolling, allocating and transferring labour, both male and female. The Ministry of National Service was to determine priority demands for labour, subject to necessary arrangements with the other Departments concerned.'[9]

Policy decisions were made by a War Priority Committee of the Cabinet which decided upon industrial needs and instructed the Ministry of National Service as to the channels into which labour should be directed.

The re-organization came a little late:

'Nothing could drive out from their formidable entrenchments Departments like the Ministry of Munitions and the Admiralty, with at least two years of experience of the problems to which the new Department was to address itself.'[b]

In practice the Ministry of National Service left their usual spheres of activity to the Ministry of Munitions and the Admiralty and worked through the Employment Exchanges, making the Chief Executive Officer of the Exchanges Director General of the National Labour Supply. In this position he was a co-ordinator of all the departments concerned. The new system was 'the nearest approximation to the ideal of a single central authority that the War produced'.[10]

Food and Agriculture

The formation of the Ministry of Food and the Food Production Department can safely be attributed to the eventual realization of the size and character of the emergency which faced the country. The unsatisfactory diffusion of responsibility for the procurement of food from overseas and for other aspects of food supply was largely remedied by the appearance of the Food Controller and his Ministry. The two executive Royal Commissions remained: the Sugar Commission went its own way, but the Wheat Commission became in practice the Cereals Division of the Ministry, though the Commissioners resisted all attempts to reduce their independence as a trading organization, and their relations with the Food Controller were 'complicated and at times delicate'.[11] From other departments, however, the Controller took over a large number of tasks. The control of oils and fats was transferred from the Ministry of Munitions: responsibility for cheese and frozen fish came from the Board of Trade, but the latter retained responsibility for refrigerated meat: food preservation was taken from the Board of Agriculture, and the Food Economy Campaign from the War Savings Committee. The War Office relinquished its responsibility for oats and along with the Admiralty worked through the Ministry of Food instead of obtaining supplies independently. The Ministry gradually assumed responsibility for the

[b] H. Wolfe: *Labour Supply and Regulation*, p. 52. In February, 1918, Mr (now Sir) Winston Churchill proposed that the Labour Departments of the Ministry of Munitions and of the Admiralty should be transferred to the Ministry of National Service in order to secure 'a single policy for war labour'. The proposal came to nothing, but it is interesting to note that the Ministry of Labour was apparently not considered as a candidate. *History of the Ministry of Munitions*, Vol. 2, Supplement to Pt. I, p. 9.

C

purchasing of nearly all the remaining imported foodstuffs during 1917 and 1918. By the end of the war practically 'everything eatable or drinkable that reached this country came as the property of the Government or became its property on arrival'.[12]

Food imports were relatively easily brought under the Food Controller's hand, as in fact he was so often the purchaser of overseas supplies. Home-produced food had first to be taken from the hands of the producers into the control of the Ministry. In the case of meat and cheese all supplies were bought by the Government. Cereals were not purchased but control was ensured by restrictions on the uses to which they could be put, by price fixing and by taking over the flour mills. Of the rest, the prices of all but a few items were fixed but no direct regulation of supplies was attempted: in addition, some commodities such as milk, bacon, butter and potatoes were subjected to varying physical controls over distribution. Rationing was slow to develop. Sugar was the first commodity rationed nationally – on December 31, 1917 – and rationing reached its peak in the month of July, 1918, when there were national schemes for sugar, butter, margarine and lard, meat, bacon and ham. Some items, such as tea, were rationed locally but not nationally.

The advent of the Food Production Department in January, 1917, marked the end of a policy of advice and exhortation and the beginnings of a policy of direction in agriculture. The Department was made responsible to the President of the Board of Agriculture but was entirely separate from the Board itself. The new Department had comprehensive powers of directing the use to be made of agricultural land in England and Wales: it delegated those powers to County Agricultural Executive Committees. The latter were composed partly of members appointed by the Board of Agriculture and partly of members nominated by advisory County War Agricultural Committees which had been in existence for some time. In 1917 a Corn Production Act was passed authorizing a subsidy to be paid in order to guarantee corn prices. As a *quid pro quo* to farm workers, Agricultural Wages Boards and County Wage Committees were set up to fix minimum rates of pay.

The Food Production Department was at first set up as part of the Board of Agriculture. Its rapid growth and the fact that its new powers were quite distinct from those of the 'peace-time' Board seem to have been the main reasons for making it a separate organization. There were no similar departments for Scotland and Ireland, but powers similar to those exercised by the Food Production Department were exercised by the Board of Agriculture for Scotland and by the Irish Department of Agriculture and Technical Instruction.

Shipping

The lack of a comprehensive administrative authority to control merchant shipping during the first two years of the war was remedied by the appointment of a Shipping Controller in December, 1916. It had become plain that only a single control would be able to secure the greatest possible economy in the disposition of cargo space, and that such control should be in the hands of an authority which was not one of a number of claimants for shipping. The Admiralty had indeed become the most important controller, but its own requirements naturally tended to take precedence over those of the other Services and over civilian imports. The Admiralty's Transport Department was therefore transferred to the Ministry of Shipping. The Board of Trade's Mercantile Marine Department, however, remained where it was. This was mainly due to the real distinction between the emergency functions and the duties imposed by the Merchant Shipping Acts: and to the wish to avoid any not absolutely necessary uprooting in the midst of war. In addition, the Mercantile Marine Department was working very smoothly, and the Shipping Controller, Sir J. P. Maclay, was unwilling to enter Parliament: there might well have been parliamentary objections to the concentration of all shipping functions in a Minister who was not a Member of either House.

The Shipping Controller also brought in a much needed supervision of shipbuilding and introduced a programme of constructing standard ships. This responsibility did not remain with the Controller for very long. The terrible losses at sea during the early months of 1917 made a great acceleration of construction essential, and it was considered desirable to place the whole of shipbuilding, both naval and civil, under a single department. The Admiralty was the chosen instrument, and the transfer was made in May, 1917.

The Board of Trade

The Board of Trade was thus suddenly relieved of a good many responsibilities at the end of 1916. Only the labour functions were lost permanently, but the Board was for the rest of the war not directly concerned with the more spectacular jobs of controlling food and shipping. Its sphere of operation was the area of civil trade and industry left after the claims of the new departments and the Service departments had been met. The Board became more directly concerned with the control of a number of industries – exercising its powers through *ad hoc* bodies which dealt with cotton, timber, paper, tobacco and matches, etc. The coalfields were taken over in February,

1917, and the production, price and distribution of coal, the management and development of collieries and the employment of miners were made subject to the direction of a Coal Controller who worked through a Mines Department within the Board of Trade. The railway system of the country had been taken over by the Government at the outbreak of war, but it was run by a Railway Executive Committee which, though it worked under the auspices of the Board of Trade, never formed an integral part of that department's organization.

It is not the war-time work of the Board of Trade which is of primary interest in this context. During 1917 and 1918 certain changes were made within and without the Board which reflected ideas and influences concerned more with the peace beyond than with the immediate wartime problems. The full effect of these ideas and influences was not manifested in the structure of the trade and industry departments until after the Armistice, but what happened at the Board of Trade was a first instalment and may therefore serve to introduce the rest.

The main theme of those who, during the war, thought about the organization of the trade and industry departments and wanted to change it was simple: the Board of Trade of 1914 had been too big and too comprehensive. Its regulatory work relating to transport and public utilities was not akin to what one committee called 'the safeguarding and extension of British industry and trade',[13] while the labour functions were different again. There should be a department charged with nothing but the promotion of commerce and industry. Regulatory work connected with utilities should go elsewhere, labour functions should go elsewhere, and if – as appeared highly probable in the later stages of the war – the railways and mines passed into public ownership, then probably each of them should become the responsibility of a separate department. A refinement of this latter point was the insistence of the Haldane Committee on the Machinery of Government[14] that public and private sectors of the economy should be allocated to different departments.

We have already seen that one of these ideas – that labour functions should be detached – was put into practice in December, 1916: and we shall see shortly what arrangements were made after the war for dealing with the railways and the coal industry. As for the idea that there should be one department wholly concerned to safeguard and extend British industry and commerce, it is hard to imagine that those who in the First World War wanted to rid the Board of Trade of its regulatory work considered that the administration of company law, of bankruptcy, of patents, etc., should also be removed in order to leave clear the way for the 'promotion of industry and trade', whatever that phrase is interpreted to mean. In fact such routine commercial regulation has continued to be performed by the Board ever since, and nobody seems to have taken exception to that arrangement. It may perhaps be assumed here that the 'promotional' work of government with regard to trade and industry had then, as now, two major objectives: to encourage and facilitate British overseas trade, and to improve the efficiency of British industry.

Before 1914 the second of these objectives was scarcely recognized, and most of the early war-time interest in future departmental organization seems to have been concerned with the machinery needed for the promotion of overseas trade. The position before the war was based on an agreement reached during the late 19th century between the Foreign Office and the Board of Trade. In principle the 'Foreign Office and its representatives in foreign countries should be responsible for the conduct of all negotiations, while depending on the Board of Trade for guidance and information on commercial conditions and policy'.[15] This division of functions had been complicated by the appearance of a special organization for commercial relations with the Dominions in 1908. The work of collecting, analyzing and distributing intelligence about overseas trade conditions, of conducting commercial negotiations at Cabinet level, and of protecting the interests of British traders abroad, was in 1914 carried on by the Consular Service and eight Commercial Attachés appointed by the Foreign Office, and by four Trade Commissioners, one in each Dominion, appointed by the Board of Trade. There were Commercial Departments in both the Foreign Office and the Board of Trade, and a Commercial Intelligence Branch at the Board which acted as 'a clearing house for official information', initiated 'inquiries in overseas markets as to openings for trade and similar matters', and communicated 'the results to the commercial public'.[16] The whole system thus depended on smooth inter-departmental relations: the Board of Trade, which needed information for assisting British traders, had no control over the organization of the overseas representatives (except in the Dominions) who alone were in a position to supply such information.

The creation of the Department of Overseas Trade at the end of 1917 was therefore only one more in a long series of compromises between the Board of Trade and the Foreign Office over the question of who should control the commercial representatives abroad and the making of commercial policy. Acute controversy preceded and followed the establishment of the new department. No less than five committees examined the subject between 1916 and 1921, but no acceptable alternative could be found. The new department, under a

Parliamentary Secretary called the Secretary for Overseas Trade, jointly responsible to the Foreign Secretary and the President of the Board of Trade, was the effective headquarters of the overseas commercial services, which were considerably extended after the end of the war. Nonetheless the Commercial Diplomatic and Consular Services remained ultimately under Foreign Office control and carried on their work in the name of the Foreign Secretary, while the Trade Commissioners were appointed by, and the service was administered in the name of, the Board of Trade. Nor did the new department take all the commercial functions from its two parent authorities. In the late 1920s it was said that:

'The result of delegating responsibility for Commercial Intelligence to the new Department of Overseas Trade has been to emphasize the distinction between two forms of government action taken in the interests of British trade. Services rendered directly to traders in their relations with other traders abroad have become the care of the Department of Overseas Trade. On the other hand, action taken in relation to foreign governments, whether by way of representation designed to protect the interests of British traders prejudiced by the laws or administration of those governments, or by the negotiation of commercial treaties or other agreements designed to afford security to British interests in such matters, has remained the function of the Commercial Department of the Board of Trade.'[17]

At the same time the Foreign Office retained responsibility for 'the connection of political relations with our commercial policy'.[18]

So far as the promotion of overseas trade is concerned, therefore, those who wanted a specialized Department of Commerce and Industry were rewarded in 1917 with a 'half-way house'. Those concerned with the interests of home industry, on the other hand, had to be content with a new department within the Board of Trade. The Board was thoroughly reorganized in the winter of 1917–18. A major division was made: a Commerce and Industry Department was set up and a Department of Public Services Administration. The Public Services side dealt with marine, railway and public utility regulation, etc., while the Department of Commerce and Industry comprised the Department of Overseas Trade and the Commercial Relations and Treaties Department, one or two departments which did not survive the immediate post-war years, the Statistical and Industrial Property sections and the new department with which we are here most concerned – that dealing with Industries and Manufactures.

'The governing idea was that at the end of the war . . . a special administrative organ would be necessary to deal with reconstruction problems affecting British manufactures, as distinct from external commerce, and at the same time to deal with questions of policy connected with trade monopolies and combinations, the supply of raw materials, the simplification and standardization of production and similar matters.'

In fact the Department of Industries and Manufactures 'owed its birth to the experience gained during the Great War, and the acute realization of certain weaknesses in our industrial position revealed by that experience'.[19]

POST-WAR RE-ARRANGEMENTS

In the immediate post-war years the Ministries of Munitions, Blockade, Food, Shipping, and National Service, and the Food Production Department were all wound up. Two new departments – the Ministry of Transport and the Mines Department – were established, and there were some important transfers to and from the permanent departments. The Service ministries lost their 'economic' functions very quickly, except the new Air Ministry which, as will be seen, was entrusted with the government's functions in regard to civil aviation. The main structural changes were made by the middle of 1921.

Food and Agriculture

There was no hope of permanence for the Ministries of Blockade, Food, and National Service, or for the Food Production Department. Only the Ministry of Food of those four survived the year 1919. Food supply had been so disorganized by war that rationing had in some cases to be continued until the end of 1920: the Controller was also concerned in an attempt to stabilize the cost of living during 1919 and 1920 by subsidizing imported meat, bacon, butter and dried fruit. Similarly the bulk purchase of sugar and wheat kept the Sugar and Wheat Commissions active until early in 1921: the Wheat Commission was in fact revived in December of that year with new powers mainly concerned with the liquidation of stocks and controls – work which lasted until July, 1925. The Ministry of Food itself disappeared in March, 1921.

The Food Production Department was wound up in March, 1919, and a few months later, by virtue of the same Act which converted the Board of Agriculture and Fisheries into a Ministry, the County Executive Committees were abolished and replaced by Agricultural Committees of the County Councils. The new Committees were of some constitutional interest in that their members had all to have practical, commercial, technical or scientific knowledge of agriculture or an interest in agricultural land, and that while most of them were appointed by the Councils, up to one-third could be nominated by the Minister. The Committees had no powers of direction such as their predecessors had enjoyed, but they exercised all the limited agricultural powers of the County Councils. The Agricultural Wages Boards and Committees which had been set up in 1917 were abolished when the Corn Production Act was repealed in 1921, minimum wage regulation and guaranteed prices ending simultaneously. In their place, Conciliation Committees were set up, but they had no power to fix wage levels.

The agricultural departments themselves were as compact and self-contained in 1922 as they had been in 1914. A few lonely voices had been raised in favour either of their union with the Board of Trade, or at least of the amalgamation of the national units into a single United Kingdom department, but neither idea was seriously considered.[20] It would not have been feasible to add so much extra work to the Board of Trade, and there would have been political difficulties about amalgamating the English, Irish and Scottish departments. It was, however, decided to entrust forestry to a separate authority organized on a Great Britain basis: the Forestry Commission was set up by an Act of 1919.[21]

Blockade, National Service, Munitions

The Ministry of Blockade had no *raison d'être* after November, 1918, and was soon disbanded. The rapid demobilization of the armed forces and the relaxation of controls on employment quickly made the Ministry of National Service obsolete. The Ministry of Munitions came within a stone's throw of permanent status as a Ministry of Supply, but that is a story for Chapter VI. The Ministry was wound up on March 31, 1921. On the same day came the end of the Ministry of Shipping, but the demise of that department may best be treated as part of the narrative of re-arrangement of the government's transport functions.

Transport, Electricity, Shipping

The Minister of Transport was appointed in August, 1919. Practically all the powers of the Board of Trade relating to railways, tramways, canals, and electricity supply were vested in the new Minister. So were most of the Board's powers relating to harbours, docks and piers, though the Board retained its functions in connection with lighthouses, pilotage and kindred matters. The new department also took over the functions of the Road Board – the Board itself was abolished – and most of the powers with regard to roads, etc., previously exercised by the Local Government Board and by the Secretary for Scotland. A number of Irish transport functions were also transferred, but these were later handed back to Irish authorities. It can be seen from this brief list of functions that the new department might more precisely have been called the Ministry of Inland Transport.

It may well be that just as the growth of employment functions would eventually have made a separate Ministry of Labour necessary even if there had been no war in 1914–18, so the growth of road transport and its consequent effect on railway economics might in time have created an unanswerable demand for a separate transport department. But certainly that stage had not been reached in 1919. In all the somewhat scanty discussions about transport affairs during the war there was little to show that any pressure was exerted to shift responsibility for roads, ports and harbours, etc., to any new or existing department. Indeed only occasionally was there any indication that the regulation of all forms of transport was thought of as a separate field of governmental work. Frank Pick did suggest, in a reservation to the *Report of the Committee on Civil Aerial Transport* in May, 1918, that there should be a Ministry of Communications to deal with all transport utilities 'as a definite integral group', but this view was not common.[22] The advisability of having a Ministry of Transport was usually only admitted in the event of railway nationalization. Such a ministry would be responsible for running the railway system, just as the Post Office ran the postal service. This reflected the current attitude towards the administration of nationalized industries and the belief expressed by the Haldane Committee that there should be separate departments to regulate private industry and to run nationalized services. In the absence of nationalization there was a general acceptance of the departmental *status quo*, and this was manifested in 1918 when, in the re-organization of the Board of Trade, a Power and Transport Department was established within the greater Department of Commerce and Industry.

The dominant factor in the creation of the Ministry of Transport in 1919 was the position of the railways. In 1914 more than a hundred companies provided railway services. As we have seen, during the war practically all of them were taken over by the Government and controlled, subject to the general direction of the Board of Trade, by a Railway Executive Committee whose members were the General

Managers of the dozen leading companies. This enforced concentration of railway administration stimulated two movements of opinion which had already existed before 1914. In some parts of the railway world there was pressure for amalgamation on commercial and technical grounds, and in the Labour movement there was pressure for nationalization. Moreover any possibility of an immediate lapse of controls at the end of the war was prevented by the financial agreement between the Government and the companies, which provided that the Government would continue to guarantee the companies' receipts for a two-year period after hostilities ended. By the last year of the war, it appeared to a Select Committee on Transport that a return to pre-1914 conditions was impossible and that unification of the railway system was desirable whether the industry was privately or publicly owned.[23]

There is little doubt that the Government intended to promote some form of national control of the railway system. Apart from the later comments of Ministers who were closely concerned, the original staffing of the Ministry of Transport – with a Director-General of Traffic, a Director-General of Development, a Director-General of Civil Engineering, and a Chief Mechanical Engineer, each with a very adequate supporting staff – was clearly on the basis that it would have considerable executive functions, and was not designed merely with an eye to legislation for the re-organization of the railways which was eventually agreed in 1921.

The Government's intention to launch some form of nationalization may well have been based on the current technical, economic and financial condition of the railways, and with the advantages of co-ordinated operation of the whole system and the political advantages of public ownership in mind. Undoubtedly these ideas were in the mind of Eric Geddes, the first Minister of Transport. Geddes, according to his brother, was 'given the choice of remaining First Lord of the Admiralty or of becoming chief of the projected Ministry of Transport' after the 'Coupon' Election of 1918. 'Unhesitatingly he chose the junior post, his ambition being to amalgamate the railways of the Kingdom, and thus secure efficiency and economy'.[24] So strongly did he feel about the question that when it became apparent in the autumn of 1919, that the railways were not to receive the amount of governmental attention and support which he wished, he contemplated resignation,[25] and when the railways were restored to private ownership in 1921 he wrote to the Chancellor of the Exchequer expressing the view that there was no remaining justification for retaining a separate Ministry of Transport.[26]

While the intention to have some form of nationalized railway system explains the origins of the Ministry of Transport, it does not wholly explain why the new department was given other transport functions, nor why it did not take over the control of shipping and civil aviation, nor why it became responsible for matters concerning the supply of electricity.

It is difficult to find a full explanation of why responsibility for the functions relating to roads, tramways, canals, harbours, docks and piers was concentrated in the Ministry of Transport. We need not doubt the sincerity of the intention to establish, as well as a national-ized railway system, a central authority to co-ordinate the improve-ment of all forms of inland transport. This was the principal argu-ment used in the debates on the enabling Bill. But there were more immediate and practical aspects of the position of docks and canals. Many of these were owned or managed by, or came within the finan-cial and managerial boundaries of, the railway companies, and this close connection may well have weighed heavily in favour of trans-ferring responsibility for them to the department which would hence-forward have the main interest in railway administration. Moreover the widely held view that the Board of Trade was an overweighted department no doubt encouraged the movement of as many transport functions as possible away from it. There may have been some realization of the potentialities of road traffic and the size of the problems which would arise in connection with it which influenced the decision to include the powers of the Road Board and of various other authorities in the powers of the Ministry of Transport. This is not, however, likely to be the whole story, as it seems that Geddes never envisaged the great development of road transport which in fact took place in the inter-war years. The new arrange-ments for exercising the central government's powers with regard to health services almost certainly had something to do with the transfer of road functions to the Ministry of Transport.[c] The Ministry of Health, which succeeded the Local Government Board in 1919, was primarily intended to act as the guardian and promoter of the public health, and while it was in addition the central department which had the most general responsibility for local government, it was obviously only too ready to be rid of powers, such as those in con-nection with roads, which had no close relationship with health matters.

More definite explanations can be offered about the location of shipping powers, about the transfer of certain functions concerning electricity to the Ministry of Transport, and about civil aviation. It has already been shown that the Board of Trade retained the per-manent powers of regulating the Merchant Navy after the Ministry

[c] For the establishment of the Ministry of Health, see Chapter IV.

of Shipping was set up, and that the powers of the two departments were quite distinct. The only permanent section of the Ministry of Shipping was that part of it which had formed its nucleus – the old Transport Department of the Admiralty, whose job it had been to arrange for the peace-time transportation of troops, etc. At the end of the war, although there were those in the shipping world who felt that the shipping industry would secure more governmental attention from a separate shipping department, they were in a distinct minority. Majority opinion was that the emergency powers should go as soon as possible, and that the pre-1914 powers of the Board of Trade were perfectly adequate for peace-time.

Nonetheless the concept of a co-ordinated control of transport can scarcely exclude shipping, and it seems certain that Eric Geddes cast envious eyes on the Mercantile Marine Department. At the same time he was extremely concerned with another subject which came partly under the control of the Board of Trade – electricity supply – and to understand the eventual settlement of shipping we must first look at previous administrative developments in connection with electricity.

During the war a great deal of thought was devoted to the future of the rapidly expanding electricity industry. Almost all the discussion was devoted to the need for technical reorganization, and a number of committees presented the case for setting up a regulatory board with a high degree of independence. In the early stages nobody appears to have suggested that the central department which should keep a paternal eye on the new regulatory board should be any but the Board of Trade. The development of electricity supply was not itself a political issue, and in 1919 the view of the technical experts that a non-departmental scheme-making body was desirable was accepted and incorporated in an Electricity Supply Act. A newly established Electricity Commission took over most of the regulatory powers, leaving very little work for a department to do. Some work was left, however, and it was the departmental location of that work which became part of the general issue about the powers of the new Ministry of Transport.

Eric Geddes was convinced that the main railway routes would all be electrified within a few years. He foresaw the need to give direct encouragement to the electricity industry, not merely regulation or supervision, and argued that such encouragement would best be provided by the electrification of the railway system. It was also believed in some quarters that even if the railways were not electrified, the railway lines would provide ready made wayleaves for a national electricity grid. Geddes therefore urged that central departmental authority for electricity should be vested in the Minister of Transport.

In the course of 1919 the new Minister of Transport thus made heavy demands on the Board of Trade. In addition to depriving it of all its inland transport functions he wanted its electricity powers, and in order to have a single comprehensive transport department he would probably have liked the Mercantile Marine Department as well. While many weighty arguments were doubtless used in discussions about these proposed changes, it is probable that the final settlement was the result of a bargain struck between the Geddes brothers – Auckland, who was then President of the Board of Trade, offering either electricity or shipping, but not both, and Eric choosing electricity. The Mercantile Marine Department therefore remained undisturbed, except that when the Ministry of Shipping was disbanded in 1921 the work of catering for the government's direct peace-time shipping needs – i.e., the pre-war job of the Admiralty's Transport Department – was not returned to the Admiralty but was entrusted to the Board of Trade and placed under the Mercantile Marine Department. This was done because the Board of Trade was in close touch with the shipping companies and could therefore make 'more advantageous arrangements'.[27]

Civil Aviation

There remains to be discussed in the context of transport functions the allocation of powers in respect of civil aviation. All civil flying had been banned in 1914 and the ban remained in force until May, 1919. There was, therefore, literally no civil aviation until then. None the less, the war not only stimulated technical aeronautical development but also roused governmental concern for the future regulation of civil flying. As early as 1911 the Home Office had prepared an Aerial Navigation Bill containing a complete code of law based on the Merchant Shipping Acts. It provided that the Home Office should impose and enforce general regulations while the Board of Trade should be assigned duties relating to the registration and certification of aircraft and pilots, and to collisions, salvage, etc.

When the Royal Air Force was set up as an independent Service and the Air Ministry created, the interest in the potentialities of civil aviation led to the appointment of a Civil Aerial Transport Committee, under the chairmanship of Lord Northcliffe. The Committee concluded that the powers contained in the draft Air Navigation Bill should be enacted and entrusted to the Air Ministry. Most of the members believed that the 'advantages of assigning to a single Department of State the regulation of all matters relating to civil aerial transport are manifest' and that the Air Ministry was the proper department because 'the issue and administration of regulations . . . must to a great extent be governed by naval and military considerations'.[28] Only Frank Pick had misgivings: he wanted the Board of Trade to deal with the commercial side of civil aviation, the licensing of aircraft, pilots and aerodromes, accident investigation, the regulation of air traffic and the general administration of the law of air navigation, while the Air Ministry should maintain and operate aircraft and aerodromes owned by the State, should provide auxiliary services such as meteorological forecasting and wireless aids, and should undertake research and experiment.[29]

The views of the majority prevailed and the Air Ministry became responsible for civil aviation. Sir Frederick Sykes, the Chief of the Air Staff and later Controller-General of Civil Aviation, who together with Lord Weir, the Secretary of State for Air, accepted the Northcliffe proposals and submitted them to the Cabinet, has given the main reasons for the Government's decision:

'To many at the time the connection between Service and commercial flying did not appear to be clear. The Mercantile Marine had grown up independently of the Royal Navy, and to those who used this analogy there seemed to be no reason why civil aviation should not be controlled by a department of the Board of Trade. But to reason thus was to ignore the circumstances in which civil aviation would come into being. Post-war aerial transport was necessarily dependent upon the experience gained in the war. It would have, in the first place, to use military machines and personnel until it got into its stride and struck out a line of its own.'[30]

It is fair to add, moreover, that it was still an open question at that time whether there should continue to be an Air Ministry in peacetime. The addition of responsibility for civil aviation would help to produce a more viable department and strengthen the case for its continuance. Once the decision had been made against the Board of Trade it seems to have been accepted as final: there was no hint during the setting up of the Ministry of Transport that the controversy might be re-opened.[d]

The Mines Department

The re-arrangement of the work of government with regard to transport never became a matter of first-class political importance once it was realized that the idea of nationalizing the railways was quite un-

[d] The legislation regulating civil flying which was eventually enacted in 1920 was in fact based mainly on the 1919 International Civil Aviation Convention, and not on the Merchant Shipping Acts.

acceptable to Parliament. By contrast, the fate of the other industry which seemed at the end of the war a candidate for nationalization – coal – aroused passionate political concern, and a great deal of public attention was therefore paid to the administrative arrangements which were made in connection with it.

The full-scale control of the coal industry which began in 1917 and was exercised by the Board of Trade continued in force until March, 1921. During the earlier part of that period there were two overlapping ideas about the future organization of government *vis-à-vis* the industry. The main theme was that of nationalization, which in one form or other involved a Ministry of Mines. The idea of nationalization split the Sankey Commission of 1919, which produced four separate reports. Of the four, those by the Chairman and by Sir Arthur Duckham attracted the most attention. Sir John Sankey proposed nationalization with a Ministry of Mines as the major central authority. Sir Arthur Duckham suggested 'unification of the mining industry on a district basis, and under private ownership'. The Government at first favoured the Duckham proposals, but these were dropped later in 1919 'in face of the united opposition of owners and miners'.[31]

The second idea current during the later years of the war was put forward by those who, on technical grounds, irrespective of the question of nationalization, wanted a single central authority to deal with all matters concerning the coal industry. In 1918 the Controller of the Department of the Ministry of Munitions for the Development of Mineral Resources reported that the section of the Home Office which was concerned with the industry was 'too small for efficient government', and its duties and authority were 'too circumscribed'. The Controller suggested that a new authority was needed – either a separate department or a branch of some existing department – to deal with statistics, inspection, research and development, etc., and to embrace the Geological Survey.[e] A Committee on Non-Ferrous Mining reported in favour of a single administrative authority for all mining; a Mines Department should be created and 'the health and safety inspection work of the Home Office for both metalliferous and coal mining should be transferred to it'. Similar recommendations were made by the Mining Sub-Committee of the Coal Conservation Committee of the Ministry of Reconstruction in 1918 and by a Committee which inquired into the Acquisition and Valuation of Land in the following year.[32]

[e] Cd. 9184/1918, pp. 7, 45–46. The Geological Survey was under the supervision of the Board of Education until 1919, when it was transferred to the Department of Scientific and Industrial Research.

The belief that there should be a special mining department was almost the only idea shared by all the members of the Sankey Commission, and in this the Commission was in fact merely reflecting the desire of the mining industry to have a 'department of its own'. If nationalization was to be resisted, the minimum price the Government would have to pay to satisfy the mining community, with its great political importance, was the establishment of a permanent Mines Department. Moreover by the end of 1919 there was need for quick action: the Government had found no agreed solution for the future organization of the industry, and labour relations in the mines were deteriorating rapidly. It was therefore decided to set up a permanent Mines Department at the Board of Trade and to entrust to it the administration of a scheme 'which would give effect to the highest common factor in the various reports of the Coal Industry Commission'.[33] A system of joint committees and boards was introduced by the Mining Industry Act, 1920, to handle the problems of wages, conditions, output, safety and welfare. The Act transferred to the Mines Department the relevant powers of the Home Office.

The constitutional position of the new department and the status of its chief was a matter which excited much debate. The Government first proposed that a Minister of Mines should be appointed, to be

'an Under-Secretary in the Board of Trade . . . in a position of complete responsibility so far as all the routine work of the Department is concerned, and . . . only . . . responsible to the President of the Board of Trade in matters which really involve large policy.'[34]

Such a department, the Government claimed, was in accordance with the recommendations of the Haldane Committee on the Machinery of Government, which advised grouping several departments under one great Department of State. There were two guiding considerations behind this policy: first, that a completely separate Ministry would be too small to justify the overhead costs incurred: and second, that the President of the Board of Trade should be freed from routine administration to concentrate upon policy. Further, if a separate department was ruled out, the Government believed that the justification for having a Minister of Mines within the Board of Trade was that it would

'make clear to the mining industry that they have some special Minister before whom they can lay their quarrels and their difficulties, and whose sole business it is to consider and carefully to go into these difficulties. Whereas they know that, if they are only made responsible to a Minister who has a thousand and one other duties to perform, it is ten to one that he will not be able to give them the same attention. . . .'[35]

These arguments prevailed in the Commons but not in the Lords. There it was argued:

(a) That there should be appointed either a full Minister or a mere Under-Secretary, for a half-way office would lead to confusion as to parliamentary responsibility.

(b) That under the Bill all important decisions would in fact rest with the President, and therefore all other tasks could be done by an Under-Secretary without a hybrid title and an unnecessarily high salary.

(c) That a quasi-independent Ministry of Mines would be an increasingly extravagant money-spender, and 'would afford appropriate Ministerial machinery' for future nationalization.[36]

In the event, the Government accepted these objections of the Lords and reduced the 'Minister' to 'Secretary', in order not to waste time and not to risk losing the whole Bill. The exact position of the new department and its political head was defined in the first section of the Act:

'. . . there shall be established a department of the Board of Trade (to be known as the Mines Department) under a Parliamentary Secretary of the Board (in this Act referred to as "the Secretary for Mines"), and all powers and duties of the Board of Trade in relation to mines and the mining industry, whether under this Act or otherwise, shall, subject to the directions of the Board of Trade, be exercised and performed through the Secretary for Mines.'

The Factory Inspectorate

The pressure for a separate Mines Department was too strong for any protest which the Home Office may have made against the transfer of the Mines Inspectorate to the new authority. The problems of mining have always been as much technical as economic, and as in the case of shipping, the regulation of working conditions is intimately bound up with other aspects of the industry: there was, therefore, little hope of placing the Mines Inspectorate in the Ministry of Labour. That Ministry, however, had not abandoned the case for a transfer of the Factory Inspectorate from the Home Office which had been first put forward at the end of 1916. The general argument of those in favour of the change was that the supervision of labour in factories and workshops was a proper function of the department primarily concerned with employment matters. The whole question was re-opened after the war, and the chance of the transfer was increased by proposals to enforce an eight-hour working day.[37] Bills were introduced in 1919–20 – one of them by the Government – which, if passed, would probably have given the Minister of Labour powers to supervise hours of work cognate with the existing powers of the Factory Inspectorate. Had this come about it is not impossible that the Inspectorate would have been moved to the Ministry of Labour, but apparently because of the disagreement of the interested parties – in particular those concerned with employment in agriculture – none of the Bills made any progress beyond first reading. The main argument against transferring the Inspectorate did not, however, touch the proposals for regulating hours of work, at any rate directly. It was always the contention of the Home Office that a department which was often closely involved in wage negotiation should have nothing to do with the regulation of working conditions in factories, in case there should be any suspicion that such regulation might be made a bargaining point in those negotiations. The Home Office had a redoubtable champion in the person of Sir Malcolm Delevingne, then head of its Industrial Division. As early as the autumn of 1918 he was, according to one observer,

'fighting a spirited rearguard action against the Ministry of Labour, which had claimed with hardly disputable logic that it should annex the inspection of factories, and perhaps even Delevingne himself. But he was prepared to die on the steps of the Home Office rather than yield one iota of its prerogatives to any upstart department. He defended the fort with such fiery pertinacity and such inexhaustible ingenuity that he held it triumphantly. . . .'[38]

Whatever personal or institutional influences were at work, the Factory Inspectors were to answer to the Home Secretary for another twenty years.

Gas and Petroleum

Only two minor changes in the immediate post-1918 period remain to be recorded. Both concerned parts of what we have since the Second World War learned to call the fuel and power industries. When the Local Government Board was replaced by the Ministry of Health in 1919, the powers of the Board with regard to Local Authority gas undertakings were included in the transfer. It was recognized, however, that not all the functions of the Local Government Board were appropriate to a department whose major concern was supposed to be with health matters, and provision was made in the Ministry of Health Act for the transfer of such functions to other departments. The Board of Trade, which already looked after private gas undertakings, was the obvious home for the powers in respect of Local Authority gas works. The transfer was made effective in November, 1920. [f]

The First World War had given a great impetus to the use of petroleum in transport and industry. [g]. The Government found it necessary to control importation and allocation, and later encouraged the search for petroleum in this country in the hope of increasing available supplies. These two aspects of petroleum supply – allocation and production – were entrusted to different departments. At the Board of Trade a Petrol Control Committee was set up in April, 1916, and was absorbed into a Petrol Control Department which appeared a few months later. This department was responsible for controlling the distribution of petrol for civil and industrial purposes: it remained in being until towards the end of 1920, its life having been prolonged by almost a year in order to deal with refunds on unexpired petrol licences.[39] At the Ministry of Munitions a group of authorities appeared in the first half of 1917 to handle importation and supplies for munitions firms and to stimulate home production of petroleum. In the autumn of 1917, Walter Long, who was then Colonial Secretary, was asked by the War Cabinet to form a Petroleum Executive which would co-ordinate the various bodies concerned with the supply of petroleum. This Executive absorbed some of the existing authorities, and until November, 1919, when it was re-named the Petroleum Department, it worked under the aegis of the Ministry of Munitions.

By the Petroleum (Production) Act, 1918, the Minister of Munitions was empowered to license and promote searches for home supplies of petroleum. Provision was made in the Act for the transfer of this function to another department, and in March, 1921, when the Ministry of Munitions was abolished, the powers passed to the Board of Trade, to be exercised through the Secretary for Mines. Meanwhile the Petroleum Department had also come closer to the Board of Trade. For some time after November, 1919, it was apparently

f Central responsibility for water undertakings, whether municipal or private, was concentrated in the Ministry of Health at the same time.

g In 1913 the British Government had invested £2,200,000 in the Anglo-Persian (later Anglo-Iranian) Oil Company, thereby acquiring a majority holding of the shares.

regarded as a separate entity and appeared in the Estimates first as a Temporary Commission, and later under the Department of Overseas Trade. It was finally merged into the Board of Trade in October, 1922.[40] Thus by the end of that year what powers the State retained over the petroleum industry were concentrated in the Board of Trade, the powers with regard to prospecting for home sources of supply being exercised by the Mines Department.

THE NEW PATTERN

The new pattern of the trade and industry departments which had more or less emerged by the middle of 1921 did not go unchallenged during the last years of the Lloyd George Coalition. The setting up of the Ministry of Transport and the Mines Department had played some havoc with the 1918 re-organization of the Board of Trade, and the subsequent dropping of railway nationalization left the Ministry of Transport in an odd and weak position. The Geddes Committee on National Expenditure which held its inquiries in 1921–22 wanted to see the Ministry of Transport, the Mines Department and the Department of Overseas Trade wound up and their functions re-transferred to the Board of Trade, thus returning very largely to the 1914 position.[41] These drastic proposals were rejected, but the Board of Trade, while remaining the *doyen* of the trade and industry departments, had to re-arrange its internal organization to take account of the post-1918 changes. Thus the Power and Transport Department of the Board, which had been set up in 1918, had no convincing *raison d'être* after the Ministry of Transport appeared. It was first combined with the General Economic Department (an intelligence department which had also been set up in 1918). The resulting Power, Transport and Economic Department dwindled in importance all through 1919 and 1920. Its existence as an 'odd job' section of the Board was condemned by two committees, and it finally disappeared altogether in 1922.

Four years after the end of the war, the distribution of the trade and industry functions of the central government was thus much more complex than had been the case in 1914. Agriculture and fisheries had remained the business of separate departments in England and Wales and in Scotland, though the agricultural departments had lost forestry to the new Forestry Commission whose ultimate ministerial chief was the Chancellor of the Exchequer. The Board of Trade was still accepted as the main source of advice on general commercial and industrial policy, but its administrative scope had been severely reduced. It now shared its former wide jurisdiction with two new Ministries – of Labour and of Transport – and with two sub-departments – of Overseas Trade and of Mines – which in the latter case, however, did owe full allegiance to the President of the Board, and in the former case joint responsibility to the President and to the Foreign Secretary. In the light of much later developments it is interesting to note the distribution in 1922 of the government's functions with regard to transport and to the fuel and power industries. Three departments were concerned with transport: the Ministry of Transport with railways, roads, ports and inland navigation, the Board of Trade with shipping, and the Air Ministry with civil aviation. The coal industry had its own Mines Department: electricity was in fact regulated by the Electricity Commission though the Ministry of Transport acted in an appellate and confirming relationship to that body: powers relating to the gas industry were exercised by the Board of Trade, which also shared the slight governmental interest in petroleum with the Mines Department.

THE TRADE AND INDUSTRY DEPARTMENTS
1922–1939

The general character of the development of the economic functions of government between the First and Second World Wars has been sketched in the first section of this chapter. That development did not entail any major changes in the structure of the trade and industry departments, but some further brief account of the developments both in the internal organization and functions of those departments and in the circumstances and ideas of the time is essential for an understanding of later administrative changes. Moreover some minor re-arrangements of departmental work must be recorded here.

FOOD AND AGRICULTURE

We have already noted the growth, especially in the 1930s, of experiments in the subsidization and marketing of agricultural produce. Those experiments widened the scope of the agricultural departments, though the latter were not concerned directly with the administrative side of the marketing schemes. Marketing Boards were set up by the producers of hops, pigs, milk, bacon and potatoes, but the schemes of which the Boards formed a part had to be approved by the Minister of Agriculture and Fisheries or the Secretary of State for Scotland, or both in the case of Great Britain schemes, in consultation with the President of the Board of Trade who represented the interest of the consumers. The Commodity Commissions for wheat, sugar and livestock were Government-nominated, and the latter two were staffed by civil servants. The Commissions were primarily intended to administer some form of financial assistance, but all three, and in particular the Sugar and Livestock Commissions, also had certain regulatory and supervisory powers. Thus while the boundaries of the agricultural departments did not alter, the character of agricultural administration was re-orientated. The Scottish department also underwent a constitutional transition. The Board became the Department of Agriculture in 1928 under the control of the Secretary of State, and in 1939 all its powers were vested in the Secretary of State.

A somewhat similar set of developments occurred in fisheries administration. Two statutory bodies – the Herring Industry Board and the White Fish Commission – were appointed in 1935 and 1938, respectively, to re-organize and re-develop their respective industries, and both were in close relationship with the relevant central departments. The powers of the Fishery Board for Scotland were in 1939 vested in the Secretary of State for Scotland, and the Board's organization became part of the Scottish Home Department.

On the distributive side of food supply there were also significant developments. When the first Ministry of Food was abolished in 1921 the remaining staff were transferred to the Board of Trade where they formed a small Civil Emergency Food Organization which was brought into operation during big strikes. When war planning became serious in the mid-1930s the Government set up a Food (Defence Plans) Department in the Board of Trade, and among its other activities it bought stocks of wheat, sugar and other staple foodstuffs from overseas through the agency of large commercial houses. Government had not made bulk purchases of food since the end of the First World War, but governmental action had to some extent shaped the pattern of commercial importation through the research and propaganda on behalf of Empire products conducted by the Imperial Economic Committee and the Empire Marketing Board, especially during the late 1920s, and by the introduction of comprehensive tariffs and Imperial Preference in 1931–32.[42]

TRANSPORT

The work of the Ministry of Transport assumed greater importance as the use of the motor-car spread. Under the Road Traffic Acts, 1930–37, and the Road and Rail Traffic Act, 1933, extensive systems of licensing public road passenger services and road haulage were introduced and carried out by Area Traffic Commissioners. The need to enforce more stringent regulations in the interests of public safety forced on the Ministry functions relating to driving tests, traffic control, and various other methods of protecting road users. In 1937 the Ministry of Transport took from Local Authorities responsibility for 'trunk roads' – roads comprising the principal through routes of national as distinct from local importance. A second transfer (in 1946) brought the total mileage of such trunk roads to 8,200 out of a total road mileage of 183,000 throughout Great Britain. Local Authorities, however, continued as agents of the department to handle the bulk of the work of maintaining and improving trunk roads.

The rise of motor traffic had a very adverse effect on the railways, which had been grouped into four large companies in 1921. Competition from road services also had a detrimental effect on coastal shipping. Traffic on canals had been declining steadily for generations. The resulting economic difficulties convinced many people that some system of 'co-ordinated' or 'integrated' inland transport was essential. While little or nothing of the sort was attempted between the wars, the idea of an inland transport system which would provide the optimum service to the public and at the same time would avoid the alleged wastefulness of unrestricted competition, particularly between road and rail, was widespread and no doubt helped to establish the concept of 'transport' as a definite 'field' of governmental responsibility.

But however much the various media of inland transport may have been increasingly regarded as interdependent, there was little or no serious discontent with the departmental arrangements for dealing with them or with shipping. In some shipping circles there was, particularly during the worst years of the depression, a feeling that

'the shipping policy side of the Board of Trade was very much a sideshow, and that an industry of such importance to the country merited a Minister more exclusively concerned with transport problems than the President of the Board of Trade could possibly be.'[43]

Similarly some civil flying enthusiasts were unhappy because the Air Ministry was responsible for civil aviation which, in their view, suffered neglect from being attached to a military department. This criticism was met to some small extent in 1937 when the powers relating to civil aviation, which had hitherto been vested in the Air Council, were transferred to the Secretary of State for Air, though this did not affect their departmental location. There was, however, no strong political pressure to extend the scope of the Ministry of Transport by transferring to it the government's functions with regard to shipping and civil aviation. Only a few minor changes of responsibility took place. The Board of Trade inherited the Coastguard from the Admiralty in 1923, and in 1937 a statutory Air Registration Board took over from the Air Ministry responsibility for administering certain regulations about airworthiness.

FUEL AND POWER

It is clear from the description of developments between 1914 and 1922 that there was in those years little or no conception of what we now regard as the obvious unity of the fuel and power industries – or at least no feeling that those industries needed to be treated, from a governmental standpoint, as the business of a special administrative department. Perhaps the most obvious reason for the apparent lack of any appreciation of this inherent technical and economic inter-relationship was the contemporary dominance of coal mining as the basic industry of the country – coal was being produced in abundant quantities despite technical shortcomings and bad labour relations in the mines – and the comparative immaturity of what was to become at once its great partner and competitor, the electricity industry. It was to be a further twenty years, during which technical and economic developments greatly modified the national fuel and power situation, before the needs and accidents of another war provided the necessary impetus towards the unification of the relevant central governmental organizations. It was, however, consideration of the unhappy state of the coal industry – declining in prosperity, falling behind in its techniques, savagely divided within itself over its labour problems – that first produced a firm statement of the desirability of treating all aspects of the fuel and power industries together. The Samuel Commission on the Coal Industry recommended in 1926 that:

'A closer connection of mining with the allied industries should be promoted. Highly technical questions are involved, affecting a number of industries, and not electricity alone. The development of electrical supply . . . should be closely co-ordinated with the genera-tion of electricity at the mines. The heat, power and light require-ments of the country should be under the constant and compre-hensive survey of a body formed for the purpose. We propose for consideration the establishment of a National Fuel and Power Committee, with advisory powers, composed of representatives nominated by the Government from among the official and other bodies concerned.'[h]

[h] Cmd. 2600/1926, pp. 233–234. The Commission was no doubt influenced by the evidence laid before it by the Labour Party, which included a proposal for the establishment of a Power and Transport Commission to be attached to the Board of Trade. See *Coal and Commonsense: Labour's Scheme for the Future of the Coal Industry*, Labour Party, 1926.

A National Fuel and Power Committee was appointed by the Board of Trade in August, 1926, with wide terms of reference. The Committee was disbanded, however, late in 1928 after submitting two Reports which were mainly concerned with the coal and gas industries.[44] No further attempt was made to implement the recommendation of the Samuel Commission that there should be a permanent body to undertake a 'constant' survey of 'heat, power and light requirements'.

Most of the developments in government organization *vis-à-vis* the fuel and power industries between 1922 and 1939 were extra-departmental. In 1926 the Central Electricity Board appeared. Four years later a Coal Mines Act provided for the regulation of production, supply and sale of coal and set up a Coal Mines Reorganization Commission to hasten amalgamation schemes made under an Act of 1926. The Reorganization Commission failed to secure effective amalgamations and was abolished in 1938 when the State took over all royalty rights in coal. A Coal Commission was established to act as 'landlord' of the coal, without having any powers to undertake mining operations, and it also took over the functions of the Reorganization Commission. The transfer of royalties was not completed until 1942.

One of the few relevant departmental changes concerned petroleum. In 1928, on the retirement of the officer mainly responsible for the remaining petroleum functions at the Board of Trade, the work of his small branch was transferred to the Mines Department which, it will be remembered, had taken over powers relating to prospecting for home sources of supply from the Ministry of Munitions. Henceforward the activities of the Mines Department with regard to petroleum were not restricted to the small-scale British production, but were also concerned with British interests in the big oil-producing countries. Powers relating to the search for petroleum at home were consolidated and extended by the Petroleum (Production) Act, 1934, which vested in the Crown the property in petroleum and natural gas in Great Britain.

The actual constitutional position of the Mines Department during this period is of some interest. It had no formal contact with the 'official' Board of Trade. The Department was separately housed, and had its own Accounting and Establishment Officers. The official head was called the Under Secretary, and it was he who advised the Secretary for Mines and the President of the Board of Trade on mining matters, not the Permanent Secretary of the Board. The President of the Board of Trade was a very real Minister with regard to the Mines Department: he was always concerned with big policy matters and legislation, and would handle such matters in Cabinet and in

Parliament. The Secretary for Mines was definitely more than a Parliamentary Secretary, but only dealt with policy matters up to a certain level, above which the President of the Board of Trade took over. Popular opinion, however, probably regarded the Secretary for Mines as the Minister responsible for the mining industry.

EMPLOYMENT

By the fall of the Lloyd George Coalition in 1922 the functions relating to employment were largely but not entirely concentrated in the Ministry of Labour. The Ministry covered most of the field of industrial relations, though the Mines Department dealt with many disputes in the coal industry: it ran the placing service, handling several million people each year, administered the Trade Board Acts, collected employment statistics except in agriculture and fisheries, and administered Unemployment Insurance. The Ministry was also much concerned with the newly created International Labour Office, of which the British Government was a 'founder member'. The Factory Inspectorate remained in the Home Office, the Mines Inspectorate was at the Mines Department, and the Board of Trade retained its employment functions in relation to merchant shipping and seamen. In agriculture the rather weak Conciliation Committees came within the general purview of the agricultural departments.

Between 1922 and 1939 the Ministry of Labour steadily extended its scope. The function of providing a service of conciliation and facilities for arbitration became more important, especially in the early 1920s, when industrial unrest was constant and widespread. The Ministry also fostered the development of joint negotiating machinery within industries as a means of settling differences, and remained responsible for statutory wage regulation, except in agriculture. But the major concern of the Ministry throughout the period was with unemployment.

Mass unemployment dominated the inter-war years. It was a huge and apparently intractable problem. There was no remedy which the leading professional economists could evolve or agree upon, and in any case international events to some extent dictated domestic economic conditions. So far as government action was concerned, there were two necessary approaches: to do what could be done to relieve the social distress resulting from mass unemployment, and to find means of creating new employment. The relief side was in fact a combination of Unemployment Insurance Benefit with various other methods of financial assistance. The details of those schemes and the administrative changes brought about by the establishment of the

Unemployment Assistance Board in 1934 are described in Chapter IV. Here it is enough to say that the Ministry of Labour continued to be responsible for Unemployment Insurance throughout the period, and that the work constituted a major part of the department's duty. This allocation of responsibility was a recognition that an unemployed person is a potential worker and should be so regarded. The more positive side – the creation of employment and the reduction of the obstacles to greater employment – may not have made a big impression in relation to the tremendous extent of the problem, but it is notable because the devices introduced during the period were basically those which are now generally recognized as some of the essential measures for maintaining full employment.

The main administrative device was the Ministry of Labour's existing network of Employment Exchanges, where the placing of men in jobs continued at a high level throughout. Coupled with the placing of adult workers went a much extended service of vocational guidance for young persons. The central responsibility for this service was transferred from the Board of Education to the Ministry of Labour in 1927. Some of the executive work was done by the Ministry's Exchanges but in many areas Local Authorities provided the service with financial aid from the central department. A variety of vocational training, instructional, occupational and vocational centres were set up, both for juveniles and for unemployed adults. The responsibility for training disabled servicemen had passed from the Ministry of Pensions to the Ministry of Labour in 1919.

There were, however, more direct attempts to create employment. As early as 1920 an Unemployment Relief Works Act was passed and an Unemployment Grants Committee was set up by the Treasury. In 1929, by the Development (Loan Guarantees and Grants) Act the Unemployment Grants Committee was made responsible to the Ministry of Labour. The schemes were administered by Local Authorities and included the clearing of sites and building of factories, road making and bridge construction, the improvement of harbours and quays, land drainage schemes, and the establishment of trading estates. In the early 1920s it was recognized that workers should be encouraged to leave districts where no work was available, and the Ministry of Labour sponsored the idea of labour mobility. An Industrial Transference Board was set up in 1928, but the policy which it pursued had been adopted some years earlier.

In 1934 the Minister of Labour appointed four Commissioners to inquire into the problems of depressed areas, and their recommendations led to the Special Areas (Development and Improvement) Act, 1934. Under the Act two Commissioners were appointed with wide powers to stimulate the social and industrial development of Special Areas, and those powers were further extended in 1937. The Commissioner for England and Wales worked under the general control of the Minister of Labour (a Great Britain Minister for all other purposes) and the Commissioner for Scotland was under the control of the Secretary of State, who co-operated closely with the Minister of Labour.

In agriculture the Conciliation Committees set up in 1921 failed because of lack of organization among farm workers, and in 1924 a new structure of Agricultural Wages Board and local Wage Committees was re-introduced in England and Wales. A similar structure did not appear in Scotland until 1937. The agricultural departments 'serviced' these bodies, which were independently constituted and had power to determine minimum wages and to enforce minimum standards of working conditions.

Towards the end of the 1930s the probability of war brought forward the fundamental administrative problem of how to apportion responsibility for military recruitment and the handling of civilian manpower. The tragic muddles of 1914–18 had demonstrated that:

'A National Service Ministry to carry out its functions adequately must be in a position to take a complete survey of the manpower of the country, to classify it as scientifically as things human will permit of classification, and then, under the instructions of the supreme strategic authority, to direct the power thus classified into the appropriate channel.'[45]

TABLE VIII

TRADE   AND   INDUSTRY   DEPARTMENTS   1935
(With numbers of non-industrial staffs)

Ministry of Agriculture and Fisheries (excluding Ordnance Survey)	1,700
Forestry Commission	340
Ministry of Labour	23,660
Board of Trade	3,770
Export Credits Guarantee Department	90
Mines Department	375
Department of Overseas Trade	470
Ministry of Transport	1,935
Department of Agriculture for Scotland	485
Fishery Board for Scotland	220
	33,045
Post Office	165,890

The decisions taken towards attaining this ideal were of basic importance. For many years the Ministry of Labour had been averse to taking over responsibility for National Service on the ground that it would be incompatible with its conciliation duties. Nevertheless, the campaign for National Service in 1938 and the compilation of a revised schedule of reserved occupations between 1937 and 1939 were both entrusted to the Ministry of Labour, and were carried through by that department with notable success. That success demonstrated that a civil department could cope with military recruitment and no doubt influenced the Government when it decided, early in 1939, to entrust the execution of the Military Training Act of that year – which permitted the formation of a conscripted Militia – to the Ministry of Labour. Moreover the Ministry of Labour had the machinery working, whereas the Service departments had no comparable organization. In addition, it was felt that the work of reinstating conscripted soldiers into civilian life was the final stage of one process, and that the whole of that process should be the responsibility of a single department.

WAR PREPARATIONS: FOOD, RAW MATERIALS, SHIPPING

The rest of the inter-war story is wholly concerned with preparations for war which helped to fashion the structure of the departments in and after 1939. We have just seen that the Ministry of Labour was clearly destined to become the wartime manpower department. The Board of Trade's Food (Defence Plans) Department became practically independent of the Board in April, 1939, when the Chancellor of the Duchy of Lancaster was placed at its head, and its conversion into the second Ministry of Food merely awaited the outbreak of war. The sheer size of the administrative job involved in rationing and allocating all basic foodstuffs demanded a separate department. There was no possibility either that the Board of Trade could cope with it or that at that stage there could be any combined Ministry of Food and Agriculture – the division of agricultural administration between three national departments (including Northern Ireland) put the latter idea out of court politically, and in any case there were no reasonable administrative arguments in favour of it. Even if there had been a single United Kingdom Ministry of Agriculture, it would not have had the expert knowledge required for an extensive trading and regulatory organization of food supplies.

During the First World War the difficulties of maintaining supplies of raw materials were never seen as a whole and were treated in piecemeal fashion, numerous departments exercising controls, with none too happy results. In the inter-war years a Supply Organization was set up in the Board of Trade to investigate and review the raw materials position. All the plans for a future war administration of materials were closely bound up with the wider problems of defence supply, and it seemed probable well into the early 1930s, that in the event of war, while there might not be a Ministry of Supply, there certainly would be a separate Ministry of Material Resources. Details of the relevant developments are given in Chapter VI, but in short the plan which was developed later in the 1930s of having both a Ministry of Supply and a Ministry of Material Resources fell down because of the opposition of the Admiralty and Air Ministry to a comprehensive Supply Department. The Ministry of Supply which was established in the summer of 1939 was primarily a department for supplying the needs of the Army, an enormous task in itself, but not so great as the earlier idea of supplying all three Services. It was therefore argued that the new Ministry could cope with the control of raw materials as well, and a Raw Materials Department was set up within it.

Finally we return to the administration of shipping. In planning for war, the Board of Trade recognized the desirability of taking up the shipping task at the point where it had been left in 1918 – i.e., with independent control of merchant shipping from the outset. The Board already had, in the inter-war years, responsibility for military sea transport, which it had not had in 1914. The sea transport organization, of key importance in preparations for war, was bound up with technical services which existed primarily for work under the Merchant Shipping Acts. The war planning hinged largely, for example, on considerations of mercantile marine personnel, and therefore required close and continuing participation of those in the Mercantile Marine Department ordinarily concerned with crew matters. In fact internal administrative convenience pointed to the creation, on the outbreak of war, of a separate shipping department which would not only exercise emergency powers but would also take over the statutory marine duties of the Board of Trade and the Board's sea transport work.

THE TRADE AND INDUSTRY DEPARTMENTS
1939–1956

CHANGES FOR WAR
Civil and Military Departments

The fact that so much preparation had been made for the adaptation of peace to war administration is the first general point of contrast between 1939 and 1914. Another general contrast is afforded by the experience of the Service departments. In any 'total' war it is impossible to draw a firm line between administration which affects only the military machine and administration which affects the civilian economy – there is, in fact, no 'military' as opposed to 'civil' economy, there is only a single war economy. None the less, in 1914–18 the mixture of responsibility for economic affairs between military and civil departments was much more marked than in 1939–45. In the latter period there appeared a set of 'war production' authorities: the Ministry of Supply relieved the War Office of most of its 'economic' functions, and in 1940 a Ministry of Aircraft Production was established which did the same for the supply part of the Air Ministry. Only the Admiralty among the Service departments played a dual rôle, as will shortly be seen. The structure of war production departments was completed in 1942 when a Ministry of Production was set up to act, in the main, as a co-ordinating agency for the whole range of war industry. A description of this predominantly 'military' economic administration is reserved for Chapter VI: here we are concerned with the 'civil' trade and industry departments.

Labour, Food, Economic Warfare, Shipping

Within a few days of the outbreak of war a number of expected changes occurred. The new duties of the Ministry of Labour were confirmed by a National Service Act which gave the Minister power to call up men not only for training but for active service. At the same time the department was renamed and henceforward has been known as the Ministry of Labour and National Service. The Food (Defence Plans) Department formed the nucleus of a new Ministry of Food, and a Ministry of Economic Warfare, the equivalent of the Ministry of Blockade of 1916–19, appeared. After an interval of a few weeks a Ministry of Shipping was established: it took over all the shipping work of the Board of Trade and in addition was made responsible for merchant shipbuilding. This latter arrangement, however, worked no better than it had in the early months of 1917, and in February, 1940, responsibility for merchant shipbuilding and repairs passed to the Admiralty, thus placing all shipbuilding under one control. Another transfer between the same two departments was made in May, 1940, when control of the Coastguard was handed over to the Admiralty for the duration of the war.

The Factory Inspectorate

We have seen that in its early years the Ministry of Labour had been

TABLE IX

TRADE AND INDUSTRY DEPARTMENTS
Chronology of Major Changes 1939–1956

1939

August	Establishment of Ministry of Supply
September	Establishment of Ministries of Economic Warfare and Food
October	Establishment of Ministry of Shipping

1940

May	Establishment of Ministry of Aircraft Production
June	Transfer of Factory Inspectorate from Home Office to Ministry of Labour and National Service
October	Merging of Office of Works into a new Ministry of Works and Buildings which became the Ministry of Works and Planning in July, 1942, and the Ministry of Works in February, 1943

1941

May	Ministry of Shipping combined with Ministry of Transport to form Ministry of War Transport

1942

February	Minister of Production appointed: Ministry set up in following July
June	Establishment of Ministry of Fuel and Power, in which Mines Department was merged

1945

April	Transfer of Unemployment Insurance from Ministry of Labour and Nat. Service to Ministry of Nat. Insurance
April	Establishment of Ministry of Civil Aviation
Summer	Disbanding of Ministries of Production and Economic Warfare

1946

April	Merging of Ministry of Aircraft Production into Ministry of Supply: disbanding of Department of Overseas Trade

1951

July	Establishment of Ministry of Materials

1953

October	Ministry of Civil Aviation combined with Ministry of Transport to form Ministry of Transport and Civil Aviation

1954

August	Ministry of Materials disbanded

1955

April	Ministry of Food merged into Ministry of Agriculture and Fisheries to form Ministry of Agriculture, Fisheries and Food
July	Transfer of responsibility for iron and steel and engineering industries from Ministry of Supply to Board of Trade

eager to absorb the Factory Inspectorate into its organization, but had failed in its attempts to promote the transfer. The move eventually came in June, 1940, mainly as a result of developments in the war-time direction of labour. Power was taken to direct workpeople into jobs which they could not leave voluntarily, and which might involve moving their homes. Mr Bevin, the Minister of Labour, insisted that this power could not be exercised unless the welfare of the workpeople concerned was very carefully safeguarded. Housing, travelling and feeding facilities had to be provided. Mr Bevin considered that the Factory Inspectors were the proper officials to see that facilities were properly supervised within the factories and that they could only satisfactorily perform their extended tasks if they were placed under the command of the Minister of Labour. The supervision of amenities outside the factories was to be the responsibility of Welfare Officers. The Home Office opposed the transfer on the traditional grounds that responsibility for safeguarding working conditions should rest with a department which had no other interest in the industry or trades concerned and which could be relied upon to act as an impartial referee. In short, the enforcement of safety and welfare regulations should not be a responsibility of the same department which was concerned with conciliation, arbitration and the promotion of good labour relations. The argument was only settled at Cabinet level, Mr Bevin's view prevailing, but at first the transfer was regarded as temporary. In 1946, however, it was made permanent.

The Ministry of Works

Mr Bevin was also in part responsible for a new administrative arrangement which had no parallel in the First World War. This was the conversion of the old Office of Works into a Ministry of Works and Buildings in October, 1940.[j] The idea was not entirely original, as Mr Churchill had proposed in 1918 that the building departments of the War Office, Air Ministry and Ministry of Munitions should be concentrated under the First Commissioner of Works.[46] The 1940 scheme was first pressed by Mr Bevin, who wanted a central authority which would 'plan and execute all building and civil engineering work for the Government'.[47] In practice, however, the new department did not assume all responsibility for government building, largely because the Service departments continued to supervise most of their specialized constructional work. The new Ministry became nonetheless the main governmental building agency and the recognized cen-

[j] The title was changed to 'Works and Planning' in June, 1942, and to 'Works' in February, 1943.

D

tral authority for dealing with the building and civil engineering industries and industries producing building materials.

Transport

The next set of changes, in chronological sequence, concerned transport functions. The Ministries of Transport and of Shipping were merged into a Ministry of War Transport in May, 1941, at a time when enemy air attack on our ports and shipping was intense. The reasons for this merger have been given succinctly by two eminent transport administrators. Lord Hurcomb, speaking long after the event, said:

'Shipping and inland transport touch in the ports, and the docks were debatable land, where the work of the Ministry of Shipping to some extent overlapped that of its inland partner. In war, when the time of every ship is precious, the interest and duty of the Minister responsible for shipping must follow each ship, wherever she goes. On the other hand, inland transport has an interest in knowing that ships are loaded and stowed abroad with the greatest practicable regard to the situation at the receiving end, and to the ultimate destination of the goods, so that unnecessary internal hauls by rail or road may be avoided. The contacts between the two Departments thus came closest in the common task of allocating incoming ships to the ports where they could best be handled.'[48]

The new Minister of War Transport, Lord Leathers, explained at the time of the change that

'. . . the organization of our national economy for the maximum war effort demands that the entire transport system of this country should be considered as a unit. . . . Hitherto this vast organization has been the concern of two Government Departments, and this has meant the drawing of an arbitrary line in what should be one continuous process. This line was drawn at the ports, but the distinction was never very satisfactory. The internal and external transport systems are interlocking and interdependent. The fact that the full information of ships' movements and cargoes is not under the same roof as the full information about internal transport inevitably leads to certain delays. These have been steadily reduced to a minimum by the friendly co-operation of the two Departments, but it is not possible completely to integrate the transport processes of the country under the control of two separate Ministries.'[49]

The views of Lord Leathers, who was invited by the Prime Minister to become the first Minister of War Transport, were in fact probably decisive.[50] The combined jurisdiction of the department enabled more effective action to be taken to overcome the difficulties which were at the root of the transport delays. By the middle of 1941, therefore, one department was responsible for the whole range of governmental functions relating to land and sea transport. Only civil aviation – practically non-existent during the war – remained beyond its boundaries.

Fuel and Power

One of the by-products of the combination of the Ministries of Transport and Shipping was a significant preliminary move in the next big administrative re-adjustment which has to be recorded – the establishment of a Ministry of Fuel and Power. The powers of the old Ministry of Transport included some relating to the supply of electricity. They were no doubt among those powers which the Government considered to be 'only remotely connected with communications' (a far cry from 1919!) and which were, after the creation of the Ministry of War Transport, to be 'transferred to the Board of Trade or other Departments'.[51] The electricity powers were in fact transferred to the Board in September, 1941. Another preliminary move in the fuel and power story happened at the beginning of the war when a Petroleum Board was set up by the industry, with the blessing of the Government. It was a trade organization registered as a Company limited by guarantee without share capital, and had as its purpose the securing of 'maximum efficiency in the distribution of petrol and oil'.[52] The need to control the importation, distribution and price of petroleum also greatly increased the work of the Board of Trade, and in May, 1940, a Petroleum Department was placed alongside the Mines Department of the Board, under the direction of a junior Minister, a Secretary for Petroleum. The Mines Department was relieved of extra work at a time when the coal industry demanded its whole attention.

Thus in the autumn of 1941 the powers of the central government with regard to fuel and power were in a loose way gathered into the Board of Trade, coal and petroleum being the business of special sub-departments each with its own political head. This concentration came at a time when there was a growing need to co-ordinate the numerous regional organizations which had been set up during the first two years of the war to handle questions of fuel and power from the standpoint of civil defence. The Mines Department had Coal Supplies Officers in the coalfields, Divisional Coal Officers and House Coal Officers in the civil defence areas, and Coal Export Officers in the principal shipping districts. There were Divisional Petroleum Officers and Regional Managers of the Petroleum Board, and a number of advisers representing electricity and gas interests in the civil defence regions. The President of the Board of Trade therefore set up a Fuel and Power Controller in every Civil Defence Region to co-ordinate the work of the existing officers, to provide liaison between the industries and the Regional Commissioners, and to organize emergency plans for fuel and power services in the event of invasion or air attack.[53]

The events which led from this point to the creation of the Ministry of Fuel and Power in June, 1942, were almost entirely concerned with problems of coal supplies. At the beginning of the war the Secretary for Mines had been authorized by Defence Regulations to give directions to colliery managements and to exercise wide powers over production, storage, transport and distribution of coal, but these powers had in fact been sparingly used. A highly indirect system of control making the minimum use of statutory regulations was established,

'. . . in the belief that normal peace-time methods of production and distribution would for the most part suffice and that the work of the control could be limited to watching for and eliminating the sort of distortions which war-time conditions might breed. Direct control of the operations of the mines, still more of their finances, was to be avoided.'[54]

Circumstances were soon to demand a more rigorous application of the existing powers. The first phase of the story concerns the proposals to ration fuel.

Since July, 1941, domestic coal consumers had been restricted to a maximum coal delivery of one ton per month, and at the beginning of 1942 the Secretary for Mines took additional powers to control supplies for all domestic and small industrial premises. These measures did not allay anxiety over what appeared to be an impending shortage of coal: a much more detailed scheme for rationing all fuel was discussed, and the intention of the Government to introduce it was announced in March. Sir William (now Lord) Beveridge produced a rationing scheme at the request of the President of the Board of Trade, which was published in April, and it was proposed to put the scheme into effect in June.

Meanwhile the anxiety over the potential shortage of coal became acute. The shortage was due to reduced production resulting from a big drop in the labour force, and from the troubled state of labour relations in the mines. There were two possible remedies: to release men from the Army or from other industries in order to build up the mining labour force, or to re-organize the industry in order to make the best use of the labour available. The Cabinet decided to follow the second course, and in April, 1942, set up a strong committee over which the Lord President of the Council, Sir John Anderson (now Lord Waverley) presided, to make recommendations. While the committee deliberated, two events aggravated the whole fuel situation – the House of Commons showed itself very hostile to the rationing proposals, and a fresh wave of strikes further threatened production prospects. The committee reported to the Cabinet at the end of May, and recommended certain vital changes – the pooling of technical advice, further mechanization, and concentration of manpower in the most productive mines. These were to be accompanied by reform of the methods used to discipline absentee miners and by recognition of work in the mines as national service. This amounted to the assumption of full control over the operation of the coal industry.

The Government therefore had two big proposals on hand: to ration fuel and to re-organize the production of coal. It would not appear that there was any overwhelming pressure being exerted to alter departmental arrangements as well, although as long ago as August, 1941, when the Ministry of Transport's electricity powers were about to be transferred to the Board of Trade, the Lord Privy Seal (Mr – now Earl – Attlee) had remarked that the transfer would not 'preclude consideration at some later stage of a more comprehensive realignment of Departmental responsibilities for fuel and power services'.[55] Whatever consideration was being given, the Lord President's Committee certainly made no suggestions for high-level administrative change, though it advocated an extended regional organization as the *sine qua non* of effective control of the coal mines. Even the Government's White Paper, published on the eve of the creation of the Ministry of Fuel and Power, which laid down the new policy for coal, made no mention of the forthcoming department.[56] The Cabinet in fact decided to accept the recommendations of the re-organization committee, to reject for the time being the rationing proposals, and to set up a Ministry of Fuel and Power. A number of reasons may be advanced for these decisions.

In the first place there was a growing feeling – no doubt in part reflecting the changed national mood which brought about the fall of the Chamberlain Administration – that something should be done to co-ordinate the handling of coal, gas and electricity – that national fuel and power problems were indivisible. The very proposal to ration all types of fuel was the most striking symptom of this new awareness. The Labour Party had been thinking in terms of a separate department since at least the time of the Samuel Commission. Mr Bevin almost certainly shared this view, and it is possible that Sir John Anderson had come to favour the idea. Moreover the nationalization of the coal industry was pressed in some Labour quarters as a solution to the threatened coal shortage. The full operational control of the industry and the creation of a Coal Board attached to the Ministry of Fuel and Power was in some degree an alternative to immediate nationalization.

The need for some more comprehensive fuel and power organization was increased by the effects of air attack. Disorganization of gas and electricity supplies by bombing called for close liaison between the various authorities for dealing with technical matters. As we have seen, there was a group of Regional Fuel and Power Controllers for civil defence purposes whose presence was an admission of the necessity of treating those industries together. When fuel rationing was being planned it was found that no single department was able to cope with all types of fuel, and the Board of Trade had therefore to set up a shadow organization drawn from the various departments concerned. A combined machinery was thus already largely in existence.

There were other influences at work. The new coal policy would require leadership of a high order. The Mines Department was not likely to provide such leadership. Its position as a minor department with a junior Minister of its own had been experimental, and it was now generally felt in Whitehall that this type of organization had not been successful and should not be repeated. An official historian has claimed that the Mines Department, with its 'severely limited powers', had

'no great record of success to its credit in dealing with an industry well organized to resist intervention even when it was incapable of dealing with its own problems. The war years had called upon a Department with this uninspiring past to face administrative problems of the first order, without the quantity or the quality of the staff which was required for the successful discharge of its new functions.'[57]

Moreover the relations between the Mines Department and its parent body, the Board of Trade, had been unsatisfactory for some time. A ministry organized on a new basis might regain the confidence of the coal industry. At the same time the Board of Trade, already overburdened with other wartime work, was probably only too glad to part with a coherent group of functions already largely organized in separate sub-departments.

Lastly, the Government felt that it would be better to tackle the re-organization of the coal industry first, and not to complicate that big task by embarking simultaneously on a controversial rationing scheme. This meant repudiating the advice of the President of the Board of Trade, Mr Dalton, who had championed the rationing proposals: there was a sharp political crisis, 'not without offers of resignation if political gossip is to be believed'.[58] An added political complication was the attitude of Mr Grenfell, the Secretary for Mines, who thought that the re-organization scheme was 'impractical and unwise'.[59] He obviously could not be expected to administer the new policy, and the resulting vacancy at the Mines Department thus offered an opportunity for re-allocation of ministerial responsibility.

It is a little doubtful whether the establishment of the Ministry of Fuel and Power in 1942 was considered as the beginning of a permanent department for peace-time purposes. It was rather the reaction to an immediate wartime problem. Nonetheless, though few at the time would have been prepared to prophesy that a Minister of Fuel and Power would still be with us in 1956, it was apparent in 1942 that the bringing together of the fuel and power functions of the central government into a single administrative unit was a step which could not easily be retraced.[k]

The Board of Trade and the Agricultural Departments

The Ministry of Fuel and Power was the last big innovation in the sphere of trade and industry administration which was made primarily for war purposes. Later changes within the war period were the results of re-arrangements made with an eye to the post-war world. This is a good point, therefore, to look generally at what had occurred since 1939, particularly in the context of the greatest of the permanent trade and industry departments, the Board of Trade.

Within three years of the outbreak of the Second World War the process of relieving the Board of Trade of its functions relating to utilities and transport, which had begun in 1916, was completed. The Board itself was left with a general responsibility for commercial policy and for many aspects of the regulation of commerce and industry, and with a special responsibility for all those trades and in-

[k] Whatever doubts there may have been about the permanence of the Ministry of Fuel and Power in 1942 had apparently disappeared by the early months of 1945, for shortly before the end of the European War a brief Act confirming the status of the department received the Royal Assent. The Ministry of Fuel and Power Act was a formal measure designed to give statutory authority for a permanent department. The Bill passed through Parliament without arousing either enthusiasm or criticism.

dustries which did not fall within the jurisdiction of other departments. Within this still wide area, the Board underwent no small conversion as a result of war. It became an executive department, administering directly a mass of detailed controls, including such schemes as the rationing of clothing and furniture which were unknown in 1914–18.

Responsibility for the home production of food was vested in the agricultural departments. There was no repetition of the Food Production Department as a separate entity.[m] County War Agricultural Executive Committees were appointed by the Ministers and given wide powers for directing the cultivation and management of land. The departments were in fact the headquarters of a decentralized system of administration in which the Executive Committees acted as the Ministers' agents.

Some characteristics of war-time controls

The closely supervised economy of the war and the early post-war years, when physical controls were of great extent and importance, was responsible for the development of the concept of the 'production authority'. Each industry was placed in the care of a department which was the 'production authority' for that industry. The department had a general responsibility to promote by any means in its power the interests of the industries within its care, and provided a point of contact in the government machine through which its industries' needs and problems could be discussed and as far as possible overcome.

In the later stages of the Second World War the full panorama of governmental control of the economy can be represented in departmental terms. Food production and food distribution were being handled by the agricultural departments and the Ministry of Food respectively. The fuel and power industries had their own department: so did the builders. Ships were built under Admiralty auspices: aircraft by direction of the Ministry of Aircraft Production. The metal and engineering industries were otherwise looked after by the Ministry of Supply. Over all the range of war industry roved the Minister of Production, acting in the main as a co-ordinator of productive activity. He was specially concerned with the supply of raw materials from overseas, but the executive control of those materials at home

[m] In 1935 it was considered that a separate department would be needed in wartime, but the growth of contacts between farmers and the agricultural departments during the 1930s prepared the latter for the exercise of the executive powers imposed in the emergency. See K. A. H. Murray: *Agriculture*, pp. 319–20.

was the responsibility of the Ministry of Supply. For the area of trade and industry not covered by any other department the Board of Trade was in charge. All transport except civil aviation was the business of one department. The allocation of manpower was the function of the Ministry of Labour and National Service.

PREPARING FOR PEACE

The Ministry of Labour: Unemployment Insurance and the Distribution of Industry

The last big administrative changes in the economic sphere during the war might almost be viewed as part of the post-war rearrangements, in that they were mainly concerned with the preparations for post-war action. The acceptance by the Government of the idea of comprehensive social security first formulated by Sir William Beveridge in 1942[60] led to the appointment of a Minister of National Insurance and the establishment of a Ministry of the same name in November, 1944. In March, 1945, the responsibility for Unemployment Insurance was transferred from the Minister of Labour and National Service to the Minister of National Insurance, though the Employment Exchanges continued to do much of the day-to-day administration of Unemployment Insurance on an agency basis. Claims and payments of unemployment benefit are, in fact, still handled across the counters of the Exchanges. The position of the Exchanges under the new National Insurance scheme was the subject of some controversy in 1943–44. Sir William Beveridge in his Report suggested either that the registration and placing functions of the Ministry of Labour should be transferred to a Ministry of Social Security, or that those functions should be retained by the Ministry of Labour but that the staffs concerned should be housed in local offices of the Ministry of Social Security. The Government refused to accept either of these alternatives. They argued that

'Unemployment benefit is designed merely to fill a temporary gap in wage-earning employment. The latter should represent the insured person's normal condition. The employment service fulfils two functions: it helps the worker to secure suitable employment and it enables industry to obtain labour as quickly as possible. There must be a close connection between paying unemployment benefit and placing people in work, but to make the organization of the latter dependent on that of the former would be to put the emphasis in the wrong place. The employment service should remain in the Employment Exchanges and under the Ministry of Labour.'[61]

During the war new thinking about the control of the distribution of industry prepared the way for an extension and a fresh alignment of central departmental responsibility which came to fruition in 1945. The Special Areas which had been defined before the war and placed in the charge of Commissioners who were to encourage their re-development, were renamed Development Areas in 1944. The concept of redeveloping depressed areas had in fact been merged in the greater idea of controlling the whole distribution of industry. It was admitted that 'no single department could conveniently undertake the responsibility for formulating and administering the policy for the distribution of industry . . . there should be a single channel through which Government policy . . . can be expressed. It would not be satisfactory if the public were left to deal with a number of different Departments on different aspects of the same problem.'[62] The Board of Trade was therefore given primary responsibility, obtaining the advice of other departments as necessary. The new rôle of the Ministry of Labour and National Service was – as it still is – to advise the Board of Trade about the desirability of industrial development in any area from the employment aspect.

Civil Aviation

We have mentioned earlier the discontent which existed in some circles in the inter-war years over the Air Ministry's alleged neglect of civil aviation. That discontent had naturally been silenced for the first part of the war: civil flying was restricted and the newly nationalized British Overseas Airways Corporation, though its resources were fully employed, was placed entirely at the disposal of the Secretary of State for Air and operated alongside RAF Transport Command, under the direction of the Air Ministry. As the war progressed and ultimate victory became assured, the old controversy broke out again. It was inflamed by two factors; the remarkable technical developments in aeronautics, which ensured that air transport would have a much greater importance in the post-war than in the pre-war world: and the agreement between Britain and the United States over the pooling of resources whereby Britain had neglected the development of civil and transport aircraft, in order to devote all her energies to making bombers and fighters. From 1943 onwards concern about British prospects in post-war civil aviation grew rapidly. It seemed that as things stood, the Americans might establish a commanding lead in the production of civil aircraft, and that the future of our own newly-developed aircraft industry therefore needed the stimulus of an extended British interest in civil flying. The potential use of air travel to promote Commonwealth co-operation was another factor which kept the future of civil aviation well to the fore. A major theme of those most interested – including members of all political parties – was that either a separate department should be created or that at the very least civil flying should cease to be a responsibility of the Air Ministry.

The Air Ministry tried hard to keep civil aviation, but after the whole future of civil air transport had been discussed by a committee under the chairmanship of Lord Beaverbrook, a Minister of Civil Aviation was appointed in October, 1944, and a new department established early in 1945. While the underlying reason for these developments was without doubt the general conviction that civil aviation had to be separated from the control of a military department if it was to receive its proper share of attention and resources, the immediate cause of the appointment of a Minister was the need to send a powerful representative to an international conference on post-war civil aviation which was convened by President Roosevelt in November, 1944. The President's invitation, as Lord Swinton, the first Minister of Civil Aviation, has said, 'brought matters to a head'.[63]

The question which arises out of these events is: Why a separate Ministry of Civil Aviation, why not a transfer of the relevant powers to the obvious alternative department – the Ministry of War Transport? Mr Bevin wanted this latter course to be adopted, and Mr Lennox Boyd has recalled that there was at the time 'always in the minds of many people' the idea that there would eventually be a ministry of all civil transport.[64] The biggest negative reason why civil aviation did not go to the Ministry of War Transport in 1945 was simply that the latter did not want it, mainly because the department already had quite enough to do. But there were several positive reasons why a separate department was set up. Civil aviation was still widely regarded as a fledgling, an intricate industry needing the psychological boost which individual departmental attention provides. There was a great deal of preliminary work of a specialized nature to be done, and much of that preliminary work was concerned with international and Commonwealth negotiation and organization. This latter task involved a lot of travelling 'which it would have been difficult for a Minister who had any other responsibilities to undertake'.[65] Moreover there were obviously problems to be faced about the future organization of civil flying, involving issues of public ownership and relations with the aircraft builders, which may have been felt to warrant the full-time activity of a Minister.

POST-WAR REARRANGEMENTS: THE LABOUR GOVERNMENT

Administrative Contraction: Economic Warfare, Production and Aircraft Production

Between the end of the war in Europe in May, 1945, and the end of the Japanese war some three months later, the inevitable process of administrative contraction began. The 'Caretaker' Government of May–July did not include a Minister of Economic Warfare, and the department over which the holders of that post had presided disappeared quietly in the course of these months: its functions were wholly born of international conflict and its career has had no influence on the permanent structure of the central administration. Much the same sentiment may be expressed about the Ministry of Production. After May, 1945, one man held the two posts of President of the Board of Trade and Minister of Production, prior to the merging of the Ministry into the Board. By June 5 the Ministry was 'either being wound up or swallowed up'[66] and its disappearance symbolized both the release of industry from its obligation to concentrate all its energies on war output, and the return of general supervision of the whole range of industry to the department traditionally most concerned with industrial affairs.

The process of administrative contraction did not, however, go far beyond this as soon as the war with Japan ended. The main early changes concerned the Board of Trade and the Ministries of Supply and Aircraft Production. The Labour Party came into office firmly intending that departments generally should continue to be closely concerned with industry in peace-time, and that the Ministry of Supply in particular should do much more than look after the provision of military equipment. In fact the post-war Ministry of Supply was conceived by the Labour Government as a department for engineering and heavy industry. The sponsorship of the engineering industry and certain engineering responsibilities which had been retained by the Board of Trade throughout the war were handed over to the Ministry of Supply in August, 1945. Moreover there was no intention of retaining a separate supply department for aircraft, and Mr Attlee's list of Ministers included one man who held both the Supply and Aircraft Production portfolios. The final rearrangements took effect on April 1, 1946. The post of Minister of Aircraft Production ceased to exist and his responsibilities were vested in the Minister of Supply. The 'new' Ministry of Supply did not, however, continue to have a monopoly of the controls over raw materials. It retained the controls over iron and steel and non-ferrous metals, but responsibility for petroleum and petroleum products passed to the Ministry of Fuel and Power, and responsibility for all other raw materials was transferred to the Board of Trade. To some extent this distribution of responsibility for materials was due to a partial acceptance of the view that departments should deal with all aspects of the industries in their care. At the same time the realization of an ultimate relaxation of governmental control – and especially of governmental bulk purchase – of materials may have given an impetus to the disbanding of a comprehensive raw materials unit.

Overseas Trade

The old mechanism for dealing with overseas trade did not long survive the Second World War. The joint Department of Overseas Trade was swept away in 1946 and its functions handed over to the Board of Trade, where the transferred staff comprised an Export Promotion Department. The Secretary for Overseas Trade, who had hitherto been jointly responsible to the Foreign Secretary and the President of the Board of Trade, was henceforward to be responsible directly to the President. There were a number of reasons for this change. In 1943 the Government had reorganized the Diplomatic, Commercial Diplomatic and Consular Services, merging all three and the Foreign Office into a unified Foreign Service. This must have made the position of the Department of Overseas Trade very difficult, as until then it had in practice administered and controlled the Commercial Diplomatic and Consular Services whose members henceforward were to constitute an integral part of the Foreign Service. At the same time the Board of Trade's control of the Trade Commissioner Service in the Commonwealth was not disturbed. Secondly, the rather peculiar distribution of functions between the Foreign Office, the Department of Overseas Trade and the Board of Trade described earlier had serious limitations in the new economic situation, which demanded an all-out concentration on restoring and extending the export trade, which in turn depended on the efficiency of home industry and the condition of the home market. As Mr Oliver Lyttelton (now Lord Chandos) put it in August, 1945:

'There cannot be export policy in one compartment and trade policy for the home market in another. Nearly always the product for export comes from the same factory as the product for the home consumer, and the artificial line drawn in Whitehall between exports and home markets is, from an organizational standpoint, entirely unsound.'[67]

In the third place, the Department of Overseas Trade had from the start been a compromise owing to the inability of two major departments to co-operate closely without formal machinery. Since 1917 the development of inter-departmental liaison had advanced so far that the Foreign Office could confidently let go its formal hold on overseas trade, knowing that it would not on that account lose either contact or influence.

Two further developments at the Board of Trade round off the story of Overseas Trade. The abolition of the Department of Overseas Trade had left the Board with two departments concerned with overseas trade. The Export Promotion Department, which as the successor to the Department of Overseas Trade was the executive instrument for fostering exports and for providing economic intelligence: and the Commercial Relations and Treaties Department which was concerned with the actual formation of external commercial policy. In short, the first provided the 'trader to trader' channel: the other was the 'Government to Government' spokesman. On January 1, 1949, these two departments were merged into one Commercial Relations and Export Department in order that both trade policy and matters of trade promotion would be the responsibility of a single administrative unit. The post of Secretary of Overseas Trade was retained until September, 1953, when it was replaced by a new office of Minister of State at the Board of Trade.

Trade and Industry Departments under the Labour Government

For the greater part of the Labour Party's tenure of office the departmental picture remained similar to what it was by the spring of 1946. The Board of Trade had reassumed its traditional rôle as the leading department, proffering advice on the whole range of industrial and commercial policy. The Ministry of Labour and National Service was a vastly more important department than it had been in 1939. The Ministry of Supply was both the supply department for the Army and the Air Force and the department concerned with the metal, engineering and aircraft industries. The Ministry of Transport (the word 'War' was dropped from the title in 1946) gave nothing away when the fighting ended, and received back into the fold the Coastguard Service which had been under Admiralty control since 1940. The Ministry of Civil Aviation kept its separate status throughout Mr Attlee's Administration. The Ministry of Fuel and Power became more prominent as the coal situation failed to improve after the fuel crisis of 1946–47. The Ministry of Works and the Admiralty continued to be closely concerned with building and shipbuilding respectively, and the idea of placing each industry under the eye of a central department brought new responsibilities to the Ministry of Health, which looked after the manufacturers of drugs and medical appliances. The extensive nationalization measures of the Labour Government, while they added greatly to the responsibilities of the Ministers concerned, did not in fact have any outstanding effect on the distribution of departmental functions.

The agricultural departments became immeasurably more important than ever before in peace-time when in 1947 Parliament passed an Agriculture Act which is likely to be regarded as a landmark in the history of farming in Britain. It provided for the implementation of two major policies – to provide the farmers with guaranteed markets and assured prices, and to encourage and if necessary to enforce high standards of estate management and husbandry by empowering the Ministers to supervise, direct or even dispossess landowners and farmers who failed to maintain such standards, and by providing the good tenant farmer with far greater security of tenure than he had hitherto enjoyed. The executive machinery for pursuing these policies was provided by the Agricultural Executive Committees, which became a permanent feature of agricultural administration. They continued to be appointed by the Ministers, and their staffs, together with the various technical advisory officials scattered all over the country, enormously increased the establishments of the agricultural departments. As a corollary of the permanent establishment of the Executive Committees, the old Agricultural Committees of the County Councils, which had first been set up in 1919, were abolished. Fisheries administration remained a responsibility of the Ministry of Agriculture and Fisheries in England and Wales, and of the Scottish Home Department. The Forestry Commission continued to work on a Great Britain basis, but from 1945 onwards was made subject to the direction of the agricultural Ministers. The Labour Government announced its decision to make the Ministry of Food a permanent department on November 7, 1945.[68] The Ministry maintained its wartime functions of procuring supplies of the principal foodstuffs, and allocating and rationing them, and had an active share in operating the system of financial assistance inaugurated by the Agriculture Act of 1947.

Raw Materials

The last big change initiated by the Labour Government concerned raw materials. As we have seen, from 1946 onwards such controls as remained on raw materials were exercised by the Board of Trade, the Ministry of Fuel and Power, and the Ministry of Supply. In 1947 the bulk purchase and distribution of raw cotton had been entrusted to a non-departmental body, the Raw Cotton Commission. Early in 1950 the idea that each department should look after the raw material supply for each of the industries under its care was carried a stage further. At the Board of Trade itself the single raw materials organization, which had the responsibility for a wide range of materials for all industries, was split up. Its work was distributed among the various branches dealing with individual industries. This arrangement was destined to be short-lived. Within a year the economic and political situation arising mainly from the outbreak of the Korean War had so changed the conditions governing the supply of raw materials that the Government were convinced of the necessity of re-establishing a separate organization. A Cabinet Minister – Mr Richard Stokes, the Lord Privy Seal – was first given special responsibility for watching over the supply of raw materials, and in July, 1951, while retaining his original post, was also appointed Minister of Materials and provided with a department. The new organization was to be generally responsible for the supply of materials up to the point at which they entered into manufacturing industry, but there were exceptions to this and the jurisdiction of the Ministry was not fully comprehensive. Thus the Ministry of Supply remained the central authority concerned with iron and steel and with certain other metals, though responsibility for most non-ferrous and light metals in unwrought forms, including ores and concentrates, passed to the Ministry of Materials. All the Board of Trade's raw materials business went over to the new department, except the responsibility for some chemicals and for diamonds and tobacco, and the Board's powers with respect to the Raw Cotton Commission were also transferred.

SINCE 1951: THE CONSERVATIVE GOVERNMENT

Civil Aviation

The Conservatives returned to power at the end of 1951 intent on 'freeing' the economy. Not only was there general pressure to get rid of as many of the remaining economic controls as possible, but there was also a desire to reduce the number of government departments. There were three obvious departmental candidates for abolition – the Ministries of Civil Aviation, Materials and Food. The eventual combination of the Ministries of Civil Aviation and of Transport was foreshadowed by the appointment of a single Minister to look after both departments in October, 1951. The merger duly followed in October, 1953. Neither department advocated this change, which was prompted by the Government's concern to reduce the number of ministries. Civil aviation was overcoming its 'teething troubles' and its technical developments were no longer unique. International and Commonwealth organization was now firmly established, and a Minister concerned only with civil aviation would be less fully occupied than in the immediate post-war period. Civil air transport had, in fact, settled down: the political controversy over public ownership of air lines had died away, and the industry did not warrant the continued attention of a special department.

The Ministry of Materials

The second trade and industry department to disappear was the Ministry of Materials. It had been set up at a time when there was a shortage of materials, but no sooner had it been properly established than the world position began to improve. The controls on raw materials were soon whittled down, and by the end of 1953 private trading had been resumed in almost all the materials which had come within the purview of the department. The *raison d'être* of a separate Ministry of Materials had therefore disappeared, and the department was wound up in August, 1954.[n] The Raw Cotton Commission was abolished at the same time. All the functions of the Ministry of Materials were transferred to the Board of Trade.

The Ministry of Agriculture, Fisheries and Food

The third department to lose its separate identity was the Ministry of Food. Rationing of basic foodstuffs was coming to an end, supplies of food generally were becoming easier, and bulk purchase of overseas supplies had fallen out of favour. At the same time there was no question of all the functions of the Ministry of Food simply disappearing. The nature of food administration had changed radically since 1939. There was a considerable amount of continuing work to be done on food policy in connection with the administration of financial assistance to farmers: there were still some overseas contract commitments to wind up: and the Ministry of Food had fostered a new governmental concern for food hygiene and for the maintenance of nutritional values. There were three alternative courses open to the Government. They could leave the Ministry of Food, shorn of its

[n] The post of Minister of Materials was held by Lord Swinton together with the Chancellorship of the Duchy of Lancaster from November, 1951, to November, 1952; it was then held separately by Sir Arthur (now Lord) Salter; and from September, 1953, until its abolition it was held by Lord Woolton together with the Chancellorship of the Duchy of Lancaster.

local organization and relieved of its responsibilities for rationing, as a small separate department. This was probably overruled by the pressure in favour of reducing the number of Ministers and departments. The second alternative was to close down the Ministry of Food and to transfer its continuing work to the Board of Trade, which had been responsible for emergency food administration in the inter-war years. This course was unacceptable mainly because the Board of Trade already had quite as much responsibility as it could handle. The third idea was to combine the continuing functions of the Ministry of Food with the functions of the agricultural departments (in fact many of the continuing functions of the Ministry of Food were probably more germane to the agricultural departments than to any others) and to form departments in England and Scotland which would reconcile the interests of the producers and the consumers and thereby help to meet the criticism that the agricultural departments were liable to be unduly influenced by strong producers' pressure groups. This idea was put into practice: the Ministries of Agriculture and Fisheries and of Food were merged to form a Ministry of Agriculture, Fisheries and Food in April, 1955, and the former responsibilities of the Ministry of Food in Scotland were transferred to the Secretary of State, who in turn entrusted them to the Department of Agriculture for Scotland and the Fisheries Division of the Scottish Home Department. Certain functions of a general character were to be exercised henceforward by the Minister of Agriculture, Fisheries and Food and the Secretary of State jointly. A few months later a number of functions concerned exclusively with food hygiene were transferred to the health departments.

The Ministry of Supply

The last major change which has to be recorded was the narrowing of the economic functions of the Ministry of Supply. When the Conservatives came into office the Ministry of Supply was still concerned, apart from its military work, with the metal, engineering and aircraft industries, and it had also been responsible since 1946 for research into and development of atomic energy for industrial as well as for military purposes. As we have already seen, the Ministry of Supply had been relieved of its responsibility for maintaining supplies of certain raw materials when the Ministry of Materials had been set up in 1951, though it retained control of iron and steel and some other metals. By the middle of 1955 the Ministry of Supply had lost, through a number of transfers, almost all its 'civil' economic functions.

The first transfer took place on January 1, 1954, when the powers of the Minister of Supply under the Atomic Energy Act, 1946, and the Radioactive Substances Act, 1948, were handed over to the Lord President of the Council. This followed a decision, based on the recommendations of a committee under the chairmanship of Lord Waverley, to set up a non-departmental Atomic Energy Authority for which the Lord President would bear parliamentary responsibility. The Minister of Supply remained responsible for the provision of complete atomic weapons, but research, development and production were the business of the new Authority. The crux of the argument lay in the Government's belief that 'the necessary flexibility and speed of decision can best be obtained from the Board of an organization run on industrial lines, and with no responsibility outside the field of atomic energy'. The Lord President was chosen to be the Minister responsible to Parliament because it was felt that a high-ranking Minister with 'no departmental responsibilities which encroach upon the field of atomic energy' was preferable to the Minister of an interested department.[69]

When the Ministry of Materials was abolished in August, 1954, the functions which it had taken from the Ministry of Supply in 1951 were not returned to that department, but were handed over to the Board of Trade. The Ministry of Supply was thus left with control only over supplies of iron and steel and certain other metals – control which formed part of the general supervision which the department exercised over the iron and steel and engineering industries. The denationalization of iron and steel was, however, one of the main 'planks' in the Conservatives' programme, and the necessary legislation had been passed in 1953. In place of the Iron and Steel Corporation set up by the Labour Government, a regulatory Iron and Steel Board was established, though at that time the Minister of Supply continued to bear responsibility for the functions of government in relation to the industry. Finally in July, 1955, the Minister of Supply's responsibilities for iron and steel, non-ferrous metals and the engineering industries were transferred to the Board of Trade, leaving the Ministry of Supply with responsibility for the aircraft, light metal and electronics industries. The transfer was partly due to a wish that the Ministry of Supply should be relieved of duties extraneous to the department's main job of supplying the Services. It also reflected a shift of economic emphasis. In the early post-war years the basic problems of heavy industry were mostly in the field of production and especially in connection with the supply of raw materials: more recently commercial aspects such as export incentives, tariff arrangements, etc., had come to the fore, and those aspects of commercial policy were a primary concern of the Board of Trade. The retention of responsibility for the aircraft, light metal and electronics industries by the Ministry of Supply was due to the fact that the civil and military problems of those industries were considered to be inextricably linked, at least for the immediate future.

TRADE AND INDUSTRY FUNCTIONS IN SCOTLAND 1939–1956

One of the main characteristics of the distribution of functions relating to trade and industry has been that, with the exception of agriculture and fisheries, most functions have been entrusted to departments with a jurisdiction over the whole of the United Kingdom or Great Britain. Since 1939 there has been a tendency to delegate administrative powers concerning trade and industry to Scottish authorities. The transfer of some of the remaining powers of the Ministry of Food to the Secretary of State has been mentioned already, as has the new joint responsibility of the agricultural Ministers for forestry. In 1943 the Secretary of State was the Minister appointed to deal in Parliament with the work of the new North of Scotland Hydro Electric Board, whose area covered a large part of the country. Twelve years later a reorganization of the nationalized electricity supply industry placed the rest of Scotland under a South of Scotland Electricity Board quite independent of the British Electricity Authority (henceforward known as the Central Electricity Authority). Ministerial responsibility for electricity in Scotland was at the same time transferred from the Minister of Fuel and Power to the Secretary of State. On the recommendation of the Royal Commission on Scottish Affairs, which reported in 1954, some transfers of agricultural powers were made from the Ministry of Agriculture, Fisheries and Food to the Secretary of State, and in April, 1956, the powers of the Minister of Transport and Civil Aviation relating to the construction, maintenance and management of roads, bridges and ferries in Scotland were similarly transferred. This latter transfer made the Secretary of State responsible for all trunk roads in Scotland and for making grants to local highway authorities in respect of classified roads: it was a change which very largely restored the position as it was prior to the creation of the Ministry of Transport in 1919, though the road functions of the Scottish authorities at that time were not so extensive. Despite these transfers, however, all the general powers relating to trade and industry rest with the Board of Trade for the whole of Great Britain, though the Secretary of State, as 'Scotland's Minister', has a wide interest in the Scottish economy.

THE TRADE AND INDUSTRY DEPARTMENTS AT THE END OF 1956

THE OVERALL PICTURE

In 1914 it could fairly be said that with a few exceptions the work of government in regulating, aiding and advising on the processes of production and exchange, finance apart, was carried on by a group of departments concerned with agriculture and fisheries, by the Board of Trade and by the Post Office. The scope of the Board of Trade was very great, covering all manufacturing industry, most of the transport work, overseas trade intelligence, and employment functions. Forty-two years later the vastly expanded economic functions of government are distributed over an equally expanded administrative structure.

The Post Office, despite a considerable internal expansion, still remains essentially self-contained, and stands alone. The Board of Trade and the Ministry of Labour and National Service primarily perform functions touching all sections of trade and industry, but the Board also takes a close interest in a very large number of particular trades and industries. The Ministry of Agriculture, Fisheries and Food, the Department of Agriculture for Scotland, and the Fisheries Division of the Scottish Home Department deal almost exclusively with the production, procurement and distribution of foodstuffs. The Ministry of Transport and Civil Aviation and the Ministry of Fuel and Power are largely concerned with industries which are under public ownership and control.*o* The Ministry of Supply, the Ministry of Works, the Admiralty and the Ministry of Health are not regarded as 'trade and industry' departments but they are the recognized governmental authorities for dealing with certain industries.

THE BOARD OF TRADE

The Board of Trade remains the *doyen* of the trade and industry departments, and its President is a Cabinet Minister of very senior status. The Board advises on all aspects of commercial policy, looks after the general wellbeing of trade and industry, and is generally

---

o In January, 1957, when a new Government was formed by Mr Macmillan, the Ministry of Fuel and Power was renamed Ministry of Power and the functions of the Board of Trade concerning iron and steel were transferred to it. The new Minister of Power was also charged with responsibility 'for extending the use of atomic energy as a source of industrial power'. (*The Times*, January 14, 1957.) The renaming of the Ministry and the transfer of the functions relating to iron and steel were authorized by SIs 48 and 95/1957, under the Ministers of the Crown (Transfer of Functions) Act, 1946.

responsible for promoting the external trade of the nation: it is charged with the regulation of commercial practices and property, etc.: and it is the main point of contact inside the central government for all those industries which do not fall within the boundaries of other departments. It would need a great deal of space to do full justice to all the functions of the Board, but special mention must be made of such important work as that concerned with export production in the widest sense, commercial policy issues, tariff and import licensing (the tariff work may well become of relatively greater importance in future), the operation of strategic controls, patents administration, productivity, monopolies and restrictive practices (the Board is responsible for the work of the Monopolies Commission) and the Board's responsibilities under the 1945 legislation for distribution of industry policy (which involves the issue of an Industrial Development Certificate for every new factory of any size and the operation of large trading estates in Development Areas). Stress must also be laid on the crucially important statistical work, especially the censuses of production and distribution. In addition, certain agencies which come within the Board's jurisdiction play an important rôle – British Travel and Holidays Association, National Research Development Corporation, Council of Industrial Design, British Standards Institution, National Film Finance Corporation, etc. The Export Credits Guarantee Department has developed enormously with the expansion of the export trade. It is separately organized and has its own Accounting Officer who reports to the Board of Trade Ministers. The Department appoints its own staff and the Permanent Secretary to the Board of Trade has no responsibility for it. Its policy is directed jointly by the Board of Trade and the Treasury. Guidance on routine insurance is provided by a committee drawn from the City, but special risks can only be covered on the authority of the Board of Trade and the Treasury acting jointly.

Though the Board of Trade has been relieved of a number of major functions since 1914, within its more compact jurisdiction its work is far more extensive than was the case forty years ago, and the Board is even now in a constant dilemma over the size of its staff and over its internal organization. Changing economic conditions often produce emergencies which involve calling on a reserve of officials, while in stable economic situations the staff retained to cope with emergencies may be too large for the work in hand. A very great deal of the work of the Board is concerned with policy issues which have to be handled by senior officials. The device of having bodies such as the Monopolies Commission takes some work off the department's shoulders but does not relieve it of responsibility for policy decisions. The load on the President and the Permanent Secretary is a basic and continuing problem.

EMPLOYMENT

As has been the case throughout its career, the Ministry of Labour and National Service today carries out most of the governmental functions which relate to employment. But other departments have a share in employment matters, and the distribution of functions is far from simple. The Ministry of Labour looks after what are usually called the Employment Services – the machinery of placing, the transfer of workers, and the Youth Employment Service. It runs a number of training schemes, has wide responsibility for making arrangements for the employment of disabled persons, and is responsible for registering, calling-up and reinstating in civilian life persons liable for military service. It is the department entrusted with the conduct of external labour relations and is concerned with the controlled immigration of foreign workers. It is also the main collector of employment statistics, and it acts as the agent of the Ministry of Pensions and National Insurance in connection with Unemployment Insurance.

The Ministry of Labour is concerned to encourage good industrial relations and offers services of conciliation and facilities for arbitration. In the conciliation field the Minister's Conciliation Officers at Headquarters or in the Regions are available to advise and assist employers and workers in connection with problems which may arise between them. Each year a large number of disputes is settled following action taken by the Conciliation Officers. The Minister will not, however, conciliate if any negotiating machinery suitable for dealing with a dispute has not been fully used. The overriding principle is that where there is procedure drawn up by an industry for dealing with disputes that procedure should be followed. The department does not act as a conciliator in direct disputes between the Government and trade unions as might happen in the case of industrial or non-industrial government employees, nor does it deal with leaders of unofficial strikes since to do this would be to weaken the authority of the official union leadership. As regards arbitration, facilities for arbitration by consent of both parties are available under the Industrial Courts Act, 1919, and the Conciliation Act, 1896. The Industrial Disputes Order, an experimental modification of wartime practice based on emergency legislation, provides facilities for arbitration at the request of one of the parties to an industrial dispute.

The field of statutory wage regulation has greatly increased since 1939. The Catering Wages Act, 1943, made provision for the establishment of Wages Boards in the catering industry. The Wages Councils Act, 1945, replaced the Trade Boards by Wages Councils with wider powers; an amending Act of 1948 converted the Road Haulage Central Wages Board into a Wages Council. A number of new Wages Councils were established in the retail distributive trades during the period from 1947 to 1953, and a Wages Council for the Rubber Proofed Garment Making Industry was set up in October, 1956. Four Wages Councils (all former Trade Boards) have been abolished because voluntary negotiating machinery had become established which was adequate for the regulation of wages and conditions in the trade concerned. There are now fifty-nine active Wages Councils and four active Catering Wages Boards. The Wages Inspectorate now deal with over 500,000 establishments (employing some three million workers) instead of the 100,000 establishments covered by the pre-war Trade Boards.

The employment functions of the agricultural departments have also increased. The State purchase and control of farm produce during the war and the agricultural legislation of 1947, guaranteeing prices, brought the entire economy of agriculture on to a national basis. Two Acts of 1940 had already centralized the control of agricultural wages, although there is a separate Wages Board for Scotland. The Wages Boards continue to hold an important place and, in addition, various training schemes for agricultural workers are administered by the agricultural departments. During and for some time after the war those departments had large responsibilities for organizing seasonal

---

TABLE X

TRADE AND INDUSTRY DEPARTMENTS 1956
(With numbers of non-industrial staffs)

Ministry of Agriculture, Fisheries and Food (excluding Ordnance Survey)	16,610
Forestry Commission	2,490
Ministry of Fuel and Power	2,030
Ministry of Labour and National Service	22,210
Board of Trade	7,285
Export Credits Guarantee Department	715
Ministry of Transport and Civil Aviation	11,135
Department of Agriculture for Scotland	1,990
Scottish Home Department (Fisheries Division)	240
	64,705
Post Office	252,940

labour schemes and for dealing with questions of deferment of national service for farm workers. Until recent years there has been relatively little need of regulations regarding the physical conditions of work in agriculture, but safety measures have been introduced since 1952 which must be adopted when toxic substances are used in farming operations. The agricultural departments are empowered to enforce these regulations. The same departments have Wages Inspectors of their own mainly because it is convenient that only one authority should deal with the farming community.

The inspection of working conditions is done by several departments. In general it is the case that the Ministry of Labour is responsible except where there are very good reasons why it should not be. The inspection of mines and quarries is a highly technical business and is the concern of the Ministry of Fuel and Power. Similar technical factors are involved in shipping, where the interest of the Ministry of Transport in the welfare of seamen is inseparable from its wider concern for the equipment and seaworthiness of vessels. The Home Office and the Scottish Home Department are responsible for conditions in shops, being the central departments concerned with the general administration of the Shops Acts.

THE SCOPE OF THE TRADE AND INDUSTRY DEPARTMENTS

By comparison with the widespread responsibilities of the Board of Trade and the Ministry of Labour and National Service the other trade and industry departments have relatively compact fields to deal with, and their functions do not therefore need to be enumerated here. Similarly the 'economic' responsibilities of the Ministries of Supply, Works, and Health, and of the Admiralty, are restricted to acting as guide, philosopher and friend to the light metal, aircraft and electronics industries, the building, civil engineering and certain building material industries, the drug and medical appliance trades, and the shipbuilding community respectively. It is very necessary to stress that while each industry still has a departmental sponsor, the concept of the 'production authority' no longer has the same importance as it had in the war and immediate post-war era of direct physical controls. Now that those controls have largely disappeared, the relationship between a department and the industries allotted to it are necessarily more indirect and more difficult to maintain. Perhaps the position could best be described by saying that the department is the main, but not the sole, contact point between its industries and government, that it is expected to know about those industries and to help and advise them as may be necessary. This is an important rôle, and the very fact that such a relationship continues after direct controls have largely been lifted is a highly significant symptom of the contemporary position of government *vis-à-vis* industry.

III

LAW, JUSTICE AND PUBLIC ORDER

THIS chapter deals with the maintenance of public order, with the appointment of judges and the organization of courts, with the conduct of litigation and prosecutions, with the provision of legal advice to administrators, with the reform and revision of the form and content of the law, and with the carrying out of certain administrative tasks which demand the continuous use of expert legal knowledge. The distribution of the work involved under these headings is, and has been throughout our period, complicated – numerous Ministers and departments being concerned – and while some important changes have been made the overall picture in 1955 is not markedly dissimilar to what it was in 1914. Because of the relative stability of administrative arrangements in this field an entirely narrative approach is of little use. Instead, each of the sections defined above is taken in turn and the relevant distribution of functions is described, changes since 1914 being mentioned in the course of that description. There are in addition, however, a number of wider aspects which are considered at the beginning and end of the chapter.

The distribution of administrative functions concerning law and justice in Britain can only be comprehended if a number of important general factors are kept in mind. The first of these is the widely felt dislike of the idea of a centralized police. Only the police force for the metropolitan area of London is directly under the control of the central government, though even here the Government cannot intervene in prosecutions. The rest of the country is divided between over 150 police forces. A force for a large town in England or Wales is responsible to a committee appointed by the elected Local Authority. A county force in England and Wales is responsible to a Standing Joint Committee comprising equal numbers of representatives of the elected Council and of the Justices of the Peace for the county. Urban forces in Scotland are responsible to their Town Councils, and county forces to their County Councils. In all three countries some forces operate in areas covering either more than one county or a county and a large town: such forces are responsible to combined police authorities drawn from the constituent areas. The central government does exercise some influence over the administration of provincial police forces and is responsible for providing certain central services and for a grant-in-aid, but that influence is quite different from having direct control. Moreover the importance and independence of the locality in matters of public order and justice is enhanced by the existence of the Justices of the Peace – unpaid lay magistrates who, except in the largest towns and in most of Scotland, constitute the courts of first instance and in the counties also sit at Quarter Sessions.

Equally important as the diffusion of police power is the unquestioned assumption that the Judiciary should be as far as possible independent of the Executive – and indeed of Parliament as well. In England and Wales judges of the Supreme Court are appointed by the Crown, but they hold office during good behaviour and can be removed only on a joint address to the Crown of both Houses of Parliament. Holders of lesser judicial offices in England and Wales can be removed more easily, but both the appointment and dismissal of all but a few are now (though not in all cases during most of our period) the responsibility of the Lord Chancellor, a Minister who has invariably been a barrister of the highest standing. All High Court judges in England and Wales are drawn from the ranks of practising barristers. The judges of the Scottish High Court and Court of Session[a], who in practice have always been members of the Scottish Bar, are also appointed by the Crown and hold office during good behaviour, but there is no statutory provision for their removal on a joint address of both Houses of Parliament, and it is possible that special legislation would be needed to effect a dismissal. Holders of lesser Scottish judicial offices are appointed and can be dismissed by the Secretary of State. The fact that judges are drawn from the ranks of the legal profession and the impressive solidarity and predominantly conservative character of that profession are powerful and widespread influences which help to safeguard the independent status of the Judiciary.

To the diffusion of police power and the independence of the Judiciary must be added the almost complete separation of legal practice and legal administration between England and Wales on the one hand and Scotland on the other hand. Scotland has its own laws, its own system of courts, and its own central legal administration, all quite different from what is found in England and Wales.

Lastly there is the earlier development of administration connected with law and justice. No more complex chapter of English administrative history will be found than that concerning the organization of the Judiciary, and despite extensive reforms towards the end of the

[a] The Court of Session is the Supreme Civil Court and the High Court of Justiciary is the Supreme Criminal Court of Scotland. ⟨WRONG!⟩

19th century the administrative offices of the courts remain something of a mystery to the layman. They are indeed a most colourful repository of British institutional traditions, and on this storehouse the tidy-minded administrative reformer has made little impression during our period.

The Home Secretary and the Secretary of State for Scotland are the Ministers responsible for the functions of the central government which concern police and prison administration. The Metropolitan Police is headed by a Commissioner responsible to the Home Secretary. Other police forces are inspected periodically by Inspectors of Constabulary attached to the Home Office. In Scotland similar functions were until 1939 performed by the Scottish Office and since the reorganization of that year have been the business of the Scottish Home Department. The departments, while not encroaching on the independence of local forces, have become 'clearing houses' for the exchange of ideas and experience: they provide services of advice, research and other special assistance to those forces, and encourage liaison with them and between them.[1]

Prison administration has been centralized throughout our period. In England and Wales it is, and has been since the later part of the 19th century, the concern of a separate body of Prison Commissioners who are answerable to the Home Secretary. In Scotland the Prison Commission of 1914 became the Scottish Prisons Department in 1928 and in 1939 its powers were vested in the Secretary of State, who exercises them through the Scottish Home Department. These Scottish changes have, however, only been changes of internal organization, and involved no transfer of ministerial responsibility. Closely related to prison administration is the probation service and the detention and treatment of juvenile delinquents. In England and Wales these are Home Office responsibilities, but in Scotland, while most of them are the business of the Scottish Home Department which took over from the old Scottish Office in 1939, 'approved schools' have since 1920 been looked after by the Scottish Education Department. The Home Secretary was until 1948 wholly responsible, in England and Wales, for the detention of criminal lunatics in a special institution – Broadmoor. In 1948 the management of Broadmoor passed to the Board of Control, which is answerable to the Minister of Health, and the inmates have since been called 'Broadmoor patients'. Questions of release from Broadmoor are, however, still decided by the Home Secretary. In Scotland, full responsibility for criminal lunatics is still vested in the Secretary of State, but it is expected that a new State Mental Hospital will be completed very soon. It will be managed by the General Board of Control for Scotland, which is closely linked with the Department of Health for Scotland. The term 'criminal lunatic' will then cease to be used. Questions of the release of persons detained in the State Mental Hospital will continue to be decided by the Secretary of State for Scotland through the Scottish Home Department.

It would be very wrong to leave the reader with any impression that police and prison administration constitutes the whole or even the greater part of the responsibility of the Home Secretary and the Secretary of State for Scotland for maintaining public order. 'Public order' is used here to denote a much wider concept than what is covered by the police function. It covers a host of duties, by no means all markedly legal or judicial or repressive in character, whose administration has some common bearing on the general well-being and safety of the people, and particularly on the status and the liberty of the individual citizen. Most of them – there are marginal cases which have been the subject of controversy – have continued to be entrusted to the Home Secretary (and in Scotland in more recent times to the Secretary of State) mainly because of the peculiar constitutional status of his office. In the early part of the 19th century the Home Secretary was the principal Minister concerned with all domestic affairs – which affairs were basically those of preserving law and order. His writ ran throughout the United Kingdom, and it was not until 1887 that the Secretary for Scotland (first appointed in 1885) took over nearly all his responsibilities in that country. Ireland had its own Chief Secretary throughout the period of the Union. As the work of government extended so the Home Secretary's near monopoly of domestic administration was necessarily reduced. Special departments sprang up to handle the newer tasks, and the Home Office gradually assumed a more restricted dual rôle. Its work in maintaining public order forms its major continuing functions: in addition it is regarded as the 'residuary legatee' – the department to which fall all those miscellaneous duties in the domestic sphere for which no other department has a strong or clear claim. We have already seen in the previous chapter how responsibility for enforcing the safeguarding of working conditions in mines and factories was taken from the Home Secretary during our period – work which had originally been entrusted without question to the Home Secretary in the 19th century as the Minister generally concerned with the well-being of the people. At the same time it is worth recalling that the inspection of working conditions in shops remains the business of the

Home Secretary (and in Scotland of the Secretary of State) as one of his 'residual' responsibilities.

Various subjects additional to police and prison administration are generally accepted as forming, together with that administration, the body of functions collectively describable as concerning public order. The Home Secretary and Secretary of State for Scotland advise the Crown on the exercise of the prerogative of mercy. Other duties include central responsibility for local fire services (from 1941 to 1947 there was a National Fire Service): the control of aliens[b]: questions of nationality and naturalization: the administration of elections (transferred in England and Wales from the Minister of Health in 1921): the enforcement of various safety regulations: liquor licensing: and work connected with betting and lotteries, dangerous drugs and poisons, obscene publications, etc. The Ministers also have a general responsibility for dealing with all disasters such as major flooding, and each convenes an inter-departmental committee on Civil Emergencies. We shall see in Chapter VI that since the 1930s the Home Secretary and the Secretary of State for Scotland have been the Ministers mainly responsible for Civil Defence.

The present 'residual' functions of the Home Secretary (and in some cases the Secretary of State for Scotland) include dealing with constitutional matters relating to outlying parts of the United Kingdom – Northern Ireland, the Channel Islands and the Isle of Man – certain international work under conventions and treaties, the approval of various classes of Local Authority bye-laws, and a group of other miscellaneous duties. The functions of the Ministers which have not been mentioned so far are those which are concerned with the judicial process. It is those functions whose departmental location is of particular interest in the context of this study.

THE APPOINTMENT OF JUDGES AND THE PROVISION OF COURT FACILITIES

The independence and integrity of the Judiciary is a paramount consideration in a democratic country. In Britain these qualities are safeguarded by institutional practices – appointment during good behaviour and removal only by parliamentary action (in England and Wales on a joint address of both Houses of Parliament) – backed by the strength of the legal profession and by high standards of morality in public affairs. Judges are, however, only at the apex of an organization – called hereafter 'the courts' – which exists to facilitate

[b] Aliens administration and matters concerning explosives are dealt with by the Home Office for the whole of Great Britain.

the judicial process. Courts have to meet in buildings, and have to be staffed by numerous officials whose duties are only ancillary to the hearing of disputes. In short, there is an administrative organization whose function is to facilitate judicial proceedings. It is with the distribution of responsibility for organization and appointment that this section is concerned.

Throughout our period the appointment of judges in the House of Lords and of judges in the English Court of Appeal and High Court and the Scottish Courts of Session and Justiciary has been made by the Crown. The appointment of the most senior of these judges is made on the advice of the Prime Minister, who normally in turn seeks the advice of the Lord Chancellor or of the Secretary of State for Scotland. The other judges are appointed on the direct advice of the Lord Chancellor in England and Wales, and in Scotland on the advice of the Secretary of State after nomination by the Lord Advocate. Judges of the lower civil courts – the County Courts – in England and Wales were until 1956 appointed by the Lord Chancellor, except within the area of the Duchy of Lancaster, where appointments were in the gift of the Chancellor of the Duchy. These appointments will henceforward be made by the Crown on the recommendation of the Lord Chancellor or the Chancellor of the Duchy of Lancaster as the case may be. Until 1950 Recorders and Stipendiary Magistrates, who preside over minor (mainly criminal) courts in the big towns of England and Wales were appointed by the Crown on the advice of the Home Secretary, but since 1950 the appointments have been made by the Crown on the recommendation of the Lord Chancellor. In Scotland the Sheriff Courts combine the civil work of the English County Courts (but with no upper value limit) with much of the criminal jurisdiction of the English Justices. The Sheriffs and Sheriffs Substitute are appointed by the Crown on the recommendation of the Secretary of State after nomination by the Lord Advocate. JPs in England and Wales other than those whose commissions lay wholly within the Duchy of Lancaster are appointed by the Lord Chancellor, who also appointed JPs in Scotland until 1955, when the responsibility was transferred to the Secretary of State. The Lord Chancellor and, in Scotland, the Secretary of State or the Lord President of the Court of Session, also appoint members of certain specialized tribunals, and since 1948 the Lord Chancellor has been responsible for advising the Crown on the filling of the chief judicial appointments in the armed forces – the Judge Advocate General and the Judge Advocate of the Fleet. There has thus been a concentration of the power of judicial appointment in the Lord Chancellor and the Secretary of State for Scotland. The former now appoints or advises on the appointment of all judicial officers in England and Wales other than County Court judges and JPs in the Duchy of Lancaster. The latter appoints or advises on the appointment of all judicial officers in Scotland, though he would normally accept the nominations of the Lord Advocate.[c]

The division of the appointing power in England and Wales until recent years reflected a general, though not a precise, division of responsibility for administrative matters concerning the civil and the criminal law, which is still maintained in other respects to some extent. The Lord Chancellor is concerned with everything relating to civil law and has some powers over most courts, especially in matters of procedure, either through his chairmanship of Rules Committees or because rules must receive his approval. The Treasury had a large share in the organization of the County Courts until 1921, when the County Courts Department was transferred to the Lord Chancellor. The establishment work of the higher courts and of the County Courts was in 1914 performed by a number of authorities, and in the Royal Courts of Justice in London, though the Lord Chancellor had considerable powers, individual judges exercised some patronage, as they still do to a far less degree. Since the end of the First World War the character of the staffs of these courts has changed somewhat – thus for example the majority of the Registrars of County Courts have become full-time officers and since 1946 the Clerks of Assize have been regarded as officers of the Supreme Court. These and similar changes have modified a system of patronage which some critics had condemned, and have also increased the administrative responsibilities of the Lord Chancellor. The Lord Chancellor's Department has in fact grown during the last forty years from a small private office to a still relatively small but distinct administrative department.

The Lord Chancellor has throughout our period had a say in certain matters concerning the lower criminal courts in England and Wales[d] – i.e., the magistrates' courts – notably in connection with the making of rules governing their practice and procedure, their size and composition, and the instruction and discipline of magistrates. The Minister with the main interest in those courts, however, has been the Home Secretary. He makes rules which are confined to such ancillary matters as the keeping of accounts by justices' clerks, and

[c] Coroners in England and Wales are appointed by Local Authorities who must inform the Home Secretary of their appointment. The Lord Chancellor (and in the Duchy of Lancaster the Chancellor of the Duchy) has power to remove coroners for inability or misbehaviour. There are no coroners in Scotland, where the corresponding duties are performed by the Procurators Fiscal.

[d] The magistrates' courts are not exclusively criminal courts. They have some civil jurisdiction, but their main work is concerned with criminal matters.

E

TABLE XI

DEPARTMENTS CONCERNED WITH LAW, JUSTICE AND PUBLIC ORDER
(With numbers of non-industrial staffs)

	1914	1935	1956
(a) *Answerable to the Lord Chancellor or to the English Law Officers*			
Lord Chancellor's Office/Department[a]	10	25	140
Supreme Court Offices[b]	900	1,170	1,535
County Courts (including County Courts Department)		2,445	2,250
Pensions Appeal Tribunals		5	30
Department of Judge Advocate General and Judge Advocate of Fleet			60
Lands Tribunal			20
Land Registry	225	1,000	1,075
Public Trustee	435	765	660
Law Officers' Department	5	10	10
Director of Public Prosecutions	5	45	75
(b) *Answerable to the Secretary of State for the Home Department*			
Home Office	275[c]	1,065[d]	3,415[d]
Prison Commission	3,400	3,290	6,710
(c) *Answerable to the Chancellor of the Exchequer*			
County Courts (including County Courts Department)	585		
Friendly Societies' Registry	120	155	105
Office of Parliamentary Counsel	5	20	25
Treasury Solicitor	65	175	315
Statute Law Committee/Statutory Publications Office[e]		5	20

(a) The Lord Chancellor's Office in 1914 was merely the personal secretariat of the Lord Chancellor in the House of Lords, together with the Crown Office, and indeed most of the officials concerned were listed as comprising one group of the Officers of the Judges. In 1935 the Lord Chancellor's Department included the Crown Office and the Supreme Court Vote Office as well as his personal officers. In 1949 the Copying and Typing (or Scrivenary) Department, which performs the copying work of all departments of the Supreme Court, was moved from the Central Office of the Supreme Court to the Lord Chancellor's Department. The 1956 staff employed in the Lord Chancellor's Department is thus made up of the personal staff of the Lord Chancellor, the Vote Office, and the Copying and Typing Department.

(b) In all three years the Supreme Court Offices included the following: the Officers of the Judges: Central Office of the Supreme Court: Taxing Office: Chancery Division: Probate, Divorce, and Admiralty Division: Bankruptcy (Winding-up) Department: Court of Protection (under different names in 1914 and 1935): Official Solicitor's Department: Supreme Court Pay Office: Attendant

(d) Independent department
(England and Wales only)

Charity Commission	90	120	125

(e) Scotland

Scottish Office/Scottish Home Department	50	90	1,670(f)
Scottish Prison Commission/ Department	615	485	
Lord Advocate's Department and Crown Office	20	25	25
Courts of Session and Justiciary	75	70	75
Pensions Appeal Tribunals		5	10
Land Court	15	20	20
Accountant of Court	20	20	20
Department of the Registers of Scotland(g)	205	210	220
Procurator Fiscal Service		95	120
Sheriff Clerk Service		220	235
	7,120	11,535	18,965

(f) Ireland

Irish Office	65		
Charitable Donations and Bequests Office	15		
Chief Crown Solicitor	5		
Prisons Board	590		
Supreme Court	300		
County Courts	30		
Magistrates	65		
Land Registry	145		
Registry of Deeds	90		
	8,425	11,535	18,965

and Messenger Staff at the Royal Courts of Justice: and the District Probate Registries. Official Referees are included for 1935 and 1956. The District Registries of the High Court at Liverpool and Manchester are included for 1935, and the District Registry for Manchester is included for 1956. Other District Registries were – and are – served by the staffs attached to the County Courts.

(c) Excluding Mines and Factories Inspectorates.

(d) Total staffs.

(e) In April, 1956, the Statutory Publications Office was incorporated in the Treasury Solicitor's Department.

(f) Excludes Fisheries staff and road engineering technical staff but includes Prisons staff and staff required for duties other than those concerning law, justice and public order.

(g) The figures for 1914 and 1935 include the staff of the joint Records Department. Since 1949 there has been a separate Scottish Record Office.

the payment of allowances to JPs and to witnesses. He has many and various other supervisory duties, and since 1953, when the magistrates' courts became a grant-aided service, his responsibility to Parliament for the spending of the public money involved has necessarily made him concerned with the organization of the courts. At the same time the Home Secretary's powers do not enable him (or perhaps it would be more exact to say are not used in such a way as) to impose a rigid centralization – the courts, for instance, are staffed and maintained locally.[2]

In Scotland all the establishment work involved in the appointment, transfer, promotion, etc., of the staffs of the courts (other than the local police courts) is now done by the Scottish Home Department. The Sheriff Clerk Service and the Procurator Fiscal Service were established on a Civil Service basis in 1928. Some of the rule-making functions of the Lord Chancellor in England and Wales are vested in Scotland in the Court of Session.

THE GOVERNMENT IN COURT

The duty of conducting the most important Crown prosecutions devolves on the Law Officers of the Crown – the Attorney General and Solicitor General in England and Wales, the Lord Advocate and Solicitor General in Scotland. In England and Wales, while most criminal proceedings are instituted by the police, they can be instituted by other public authorities and by private individuals. This enables many government departments to take action themselves through their own legal officers or through the Treasury Solicitor who acts for them. (The Treasury Solicitor provides a legal 'common service' to a large number of departments, as will be seen later.) A department which does initiate proceedings itself normally only does so when cases arise under the particular code of law administered by the department. Offences against the general law of the land are left to the Director of Public Prosecutions, an officer appointed by the Home Secretary but working under the supervision of the Attorney General and subject to his direction. In some cases, the Director's consent is needed before proceedings can be instituted. The Attorney General has an unfettered discretion to institute or stay proceedings, and his consent is required to the institution of proceedings under a number of Acts, and to appeals from the Court of Criminal Appeal and from the Courts Martial Appeal Court to the House of Lords.

In Scotland private prosecutions are virtually excluded: practically all prosecutions are instituted in the public interest by the Lord Advocate and his officers. The central department responsible for prosecutions is the Crown Office, under the control of the Lord Advocate, and in each Sheriff Court district there is a public prosecutor – the Procurator Fiscal – who is appointed by and answerable to the Lord Advocate. The Burgh Courts and the Justices of the Peace Courts have their own prosecutors who are not appointed by the Lord Advocate. The police in Scotland do not prosecute.

Ultimate responsibility for the conduct of all litigation to which the Crown or a government department is a party rests on the Attorney General or the Lord Advocate. The Law Officers themselves appear in the most important cases: they appoint counsel to the various departments and have the right to nominate counsel to appear for the Crown in any cases, civil or criminal. The Law Officers have small professional staffs to help them.

PREPARING LEGISLATION AND KEEPING THE LAW UP TO DATE

The process of law-making in Parliament does not find a place in a study of the structure of executive government. But the Government has a big part to play in the formulation of statute law – in producing the draft Bills which are placed before Parliament by Ministers. Government Bills referring to the United Kingdom, to Great Britain and to England and Wales are prepared by the Office of the Parliamentary Counsel to the Treasury, which also drafts such Statutory Instruments as may be referred to it. Government Bills concerning Scotland only, and the provisions of any Government Bill extending to the United Kingdom or to Great Britain insofar as it applies to Scotland, are drafted by the Lord Advocate's Department. Parliamentary Counsel and the Lord Advocate's Department are closely concerned with the amendments which may be made during the passage of legislation, and they prepare financial and other resolutions connected with Bills.

Since 1914 there has been a growing interest in the problem of law reform. In that year the only official body concerned with the revision of the law was the Statute Law Committee, first appointed in 1868, when its terms of reference imposed on it the restricted duty of making 'the necessary arrangements' and superintending 'the work of preparing an Edition of Statutes revised'. Alongside this body there was established in 1934 a Law Revision Committee in effect replaced since 1952 by the Law Reform Committee with the following terms of reference:

'To consider, having regard especially to judicial decisions, what changes are desirable in such legal doctrines as may be from time to time referred to it.'

An informal group appointed by the Lord Advocate did similar work on Scottish Law until 1955, when it was given a formal status as a Scottish Law Reform Committee.

In 1947 the scope of the Statute Law Committee was widened. Henceforward it was to consider 'the steps necessary to bring the Statute Book up to date by consolidation, revision or otherwise', and to superintend 'the publication and indexing of Statutes, Revised Statutes and Statutory Instruments'. Consolidation involves the combining in one statute of provisions contained in a number of statutes without altering the law: it is often a very difficult process, and is handled by a separate Consolidation and Codification Branch of the Office of Parliamentary Counsel. Since 1949 a special procedure for passing Consolidation Bills has been in operation. A less difficult but related job – that of preparing Statute Law Revision Bills and of preparing and publishing editions of Revised Statutes, annual indexed volumes of Public General Acts and Measures and of Statutory Instruments, and an annual index to Statutory Instruments – is entrusted to another sub-department of the Treasury, the Statutory Publications Office, which in 1956 was incorporated in the Treasury Solicitor's Department. Both the Consolidation Branch and the Statutory Publications Office work under the eye of the Statute Law Committee. In Scotland all such work is done by the Lord Advocate's Department: the Lord Advocate himself is a member of the Statute Law Committee.

In addition to the Law Reform Committees and the Statute Law Committee there has been, since 1952, a standing committee called the Private International Law Committee. This structure of committees constitutes a formidable organization devoted to law reform. The whole process of improving the Statute Book especially has, in fact, become 'an accepted part of governmental activity, and not just something that received attention if there should be time to spare', as had tended to be the case before the Second World War.[3]

The responsibility of the Home Office and Scottish Home Department for the general maintenance of public order, and their particular interest in the police and prison systems and the magistrates' courts, are only the more obvious manifestations of the close concern which those departments have for the whole range of the criminal law. They are in a good position from which to see clearly the working of the law and to observe where reform is needed; and if there are any proposals for change the two departments have a recognized right throughout the central government to be consulted.

LEGAL WORK IN THE DEPARTMENTS

The Lord Chancellor and the four Law Officers are the main sources of legal advice to the Government as a whole, but each of the major departments relies on its own legal staff or on the staffs of the Treasury Solicitor and the Lord Advocate for the usual run of departmental legal work. That work includes some which has already been mentioned – drafting, preparation of litigation and prosecutions and the representation of departments in court – but it also covers general advice on interpretation and application of the law, and a considerable amount of conveyancing duties involved in the transfer of real property.

Departments fall roughly into three groups so far as the sources of their legal advice are concerned. Some departments are self-contained – though all but one or two of those with a United Kingdom or Great Britain jurisdiction depend either on the Lord Advocate's London Office or on the Solicitor to the Secretary of State for Scotland for advice on Scottish legal matters. Some departments are wholly dependent on the Treasury Solicitor and the Lord Advocate's Department. The third group comprises departments which have legal officers who deal with only a proportion of the legal work, and which draw on the Treasury Solicitor and Lord Advocate's Department for special advice – and often for conveyancing. The Scottish departments look either to the Lord Advocate's Department or to the Solicitor to the Secretary of State for legal advice on Scottish questions.

This threefold division has been commonplace throughout the period. When a department has a set of administrative tasks which are based on or involve dealing with a code of specialized law, or when a department has a very great deal of legal work, then the department has its own legal section. This is the case, for example, with the Board of Inland Revenue (which even has its own Solicitor in Scotland), the Ministry of Agriculture, Fisheries and Food, the Board of Trade, the Ministry of Labour and National Service, etc. There are cases – e.g., Health and Housing and Local Government – where one legal branch serves two or more departments. The departments which have legal officers but also rely on the Treasury Solicitor include the Ministry of Education and the three departments exclusively concerned with external affairs – the Foreign, Colonial, and Commonwealth Relations Offices. The departmental Legal Advisers of the three latter offices concentrate on the special aspects of law peculiarly relevant to external affairs – e.g., the drafting of treaties, advice on international law, etc. – and leave the more routine domestic legal business of their departments to the Treasury Solicitor. The Defence departments, the Ministry of Fuel and Power, the Ministry of Transport and Civil Aviation and a large number of small departments rely entirely on the Treasury Solicitor, either because of the general and miscellaneous nature of the legal advice which they require and which can most conveniently be provided by a 'common service' organization, or because they have insufficient legal work to justify separate legal establishments.

During the past forty years departments have on occasion shifted from one of the three groups to another as the size or nature of their legal needs have changed. New departments have tended to rely on the Treasury Solicitor, though the Ministry of Labour and the Ministry of National Insurance are among the exceptions.

ADMINISTRATION DIRECTED BY LAWYERS

The Lord Chancellor's Department and the small departments attached to the Law Officers are staffed almost entirely by lawyers, understandably so considering the highly legal nature of the work. There are four small departments which are also largely preserves of the legal profession because the work they do demands the continual application of expert legal knowledge. The Lord Chancellor has parliamentary responsibility for the Public Trustee's department and for the Land Registry: the Chancellor of the Exchequer is answerable for the Friendly Societies' Registry. The Charity Commission has throughout the period been an independent department, though the Government announced in July, 1955, that

'a Minister should be appointed to represent the [Charity] Commissioners in Parliament and in the Government with power to approve rules and regulations made by the Charity Commissioners but . . . to give them general guidance only, not direction. It is proposed that the Home Secretary should undertake these functions.'[4]

The necessary legislation has not yet been introduced.

THE IDEA OF A MINISTRY OF JUSTICE

The arrangement of work in this rather diffuse field of public order, justice and legal administration has never been the subject of major public or parliamentary controversy during the last forty years, but some aspects of it have been the subject of continuous if mild, leisurely, and somewhat academic discussion arising from a proposal made by the Haldane Committee on the Machinery of Government in 1918 that a Ministry of Justice should be established.

It must immediately be emphasized that the Ministry of Justice which the Committee and later writers envisaged was a peculiarly British concept, owing little or nothing to the experience and practice of other – notably European – countries. The Haldane proposals are representative of all those which came later – few if any of which, in fact, have included detailed suggestions. Those proposals were, in essence, to reshuffle the functions of the Lord Chancellor and the Home Secretary: Scottish arrangements were not dealt with by the Committee.

The Haldane Report suggested that the Lord Chancellor, relieved of his duties as Speaker of the House of Lords and 'freed from the duty of daily or even frequent judicial sitting', should become responsible for the appointment of all judges, after consultation with a small advisory committee: should continue to be 'the principal legal and constitutional adviser of the Cabinet': and should have sufficient time to 'watch and master all questions relating to legislation'. All the other functions of the central government which were connected with the administration of justice and with what we have called public order should be concentrated in the Home Office. The Home Secretary should at the same time be 'relieved of functions pertaining to other national services, such as those concerned with health and with production in Mines and Factories', and should take from the Local Government Board its 'general jurisdiction in regard to local areas and powers', and its responsibility for electoral administration. In short the Haldane Committee's Home Office or 'Ministry of Justice' would have been responsible for all the central government's administrative arrangements for facilitating the judicial process other than the appointment of judges, and for maintaining public order, and at the same time would have been the department with a special overall interest in the structure and constitutional arrangements of the local government system.

The Haldane proposals were a result in part of applying the Committee's 'principle' of concentrating the functions of government, but they were also based on other considerations. First was the opinion, drawn from the personal experience of Lord Haldane, that the Lord Chancellor had far too much to do. Second was the objection to what appeared to the Committee as a very diffused and untidy arrangement of functions concerning law and justice: it seemed to them improbable that such a patchwork could really be efficient. Third was the belief that the reform of the law would receive more attention from government if a Ministry of Justice as defined was in fact established.

With the validity of these arguments, either in 1918 or later, this study is not concerned, but it is of some interest to compare what has in fact happened with the Haldane Committee's recommendations. The Lord Chancellor has indeed collected to himself practically all the power of appointing or advising the Crown on the appointment of judges in England and Wales, but whereas the Haldane Committee wanted him to be relieved of most of his other administrative work, in fact he has been made responsible for much more, and his original personal office has in the process become a small but distinct department. Meanwhile the division of responsibility between the Lord Chancellor and the Home Secretary has been considerably clarified. The Home Secretary has in turn lost some of those 'unrelated' functions such as the regulation of working conditions in factories and mines which he had in 1918, and has also, as the Haldane Committee wished, become responsible for electoral administration; but the general concern for the local government system remains with the successor to the Local Government Board. The Home Secretary remains the 'residuary legatee', and counts among his present functions some which the Haldane Committee might have regarded as properly belonging elsewhere.

Scottish arrangements might well be regarded as 'out-Haldaning' Haldane. In the Scottish Home Department are concentrated even more comprehensive powers than it was thought desirable to vest in a Ministry of Justice for England and Wales. The Department does most of the establishment work concerned with the staffs of the Scottish courts (except the local police courts), exercises the central powers relating to police and prisons, and has a general oversight not only of the structure of the local government system but also of its finance, which the Haldane Committee considered should be the business of the Treasury. The ministerial head of the Scottish Home Department – the Secretary of State for Scotland – is responsible for the appointment, or for advising the Crown on the appointment, of almost all the judges (though normally they are first nominated by the Lord Advocate). The Haldane Committee had insisted that the appointing power should not be wielded by the departmental minister responsible for 'Justice', but they did not include Scotland in their purview.

IV

SOCIAL SERVICES

THE expression 'Social Services' is used loosely at the present time to cover those activities of the State which are either concerned with intimate aspects of the life of the individual citizen – his education, his health, his financial security in sickness, unemployment or old age, etc. – or are concerned with some aspects of the physical surroundings and conditions in which the citizen passes his life – the provision of houses, the enforcement of public health regulations, the layout of towns, and so on. Social services are, in fact, those services which are directed towards sustaining an acceptable minimum and promoting a progressively better physical and moral 'condition of the people'. If this wide and somewhat rhetorical definition is translated into terms suitable for a study of the administrative work of the central government, it is to-day usually taken to mean, on the 'personal' side, education, the National Health Service, the national schemes of insurance, family allowances, and assistance, etc.: and, on the 'environmental' side, housing, town and country planning, public health and related matters.

These social services have come to be thought of as forming a coherent group of governmental functions in the field of domestic affairs. They are not as clearly connected with each other, as far as policy work is concerned, as the defence or economic functions; but they are essentially a single concept. This is particularly true of those services which involve the payment of financial benefits and the provision of free medical attention: these personal services are indeed now regarded as part of the 'British way of life', most of them having a universal application. Every citizen at some time or other, whatever his status in the community, comes into contact with one or other of those numerous practices which are frequently referred to as forming, collectively, the Welfare State. This attitude is, however, of very recent growth: it is, in fact, only characteristic of the post Second World War years, and reflects in large part the impact of that thought and planning during the war which had as its major manifestation the Report by Sir William (now Lord) Beveridge on *Social Insurance and Allied Services*.[1]

Before the Second World War each service grew up separately, in response to different social and political pressures: each service applied only to particular sections of the community: and the work of administering each service was, by and large, self-contained. It is only in the last few years that we have come to think of the social services, in the context of the central government, as concerning primarily four departments or sets of departments concentrating on education, personal health, environmental conditions, and 'cash payments' (i.e., pensions, health and unemployment benefits, family allowances, and assistance) respectively. These functional divisions existed before the Second World War, but each was not necessarily the exclusive business of one or a set of departments. It would be possible to trace the history of each of these four 'fields' from 1914 to the present day in separate narratives, but slavish application of this idea would distort the true picture of how each service and its administration fitted into the structure of government as a whole at various times. The method of presentation adopted, therefore, is to divide the narrative into sections which are each devoted to a clear period of development, either of a particular department or of a particular service or group of services. In the case of education the service and the departments are, except in regard to the universities and to certain aspects of agricultural education, synonymous, and a continuous narrative section on all education covering the whole period is therefore possible.

The subject matter of this chapter is not restricted to those functions of the central government which concern the three basic ingredients of the Welfare State – education, health, and the various financial benefits. It also covers the administration of war disablement pensions and the care of war pensioners, which in recent years has been entrusted to the social service departments: and the central government's responsibilities for the care of children deprived of a normal home life.

Since the social services are provided for the individual citizen, they have to be administered locally, and a very large part of the administration of the social services is and always has been the business of Local Authorities. With the internal organization of those Authorities and with the nature of the relations between them and the central departments this study is not concerned.[a] Transfers of responsibility

[a] The central government's relations with Local Authorities range from detailed control of some services to practically no control of other services. It is quite impossible to generalize but in this short chapter it is equally impossible to give an accurate description of the central government's powers and influence in the case of each of the Social Services. This should be remembered in reading the following pages: expressions like 'central supervision', or 'the central government

between local and central government are recorded, but rearrangement of functions among the various classes of Local Authorities is either ignored or receives only passing mention. It may, however, be mentioned that so far as England and Wales are concerned, the principal department dealing with social services has, throughout our period, been the department which the Government has generally regarded as the major central authority interested in local government as a whole – i.e., with the broad constitutional aspects of local government, its structure, its finance, and its functions. That department in 1914 was the Local Government Board: its successor from 1919 until 1951 was the Ministry of Health: and the present department responsible for this local government work is the Ministry of Housing and Local Government. Each of these departments has been concerned with environmental services and, until 1948, with the central supervision of the administration of the Poor Law. In contrast to English experience, the general constitutional and financial oversight of local government in Scotland has throughout our period been the business of a department not mainly concerned with social service administration – the Scottish Office until 1939 and thenceforward the Scottish Home Department.

EDUCATION 1914–1956

Responsibility for central educational administration has been remarkably static and compact since 1914. While governmental concern for and expenditure on education has steadily increased, and while great changes have been made in the concept of education, the present functions of the central departments are no more than an extended version of the work they were performing forty years ago.

The three Irish education departments – the Commissioners of National Education, the Intermediate Education Board, and the Endowed Schools Commission – remained unchanged in status until the end of the Union in 1922, but the two departments serving England and Wales on the one hand, and Scotland on the other hand, have both undergone some constitutional transition. The Board of Education for England and Wales became a Ministry in 1944, though this made no real difference to the position of the political head of the department, who as President of the Board had been its virtual chief – the 'Board' was in fact the last of the 'phantom' Boards of the 19th

---

had certain powers in respect of', when applied to services run by Local Authorities mean only one of a wide range of central/local relationships.

century to give place to the 20th century idea of the 'Ministry'.[b] The Scottish Education Department was from 1914 to 1939 under the control of a Committee of the Privy Council on Education in Scotland, but the Committee never met after 1913 and the Secretary/ Secretary of State for Scotland was its only active member.[2] In 1939 the Privy Council's powers were transferred to the Secretary of State, who has continued to exercise them through the Scottish Education Department.

School administration has remained throughout primarily a local government service carried out subject to certain supervisory powers of the central departments. The concern of the State with the universities has been, in the main, confined to granting increasingly large sums of money for their development and administration. From 1914 to 1919 the Board of Education and the Scottish Education Department made grants to universities, but in 1919 this work was transferred to the Treasury, where it has since been carried out through a University Grants Committee. That Committee was originally intended only to be an advisory body, and though this is still the case formally, in practice the Committee has won the confidence of the Treasury to such an extent that the allocation of money has been almost entirely entrusted to it. The evolution of this unique machinery for giving State aid to universities without trespassing on the academic independence of those institutions is perhaps the most important development which has occurred in the field of educational administration. Responsibility for the provision of and for financial assistance to agricultural education below the university level is, at the centre, shared between the education and agricultural departments.

Other relevant changes in departmental responsibilities have been concerned with minor and marginal activities. The Board of Education parted company with the Geological Survey in 1919, when the latter passed into the fold of the recently created Department of Scientific and Industrial Research. Certain medical functions concerning children were taken from the education departments in 1919 and handed over to the newly-established Ministry of Health and Scottish Board of Health.[c] Until 1927 the Board of Education was

[b] The Boards of the Treasury, the Admiralty and of Trade, still with us, are survivals from before 1800. The Board of Admiralty has never been a 'phantom'. The Treasury Board does not meet to transact business, but its members – the Prime Minister (First Lord), the Chancellor of the Exchequer (Second Lord), and the Junior Lords (Government Whips) – all have Treasury duties of some kind. The Board of Trade never meets and none of its members except the President takes any part in its work.

[c] These changes are dealt with more fully in the following sections on health and welfare services.

responsible for youth employment work in those areas where it was done by local education authorities, but in that year the central powers were transferred to the Ministry of Labour. In 1946 the Central Youth Employment Executive was set up. It consists of representatives of the Ministry of Labour and National Service, the Ministry of Education and the Scottish Education Department, and is responsible to the Minister of Labour and National Service. In 1953 financial responsibility for education in prisons and Borstals was transferred from the Ministry of Education to the Prison Commission.

In return, as it were, for these losses, the education departments gained a few similarly minor functions. Power with regard to public libraries passed from the Ministry of Health to the Board of Education in 1920, and from the Scottish Office to the Scottish Education Department in 1939. In 1920 the supervision of reformatories and industrial schools in Scotland was transferred from the Scottish Office to the Scottish Education Department.[d] In 1949 the Ministry of Education was entrusted with jurisdiction over quasi-educational trusts which had previously been exercised by the Charity Commission: charitable trusts whose purpose was wholly educational had been handled by the Board of Education since its establishment at the turn of the century. In Scotland, when the Commissioners under the Educational Endowments (Scotland) Act, 1928, ceased to hold office in 1936, the powers vested in them were transferred, as provided by the Act, to the Scottish Education Department.

HEALTH AND WELFARE SERVICES TO THE END
OF THE FIRST WORLD WAR

The Position in 1914

In the nine years prior to the outbreak of war in 1914 Liberal Governments had extended the restricted health and welfare services which existed when they took office and had introduced vast new schemes based on principles hitherto untried under governmental auspices in this country. At the centre these services were by 1914 the concern of a varied group of departments.

The oldest of the welfare services was also the most comprehensive. Under the Poor Law, which in England and Wales dated from 1601, though it had been reformed and reorganized in 1834, any citizen who had sunk to a sufficiently low material condition was

[d] Such schools in England and Wales have always been under Home Office control.

eligible either for *ad hoc* payments in money or in kind, or for the Spartan comforts of the workhouse. Medical attention was available under the Poor Law, and some of its more enterprising local admini-strators in England and Wales – the Guardians of the Poor – had developed general hospitals. In England and Wales the Guardians were supervised by the Local Government Board, and similar local provision in Scotland and Ireland was made under the eyes of Local Government Boards in Edinburgh and Dublin.[e] The three Local Government Boards were, however, not only Poor Law authorities. They also had powers in respect of the local administration of that mass of public health legislation which had been one of the great social achievements of the Victorian age. Concern particularly for the health of towns had produced a code of sanitary law: permissive power to build houses had been given to Local Authorities towards the end of the 19th century in order to stimulate slum clearance, though little municipal building had in fact been undertaken by 1914: and in 1909 the first town planning legislation found a place in the Statute Book. The environmental health services did not, how-ever, constitute all the functions carried out under public health powers. Those powers enabled – and indeed often commanded – Local Authorities to provide health services of a personal nature, such as the isolation and treatment of sufferers from infectious diseases, public vaccination, and quarantine administration in the ports.

Since 1905 the education departments had developed a very con-siderable interest in health matters. An Act of 1907 made the medical inspection of all schoolchildren compulsory in England and Wales, and a School Medical Service grew up, administered by the Local Authorities with the help and under the eye of the Board of Educa-tion, which also helped and encouraged voluntary bodies to run maternity and child welfare services. Similar provision was made in Scotland under Acts of 1908 and 1913. The Privy Council had certain powers relating to the governing body of the medical profession – the General Medical Council – and was also responsible, through the Central Midwives Board, for regulating the practice of midwifery in England and Wales. Similar regulation was not extended to Scotland until 1915.

The Home and Scottish Offices had a mixed group of health and welfare responsibilities. They had what departmental powers there were concerning lunacy and mental deficiency: those powers in-cluded some relating to the largely independent bodies which did

e There were no Guardians in Scotland, where Poor Law functions were exercised originally by the Kirk Session and latterly by the Parish Council.

most of the governmental work in this connection – the Board of Control for England and Wales and the General Board of Control for Scotland. These Boards had a predominantly independent status because the control and treatment of persons suffering from mental disorders called not only for a medical but also for a judicial approach: persons could only be deprived of their liberty on account of their mental condition after the most careful legal and procedural safeguards had been applied. The Home and Scottish Offices supervised local administration of Acts governing certain aspects of the treatment of infants who were deprived of a normal home life. This work was usually referred to as 'infant life protection'. Lastly, the Home Office exercised a general oversight of the scheme of Workmen's Compensation for industrial injury. Under this scheme, which covered all manual and lower paid non-manual workers, the employer was liable

'to pay compensation to a workman injured by accident arising out of and in the course of his employment, or to his dependants if the accident resulted in death, whether or not there had been negligence on the part of the employer or anyone employed by him.'[3]

The Government made no financial contribution.

In 1908 the Liberals had introduced a scheme for the payment of non-contributory pensions to persons of seventy or more years of age who had limited means. The Treasury was responsible for these Old Age Pensions, but delegated the execution of the scheme to the Board of Inland Revenue because that department was the only one with a suitable network of local offices. Those offices were primarily used for the collection of excise duties, and in 1909 the excise and pensions work was transferred to what had hitherto been called the Board of Customs and henceforward was known as the Board of Customs and Excise.

Legislation passed in 1911 inaugurated two schemes based on the insurance principle – i.e., benefits were provided in return for actuarially calculated contributions from employees and employers which were augmented by a contribution from the State. Workers in certain trades were covered by an Unemployment Insurance Scheme. Unemployment Insurance was conceived as a wholly governmental device, not dependent for its administration on private institutions, though trade unions were permitted, in certain circumstances, to handle the benefits. It was regarded as complementary to the provision of a service for placing workers in jobs, both functions being dealt with by the new nation-wide structure of Labour Exchanges. The Board of Trade was at that time the obvious department to handle these new tasks as an extension of its existing labour functions.

The second insurance scheme – Health Insurance – was a more complicated affair. In return for contributions all manual and lower paid non-manual workers were eligible to receive medical attention and money benefits when they were sick and could not work, and the scheme also included a very limited system of maternity benefits. Medical attention and money benefits were thus tied to the payment of contributions. Medical attention required the full co-operation of the medical profession and arrangements for handling the collection and payment of money had to be made. The Government did not set up a special local office organization. Instead it 'farmed out' the routine work of collecting contributions and making payments to a

TABLE XII

DEPARTMENTS CONCERNED WITH SOCIAL SERVICES
(With numbers of non-industrial staffs)

1914

(a) *United Kingdom*

Joint Committee of the Insurance Commissions	35

(b) *England and Wales*

Board of Education	1,655
Local Government Board	920
English Insurance Commission	1,310
Welsh Insurance Commission	140
Board of Control	50

(c) *Scotland*

Scottish Education Department	245
Local Government Board for Scotland	80
Scottish Insurance Commission	275
Highlands and Islands Medical Services Board	5
General Board of Control for Scotland	20

(d) *Ireland*

Commissioners of National Education	270
Intermediate Education Board	45
Endowed Schools Commission	5
Irish Local Government Board	245
Irish Insurance Commission	215
	5,515

Note: Over 4,000 Board of Trade officials were concerned with employment matters, which included the Unemployment Insurance Scheme.

large number of friendly societies, trade unions, medical aid societies and industrial assurance companies. These organizations so far as their health insurance activities were concerned were henceforward called Approved Societies, and operated on a non-profit-making basis. Thus the clerical and executive organization needed was kept quite outside the Civil Service. There remained the need to have a central authority within the governmental hierarchy to deal with matters of high policy and finance. To meet this need a group of four separate Insurance Commissions was set up, one Commission for each of the four units of the United Kingdom, while a Joint Committee of the four was established to ensure uniformity of practice. The Treasury was the 'parent' department of all these bodies, but the bulk of the responsibility for administering the scheme fell on the Chairman of the Joint Committee, who was eligible to sit in the House of Commons and was, in fact, always a member of the Government. In order to make his position tenable in Parliament the first holder of the post asserted his sole responsibility by refusing to defend decisions of the Commissions which did not have his approval.[4] Once the worst 'teething troubles' of the scheme were overcome the Joint Committee took a less important part in its administration.

In 1913 a Highlands and Islands Medical Services Board was set up to administer a Fund for subsidizing medical services in the remote parts of Scotland. The Secretary for Scotland had certain powers concerning the Board.

The group of departments described above did not have a monopoly of all the health and welfare services, insofar as a number of departments – the Admiralty and War Office, for example – provided some such services in special circumstances and to special occupational categories of people. Apart from the administration of disablement pensions and the medical treatment of persons receiving such pensions, which will be dealt with later, the health functions of these other departments have never been regarded as part of the general social services, and therefore do not receive any further mention in this chapter. We must now begin to trace the administrative fortunes of the various component parts of the general social services after 1914.

Unemployment Insurance and the Ministry of Labour

When the Ministry of Labour was set up at the end of 1916 it took over all the labour functions previously discharged by the Board of Trade, among them the administration of the Unemployment Insurance Scheme. This was an obvious arrangement: as we have seen,

Unemployment Insurance was regarded as the partner of the placing service, and both were handled by the same administrative machinery, the Labour Exchanges.

The Establishment of the Ministry of Health and the Scottish Board of Health

In 1919 a Minister of Health and a Scottish Board of Health were appointed. Either immediately on the passing of the Ministry of Health Act in June, 1919, or within three years of that date, there were transferred to the Minister of Health all the powers of the Local Government Board and of the English and Welsh Insurance Commissions: the powers of the Privy Council and of the Lord President of the Council concerning midwives in England and Wales: the powers of the Home Secretary relating to infant life protection, to the practice of anatomy, and to the treatment of lunacy and mental deficiency in England and Wales, and certain powers under the Factory and Workshop Act, 1901: the powers of the Board of Trade concerning private water undertakings: certain powers of the Ministry of Agriculture and Fisheries relating to infestation in ports and vessels: and the powers of the Board of Education regarding medical examination and treatment of young persons and regarding maternity and infant welfare services. Special arrangements were simultaneously introduced between the Ministry of Health and the Board of Education which ensured that the School Medical Service continued to be administered by the Board: various methods were adopted to prevent friction between the two departments, one of the most prominent being the appointment of a single Chief Medical Officer who served both authorities. The new Ministry of Health completed the definition of its functions by getting rid of certain duties not closely concerned with health and welfare – some transport powers went to the new Ministry of Transport, supervision of public libraries became the responsibility of the Board of Education, and the regulation of municipal gas supply was transferred to the Board of Trade. A Welsh Board of Health was set up, composed of officials of the Ministry of Health, to exercise such powers in Wales as the Minister thought fit.

A broadly similar set of transfers was effected in Scotland, where the new Board of Health took over the powers of the Local Government Board for Scotland, the Scottish Insurance Commission, the Privy Council's and Lord President's powers relating to midwives, and the Scottish Education Department's health functions. In addition, however, the Board took on the Secretary for Scotland's powers concerning the Highlands and

Islands Medical Service, and a number of public health functions previously vested in the Secretary for Scotland, including supervision of the registration of births, deaths and marriages, which in England and Wales had been part of the responsibility of the President of the Local Government Board. The Secretary for Scotland was the President and political head of the new Board of Health, and a Parliamentary Secretary for Health was appointed as Vice-President – the first junior minister (apart from the Solicitor General) to be allotted to Scotland. *f*

The establishment of two departments overwhelmingly concerned with health matters was the partial triumph of an idea – the idea that the main existing health services should be unified and placed under the general supervision of a Minister in each national area whose purpose would be, in the words of the Ministry of Health Act, to promote 'the health of the people' and whose duty it would be to take 'all such steps as may be desirable to secure the preparation, effective carrying out, and co-ordination of measures conducive to the health of the people'. The creation of these departments was, however, only a partial triumph because while it achieved unity at the centre it left a division in local administration between those services provided under the Poor Law and those developed by the general Local Authorities. It was not until ten years later, with the abolition of the Boards of Guardians in England and Wales and the Parish Councils in Scotland, and the merging of their functions with those of the henceforward comprehensive Local Authorities that the whole administrative reform was completed. Moreover the departmental reorganization at the end of the First World War was only a reorganization – it did not involve any major extension of governmental functions save in the case of housing.

The creation of the Ministry of Health was, indeed, merely one more stage in that long and complicated development of the rôle of the State in the field of social welfare which came to full fruition after the Second World War. To tell the whole story of the origins of the Ministry of Health would therefore be to tell the story of all the contemporary developments in the ideas about, and in the organization of, all the welfare services. We cannot attempt such a task here, and what follows is only the barest recital of the major influences and occurrences which led to the administrative changes of 1919. The story is an English story, but there was a similar outcome in Scotland.

A single theme which runs through the complex administrative

---

f Irish departmental arrangements were not disturbed. The Irish Local Government Board and Irish Insurance Commission remained in existence until the end of the Union.

changes and innovations of the years from 1906 to 1919 was the consistent belief in the necessity and inevitability of a Ministry of Health which was held by Sir Robert Morant, whose influence was undoubtedly a big factor in the establishment of the new department. He was first impressed with the desirability of unifying the health services when, as Secretary of the Board of Education, he played a notable part in launching the School Medical Service in 1906–7. He then began to think of 'health as the identical twin of education, two great services to be developed side by side'. By 1915, when Chairman of the English Insurance Commission, he was sure of his ultimate aim – 'In a sentence it is the gradual building up of a rational organization, in London, of a Central Department of Health'.[5]

The unification of health services under the auspices of a single department, which did not perhaps seem too far away in the first years of the Liberal Administration, was delayed and made more difficult to achieve by three major factors – the controversy over the future of the Poor Law, the introduction of National Health Insurance, and the outbreak of war. The famous Royal Commission on the Poor Laws reported in 1909 and was clearly divided. All members were agreed on the need for reforms in the Poor Law medical service, but the influential minority wanted a 'root and branch' reform based on the 'breaking up' of the Poor Law which, among other things, would permit the unified control of local health services and thereby avoid that overlapping between the Poor Law Guardians and the Local Authorities which was already apparent.

One effect of the controversy which broke out over the future of the Poor Law was to weaken the position of the Local Government Board. Even if full allowance is made for the enthusiasm and bias of the partisan, there was considerable justification for Beatrice Webb's contention in 1917 that 'since the issue of the two reports (1909) the status of the Local Government Board had gone from bad to worse', and for her belief that the department was 'being throttled by its connection with an obsolete and emasculated Poor Law. No Government dared to give any function to a Poor Law authority – central or local'.[6] A contributory factor in the decline of the Local Government Board was the presence of John Burns at its head during the crucial period up to 1914. Viscount Samuel has written this sketch of the departmental career of that early leader of the Labour Movement:

'The first manual worker ever to become a Cabinet Minister, he had set about his work in an energetic reforming spirit; but as time went by the pace slackened; and after eight years' continuous service the Minister had become more and more bureaucratized, and the Department less and less active. Lloyd George, with his unresting zeal, found himself without effective co-operation from the Ministry with which many of his plans were closely concerned, and chronic friction developed.'[7]

It is not surprising, therefore, to learn from another source that Lloyd George's distrust of Burns was one reason why the Local Government Board was not chosen to handle Health Insurance, though that distrust may well have extended beyond Burns himself to the department as a whole.[g]

The introduction of Health Insurance with a separate organization undoubtedly complicated and retarded the unification of health services administration. Morant only reluctantly agreed to become Chairman of the English Insurance Commission in 1911 because though he saw the chance which the post ultimately gave him of working towards unification, he felt insurance to be 'an oblique and unsatisfactory entry' into the difficult field of comprehensive health services.[8] The effects of the decisions taken in 1909–11 have been appraised by Sir Arthur Newsholme, who remarks that when the Insurance Act was passed

'both the Local Government Board and the Board of Education were already actively engaged in medical and hygienic work, in considerable measure for the same persons. The addition of the Insurance Medical work, in a third compartment, multiplied confusion and seriously impeded satisfactory work. Incidentally it also postponed the poor law medical reform, in favour of which the Royal Commission on the Poor Laws had reported, and so a momentous opportunity for unifying the medical work of government was allowed to slip.'[9]

At the beginning of the First World War, therefore, the problem facing those who wished to see all the elements in health administration concentrated in a single department was, primarily, how to bring together the Insurance Commission and the Local Government

g Sir Almeric Fitzroy: *Memoirs*, Vol. II, p. 646. The Webbs and apparently Mr Winston Churchill – and Morant himself – had hoped that the latter would become Secretary of the Local Government Board in 1909, but his known sympathy for the Minority Report of the Poor Law Commission, which was not shared by Burns, helped to put this out of court. It is interesting to speculate on whether Lloyd George might have been more willing to entrust Health Insurance to the Board had this happened, in view of the fact that he chose Morant to help him in 1911. See B. M. Allen: *Sir Robert Morant*, p. 248; B. Webb: *Our Partnership*, pp. 379, 411, 437, 443; and comments by D. N. Chester in 'Robert Morant and Michael Sadler', *Public Administration*, Summer, 1950.

Board. Even as early as July, 1914, Lloyd George had apparently recognized the weakness of the existing division and expressed the wish that Insurance should be moved to the Local Government Board,[10] but it was not until 1917 that firm proposals reached the Cabinet and received a blessing in principle, and agreement on a draft Bill was not achieved until the middle of 1918. It is unnecessary to describe at length the progress of the negotiations. The chief proponents of the Ministry of Health were, apart from Morant, Dr (later Lord) Addison and Lord Rhondda, who provided the main pressure at Cabinet level, where they were supported by Lord Milner.[11] Public opinion was by this time running in favour of the reformers. Morant made the point in 1915 that medical treatment was the vital thing in the Insurance Scheme and that it had caught the popular imagination.[12] Moreover a sign of political support was the formation of a group of enthusiastic Unionist MPs who came to agree on the need for a single department of health.[13] Apart from some institutional unwillingness on the part of the Local Government Board and the Insurance Commission to accept the idea of a merger, the main obstacles in the later negotiations were the fear of the Approved Societies that the new régime might deprive them of their privileged positions as distributors of insurance benefits, and a more general fear that the new concept of health services under the Insurance Scheme might be tainted through such close departmental association with the Poor Law. All these objections were met sufficiently for the Ministry of Health Bill to be given an enthusiastic reception, mingled only with regret in some quarters that the problem of the Poor Law had still to be faced.

WAR DISABLEMENT PENSIONS: THE ESTABLISHMENT OF THE MINISTRY OF PENSIONS

We must now turn back and describe the development of another activity which was eventually to be merged, administratively, with the general health and 'cash payment' services. Responsibility for the support of dependants of Servicemen who had been killed or disabled had only been assumed by the State since the South African War. The public conscience had, however, been roused on this subject during the Crimean campaigns, and a body of Commissioners had been appointed at that time to manage on behalf of dependants the large sums of money subscribed. The Royal Patriotic Fund Commission provided benefits not only for the victims of the Crimean battles, but also, in later years, for the dependants of those killed or disabled in the small Colonial Wars of the latter decades of the 19th century. The Fund was extended during the war in South Africa and was used to supplement the new dependants' pensions then awarded by the State. In 1903 the Commission was reorganized and was henceforward known as the Royal Patriotic Fund Corporation. Under that name it was to play no small part in the history of pensions administration during the First World War. The State disablement pensions, such as were awarded, were administered by the two Service departments: the War Office entrusted their share of the work to a satellite body, the Commissioners of Chelsea Hospital, whose duties included the care of the 'in-pensioners' of that famous institution.

This organization for administering what may be called war disablement pensions remained substantially unaltered during the first two years of the war which broke out in August, 1914. As in other fields, the scale of the conflict was not at first realized, and the inevitable result was that the pensions machinery of the Service departments was overwhelmed. Moreover, new ideas about what benefits should be made available by the State were voiced, and the Government was gradually pushed into accepting increasingly heavier financial burdens. The first major change in the administrative structure came late in 1915 when Parliament, acting on the advice of a Select Committee, set up a Statutory Committee of the Royal Patriotic Fund Corporation and a whole network of local committees. The functions of the new organization were threefold. It was to decide any question of fact on which the payment of pensions from public funds depended: it was to regulate and to pay supplementary grants, pensions and separation allowances in exceptional cases where the official payments were inadequate: and it was to provide medical and after-care, training and employment for the disabled and their dependants. The Treasury refused to give public money to the Statutory Committee at first, hoping that sufficient funds would be forthcoming from private subscriptions. It was claimed that what was needed was 'a voluntary body not under Parliamentary control', that the power of granting benefits was best removed from the sphere of 'politics', and that the alternative course of amalgamating all the scattered departments of the War Office and Admiralty and creating a wholly unified central administration was too difficult.

The Statutory Committee and its local committees began to function early in 1916, and throughout that year there was increasing overlapping and delay resulting from the heavy and continuous influx of new cases and from the existence of three separate organizations, two under full ministerial control and one having a peculiar quasi-governmental status. The position was not improved by the realization that insufficient money was being subscribed privately to meet the needs of the Statutory Committee. The Government paid over £1 million at the end of March, and when the Committee assumed responsibility for the payment of supplementary separation allowances in July the Treasury undertook to provide all the necessary money. Finally the Treasury agreed, in August, to ask Parliament for £6 million for the Statutory Committee, but by then the whole situation had become so complex and unsatisfactory that drastic administrative reorganization was foreshadowed.[14]

The Asquith Government brought in a Board of Pensions Bill in November, 1916. It provided for the creation of a Board to deal with Army cases only and left the payment of separation allowances and the provision of after-care, training and employment to the Statutory Committee. The Bill was obviously a compromise measure, and one Government spokesman admitted that it was merely a 'half-way house towards unification' of pensions administration. The House of Commons was in no mood to accept such a Bill. It was agreed that a real unification was essential to avoid overlapping jurisdictions with their consequent delays and anomalies, to free the Service departments of what was predominantly civil work, to enable all the related problems of payment, after-care, training and employment to be treated together, and to end the arrangement whereby the Statutory Committee, an authority almost independent of Parliament, was spending huge sums of public money. These arguments carried the day, and the renamed Bill, considerably modified, was passed in December to authorize the creation of a Ministry of Pensions.

The new Ministry took over from the Admiralty and War Office in February, 1917, the functions relating to the administration of all disablement pensions and allowances, including pensions awarded prior to 1914.[h] The Statutory Committee and the local committees were brought under the general control of the Minister but retained the initiative in some matters and a good deal of practical autonomy in their administrative work. This continued duality soon proved unworkable. The local committees felt that they were answerable to two masters and there was irritating overlapping on some aspects, such as the provision for after-care and training. The Statutory Committee ceased to exist in September, 1917, with apparent agreement in all quarters, some of its judicial work passing to an independent special Grants Committee. At the same time a firm line was

[h] The Ministry of Pensions also dealt with pensions for the Nursing Services. The 'in-pensioners' at Chelsea remained a responsibility of the Commissioners of the Hospital.

drawn once again between public and private funds: all money held by the Statutory Committee which had been voluntarily subscribed was handed over to the Royal Patriotic Fund Corporation.

The almost complete unification of the administration of disablement pensions lasted for three years. During that period only one type of disablement pension – that awarded to officers on account of wounds – remained the business of the Service departments. The idea of having a comprehensive department which would deal with all aspects of pension work did not long survive the end of the war. The work of providing training for disabled ex-servicemen was transferred from the Ministry of Pensions to the Ministry of Labour in May, 1919. In the following year the Government decided to reduce the scope of the Ministry of Pensions' functions by retransferring to the Service departments the administration of pensions awarded for disablement arising out of service in peace-time prior to 1914 and for service in peace-time following the end of the Great War – the date of which was later fixed for pension purposes as September 30, 1921.

The curtailment of the functions of the Ministry of Pensions was partly the result of a conviction that the department should be concerned only with pensions awarded for service in the Great War, though the Government in fact gave way to the Commons while the enabling Bill was passing through Standing Committee and agreed that disablement pensions awarded for service during wars prior to 1914 should continue to be administered by the Ministry. There were, however, additional reasons of a more substantial nature why responsibility for peace-time disablement pensions was returned to the Service departments. In the first place, such pensions would be awarded to regular soldiers, sailors and airmen who would, in addition to their disablement benefits, receive service pensions based on years of service and good conduct qualifications, etc. As the records of such service qualifications were held by the Service departments it would be more convenient for those departments to deal with disablement pensions as well, and thus avoid the necessity for treating each case in two ministries. Another point made against those who wished to see the Ministry of Pensions left with all its original powers was that since the transfer of the duty of training disabled ex-servicemen to another department, the Ministry could no longer be regarded as a comprehensive pensioners' agency and that its separate existence was merely temporary.

While the functions of the Ministry of Pensions were thus pruned by the War Pensions Act, 1920, some sections of that statute vested fresh powers in the department. The anomaly of officers' wounds pensions was cleared away. Those pensions were paid to officers in addition to disablement retired pensions: the latter had since 1917 been dealt with by the Ministry of Pensions and in 1920 the administration of wounds pensions was transferred to the Ministry from the Service departments, thus avoiding dual jurisdiction.

A scheme for the administration of disablement pensions for or in respect of merchant seamen and fishermen killed or injured in 1914–18 was operated by the Board of Trade.

PERSONAL HEALTH AND WELFARE SERVICES 1920–1942

During the inter-war years the health and welfare services were steadily extended, but mostly in accordance with principles already accepted and, in the context of the central government, with only one major administrative innovation – the Unemployment Assistance Board. The Health departments continued throughout as the main social service authorities in Whitehall and Edinburgh. The Health Insurance scheme was opened to further categories of persons, and in 1925 a scheme of contributory Old Age, Widows' and Orphans' Insurance was introduced.

Medical Services

Medical and welfare services provided by Local Authorities grew in quality and quantity in the 1920s and 1930s. A great opportunity for advance in local health administration was offered by the abolition of the Guardians of the Poor in England and Wales and the Parish Councils in Scotland and the transfer of their powers, under which the Poor Law Medical Service had been built up, to the larger Local Authorities. This took place on April 1, 1930, and henceforward it was possible for the main personal health services – which were those provided under the Poor Law – to be administered along with the other health services, though councils could, at their discretion, continue to restrict Poor Law services to the poor alone, administering them through their Public Assistance Committees.

While each Local Authority extended its health services at its own pace, the central government moved further into the field of medical administration in connection with war planning. In 1935 an Air Raid Precautions Department was set up in the Home Office. Its duties included the organization of casualty clearing hospitals, first-aid posts and ambulance services, etc., in the vulnerable centres of population. Base hospitals were to be provided in the less dangerous areas, but it was not until December, 1937, that responsibility for them was vested in the Ministry of Health in England and Wales and the Department of Health in Scotland. The division of interest between the Home Office and the Health departments, and the distinction between casualty and base hospitals, both broke down before war was declared. In June, 1938, it was decided that in the event of war all hospitals should come under the Health departments, and in December of the same year responsibility for first-aid posts and ambulance service was also vested in those departments. Finally, three months after the outbreak of war, the Health departments took over from the Home Office the supervision of collective training and exercises for first-aid personnel. All these services came to be known as the Emergency Medical Services. The Emergency Hospital Service was administered directly by the Health departments: it embraced Local Authority and voluntary hospitals which in the course of the war were opened to Service casualties.

Unemployment Insurance and Assistance

The steady growth in the numbers of people eligible for general practitioner services under the Health Insurance Scheme, the developments in Local Authority health administration, and the partial unification of hospital services to meet the compelling needs of the Second World War, were pointers to the eventual concept of a comprehensive medical service for the whole population. This dramatic step forward in the scope and administration of health services was not to be taken until after 1945, however. The major developments in the administration of the social services between the wars were due to the effects of mass unemployment on the Unemployment Insurance scheme and on the local provision of poor relief.[j] The Unemployment Insurance scheme was badly disorganized by mass unemployment: as early as 1921 it was decided to go beyond the strict actuarial basis of the scheme and to pay 'uncovenanted' or 'transitional' benefits and dependants' allowances to those who were out of work. Thus the relief of unemployment became a mixture of insurance and assistance. Unemployed persons who had no insurance rights at all were supported until 1929 by the Poor Law Guardians and after 1929 by the Public Assistance Committees of the larger Local Authorities.

Towards the end of 1931, in an effort to stop the drain on the

[j] The Unemployment Scheme had been extended in 1916 and again in 1920. The extensions brought all workers whose remuneration was not more than £250 a year into Insurance. The financial limit was raised to £420 a year in 1940. The number of persons covered rose from 2½ million in 1914 to 11 million in 1921 and to over 15 million by 1938.

Unemployment Insurance Fund, 'transitional' benefit was abolished and a temporary system of 'transitional payments' was introduced. Those payments were to be limited to persons who had either exhausted their insurance benefits or had not paid enough contributions to qualify for benefit. The persons concerned had to pass a means test, and the scheme was administered by the Public Assistance Committees. The money was provided from the National Exchequer.

A Royal Commission on Unemployment Insurance, which reported in 1932, recommended that the Unemployment Insurance Scheme should be redesigned to cope only with short-term unemployment, but that for those persons who had exhausted their insurance benefits the transitional payments scheme should be continued and administered by the Local Authorities. The latter scheme should continue to be financed by the central government: the Royal Commission did not think it advisable to entrust the administration of such discretionary payments to the Ministry of Labour, but wanted that department to exercise close control over the Local Authorities.[15]

The Government accepted the idea of a separate, 100 per cent centrally financed scheme of Unemployment Assistance outside the Unemployment Insurance Scheme and the Poor Law, but refused to allow the Local Authorities to administer it. The brief experience of permitting Public Assistance Committees to spend money provided by the National Exchequer had been disturbing. Many Committees had applied no means test at all, and in Durham and Rotherham the Committees had so flagrantly disregarded their obligations that the Government had replaced them by Commissioners. The Minister of Labour thought that there were three possible alternative courses. Two of them were either to administer the new Unemployment Assistance Scheme through his department, or to appoint an independent Board to administer it. Both these ideas were unacceptable: the first because it was felt that a Minister should not be answerable in Parliament for decisions about individual cases, the second because Parliament would not abdicate its overall responsibility for the unemployed. The third course, which was favoured by the Treasury, was chosen: it entailed the creation of an Unemployment Assistance Board which took responsibility for individual decisions but was subject to the Minister of Labour and to Parliament for the general policy which was to be implemented.

Apart from the overriding need to take from the Unemployment Insurance Scheme and the Poor Law authorities the job of relieving mass unemployment, the causes of the creation of the Unemployment Assistance Board might be summarized as follows:

(*a*) The desire to keep the detailed administration of the new system 'out of politics'.

(*b*) Governmental distrust of over-generous Public Assistance Committees, and the need to control the expenditure of money provided wholly by the Treasury.

(*c*) Confidence in the idea of a semi-independent board which had been fostered by the experience of the work of bodies such as the BBC, the Central Electricity Board and the London Passenger Transport Board.

(*d*) The experience of the Commissioners appointed to administer Unemployment Assistance in Rotherham and Durham.

The Unemployment Assistance Board was set up in 1934: it took over responsibility for the support of the able-bodied unemployed who were receiving transitional payments in January, 1935, and those receiving assistance from Public Assistance Committees in April, 1937. Thus was Unemployment Insurance rescued from its association with assistance and the Local Authorities relieved of a burden which they considered to be national in character.

Pensions and Supplementary Pensions

In 1920 blind persons were made eligible for non-contributory pensions when they reached the age of fifty – the age limit was lowered to forty in 1938. These pensions, being the same in character as the Old Age Pensions introduced in 1908, were administered with them by the Board of Customs and Excise.

Membership of the scheme of contributory Old Age, Widows' and Orphans' Insurance introduced in 1925 was obligatory on all those insured under the National Health Insurance Acts and on certain other persons who were 'excepted' from Health Insurance. In addition, in later years certain categories of persons were made eligible for voluntary membership of the scheme. The detailed administration of the new pensions was shared between the Health departments and the Approved Societies. The same system of collecting and accounting for contributions as was used for Health Insurance (i.e., the affixing of adhesive stamps purchased at Post Offices to Insurance Cards) was applied to the new contributory pensions scheme, and the clerical operations of the two schemes were interlocked. As a result, the administration of contributory pensions was 'virtually "lost" in Health Insurance up to the point at which title to pension' accrued and insurance ceased.[16] This meant in practice that while general responsibility for the new pensions scheme and much of the administrative work involved rested with the Ministry of Health and the Department of Health for Scotland, a good many of the routine processes were in fact handled by the Approved Societies in return for a small payment in each individual case. The duties of the Approved Societies in this context were, however, almost exactly the same as those which they would have performed in the ordinary course of Health Insurance administration, even if there had been no pensions scheme. The need for separate records for Health and Pensions Insurance was thus avoided, except in the case of those persons who paid pensions contributions but were not eligible for Health Insurance. The latter were dealt with directly by the Health departments. All claims to pensions were made to the departments: order books were issued to pensioners by the departments, and payments were made over the counters of Post Offices.

When persons could not live on their pensions alone, their incomes were supplemented, subject to a means test, by the Public Assistance authorities. In 1940, however, in response to considerable agitation, the Government decided to augment all flat rate pensions, whether contributory or non-contributory. A scheme of nationally financed and administered supplementary pensions came into operation in August, 1940, and the Public Assistance Committees of the Local Authorities were no longer permitted to supplement pensions. The new scheme eventually led to a rearrangement of functions between the Unemployment Assistance Board and the Board of Customs and Excise. The UAB already had the machinery of the means test working, and in 1940 the Board was entrusted with the administration of the supplementary pensions. The word 'Unemployment' was dropped from the Board's title, and the Board was brought into the same constitutional relationship to the Minister of Health and to the Secretary of State for Scotland, so far as its new pension work was concerned, as it already bore to the Minister of Labour in connection with unemployment assistance.

After 1940 a person receiving a non-contributory pension and also a supplementary pension had to deal with two departments: his ordinary pension was handled by the Board of Customs and Excise, while his supplementary pension was paid by the Assistance Board. Two sets of officials made visits to the homes of pensioners, and the pensioners themselves each had two separate order books for payment. In order to simplify the system and to save manpower, the Assistance Board and the Board of Customs and Excise agreed on a division of functions which came into effect on January 1, 1943. From then onwards the Board of Customs and Excise awarded the main pensions, but all cases where supplementary pensions were also paid were handed over to the Assistance Board. The Board of Customs and Excise continued to deal with all non-contributory pensions which were not being supplemented. Thus from the beginning of 1943 onwards non-contributory pensioners had only to deal with one department, either the Assistance Board or the Board of Customs and Excise. Those persons who received contributory pensions continued to receive supplementary pensions from the Assistance Board.

The introduction of nationally administered and financed unemployment assistance and supplementary pensions left the Public Assistance Committees with a relatively limited field – the provision of outdoor relief under the Poor Law for those who were neither able-bodied unemployed nor pensioners, and the provision of workhouses.

DISABLEMENT PENSIONS 1921–1939

The work of administering the claims to and award of pensions for the victims of the war of 1914–18 and of previous wars, and the provision of special medical and hospital treatment for pensioners, was left to the Ministry of Pensions throughout the inter-war period. The clientèle of the department decreased steadily, but perhaps in part because of the political importance of the clientèle the Ministry was not merged into a more permanent department which would have regarded the care of war pensioners as merely one of a number of administrative responsibilities. As it happened it was fortunate that the Ministry of Pensions did remain unscathed until 1939: an organization was ready to hand which could quickly be adapted to the potential needs of the new situation. No time was lost in making the necessary adaptation. The lesson of 1914–16 had not been forgotten: the desirability of having a single department to deal with all disablement pensions was universally admitted. An enabling Bill was rushed through Parliament at the beginning of September, 1939, transferring the relevant powers of the three Service departments to the Ministry of Pensions, which was thus endowed with all the authority with regard to compensation for wartime disablement which it had enjoyed from 1917 to 1920. The administration of disablement pensions awarded for peace-time service prior to 1914 and between 1921 and 1939 remained, however, with the Service departments. The changed character of warfare led to a widening of the field covered by the Ministry of Pensions. Disablement pensions were to be paid to members of the Mercantile Marine, to Nursing and Civil Defence personnel, and to civilians injured through enemy action. The scheme for merchant seamen and fishermen disabled in 1914–18 continued to be

F

administered by the marine division of the Board of Trade, which became the nucleus of the Ministry of Shipping in 1939 and passed to the Ministry of War Transport in 1941.

ENVIRONMENTAL SERVICES 1920–1943
Public Health and Housing

So far as the central departments were concerned there were no transfers of functions relating to environmental services during the inter-war period. Housing became a major question after the First World War, but it was always handled in Whitehall by the Ministry of Health and in Edinburgh by the Board/Department of Health for Scotland. These two departments continued to exercise supervisory powers over all the environmental services provided by Local Authorities.

Town and Country Planning

As we have seen, very limited powers to control the physical development of towns began in 1909. Between the wars those powers were extended, notably by an Act of 1932: the Ministry of Health and the Department of Health for Scotland remained the chief central departments concerned, but the Minister of Transport was given some responsibility under the Restriction of Ribbon Development Act, 1935, and the Trunk Roads Act, 1936. It must be emphasized, however, that all the planning activity taken together did not add up to very much: town and country planning was in fact not given any notable political or social priority. What interest was taken was largely academic, and discussions about amenity, about Garden Cities, and about the location of industry, etc. – the latter being linked with the problems of unemployment and the depressed areas – were only important in stimulating ideas which were not to have any very serious chance of practical application until after the Second World War.

The story which follows is concerned almost entirely with developments in England and Wales. The central responsibility for town and country planning in Scotland remained throughout the years from 1920 to 1943 – and indeed remains today – in the Department of Health for Scotland. This stability was in marked contrast to the rapid changes which took place in London in the early part of the war.

One of the first official pointers to the eventual establishment of a central planning department can be found in the *Report of the Royal Commission on the Geographical Distribution of the Industrial*

Population – known as the Barlow Commission – which was published in December, 1939.[17] The control of the location of industry obviously involves far more than 'town and country planning' in its narrowest sense, and the Commission's recommendations about the sort of central planning authority needed showed the extent to which, in its opinion, such an authority would need to poach on the existing departmental arrangements, if it was to be able to deal with 'industrial location on national lines and in the public interest'.

The majority of the Barlow Commission suggested a National Industrial Board which should have advisory, research and other non-executive functions, which should prepare a report defining what extra powers were needed to ensure progressive urban and industrial redevelopment, and which should wield limited regulatory powers in London and the Home Counties. One minority agreed but wanted regional bodies to be set up in addition, and proposed that the powers of the Commissioners for the Special Areas should be handed over to the National Board. Another minority went much further, feeling that a new Ministry 'or one evolved from an existing Department' should be established 'for the purpose of making research into and controlling the location of industry throughout Great Britain, and of

TABLE XIII

DEPARTMENTS CONCERNED WITH SOCIAL SERVICES
(With numbers of non-industrial staffs)

1935

(*a*) *Great Britain*

Ministry of Pensions	3,375
Unemployment Assistance Board	6,455
University Grants Committee	5

(*b*) *England and Wales*

Board of Education	1,770
Ministry of Health	5,755
Welsh Board of Health	430
Board of Control	105

(*c*) *Scotland*

Scottish Education Department	215
Department of Health for Scotland	750
General Board of Control for Scotland	25
	18,885

Note: The Ministry of Labour (total staff 22,360) was responsible for the Unemployment Insurance Scheme.

promoting and supervising the planning of the country for industrial, agricultural, residential and recreational requirements'. The new Ministry should take over the town planning functions and possibly some of the housing functions of the Ministry of Health, some part of the planning functions of the Ministry of Transport (there were complaints of confusion and overlapping of powers between the Ministries of Health and Transport) and all the powers of the Commissioners for Special Areas.

The critical development of the war in the spring of 1940 naturally relegated consideration of the Barlow Report to the background, but within a few months two developments brought the whole question of physical planning into the forefront of domestic affairs. The first was the effect of the blitz in the autumn of 1940. There was a very great emotional urge to plan the redevelopment of the damaged cities, and it was politically essential for the Government to show in a clear and emphatic way their concern for reconstruction. The Local Authorities in the blitzed areas were particularly keen to prepare plans for the future. All this public concern was no doubt given special emphasis in the Cabinet by the Labour members, who saw in it an opportunity to advance consideration of their wide post-war aims.

While these factors alone would no doubt have driven the Government to make some arrangement for dealing with the planning of physical reconstruction, it is very possible that such arrangements would have been different from those which did emerge had it not been for the appearance on the scene of Sir John (now Lord) Reith.[18] In May, 1940, as we saw in Chapter II, the new Minister of Labour, Ernest Bevin, began to press for the creation of a new department to absorb the Office of Works and henceforth to 'plan and execute all building and civil engineering work for the Government'.[19] The Office of Works had in fact been increasingly active with Government building since the beginning of rearmament, and was therefore the obvious department to be charged with general oversight of the building industry. In June, 1940, Mr Bevin sounded Sir John Reith to find out whether he would like to take on the new job. The latter was enthusiastic: he was already 'looking beyond the war to the problems of planning and reconstruction' and was not merely willing to organize Works for war purpose, but hoped that

'However much responsibility the new ministry might initially be given . . . it would acquire still more—by doing things that had not been thought of and for which no one else had staked claims. A real ministry of public works for construction of every sort.'

The conversion of the Office of Works into a Ministry of Works and Buildings was agreed, after stubborn resistance from the former, by September, 1940, but the question then arose whether the new Ministry should have any – and if any, what – responsibilities for post-war planning and reconstruction. Lord Reith[k] proposed that 'the Ministry [of Works] should be ready to take up responsibility for . . . planning and reconstruction arising out of the war and post-war period'. The Ministry of Health wanted the relevant paragraph of Lord Reith's memorandum either omitted or 'amended so as to make it abundantly clear that . . . [it] . . . did not imply any actual decisions as to transfer of jurisdiction' over planning and reconstruction to the new department. Mr Attlee (Lord Privy Seal) acted as arbiter, and produced a settlement which was announced on October 24 in the following terms:

'It is clear that the reconstruction of town and country after the war raises great problems and gives a great opportunity. The Minister of Works has, therefore, been charged by the Government with the responsibility for consulting the departments and organizations concerned with a view to reporting to the Cabinet the appropriate methods and machinery for dealing with the issues involved.'

In short, Lord Reith got permission to organize thinking and talking about the future while the Ministry of Health retained its executive and effective town and country planning powers.

The main reasons why this new loosely-defined function went to the Ministry of Works seem to have been that the Ministry of Works was less heavily burdened than the Ministry of Health and that Lord Reith was to become Minister of Works. The arrangement involved some duplication with the Ministry of Health, but the latter department had no time to do extensive planning work: it was 'snowed under' with emergency measures arising out of evacuation, air raid damage, and the like, and most of the staff of the Town and Country Planning Division had in fact been transferred to other jobs. Lord Reith, on the other hand, was a man of great energy, with a sense of mission, with the peculiar mental aptitude to think deeply about reconstruction at a time like the end of 1940, and with the strength of character to force his ideas on others. Moreover he stood well in many parliamentary eyes and at that time had the backing of Mr Bevin and of the Prime Minister, who admired his BBC achievements. Lord Reith was certainly not reflecting the opinions of his future officials: nobody in the Office of Works wanted planning to come to them, and an official historian has complained that the emphasis placed on the new Ministry's concern with 'vague reconstruction

k Sir John Reith was raised to the peerage as Baron Reith in October, 1940.

talk' hindered its concentration on vital wartime building.[20] The choice of Works as a home for reconstruction planning had some advantages, however, in view of the new conception of the department as the central authority concerned with building.

It is unlikely that Lord Reith was immediately concerned to take over the existing executive town and country planning powers. The whole emphasis in the early days was on the conception of a Group which would think about reconstruction, rather than on the establishment of an executive unit. Such a Group was soon formed and eventually reached a strength of about forty, including one of the principal town planning officers of the Ministry of Health who was transferred to Works. Lord Reith also appointed two committees – the Uthwatt Committee on Compensation and Betterment, and the Scott Committee on Land Utilization in Rural Areas – which were later to make influential reports, and he encouraged Local Authorities to think in terms of extensive post-war plans.[21]

The division between Lord Reith's Reconstruction Group and the Ministry of Health's executive Town and Country Planning Division was, however, only a temporary arrangement. Negotiations soon began in order to find an acceptable basis for what was usually referred to as a central planning authority. It was in the course of these long-continued negotiations that some confusion between general social and economic planning and town and country planning developed. Shortly after Lord Reith had been made Minister of Works, Mr Arthur Greenwood had been appointed Minister without Portfolio with special responsibility for all post-war reconstruction problems. It was not at first clear where the boundary was to be drawn between Mr Greenwood's jurisdiction and Lord Reith's responsibility for physical reconstruction, and for many months there was an undercurrent of bargaining and bickering over the two Ministers' respective spheres of influence. To add to these troubles, Lord Reith's early activities did not endear him to the Ministry of Health, which looked askance particularly at some of his interventions with Local Authorities.

In June, 1941, it was agreed that Lord Reith should for the present retain his personal responsibility for long-term planning policy in the sphere of physical reconstruction, while the Minister of Health and the Secretary of State for Scotland were to retain their statutory planning functions.[m] In order to ensure that the administration of the

---

[m] So far as Scotland was concerned, the work of co-ordinating the post-war planning activities of Lord Reith's Group and of the Minister without Portfolio had hitherto been done by a ministerial committee under the chairmanship of Mr Greenwood. 371 HC Deb. 856.

existing and any forthcoming legislation on town and country planning would 'proceed in conformity with long-term planning policy', however, the three Ministers were to be constituted as a council, with Lord Reith in the chair.

The search for a central planning authority continued unabated. Insofar as such an authority was only to be concerned with town and country planning, the inevitable next move was to combine the Reconstruction Group with the executive Town and Country Planning Division of the Ministry of Health. Mr Greenwood, however, was not happy about this. He at first opposed a separate department, as he felt that executive powers should be left where they were and a council set up to co-ordinate their exercise. Later he agreed to the proposal for a separate town and country planning department but insisted that an executive council for policy and development should be established simultaneously. Proposals agreed by the four Ministers chiefly concerned – Lord Reith and Mr Greenwood, Sir John Anderson and the Chancellor of the Exchequer, Sir Kingsley Wood – were drawn up for submission to the Cabinet late in 1941.

The composite scheme for a new council on policy and development and for a new department of town and country planning came before the Cabinet on February 9, 1942. It was rejected. All that the Cabinet would agree to was the transfer of the executive town and country planning powers to the Ministry of Works, which was renamed the Ministry of Works and Planning. This decision was essentially realistic. Nobody really knew what the proposed executive council would do, whereas the transfer of town and country planning powers to the Minister of Works had a readily recognizable objective – to forward the progress of preparation for physical reconstruction. So far as the transfer was concerned, the Minister of Health was by this time neutral in his attitude, no doubt because his department was already overloaded and would not have welcomed added responsibilities. Lord Reith, on the other hand, was still thirsting for more work of this kind, and by giving him executive as well as policy planning tasks the Government could meet some of the widespread dissatisfaction which was being publicly expressed about the slow progress of preparing for post-war reconstruction.

Insofar as this 'institutionalization' of planning was at least a partial victory for Lord Reith, it proved to be a hollow one: within a fortnight of the Cabinet decision he was asked to resign. The actual transfer of powers from the Ministry of Health to the Ministry of Works did not take place until July, 1942, by which time the situation had altered considerably. Lord Reith's successor was Lord Portal of Laverstoke, whose keen interest in building and war production did not extend to planning. Indeed not only was he not keen on planning, but he actively disliked it and set about getting rid of it. In addition, Parliament continued to be unhappy about the whole business, the more especially as the war position had improved and there was greater keenness to make progress with post-war plans. The nature and volume of the work was therefore rapidly changing.

In December, 1942, the Cabinet again considered the urgent need to facilitate the preparation of plans for physical redevelopment. They were faced with Lord Portal's dislike of planning, which cancelled one of the original advantages of putting the Ministry of Works in charge. They also knew that the Ministry of Health had more than enough to do. The alternative courses were to create a separate department or to set up a non-departmental body. The idea of a Commission had been discussed by a four-man committee under Lord Samuel's chairmanship which had been equally divided, and in the end the Cabinet turned it down because the sort of planning envisaged was essentially policy work and could not be removed from direct parliamentary supervision. Moreover the Secretary of State for Scotland insisted that the planning of physical redevelopment in Scotland should be handled by the Scottish departments. The scope of planning was in dispute and whereas a ministry might hold its own and avoid constant wrangling, a commission was unlikely to do so. At the same time, the control of land use was now regarded, thanks in part to the intensive study which had been undertaken, as of sufficient importance to warrant the full attention of a Minister and a department which would have no vested interest in land and would therefore be able to adopt an impartial attitude. It was also assumed, perhaps because almost no actual redevelopment could take place during the war, that planning could be divorced from execution – i.e., from building and housing powers – without excessive danger of overlapping jurisdictions.

Thus was the Ministry of Town and Country Planning argued into existence. It was set up in February, 1943: at the same time the Ministry of Works and Planning was renamed the Ministry of Works – a title which has been retained.

THE BEVERIDGE REPORT

Meanwhile an inquiry of tremendous social – and incidentally great administrative – significance was under way. The Beveridge Report on *Social Insurance and Allied Services* was published in December, 1942. It was concerned with the personal side of social welfare – insurance, assistance, medical services, etc. In order to facilitate understanding of the administrative changes which followed from the Government's decision to implement the main ideas of the Beveridge Report it is as well to lay out, in tabular form, the distribution of departmental responsibility for the various existing and relevant services in January, 1943, shortly after the Report was published and after the rearrangement of departmental responsibility for supplementing pensions had taken effect on the first day of the New Year.[n]

Health Insurance, including medical attention	Approved Societies	
Contributory Old Age, Widows' and Orphans' pensions	Approved Societies (routine processes only)	
		Ministry of Health
Miscellaneous personal health and welfare services	Local Authorities	
		Department of Health for Scotland
Ad hoc relief in money or in kind under the Poor Law, for persons who were neither able-bodied unemployed nor pensioners, and provision of workhouses	Public Assistance Committees of Counties and County Boroughs	
Unemployment Insurance		Ministry of Labour
Unemployment Assistance		
Non-contributory pensions being supplemented		
		Assistance Board
Supplementation of contributory Old Age, Widows' and Orphans' pensions		
Non-contributory pensions not being supplemented		Board of Customs and Excise
Workmen's Compensation		Home Office

The details of the Beveridge proposals are matter for the social historian. Sir William Beveridge had been appointed in June, 1941, Chairman of a Committee which was asked 'To undertake, with special reference to the inter-relation of the schemes, a survey of the

[n] *Ante*, pp. 160-161.

existing national schemes of social insurance and allied services, including workmen's compensation, and to make recommendations'.
As the inquiry proceeded it became clear that many issues of high
policy would arise, and the Government therefore decided that the
civil servants who were members of the committee should be regarded as advisers and assessors and should not be associated with
the forthcoming recommendations on questions of policy. The
Report was, in fact, Sir William Beveridge's own responsibility. He
chose to interpret his rather austere terms of reference widely enough
to recommend the introduction of a comprehensive plan of social
security, and his recommendations were received with great popular
enthusiasm. Our business is to study the implications of the Report
for the central administration.

The major administrative proposals of the Report flowed from its
author's basic idea that there should be a flat rate of benefit for un-
employment, sickness, and retirement, and a flat rate of contribution.
Such uniformity demanded unified administration, and the Report
envisaged that the new comprehensive scheme would be run by
Government and not by Approved Societies, though Sir William
Beveridge did suggest that sickness benefits might be administered by
Friendly Societies under certain conditions. If the use of Approved
Societies was to be abandoned, a big new executive organization with
a whole network of local offices would have to be created, and this
immediately raised the question of amalgamating the administration
of sickness benefit and the pension work hitherto done by the
Societies and the Health departments, with the Unemployment
Insurance work done by the Ministry of Labour.

Sir William Beveridge suggested the establishment of a Ministry of
Social Security, to which should certainly be transferred:

(a) The unemployment insurance work of the Ministry of Labour.

(b) The health insurance work of the Ministry of Health, of the Department of Health for Scotland and of the Approved Societies.

(c) The Home Office's responsibility for Workmen's Compensation:
a new scheme of Industrial Injuries Insurance was to replace the
existing system.

(d) The work of the Board of Customs and Excise with regard to non-
contributory pensions.

(e) The cash payments side of the work of the Public Assistance
Committees of Local Authorities.

The Report was not dogmatic about other transfers, and laid out the
arguments for and against, but it favoured:

(*f*) The disbanding of the Assistance Board and the transfer of its responsibilities to the new Ministry of Social Security. (It was expected that under the new scheme the work of Assistance would become progressively smaller, and this was an argument against retaining the dual organization of the Public Assistance Committees and the Assistance Board. Whereas the Report was all in favour of the transfer of Public Assistance Committee functions to the Ministry of Social Security, the possibility of keeping all Assistance administratively separate from Insurance was presented, though not approved.)

(*g*) Either that the registration and placing functions – i.e., the employment exchange work – of the Ministry of Labour should be transferred to the Ministry of Social Security; or that those functions should be retained by the Ministry of Labour but that the staffs concerned should be housed in local offices of the Ministry of Social Security.

(*h*) The combination of the Ministry of Pensions with the new Ministry of Social Security.

In addition to the detailed proposals about social security, the Beveridge Report made some big assumptions about other welfare services. In particular the Report looked forward to the establishment of a National Health Service which would ensure that 'for every citizen there is available whatever medical treatment he requires, in whatever form he requires it'. Sir William Beveridge argued that such a Service should 'be provided where needed without contribution conditions in any individual case' – i.e., that medical treatment should be 'lifted out of social insurance'. This meant that 'health' administration could be made quite independent of 'cash payments' administration: in the words of the Report, the National Health Service should be organized 'not by the Ministry concerned with social insurance, but by Departments responsible for the health of the people'.

THE MINISTRY OF NATIONAL INSURANCE AND THE
NATIONAL ASSISTANCE BOARD 1944–48

The Government, having accepted most of the main ideas of the Beveridge Report, reserved judgment about the administration of the new schemes until 1944, when they announced their decisions.[22] The Minister of Health and the Secretary of State for Scotland were to be responsible for the new National Health Service, while a new Ministry of National Insurance was to be set up to deal with cash payments – i.e., the handling of insurance contributions and the payment of insurance benefits for sickness, maternity, unemployment (though as will be seen special arrangements were made in this case with the Ministry of Labour), industrial injury, retirement, and death. The Ministry was also to administer a new scheme of family allowances. Departments were preferred to non-departmental authorities because they seemed to offer

'the most effective and the quickest way to bring the scheme as a whole into final legislative form, and to secure its smooth running during the difficult transitional period.'[23]

The Ministry of National Insurance Act was passed in November, 1944, and in March, 1945, the insurance functions of the Ministers of Labour and Health and of the Secretary of State for Scotland, and the Home Office's responsibility for Workmen's Compensation, were transferred to the new department. The Government justified its decision to transfer Workmen's Compensation from the Home Office to the Ministry of National Insurance on the grounds that though the new Industrial Injuries scheme would be separate from the general scheme of social insurance, the two 'should be integrated to the fullest possible extent', and because optimum administrative economy could be achieved by using the same staff and offices for both schemes. The payment of family allowances began in August, 1946, but the comprehensive scheme of National Insurance, the Industrial Injuries Scheme, and the National Health Service, did not come into effect until July 5, 1948.

The decisions of the Government in 1944 involved two major divergences from the Beveridge proposals. The Government turned down both of Sir William Beveridge's alternative suggestions about the Employment Exchanges – that they should either be transferred to the new insurance department or that their work should be conducted at the local offices of that department. We repeat here the statement of the Government's view already quoted in Chapter II:

'Unemployment benefit is designed merely to fill a temporary gap in wage-earning employment. The latter should represent the insured person's normal condition. The employment service fulfils two functions: it helps the worker to secure suitable employment and it enables industry to obtain labour as quickly as possible. There must be a close connection between paying unemployment benefit and placing people in work, but to make the organization of the latter dependent on that of the former would be to put the emphasis in the wrong place. The employment service should remain in the Employment Exchange and under the Ministry of Labour.'[24]

The Ministry of Labour therefore continued to handle the 'counter' business of Unemployment Insurance on an agency basis, though ministerial responsibility for insurance matters was taken by the Minister of National Insurance.

The other major divergence from the Beveridge proposals was the decision to retain the Assistance Board as a separate unit. The Board was to keep its existing functions (though the war had made the old scheme of unemployment assistance obsolete) and was also to be entrusted with the pensions work of the Board of Customs and Excise and with the remaining poor relief work of the Local Authorities. In short, all non-contributory pensions and *ad hoc* financial assistance were to be handled by the Assistance Board. The transfer of work from the Board of Customs and Excise was completed in 1947: in the following year the local Public Assistance Committees relinquished their responsibilities. The Board was at the same time renamed the National Assistance Board.

The National Assistance Board was placed in the same constitutional relationship to the Minister of National Insurance as it bore to the Ministers of Labour and Health prior to 1945. The following reasons were given in 1944 for the retention of a separate organization:

'The Government consider that ultimate responsibility for both insurance and assistance should rest upon a single Ministry; but in actual administration they attach great importance to the preservation of the distinction between insurance and assistance, and it is proposed to retain in the final arrangements separate administration for Social Insurance and National Assistance. It is true that insurance benefit arises as of right and that assistance is available only subject to proof of need and examination of means and that this is an important distinction in itself, but the Government doubt whether, if both are dealt with by the same staff, the distinction would be sufficiently preserved. Any overlapping of inspections or visits or duplication of staffs can be avoided by providing for agency arrangements between Departments . . .'[25]

Moreover different types of staff are needed for handling insurance benefits and for dealing with assistance cases – for assistance there must be local domiciliary investigation. In addition, the administrative prestige of the Assistance Board was very high at that time – the Board had most successfully handled the wartime Prevention and Relief of Distress Scheme, and had performed a large number of agency tasks for other departments. So competent an organization was well qualified to relieve the new Ministry of National Insurance –

which had an enormous initial job to do in very difficult war and post-war conditions – of an added burden. The National Insurance Act, 1946, extended the period during which new non-contributory pensions could be awarded to 1961, which gave the separate authority another, though a minor, *raison d'être*.[o]

THE CARE OF CHILDREN

Before we go on to complete the narrative of changes in the major fields of social welfare, we must record one administrative episode concerning a less widely publicized social service – the care of children deprived of a normal home life. The care of children, in this context, covers the provision of a home environment for orphans and for children separated from their parents – adoption, boarding out, children's homes, etc.: the regulation of juvenile employment: and the administration connected with juvenile courts and juvenile delinquents, approved schools, remand homes and attendance centres. In the last few years it has also included the training of people in child care work.

Between 1914 and 1947 central responsibility for child care matters was spread over several departments, each dealing with the Local Authorities and voluntary bodies which, then as now, did the actual executive work. The principal authorities were the Home and Scottish Offices and the Health departments, but the Education departments, the Board of Control and the General Board of Control for Scotland, and the Admiralty, War Office and Ministry of Pensions all had some interest in special aspects of child care. At the Home Office a Children's Branch had been set up in the middle 1920s and just before the Second World War the Office had taken the lead in organizing inter-departmental conferences on child care questions. This latter activity was a sign of the increasing realization of the importance of the subject – a realization which had been and continued to be stimulated by the long-term effects of the steadily widening coverage and tightening inter-relation of welfare services, the promised break-up of the Poor Law, and – in the Second World War – the revelation, through evacuation and bombing, etc., of the great extent of poor social conditions.

In December, 1944, some months after Lady Allen of Hurtwood had publicly expressed anxiety about the treatment of deprived

[o] Before leaving the subject of insurance it should be emphasised that a great deal of the clerical side of the work—the sale of stamps and the payment of benefits – is done by the Post Office on an agency basis. The Post Office, with its local branches throughout the country, is well suited for carrying out 'over the counter' transactions as an agent for other departments.

children, the Government announced their intention of instituting an inquiry. Committees were not set up until March, 1945, in England and Wales and April, 1945, in Scotland, and in the interval great public indignation was aroused by the death of a child due to shocking neglect on the part of his foster parents. The inquiry thus received much publicity and was assured of a sympathetic reception for any proposed reforms. Under the chairmanship of Dame Myra Curtis in England and Wales and Mr J. L. Clyde, K.C. (Lord Clyde) in Scotland, the Committees revealed a number of anomalous administrative practices, widely diffused central responsibility and great variations in the scope of governmental supervision of child welfare services. Their Reports recommended closer supervision of the Local Authorities by a single authority in each country in which all central functions specially touching the lives of deprived children shouid be concentrated.[26] This recommendation was generally accepted: it therefore remained to decide which departments were to be nominated. The Committees had not been asked to express any opinion on this point.

The Government chose the Home Office to deal with England and Wales. The Secretary of State for Scotland entrusted his powers to the Scottish Home Department, though approved schools continued to be a responsibility of the Scottish Education Department. So far as England and Wales was concerned, the choice was between the Home Office, the Ministry of Health and the Ministry of Education. The choice of a semi-independent body akin to the Assistance Board was advocated on the grounds that if child care was entrusted to any ordinary department it would only constitute a small section of the Minister's interests and would therefore tend to suffer neglect, but the proposal was impracticable because of the need for close policy supervision of the Local Authorities. In favour of the Home Office was that department's keenness to have the functions, the fact that there already was a Home Office Children's Branch capable of expansion, and the fact that the Home Office had always had a considerable concern for and therefore much experience of child care services. Moreover there was doubtless some administrative convenience to be gained by having one organization to deal with both deprived and delinquent children, since the former, as well as the latter, might come to official notice as the result of an order by the juvenile court. Even so the decision in favour of the Home Office was only reached at Cabinet level. The Ministry of Health was keen to take on the work and gained some support as the department most widely concerned with welfare services and local government. At the same time the Ministry of Health was very fully occupied in preparing for the inauguration of the National Health Service, which no doubt weakened its claim. There were those who believed that only the Ministry of Education could be relied upon to administer the relevant powers in a humane fashion, but that Ministry was not particularly keen to accept the work. Behind these alternative proposals there was, running through much of the parliamentary discussion, a feeling among those opposed to the Government's choice that the Home Office's concern with police and prisons made it an undesirable authority for dealing with all aspects of child care.[27]

The relevant statutory changes were made and the powers concentrated in the Home Secretary in September, 1947. In Scotland the concentration in the Scottish Home Department was effected administratively at the same time. The responsibilities of the Admiralty, War Office and Ministry of Pensions were not affected by the change.

HEALTH, HOUSING AND PLANNING, 1943–1951

We have seen that the new schemes of cash payments were thought to involve enough governmental activity at the centre to justify the establishment – initially at any rate – of a separate Ministry of National Insurance. The scheme for a National Health Service covering the whole population was not, on the other hand, despite the immense administrative problems involved, considered to justify the creation of a separate department. The conception of a comprehensive Ministry of Health held the field, and whereas cash payments were to be dealt with wholly by central authorities, the health service was to be administered by Local Authorities or, as was decided later, by a new structure of Regional Hospital Boards, Boards of Governors for Teaching Hospitals, and Executive Councils, with the Local Authorities playing a much less important part.[p] The Labour Government was apparently as ready as the Coalition to leave the preparation of the National Health Service to the Ministry of Health and the Department of Health for Scotland.

From the years 1943–44, when the Ministry of Town and Country Planning was set up and when the Coalition Government accepted the main aims of the Beveridge Report, until 1951 the Ministry of Health was responsible in England and Wales for all environmental services other than town and country planning, and for the personal

[p] The Ministry of National Insurance was conceived as a Great Britain department. There was no case for different standards of cash benefits in Scotland, and the need to have a single national register was overwhelming because of the constant movement of people across the Border. Health services administration, however, was always regarded as divisible between England and Wales on the one hand and Scotland on the other hand.

health services which from July 5, 1948, onwards were administered as a single co-ordinated scheme. In Scotland the Department of Health for Scotland retained a comprehensive jurisdiction over all these subjects. In England and Wales various developments led to a re-alignment of departmental work in 1951.

The establishment of a separate Ministry of Town and Country Planning was useful in that it helped planning to achieve considerable status. It enabled a Minister to devote his whole time to working out complicated legislation and its implications. But this independence was also a source of weakness. While physical reconstruction was only at the blueprint stage, the division between the central department responsible for planning and the department responsible for supervision and execution of plans – i.e., the Ministry of Health – was not very important. When the war was over, however, and new building – especially the building of houses – began in earnest, this administrative division between 'planners' and 'builders' became an obstacle. Central responsibility for housing, sewage and water supply all rested with the Ministry of Health. The Ministry of Town and Country Planning found it increasingly difficult to plan effectively without having that responsibility. In short, the Ministry of Town and Country Planning was in danger of becoming too far removed from reality: to mix planning with some 'bricks and mortar' became administratively desirable, and by combining planning with housing, sewage, water supply, etc., the necessary contact between central departments and Local Authorities would be simplified.

In the last years of the war another important problem was that of responsibility for housing – understandably so, in view of the tremendous political importance of the topic. The departments mainly concerned were the Ministry of Health, the Ministry of Town and Country Planning, and the Ministry of Works which, as the department responsible for the building industry, had experimental, technical and supply functions, and shared with the Ministry of Supply responsibility for the production, distribution and erection of most of the temporary houses which were ordered to take the strain of the immediate post-war housing demand. While in fact no change in the distribution of functions took place, between 1943 and 1945 there was very considerable public argument about housing administration. One theme predominated: that all central housing responsibility should be concentrated on one Minister. There was, however, no agreement as to which Minister should be chosen. Some people advocated a special Ministry of Housing, which would focus attention on what should be regarded as a great national emergency operation. Some wanted housing to go to the Ministry of Works because of that department's connection with the building industry and because it already had a big mobile building unit. In the light of later developments, however, the most interesting view was that put forward by the Labour Party in its election programme of 1945, *Let Us Face the Future*:

'There should be a Ministry of Housing and Planning combining the housing powers of the Ministry of Health with the planning powers of the Ministry of Town and Country Planning: and there must be a firm and united Government policy to enable the Ministry of Works to function as an efficient instrument in the service of all Departments with building needs.'

As it happened, Labour's promised merger of the housing responsibilities of the Ministry of Health with the functions of the Ministry of Town and Country Planning was delayed for six years. The Prime Minister argued, very soon after taking office, in August, 1945, that 'any drastic reorganization of Ministries would require legislation and would cause delay'. 'The Ministry of Housing and Planning,' added Mr Greenwood, was 'in cold storage'.[q] Any chance that the Ministry of Works might become the central housing authority was probably dashed by the fact that all house building was to be done by Local Authorities, whose contacts with the Ministry of Health were very intimate. Nor is it easy to imagine that so prominent a Minister of Health as Mr Bevan would willingly have relinquished his interest in housing.

The departmental situation of health, housing and planning may perhaps be seen most clearly if we look back from the end of 1948 at the relative positions of the Ministry of Health and the Ministry of Town and Country Planning as they had developed in the previous five or six years. When planning left the Ministry of Health in 1942 its loss was probably felt very slightly by that department, which had other, much greater, responsibilities. It was the major central department for dealing not only with the public health, personal health and housing services provided by Local Authorities, but also with the financial and constitutional aspects of the whole local government system. Moreover it was responsible for the supervision of National Health Insurance and of the contributory Old Age, Widows' and Orphans' Pension schemes, and it exercised a close control over the local administration of the Poor Law.[r] Between 1942 and 1948 the

[q] 413 HC Deb 110, 253. Mr Attlee made the Minister of Health and the Secretary of State for Scotland responsible for the 'housing campaign'.

[r] These were the normal functions. In addition there were the war-time emergency social services, such as evacuation and the organization of emergency hospital schemes, etc.

Ministry of Health, while retaining the greater part of its local government functions, lost its insurance and pensions work to the new Ministry of National Insurance in 1945 and some, though not all, of its Poor Law functions to the National Assistance Board in 1948. In the latter year, however, the Ministry became responsible for the administration of the new National Health Service – a huge task in itself, and one which was not really comparable to the previous limited personal health functions of the department.

In 1948, therefore, the Ministry of Health became in fact a coalition of two major interests. One half of the department was the direct successor to the old Local Government Board and the inter-war or 'first' Ministry of Health: its concern was with the local government system and the environmental services of public health and housing. The other half was the completely new organization for running the network of personal services which make up the National Health Service. The Ministry of Town and Country Planning was, by contrast, merely an offshoot of the 'local government' half of the Ministry of Health, and though planning was by now a completely different and greatly extended function as compared with pre-1939 planning, it was still a relatively narrow function and, as we have seen, was suffering from its separation from the other environmental services.

The original impulse for a re-merger of the town and country planning functions with the other environmental services came from within the Ministry of Town and Country Planning, and in 1950 an official Machinery of Government inquiry was launched. The Ministry of Town and Country Planning was found to be too small and too much divorced from the executive side of physical development, which in turn led to friction with the Ministry of Health. Its weak position made it an uninviting ministerial prospect – in fact it tended to be 'under-ministered'. The inquiry led to a recommendation that 'planning' should go back to 'health', but there were doubts whether a single Ministry of Health and Planning would as a result be too big.

The Ministry of Health (old style) was split on January 31, 1951. That part of it which was concerned with the National Health Service became a separate Ministry of Health (new style). The other part was combined with the Ministry of Town and Country Planning and became the Ministry of Local Government and Planning – a title which was changed in November, 1951, to Ministry of Housing and Local Government. Historically, therefore, the Ministry of Housing and Local Government is the modern version of the Local Government Board and of the 'first' (i.e., 1919–51) Ministry of Health. The department called since 1951 the Ministry of Health was in fact only set up in 1948 to administer the National Health Service.

We have seen that the administrative case for some such re-alignment was a strong one. Moreover, town and country planning had now been accepted and had settled down in Whitehall as a normal administrative job. It no longer required the attention of a separate Minister: one Minister could do it and could do something else as well. If administrative or political expediency dictated its transfer to another place, it could go without provoking too great a public outcry: it could go, as it turned out, home to its parent department.

But while the advisability and, indeed, the inevitability of the re-arrangement on administrative grounds may be admitted, the operation involved was complicated and widespread and would need to await a favourable opportunity for putting it into effect. The necessary impetus came from a Cabinet reshuffle in January, 1951. The Government's programme of rearmament was gaining momentum. Manpower problems were crucial and Mr Aneurin Bevan, the then Minister of Health, was appointed Minister of Labour to grapple with those problems. His departure from the Ministry of Health gave the Prime Minister the necessary chance to rearrange the functions of that department – at a time, incidentally, when the increasing cost of the National Health Service was causing anxiety – and to enlarge the responsibilities of Mr Hugh Dalton, who had been in charge of town and country planning, by making him the first Minister of Local Government and Planning. The reshuffle also involved moving Mr Isaacs from the Ministry of Labour to the Ministry of Pensions, and Mr Marquand from Pensions to the (new style) Ministry of Health.

THE MINISTRY OF PENSIONS AND NATIONAL INSURANCE

One big change in the social service departments remains to be recorded. The suggestion in the Beveridge Report that the Ministry of Pensions should be merged in a new Ministry of Social Security was not accepted in 1944. This was probably mainly due to the political importance of treating war pensioners as a special group. At the same time disability pensions were awarded on a different basis from that which was used in National Insurance, and it would have been difficult for one department to have handled them as well as integrating all the social insurance schemes at such a hectic period of administrative rearrangement. It was not until three years after the fighting stopped that a decision about the future jurisdiction of the Ministry of Pensions was announced. The Ministry was to retain all its functions with regard to pensioners of wars prior to 1914 and to First and Second World War pensioners, and in addition was to administer all pensions awarded on account of disablement resulting from future peace-time service. The major reasons for entrusting future peace-time disability pensions to the Ministry rather than to the Service departments, as had happened in 1920, were the existence of compulsory military service and the fact that the pension codes for such peace-time service were to be the same as those adopted for service during the Second World War. It was because of the difference between these codes and those governing the award of disablement pensions in peace-time prior to 1914 and between 1921 and 1939 that it was decided to leave the administration of the older pensions to the Service departments. There were no medical records of the pre-1939 peace-time pensioners and consequently their cases could not be reopened and reassessed in the light of the post-1939 codes. The necessary legislative amendments were made in 1949.

The Beveridge proposals about the Ministry of Pensions were not forgotten, however. The Ministry was abolished at the end of August, 1953, and its functions were distributed between the Ministry of Health and the Department of Health for Scotland on the one hand, and the Ministry of National Insurance – renamed the Ministry of Pensions and National Insurance – on the other hand. There were various compelling reasons for this move. The need for a separate department to deal with disablement pensioners was questionable as soon as the machinery of the new National Insurance Scheme and the National Health Service was introduced. Disablement pensioners as citizens were covered by both those schemes and consequently many of them soon came within the purview not only of the Ministry of Pensions but of the Ministry of National Insurance and the Ministry of Health as well. Above all, the number of disablement pensioners was bound to decline steadily. It was, therefore, only sensible to merge the special Ministry of Pensions hospitals into the general hospital service to ensure that the fullest use was made of all available hospital accommodation. At the same time the cash payments work of the Ministry of Pensions and of the Ministry of National Insurance was similar in nature, and economy and efficiency were likely to be increased through using a combined central and local office organization – disablement pensioners themselves would in fact benefit directly because there would be more local offices and a better 'counter' service at their disposal. There were other pointers towards amalgamation. The Ministry of Pensions had always been responsible for providing artificial limbs, surgical appliances and invalid carriages to their clients, and since 1948 the department had extended this service to National Health patients under an agency arrangement with the Ministry of Health. Lastly, an early merger would avoid the personnel difficulties which would attend the otherwise certain though gradual atrophy of the Ministry of Pensions.[28]

A final 'tidying up' operation was undertaken in April, 1954, when the small scheme for providing disablement pensions for merchant seamen and fishermen injured in the First World War was transferred from the Ministry of Transport and Civil Aviation to the Ministry of Pensions and National Insurance.

THE POSITION IN 1956

At the end of 1956, therefore, the distribution of health and welfare responsibilities was as follows:

Environmental services: housing, sewage, water supply, town and country planning, etc.	Local Authorities	Ministry of Housing and Local Government, Department of Health for Scotland
National Health Service and some aspects of public health administration.	Regional Hospital Boards, Boards of Governors for Teaching Hospitals, Executive Councils, Local Authorities	Ministry of Health Department of Health for Scotland
National Insurance. Industrial Injuries Insurance. Family Allowances. All military and war disablement pensions other than those arising out of peace-time service prior to 1914 and between 1921 and 1939.		Ministry of Pensions and National Insurance (Agency arrangement with Ministry of Labour and National Service for administration of unemployment insurance)
All *ad hoc* financial assistance. Non-contributory pensions. Provision of accommodation for 'casuals'.	Agency arrangement with Local Authorities	National Assistance Board
Care of children deprived of a normal home life.	Local Authorities	Home Office, Scottish Home Department
Disablement pensions paid in respect of peace-time military service before 1914 and between 1921 and 1939.		Service departments

TABLE XIV

DEPARTMENTS CONCERNED WITH
SOCIAL SERVICES
(With numbers of non-industrial staffs)

1956

(*a*) *Great Britain*

Ministry of Pensions and National Insurance	36,830
National Assistance Board	9,850
Central Land Board and War Damage Commission	1,240
University Grants Committee	25

(*b*) *England and Wales*

Ministry of Education	2,850
Ministry of Health (including Board of Control)	5,310
Welsh Board of Health	150
Ministry of Housing and Local Government	2,745
Welsh Office, Ministry of Housing and Local Government	195
National Parks Commission	25
Home Office Children's Department	80

(*c*) *Scotland*

Scottish Education Department	445
Department fo Health for Scotland (including General Board of Control for Scotland)	980
Scottish Home Department (Child Care)	15
	60,740

Note: The Ministry of Labour and National Service (total staff 22,210) handles the 'counter' business of Unemployment Insurance for the Ministry of Pensions and National Insurance on an agency basis.

V

EXTERNAL AFFAIRS

IN 1914 the relations between the British Government and the rest of the world fell under two main headings. There was, first, the conduct of formal diplomatic relations with foreign states. Secondly, there was the handling of Imperial affairs. The latter ranged from consultation with the Governments of five self-governing territories – the Dominion of Canada, the Commonwealth of Australia, the Dominion of New Zealand, the Union of South Africa, and Newfoundland – through a general control by means of a separate Government of India over the vast Indian Empire, to the direct administration of numerous dependent colonial territories. Responsibility for these main aspects of external affairs rested with three Secretaries of State – one for Foreign Affairs, one for the Colonies, and one for India – who presided over the Foreign, Colonial and India Offices respectively.

Even in 1914, however, these 'external' departments had not an absolute monopoly interest in external affairs. Several Ministers in charge of other departments were responsible for aspects of policy and administration within their departmental fields which concerned other countries or the very few international bodies which existed at that time. Insofar as such domestic departmental policy and administration impinged on general external policy it was of interest to the external departments – particularly the Foreign Office – and in some cases, however intimately a home department was involved in overseas affairs, the formal outcome of its overseas work was advice to the Foreign Office and to the Government's diplomatic representatives. Thus the Board of Trade, with the widest and most important external interests of all the domestic departments, was responsible for guiding and informing the Foreign Office on commercial conditions in and policy towards foreign countries, though it had its own representatives in the Dominions. Similarly the Admiralty and War Office, with their obvious interest in foreign and Imperial matters, had attachés at most of the diplomatic missions whose primary duty was to advise the heads of those missions. In some cases domestic departments had definite executive duties which arose out of their external responsibilities: the Home Office dealt with extradition, for example, and the Post Office worked with the Universal Postal Union. The extent of these domestic departmental responsibilities for special aspects of external affairs was, however, relatively very limited.

The major changes in this field since 1914 can be stated quite simply at the outset. First of all there have been changes to mark the evolution of the British Empire into the British Commonwealth. Already by 1914 the senior members were self-governing communities: between the wars 'Dominion Status' evolved further and became the recognized goal of colonial territories. During and after the Second World War the idea of 'Commonwealth' superseded that of 'Empire': self-government within the Commonwealth was extended to and accepted by several previously dependent countries and Burma, hitherto a part of the Commonwealth, became an independent foreign country. Meanwhile the whole process of preparing Colonies for self-government was accelerated.

Secondly, there are now many more international organizations than there were in 1914, and the British Government is a member of most of them. These organizations provide a new forum for inter-governmental relations and add new networks of diplomatic contact. Thirdly, domestic departments have now been drawn into external affairs to a far greater extent than in 1914. Foreign relations now embrace most aspects of human activity – social, economic and cultural as well as political and diplomatic. They therefore touch the interests of the home departments at many more points, and the staffs of our Embassies include attachés on all kinds of subjects. The Foreign Office retains the primary responsibility for relations with foreign Governments and co-ordinates the relations of other departments with them, whether directly or through international organizations. There are, however, some home departments which have the primary responsibility for relations with certain specialized international organizations: to quote one important example, since the establishment of the International Labour Organization under the Treaty of Versailles in 1920 the Ministry of Labour and not the Foreign Office has been responsible for the British Government's relations with it.

It is impossible to attempt in these pages any analysis in depth of all the effects of these developments on the organization of central government. Many of those effects have been, in any case, of more importance for the internal organization of individual departments than for the structural aspects of the central administration which are our particular concern.[1] This chapter is, therefore, in the first instance limited to a statement of the main structural changes in the external departments, based on a record of the transfers and/or re-arrangements of responsibility for conducting relations with foreign states and self-governing countries within the Empire and Commonwealth, and for administering dependencies. In addition there are sections on changes in the organization of the personnel who deal with external affairs, and on the extension of the interest of domestic departments in those affairs.

THE DISTRIBUTION OF RESPONSIBILITY BETWEEN THE 'EXTERNAL' DEPARTMENTS

At the time of the outbreak of war in 1914 the Foreign Office dealt with nearly all foreign countries directly. The exceptions were certain territories on the periphery of the Indian Empire. A number of Arab Sultanates and Sheikhdoms on the shores of the Persian Gulf and in the Aden Protectorate were then – as now – in treaty relations with the British Government. The British appointed political advisers to the rulers of these territories, but the advisers were in fact members of the Political Department of the Government of India and not members of the British Diplomatic Service. Similarly British diplomatic and consular representatives in some parts of Persia, and in Afghanistan, Nepal and Tibet were drawn from the Indian Political Service. The relations of the British Government with all these territories thus called for special liaison between the Foreign Office and the Government of India. This liaison, and indeed all contact between the British and Indian Governments, was carried on through the India Office. The Indian Empire in 1914 included Burma and the Settlement of Aden. The Foreign Office was charged with the 'protection' of Egypt and the Sudan. The Colonial Office conducted relations with the self-governing Colonies, which since about 1907 had been called Dominions. It was responsible for the British part in a newly established Anglo-French condominium for the Pacific Islands of the New Hebrides, and was the headquarters of a system of direct administration of all British dependent territories except those which were the responsibility of the Foreign and India Offices. It was not, however, responsible for the Island of Ascension, which was considered a vessel of war and was 'commanded' by the Admiralty!

The Foreign Office has remained throughout our period responsible for conducting relations with all fully independent foreign countries, and since 1914 has come to take full and direct responsibility for relations with most of the independent and protected Arab and Asian territories mentioned in the previous paragraph. The most important permanent additions to the responsibility of the Foreign Office have been due to the appearance of international political organizations, and it is convenient to deal with these additional responsibilities first. The League of Nations was set up in 1919, but during the first years of its career the British Government kept in touch with it not through the Foreign Office but through an extended Cabinet Secretariat (and less officially through Lloyd George's 'Garden Suburb') which had also dealt with the international conferences which followed the end of the war – an episode dealt with in Chapter IX. It was not until the fall of the Coalition at the end of 1922 that contact with the League of Nations became an exclusive function of the Foreign Office. No similar experiment followed the end of the Second World War when the United Nations was created: the Foreign Office formed the British departmental channel from the start.

The League of Nations held regular conferences but membership of the League did not necessarily entail the presence of a permanent national delegation at its Headquarters. Some Governments, but not that of Britain, did maintain such a delegation at Geneva. Membership of the United Nations, on the other hand, does involve the continuous representation of member states in New York. The Foreign Office provides permanent delegations both at New York and at the European branch of the United Nations in Geneva. Since 1945 other international agencies have been formed to which the Foreign Office appoints permanent (though not necessarily full-time) delegates: they are the North Atlantic Treaty Organization and the Organization for European Economic Co-operation at Paris, the Brussels Treaty Organization (since 1955 renamed Western European Union) whose headquarters are in London: the Council of Europe at Strasbourg: the High Authority of the European Coal and Steel Community at Luxembourg: the South East Asia Treaty Organization at Bangkok: and the Bagdad Pact.

We may now go back and proceed chronologically. One result of the international settlement which followed the Armistice of 1918 was a considerable increase in the work of the Colonial Office. Britain accepted mandates for several territories which had previously been German Colonies or Turkish dependencies – German East Africa (Tanganyika), Mesopotamia (Iraq), Palestine, Transjordan, and parts of Togoland and the Cameroons. The last two territories were combined for administrative purposes with the existing British Colonies of the Gold Coast and Nigeria respectively. The Colonial Office became responsible for all these territories, and in 1922 it also inherited the Island of Ascension from the Admiralty: Ascension was made a dependency of the Colony of St Helena.

Another addition to the responsibilities of the Colonial Office at this time was due to the domestic upheaval over Ireland. When the

Irish Free State was set up as a result of the signing of the Articles of Agreement in December, 1921, its relations with the British Government soon became a matter for the Colonial Secretary. The Irish Office in London was made responsible to the Colonial Secretary so far as the Free State was concerned and to the Home Secretary for Ulster affairs: the staff held acting ranks in both the Colonial and Home Offices. This was only a temporary arrangement. On April 1, 1924, the Irish Office was abolished and its functions with regard to Southern and Northern Ireland respectively were transferred to the Colonial and Home Offices.

In 1922 Egypt was recognized as a sovereign state in treaty relationship with Britain, but the Sudan continued to be a condominium – the Anglo-Egyptian Sudan – for whose administration the Foreign Secretary was responsible. Relations with Afghanistan, which had hitherto been handled through the Government of India, were made the direct responsibility of the Foreign Office on the conclusion of the Anglo-Afghan Treaty of 1921.

At the end of 1924, therefore, the work of the three departments exclusively concerned with external relations was distributed as follows:

Foreign Office	All foreign states (see, however, under India Office below)
	League of Nations
	Anglo-Egyptian Sudan
Colonial Office	Self-governing Dominions (including Irish Free State)
	Dependencies and mandated territories other than those dealt with by other departments
	Anglo-French Condominium for the New Hebrides
India Office	British India (including Burma and the Settlement of Aden) and the Indian States
	(Relations with Nepal, Tibet, the Persian Gulf Sheikhdoms, the independent Sultanate of Muscat and Oman, and the Aden Protectorate were conducted by the Government of India under the control of the India Office acting in consultation with the Foreign Office)

The first major structural change in departmental responsibility for external affairs came in 1925. We have seen that the Colonial Office's business had greatly increased since 1918 in terms of the territories which it had to administer or to deal with in other ways.

But even more significant was the change which had been affecting the whole conception of Empire during the previous generation. The large self-governing Dominions had come to take their places as equal partners of the Mother Country, and relations with their Governments were entirely different in character from the direct, paternal responsibility which the Colonial Office bore for the dependent territories. This difference had been recognized in 1907, and since then there had been a separate Dominions Division within the Colonial Office. In order to take account of the new status of the Dominions, to separate the conduct of relations with them from the direct administration of the dependent territories, and to relieve the strain on a single department, the Government divided the Colonial Office into two parts in the summer of 1925. While the long-term causes of this move are clear, the immediate impetus to set up a Dominions Office came from Mr L. S. Amery, who claimed in his memoirs that he made such a change a condition of his taking office in Mr Baldwin's Second Administration.[2] The existing Dominions Division became the Dominions Office, with its own Parliamentary and Permanent Under Secretaries of State, but until 1930 it was headed along with the Colonial Office by a Secretary of State for the Dominions and Colonies. In June, 1930, a separate Secretary of State for Dominion Affairs was appointed, and thereafter, except for two short periods in 1931 and 1938–39, the ministerial responsibility for Colonial and Dominion Affairs was divided. It was, however, not until April 1, 1947, that the staff which had since 1925 formed the joint establishment for both Offices were formally separated.

The main concern of the Dominions Office was with the Dominions – Canada, Australia, New Zealand, South Africa, the Irish Free State and Newfoundland – and with the self-governing Colony of Southern Rhodesia. In addition, the Dominions Office was responsible, through the High Commissioner in South Africa, for the direct administration of the three territories of Basutoland, of the Bechuanaland Protectorate and of Swaziland, which lie within or adjacent to the borders of the Union of South Africa. The Dominions Office also shared responsibility, on behalf of Britain, for the Pacific island of Nauru which had been under joint mandate to Great Britain, Australia and New Zealand since 1919.

Between 1925 and 1937 there were only two minor changes. In 1932 the mandate for Iraq was terminated: Iraq's full independence was recognized and henceforward relations with her were conducted by the Foreign Office. In 1927 the administration of the Aden Settlement became a joint responsibility of the Indian and British Governments. Civil administration continued to be conducted by the Indian

Government through the Resident, but responsibility for political and military affairs was vested in the British Government to whom the Resident was directly answerable, with regard both to the Settlement and to the adjoining Protectorate. The staff was drawn from both the Indian Political Service and the Colonial Service: the Resident and the Political Secretary were appointed alternately from the Indian Political Service and the Colonial Service. This dual control ended in April, 1937, when the Settlement became a Crown Colony completely removed from the sphere of the Indian Government. Both the administration of the Colony and the appointment of political advisers to the rulers in the Protectorate have since been the responsibility of the Colonial Office.

The change in the status of the Aden Settlement was only one small part of a much greater rearrangement of responsibility which took effect on April 1, 1937, when, as a result of the separation of Burma from British India, Burmese affairs were removed from the India Office and a new department – the Burma Office – was set up. No division of top responsibility was involved, however; the precedent of the Colonial and Dominions Offices was not followed. A single team – Secretary of State, Parliamentary and Permanent Under-Secretaries – remained in charge of both Indian and Burmese affairs.

In 1939 an agreement was reached with the United States of America whereby the two countries should have joint control of the Pacific Islands of Canton and Enderbury for fifty years.

On the eve of the Second World War five departments were exclusively concerned with external affairs:

Foreign Office	All foreign states (see, however, under India and Burma Offices below)
	League of Nations
	Anglo-Egyptian Sudan
Colonial Office	Dependencies and mandated territories other than those dealt with by other departments
	Anglo-French Condominium for the New Hebrides
	Anglo-American Condominium for Canton and Enderbury Islands
India and Burma Offices	India and Burma (Relations with Nepal, Tibet, the Persian Gulf Sheikhdoms and the Sultanate of Muscat and Oman were conducted by the Government of India under the control of the India Office acting in consultation with the Foreign Office)

Dominions Office	Canada, Australia, New Zealand, South Africa
	Eire[a], Newfoundland[b], Southern Rhodesia
	Basutoland, Bechuanaland Protectorate, Swaziland

Very great changes followed the Second World War. The replacement of the League of Nations by the United Nations, and the creation of other international organizations, have already been mentioned. The mandates relating to Transjordan and Palestine came to an end in 1946 and 1948 respectively, relations with the independent states of Jordan and Israel passing to the Foreign Office. Much greater changes were caused by rearrangements within the Commonwealth. The new spirit represented by the widespread use of the word 'Commonwealth' was reflected in the title of the department which dealt with that loosely defined community's 'family' relations. The Dominions Office was renamed Commonwealth Relations Office in July, 1947, immediately prior to the division of the Indian subcontinent into two independent Dominions – India and Pakistan – which have since become Republics within the Commonwealth. The India Office ceased to exist in August, 1947, relations with the new Dominions passing to the Commonwealth Relations Office. In January, 1948, Burma became a foreign country: the Burma Office was wound up and relations with Burma have since then been handled by the Foreign Office. As a result of the transfer of power in the old Indian Empire the arrangement whereby relations with Nepal, with the Sheikhdoms of the Persian Gulf and with the Sultanate of Muscat and Oman had been carried on by the Indian Political Service came to an end. All our diplomatic representatives, political advisers and consular officials in those territories now belong to the Foreign Service and are directly responsible to the Foreign Office.

In February, 1948, Ceylon, on becoming a Dominion, passed from the sphere of the Colonial Office to that of the Commonwealth Relations Office. So, too, did the Sultanate of the Maldive Islands. The Islands had previously been under the protection of the Crown through the Governor of Ceylon. Relations between the Sultanate and the British Government are now conducted by the Commonwealth Relations Office through the United Kingdom High Commissioner in Ceylon. Newfoundland chose to become a part of

[a] The Irish Free State severed some of its constitutional ties with Britain in 1937 and was renamed Eire at the same time.

[b] At the request of Newfoundland, its self-governing status was suspended in 1933 and it was administered by a Commission of Government responsible to the Dominions Office.

Canada in 1948. In the following year Eire ceased to be a member of the Commonwealth and became known as the Republic of Ireland, but the British Government decided not to treat the new Republic as a foreign State, and left the Commonwealth Relations Office to conduct relations with it. In 1953 the three territories of Southern Rhodesia, Northern Rhodesia and Nyasaland came together in a Federation of Rhodesia and Nyasaland. Relations between the Federal Government and the Government of Southern Rhodesia on the one hand, and the British Government on the other hand, are conducted through the Commonwealth Relations Office, but the Colonial Office continues to deal with the Governments of Northern Rhodesia and Nyasaland.[bb] The Foreign Office's only 'colonial' administrative responsibility came to an end in 1955 when the Sudan became an independent state. The Sudan Political Service was disbanded, and the Sudan now has a normal diplomatic mission accredited to her from Britain.

There were a few cases during and after each of the World Wars in which occupied territories were dealt with by military governments primarily responsible to the War Office. After the end of the Second World War a Control Office for Germany and Austria was established under the Chancellor of the Duchy of Lancaster. In April, 1947, the Control Office was merged in the Foreign Office under the title Foreign Office (German Section) and as such came under the direct control of the Foreign Secretary, who was assisted in discharging this responsibility first by the Chancellor of the Duchy of Lancaster, but from mid-1948 by an additional Parliamentary Under-Secretary for Foreign Affairs. Although there are no longer Control Commissions in Germany and Austria responsible for the administration of British Zones in those countries, the Foreign Secretary remains formally responsible for the administration, through the Commandant, of the British Sector of Berlin. The Foreign Secretary was also responsible in recent years for the administration by the Foreign Office of the former Italian Colonies of Tripolitania, Cyrenaica, Eritrea and Italian Somaliland, from the time when the War Office yielded responsibility until the final status of the territories was settled in the period 1950–52.

At the end of 1956 the responsibility of departments exclusively concerned with conducting formal relations with foreign and self-governing Commonwealth countries and with administering dependent territories was distributed as follows:

[bb] In March, 1957, the Gold Coast achieved independence, chose to remain within the Commonwealth, and became known as Ghana. Relations with the new state therefore passed from the Colonial to the Commonwealth Relations Office.

Foreign Office	All foreign states
	United Nations, OEEC, NATO, SEATO, Bagdad Pact, Council of Europe, European Coal and Steel Community, Western European Union
Commonwealth Relations Office	Canada, Australia, New Zealand, South Africa, India, Pakistan, Ceylon, Federation of Rhodesia and Nyasaland, Southern Rhodesia
	Basutoland, Bechuanaland Protectorate, Swaziland
	Maldive Islands
	Republic of Ireland
Colonial Office	All dependent territories not dealt with by the Commonwealth Relations Office
	Anglo-French Condominium for the New Hebrides
	Anglo-American Condominium for Canton and Enderbury Islands

This completes the record of the main changes in the distribution of responsibility among departments exclusively concerned with external affairs, but it is perhaps as well to step far enough outside the boundaries of the strictly departmental area in order to include a brief reference to the only innovation in the sphere of non-departmental organization which has been wholly concerned with contact between this and other countries. The British Council was founded in the early 1930s and with the blessing of the Foreign Office and a grant-in-aid was concerned to counteract the effects of German and Italian cultural propaganda abroad. It was granted a Royal Charter in 1940 and its function was defined as being 'the promotion of a wider knowledge of the United Kingdom and the English language abroad, and closer cultural relations between the United Kingdom and the other countries for the purpose of benefiting the British Commonwealth of Nations'. The Council arranges and helps to finance foreign and Commonwealth tours by British theatrical companies and orchestras, etc.: it organizes exhibitions: maintains offices and reading and teaching centres overseas: awards scholarships to Commonwealth and foreign students for study in Britain, and gives post-graduate scholarships to British students for study abroad: and arranges exchanges of members of university staffs, etc. It is an organization financed by a Grant-in-Aid on the Foreign Office Vote: its work may well have a notable long-term effect on foreign relations, and its activities are, therefore, of special interest to the Cultural Relations Department of the Foreign Office.[c]

[c] Another important new venture which has been the responsibility of a non-departmental organization (though not an organization wholly concerned with external matters) is the Overseas Service of the British Broadcasting Corporation.

G

THE PERSONNEL DEALING WITH EXTERNAL AFFAIRS

It has never been considered possible that the conduct of external affairs, whether diplomatic or administrative, could be handled together with the domestic business of government by a single establishment of officials whose jobs, even at the highest levels, would be readily interchangeable. There have been and are, in fact, several Services separately organized and aligned with the 'external' departments which have dealt or do deal with different aspects of external affairs. It is these Services which are considered in this section: in a later section we shall describe the overseas work of the staffs of domestic departments.

In 1914 there were three separate staffs carrying on relations with foreign countries. The Foreign Office itself was, for staff purposes, a Home department. Its personnel were only rarely posted overseas: interchange between the Foreign Office and the missions abroad was negligible. The representatives of His Majesty's Government in foreign countries were divided between the Diplomatic and Consular Services, the latter itself sub-divided geographically into five branches. There were, in addition, eight Commercial Attachés appointed by the Foreign Office.

Both the Colonial Office and the India Office were, like the Foreign Office, regarded for establishment purposes as Home departments. The Dominions Division of the Colonial Office had no

---

TABLE XV

DEPARTMENTS CONCERNED EXCLUSIVELY WITH EXTERNAL AFFAIRS
(With numbers of staff stationed in Britain)

	1914	1935	1956
Foreign Office	190	1,410	6,165*
Colonial Office	190	370	1,275†
India Office	600	500	
Dominions/Commonwealth Relations Office		100	980
	980	2,380	8,420

*The Foreign Office figure for 1956 includes the staff of the Passport Office (535), and 2,300 non-industrial civil servants employed on communications work.

†The Colonial Office figure for 1956 does not include the staffs of the Directorate of Colonial Surveys, the Colonial Products Laboratory and the Colonial Geographical Surveys. These organizations employed approximately 500 non-industrial civil servants in 1956.

concern with the internal administrative services of the four Dominions, and formal contact was maintained with their Governments through the Governors General and through the Dominions' High Commissioners in London. The title 'Colonial Service' suggests a single, tightly organized body, but in fact the officers in the colonial territories were technically the servants of the Governments of those territories. The British ('expatriate') officers could, however, be transferred from one Colony to another, and a basic code of regulations laid down by the Colonial Secretary governed their conditions of employment and action. The Indian Civil Service, on the contrary, was a compact and self-contained unit answerable to the Indian Government. As with the Foreign Office and its overseas representatives, there was little or no interchange between the staff of the Colonial Office and of the colonial Governments, or between the staff of the India Office and the Indian Civil Service.

With the exception of the India Office and the Indian Civil Service, which were still separate at the time of the assumption of independence by India and Pakistan in 1947, there has been one development common to the overseas services during our period – a growth of interchangeability between London and the diplomatic missions or colonial Governments. This development should not, however, obscure the different relationships which existed between the United Kingdom Government on the one hand and the foreign states, the Dominions and the Colonies on the other hand, and it is therefore more convenient to deal with foreign countries, Dominions and Colonies separately.

Immediately after the First World War the staffs of the Foreign Office and the Diplomatic Service were amalgamated, and the personnel of the combined Service were thus enabled to gain experience both at home and abroad. Between 1919 and 1934 the five separate Consular Services were combined. After 1918 the number of Commercial Attachés was increased and they formed the nucleus of a Commercial Diplomatic Service whose members were attached to missions as advisers and were controlled by the Department of Overseas Trade. Between the wars a body of Press Attachés grew up, composed of officers appointed to some of the important posts abroad, and in the Second World War they became an integral part of the Ministry of Information, which was responsible for all overseas information services until 1946. In 1943 a scheme was put forward for the merging of the Foreign Office and Diplomatic Service, the Consular Service and the Commercial Diplomatic Service, and those sections of the Information Services which dealt with foreign countries, into a single Foreign Service quite distinct from the Home

Civil Service. The avowed intention of this reform was to meet the widened aspects of foreign affairs and

'to create a Service which, by its composition, by the recruitment and training of its members and by its organization, shall be better able not merely to represent the interests of the nation as a whole, but also to deal with the whole range of international affairs, political, social and economic, and so constitute an adequate instrument for the maintenance of good relations and mutual understanding between the United Kingdom and other countries.'[3]

The proposals were accepted: some were put into effect immediately and the rest were introduced after the war.[d]

The creation of the Dominions Office in 1925 marked the beginnings of a new phase in the relations between the British Government and the Governments of the Dominions. Constitutional developments had by then made it impossible for the Governors General to be regarded as the usual channel of communication between the British and Dominions' Governments, and at the same time the extent of consultation between those Governments was steadily increasing and becoming more intimate. The Dominions had for some time been represented in London by High Commissioners, and from 1928 onwards the British Government began to appoint their own High Commissioners in the Dominions. Thus a new 'diplomatic' service within the Commonwealth was established. The British High Commissioners and their staffs were mainly drawn from the Dominions Office, and a career in that Office entailed agreement to serve for periods in the Dominions. The present Commonwealth Relations Service is a relatively small but distinct unit which will inevitably grow as self-government is granted to previously dependent territories. It is now a normal though not invariable practice for a member of the Foreign Service to be posted for a tour of duty on the staff of a United Kingdom High Commissioner in a Commonwealth capital. In the same way a certain number of members of the Commonwealth Relations Service are regularly posted for a tour of duty in a Foreign Office mission abroad.

In order to develop closer understanding between the staff of the Colonial Office and the Governments of the territories for which the Office was responsible, a degree of interchangeability was introduced in 1925. An amalgamation of the Colonial Office and the Colonial Service was considered a few years later but was ruled out on several

---

[d] Certain sections of the Foreign Office are still manned by civil servants who are not members of the Foreign Service. The total strength of the Foreign Service proper on September 1, 1956, was 2,620.

counts.⁴ It was decided, however, that while the Colonial Office should continue to be staffed by Home civil servants, the senior officials should be liable to serve abroad and should be attached to one of the colonial Governments for a period during their early careers. At the same time there should be a system of seconding officers of the Colonial Service to the Colonial Office for approximately two-year periods. In 1930 the structure of the Colonial Service was revised 'in order to improve recruitment and to facilitate interchange of staff in the general interest'.⁵ Thereafter there developed twenty 'unified branches' of the Colonial Service: Administrative, Agricultural, Audit, Chemical, Civil Aviation, Customs, Education, Engineering, Forest, Geological Survey, Legal, Medical, Mines, Nursing, Police, Postal, Prisons, Research, Survey (geodetic and topographical), and Veterinary.

Since the Second World War, as progress towards self-government has been accelerated, the position of the expatriate members of the Colonial Service has become a matter of serious concern to the British Government. When a Colony achieved self-government, the choice before expatriate Colonial Servants was, under the old system, between remaining in the service of a territory no longer under the control of the Colonial Office, or of accepting compensation and retiring. At the same time the new Government of the territory was often in great need of the continued services of highly qualified and experienced British officials. In October, 1954, the British Government grouped expatriate Colonial Servants into a new Oversea Civil Service and promised that when any territory attained self-government, a formal agreement would be drawn up between the government of the territory and the British Government in which certain safeguards for the tenure, pensions, etc., of expatriate officers would be embodied. Oversea civil servants, however, were to remain 'in all respects responsible to the territorial governments' under which they were serving and were to be paid by those Governments.⁶

Further proposals were published in May, 1956.⁷ They fell into two parts. The Government considered that the immediate problem was to provide officers who were already serving, and whose services were still required, with an inducement to stay on instead of deciding to retire with the compensation to which they were entitled. To this end, the Government declared that they were willing to establish a Special List of the Oversea Civil Service. Officers placed on that list would thereafter be in the service of the British Government and would serve in the oversea territories on secondment. The British Government would fix their terms of service and guarantee certain safeguards in the event of interrupted careers or premature retirements. The scheme was designed in the first instance to apply only to Nigeria, where the risk of breakdown in the event of a large-scale exodus of British staff seemed to be particularly acute; but it could be adapted for other territories if such a course appeared desirable.

The other part of the plan looked forward to new arrangements to meet the needs of oversea governments who might wish to have 'the assistance of officers who have exceptional administrative or professional qualifications', but who might not be able or willing to recruit such officers on the traditional basis. The statement declared that steps would be taken to compile a register of qualified persons 'who are ready and could be made available to accept service of this kind'. Should the scale and regularity of the demand justify such a course, arrangements would be made to recruit such persons into the regular service of the British Government for secondment overseas.

Thus it may be that the colonial and recently colonial territories will soon be served by three types of civil servant: officers of the existing Oversea Civil Service paid by and responsible to the territorial Governments, though employed under the general regulations laid down by the Colonial Secretary and available to be moved about among the territories; officers (whether recruited locally or from outside) directly engaged by and wholly responsible to the territorial Governments; and officers who, either as members of the Special List or under some other arrangement, are in the service of the British Government but seconded to the territorial Governments.

In the Middle East and in South-East Asia there have recently been interesting developments in the arrangements for conducting external relations. The British Middle East Office was first established in Cairo. It had a Political Division and a Development Division – the latter at Beirut in the Lebanon – and it was concerned to co-ordinate policy and especially to provide technical advice and assistance to developing countries in the area. During 1955, when British troops were evacuated from the Canal Zone, the Office was transferred from Egypt to Cyprus. The whole organization was revised and its name was changed to the Political Office with the Middle East Forces. The present head of the Office is known as the Political Representative and he advises the Commanders-in-Chief, Middle East. The work of the Development Division continues but now comes directly under the Foreign Office, except for local administrative matters which are dealt with by H.M. Embassy at Beirut. At Singapore after the Second World War there was a Special Commissioner for South East Asia responsible to the Foreign Office: at the same time the Governor General of Malaya, whose headquarters were at

Singapore, co-ordinated the administration of neighbouring dependent territories on behalf of the Colonial Office. The two posts were combined in 1948 to form a Commission General for South East Asia. The Commissioner General was jointly responsible to the Foreign and Colonial Secretaries and had two deputies, one drawn from the Foreign Office and the other from the Colonial Office. In 1955 the status of the Commissioner General was changed: he is now appointed by and answerable to the Prime Minister, not to the Foreign and Colonial Offices, and while he retains the personal rank of Ambassador, the Governor of Singapore and the High Commissioner for Malaya take precedence over him in Singapore and the Federation of Malaya.

THE EXTERNAL RELATIONS OF DOMESTIC DEPARTMENTS

We have seen that in 1914 the part played by domestic departments in external affairs was very specialized and not extensive. Since 1914 – and more especially since 1945 – the extent of those specialized responsibilities has greatly increased. The scope of foreign affairs is now wider and touches domestic administration at many points. The British have tried to take account of this widening of the scope of international contact by bringing as much as possible of 'foreign relations' within the competence of a unified Foreign Service. But this move, put into effect at the end of the Second World War, could not relieve domestic departments of their external responsibilities. The process of unifying the organization and personnel dealing with foreign relations has, as it were, been overtaken by the extended range of those relations. While there is little doubt that in the foreseeable future there will always be one or more specialized corps of officials concerned with general external policy, it is almost equally probable that there will be no diminution in the present degree of concern which domestic departments have with oversea business.

Few domestic departments today have no external responsibilities. The organization and character of their foreign, Commonwealth or international work is primarily an internal departmental matter which does not warrant any discussion in our context, though it is worth recording here that several such departments now have special Overseas or International Divisions or Branches. Three aspects of that work are, however, relevant to a study of the overall structure of central administration – the representation of the departments in other countries and at international organizations, their responsibility for relations with international bodies, and the co-ordination of their external business.

TABLE XVI

OVERSEAS REPRESENTATIVES OF DEPARTMENTS
OTHER THAN THOSE CONCERNED EXCLUSIVELY
WITH EXTERNAL AFFAIRS AND DEFENCE

1956

Ministry of Agriculture, Fisheries and Food
Attachés in Buenos Aires, Copenhagen and Washington
Advisers in Canada, Australia and New Zealand

Ministry of Fuel and Power
Petroleum Attaché at Washington

Ministry of Labour and National Service
Attachés at Athens, Bonn, Brussels, Buenos Aires, Cairo, Helsinki,
Madrid, Mexico City, Paris, Rio de Janeiro, Rome, Stockholm,
Teheran, Tel Aviv, Tokyo, Vienna, Washington
Adviser serving the High Commissioners in India and Pakistan and
the Commissioner General in South East Asia

Ministry of Pensions and National Insurance
War Pensions Officers in Canada and Republic of Ireland

Post Office
Telecommunications Attaché in Washington

Department of Scientific and Industrial Research
UK Scientific Missions to the Federal Republic of Germany and to
North America
Scientific Attaché in Paris
Scientific Attaché in Scandinavia (stationed in Stockholm)

Ministry of Supply
Staffs in Australia, Canada, France, Federal Republic of Germany
and USA

Board of Trade
Trade Commissioners in Australia, Bahamas (sub-office), Canada,
Ceylon, Hong Kong, India, Republic of Ireland, Jamaica, Kenya,
New Zealand, Nigeria, Pakistan, Singapore, South Africa, Southern
Rhodesia, Trinidad

Ministry of Transport and Civil Aviation

UK Representatives on International Civil Aviation Organization and Air Navigation Commission, Montreal

Civil Air Attachés or Advisers in Australia, France, Federal Republic of Germany, Lebanon, Singapore and USA

Shipping Attaché in Washington, Adviser in Singapore

Various civil aviation staff at Bahrein, Cyprus and Kuwait

Sea Transport Officers at Aden, Antwerp, Colombo, Cyprus, Hong Kong, Hook of Holland, Kure, Singapore

Treasury

Representative on UK delegation to United Nations in New York

Treasury and Supply Delegation, Washington

UK Executive Director on International Monetary Fund and International Bank, Washington

Adviser in the Middle East

Adviser in South Asia

Adviser in the Far East

The idea of specialized representation in other countries began with the Service departments and the Board of Trade. The War Office and Admiralty had attachés at most missions abroad in 1914, and the Air Ministry followed suit after its establishment during the First World War. Military Attachés are still appointed to all the major missions. The Board of Trade is now, as in 1914, responsible for the Trade Commissioner Service of commercial representation in Commonwealth countries, while the joint Department of Overseas Trade, responsible to both the Foreign Office and the Board of Trade, was responsible for the commercial and consular services in foreign countries between 1918 and 1946. We have already seen that the Press Attachés appointed between the wars were incorporated in the Foreign Service after 1946.

The appointment to missions in other countries of special representatives other than those concerned with military and commercial matters and with the Press only began on a considerable scale during the Second World War. In 1942 the first Labour Attaché was sent to Washington, and after the war, largely as a result of Mr Bevin's influence, similar attachés were sent to many other foreign capitals. In June, 1956, there were nineteen Labour Attachés and seven Assistants, covering no less than fifty missions. The first appointment of an Agricultural Attaché – again to Washington – was also made in 1942. A similar post was created at Copenhagen in 1946. Food Attachés were appointed to Washington in 1949 and to Buenos Aires in 1953. The posts of Agricultural Attaché and Food Attaché at Washington were combined in 1953. The holder of the combined post, together with the Agricultural Attaché at Copenhagen and the Food Attaché at Buenos Aires, have been, since 1955, the representatives of the combined Ministry of Agriculture, Fisheries and Food. All the other specialist attachés were appointed after the Second World War. There are not many of each type. Civil Air Attachés and Scientific Attachés are to be found in several of the most important missions. There are Colonial, Petroleum, Shipping and Telecommunications Attachés at Washington. In the Commonwealth countries the counterparts of attachés – known as advisers – are appointed to the staffs of the High Commissioners. They include, in addition to military people, advisers on economics, finance, labour, agriculture, civil aviation and scientific matters. Some domestic departments have representatives abroad other than attachés. Such representatives are the Treasury's adviser for the Middle East, the Ministry of Supply's staff in France, and the Scientific Mission of the Department of Scientific and Industrial Research at Washington. All these attachés and advisers are the employees of the departments they represent, and are not recruited as members of the Foreign or Commonwealth Relations Services.

It will be clear from the above account and from Table XVI that attachés and advisers other than those concerned with military affairs are spread widely across the world, Washington having by far the largest contingent. The attachés and advisers at a mission are responsible to its head and address reports to him on their special subjects. Official instructions to attachés and advisers go to the heads of missions through the Foreign and Commonwealth Relations Offices. At the same time attachés and advisers owe an allegiance to their home departments: copies of their reports to heads of missions are sent to their home departments, and there is usually a copious semi-official or personal correspondence between attachés and advisers and their 'opposite numbers' in Whitehall. When the departmental representatives are very numerous, as in Washington, a somewhat looser relationship to the Ambassador is inevitable, though the formal position remains unchanged.

The permanent representatives of the British Government at the post-1945 international political organizations are mainly drawn from the Foreign Service and are responsible to the Foreign Office. The Commonwealth Relations and Colonial Offices and the Treasury have representatives attached to the United Kingdom Delegation to the United Nations in New York, and some departments, including for example the Ministry of Fuel and Power, have representatives at regional international organizations such as OEEC, NATO, ECE, etc. Other departments send representatives to the permanent missions as and when required. There is not, however, any continuous representation of domestic departments at the specialized agencies of the United Nations and at other international organizations though officials of the interested departments attend the frequent conferences of those agencies and organizations.

The main point to be made here about international organizations, however, is the extent to which relations with them have become the business of domestic departments. So far as the United Nations is concerned, the position has been concisely described in a pamphlet published in 1951:[8]

'Responsibility for some of the work in connection with the United Nations, and for a good deal of the work of the Commissions of the Economic and Social Council, is allocated to the Ministries concerned with the subject matter. The degree to which responsibility is allocated depends on the nature of the business of the body and is more pronounced in the case of the purely technical Commissions. For example, the General Register Office is the Ministry responsible for dealing with the Population Commission, and the Home Office for the Narcotic Drugs Commission. In all cases, however, the Foreign Office remains ultimately responsible and provides the channel of communication with the United Nations. As regards the Specialized Agencies, however, the Ministry concerned with each Agency's field of work is responsible for relations with that agency and acts as the channel of communication between the Government and the Agencies concerned. Each Ministry is also responsible for formulating the United Kingdom policy on the matters with which its special agency is concerned.'

It should also be added that the responsibility of Ministers in charge of domestic departments concerned with the Specialized Agencies extends to responsibility for the Votes which authorize payment of the British Government's subscriptions to those Agencies. Table XVII shows the contacts between departments other than the Foreign, Commonwealth Relations and Colonial Offices and international organizations in 1956.

The policies of international bodies are in the last resort decided by the conferences at which all the member Governments are represented, and it is therefore essential that the delegations sent to those conferences should be representative of all the departmental interests concerned, and that each delegation should be well briefed so that all its members follow the same line. Moreover in a broader context it is necessary to ensure that the Government pursues a consistent policy

TABLE XVII

RESPONSIBILITIES OF DEPARTMENTS—OTHER
THAN THOSE EXCLUSIVELY CONCERNED WITH
EXTERNAL AFFAIRS—FOR RELATIONS WITH
INTERNATIONAL ORGANIZATIONS

1956

Admiralty
International Hydrographic Bureau

Ministry of Agriculture, Fisheries and Food
Food and Agriculture Organization★
International Sugar Council
European Plant Protection Organization
European Foot and Mouth Disease Commission
International Office of Contagious Diseases of Animals
International Commission for North West Atlantic Fisheries
International Council for the Exploration of the Sea
International Whaling Commission
International Fisheries Convention 1946—Permanent Commission

Air Ministry
World Meteorological Organization★

Board of Customs and Excise
Customs Co-operation Council

Ministry of Defence
Military Agencies of the North Atlantic Treaty Organization

Ministry of Education
United Nations Educational, Scientific and Cultural Organization★

Export Credits Guarantee Department
Union d'Assureurs pour le Contrôle des Crédits Internationaux

Ministry of Health
World Health Organization★

Home Office
Commission on Narcotic Drugs†
Social Commission†
International Criminal Police Commission

Ministry of Housing and Local Government
International Federation for Housing and Town Planning
International Water Supply Association

Board of Inland Revenue
Fiscal Commission†

Ministry of Labour and National Service
International Labour Organization★

Ministry of Pensions and National Insurance
International Social Security Association

Post Office
Commonwealth Telecommunications Board
International Telecommunications Union★
Universal Postal Union★

General Register Office
Population Commission†

Department of Scientific and Industrial Research
European Organization for Nuclear Research
Institut International du Froid
International Bureau of Weights and Measures

Central Statistical Office
Statistical Commission†

Board of Trade
General Agreement on Tariffs and Trade★
International Bureau at Berne for the Protection
    of Industrial Property
International Bureau at Berne for the Protection
    of Literary and Artistic Property
International Customs Tariffs Bureau
International Exhibitions Bureau
International Cotton Advisory Committee
International Tin Study Group
International Tin Council
International Rubber Study Group

Ministry of Transport and Civil Aviation
International Civil Aviation Organization
Preparatory Committee for Governmental Maritime
    Consultative Organization★
Central Rhine Commission
International Railway Conventions
Transport and Communications Commission†
International Service of Ice Observation and Patrol
    in the North Atlantic

Treasury
International Monetary Fund and International Bank★
Economic and Employment Commission†

★Specialized Agencies of the United Nations.

†Commissions of the Economic and Social Council of the United Nations.

in dealing with international organizations as a whole. While the domestic department most closely concerned with a particular international agency has the primary responsibility for maintaining relations with it and for formulating Government policy towards it, other domestic departments may also be concerned with specific aspects of those relations and that policy, while the guidance of the Foreign Office is always needed in order that proper account should be taken of the general diplomatic background. In short, there is a need for co-ordination of policy and action, and it is fulfilled in Britain by the traditional methods of inter-departmental consultation. There are numerous interdepartmental committees on the relevant special topics, and since 1946 there has been a Steering Committee on International Organizations with a senior Foreign Office official as Chairman and members drawn from all the departments primarily responsible for relations with international bodies. This ensures co-ordination between departments in respect of their relations with international organizations and provides an opportunity for the various departments concerned to discuss their difficulties and resolve any divergent points of view. The Committee's very existence is symbolic of the contemporary character of external relations and of the degree to which those relations now involve large parts of an area of government formerly almost exclusively preoccupied with domestic interests.

VI

DEFENCE

A NOTABLE feature of warfare in the 20th century has been its direct impact on the life of the whole community. Previous wars had often been limited, in large measure, to conflict between opposing naval and military forces, with comparatively small immediate repercussions in the civilian sphere except in the battle areas. During our period every department of the central government has, to a greater or lesser degree, become involved in the preparation for and conduct of war. Nor has the change in the character of warfare affected only the conventional aspects of defence administration – the raising, direction, organization and supply of armed forces. The use of the aeroplane to attack industrial plants and internal communications has forced the development of a new defensive function – civil defence – in order to protect civilian population and property. The intrusion of war considerations and the effects of war into all fields of government is apparent in the study of any branch of British administration since 1914. It is still natural and convenient, however, to use the term 'defence departments' to cover only the three Service departments – the Admiralty, War Office and Air Ministry – the Ministry of Defence, and the departments which are or were mainly concerned with military supply – the Ministries of Munitions, Supply, Aircraft Production, and Production. The departments with the major responsibility for civil defence organization have been the Home Office and the Ministry of Home Security.

The 'total' character of modern warfare and the international tension which has become commonplace since 1914 have been reflected administratively in the increased amount of work normal to Service departments. Thus conscription and the raising of the Home Guard, to mention only two instances, brought those departments great and complex tasks and have subjected them to a degree of public interest greater than existed in earlier times. For our purposes, however, the change of scale and the internal developments in the Service departments must be taken as read. In this study the developments which warrant most attention are:

(a) The evolution of the supreme directive organs responsible for strategy, direction, co-ordination, etc., pertaining to national defence as a whole, which has involved the rise of the Committee of Imperial Defence, the Joint Staffs system and, eventually, the Ministry of Defence. This evolution has, however, been closely linked with the development of the Cabinet, and it is therefore treated in Chapter IX as part of the history of the co-ordination of central administration.

(*b*) The creation of a third Service – the Royal Air Force – and its relations with the two older Services.

(*c*) The establishment of separate departments to deal with the provision of supplies.

(*d*) The growth of the Civil Defence organization.

In this chapter each of the last three subjects is dealt with in turn.

THE EVOLUTION OF A SEPARATE AIR FORCE AND ITS RELATIONS WITH THE NAVY AND ARMY

The origin of military air services ante-dates the starting point of this study by so short a period that it is desirable to deal with the whole matter from its beginnings. The Committee of Imperial Defence had recommended a unified British Aeronautical Service with military and naval wings but with common staff and training facilities, etc., in 1911, and this plan was followed when the Royal Flying Corps was set up in the spring of 1912. A permanent consultative Air Committee was formed, comprising representatives of the Admiralty and War Office, but within about two years the original idea of a unified force had been abandoned. The naval wing gradually became independent of its military counterpart, and in July, 1914, was reconstituted as the Royal Naval Air Service under full Admiralty control. At that time the RFC was to be responsible for all home defence and land operations, while the RNAS was to provide services to the Fleet and to protect naval property ashore. This arrangement was challenged by the War Office, who wanted their control of home defence to include responsibility for naval shore establishments, but the controversy was merely academic: when the war broke out all the RFC went to France, leaving the Admiralty to provide air defence for the whole of Britain. The severance of all connection between the two air services was symbolized by the disappearance of the Joint Air Committee as soon as war began.[1]

The peculiar distribution of operational functions between the air services of the Admiralty and War Office continued and was even exaggerated for several months. Under their responsibility for the air defence of the United Kingdom, the Admiralty sent a squadron of aircraft to Belgium in 1914 to attack Zeppelin bases. Some armoured car squadrons accompanied the aircraft to defend the forward air-fields. In addition the RNAS collected some armoured trains and an anti-aircraft section for home ground defence. When Mr Balfour was appointed First Lord of the Admiralty in May, 1915, he immediately handed over this military apparatus to the Army and requested that the War Office also take over responsibility for home defence – a transfer of function not put into effect until February, 1916.[2]

From the early months of 1916 until the late summer of 1917 the question which dominated all discussions of the organization of the air services concerned the supply of aircraft. At this stage the idea of a separate Air Force was little more than a vague, post-war possi-bility. Stress was laid on the avoidance of competition between Navy and Army for aircraft – in fact on the problems of allocation and priority. An ineffectual Joint War Air Committee 'to collaborate in and to co-ordinate the question of supplies and design for material for the Naval and Military Air Services' lasted from February to April, 1916. It was followed by the first Air Board, headed by Lord Curzon, which was given the same task but still no executive power. Its career, which ended in December, 1916, was marked by con-tinuous, bitter controversy with the Admiralty. In December the Board was raised to the status of a Ministry (usually known as the Second Air Board); in January, 1917, it was entrusted with the job of designing aircraft, deciding on the numbers to be ordered and allo-cating them between the Services. The manufacture and inspection of aircraft became the function of the Ministry of Munitions at the same time. The new arrangement finally settled the supply controv-ersy: in fact it settled it so successfully that the factories were soon producing more aircraft than was needed by the Army and Navy. This surplus had a profound importance for future developments.

Until 1917 air services had been regarded as essentially ancillary to the Army and Navy: the potential use of aircraft as a separate strik-ing force against industrial targets protected by their geographical position from military or naval attacks, and the effect of bombing on civilian morale, were not yet evident. The orthodox attitude was seriously modified, and the creation of an independent Air Force greatly accelerated, by two factors – the air attacks on London in the summer of 1917, and the existence of that surplus of aircraft already mentioned. The raids on London not only led to immediate discus-sion about the best means of air defence, but also provoked the natural desire to retaliate in kind, and thus encouraged those auth-orities who believed that only an air service unhampered by naval or military control could initiate and execute an effective air strategy. A

Committee headed by General Smuts was appointed after the London raids: it produced two reports in August, 1917, one dealing with the defence of the capital, the other – a paper of great historic significance – drawing attention to the immense potentialities of the use of air power and recommending the creation of a separate Air Force.[3]

The fact that enough aircraft were to hand to provide an independent bombing force without denuding the Navy and Army of 'planes for military and naval co-operation, helped to clinch the arguments and negotiations which went on during the autumn of 1917. Despite naval and military misgivings and some notable political bickering, an Air Council and Air Ministry were set up in January, 1918. Apart from the overriding strategic argument for a separate Force, it was claimed that a new organization was essential in order to prevent competition for men and material between the air services of the Navy and Army, to end duplication of staff and divergence of methods, and to provide a unified system for promoting the quickest possible scientific and technical progress in aeronautics.[4]

The Royal Flying Corps and the Royal Naval Air Service were combined to form the Royal Air Force on April 1, 1918: one authority thus controlled all the air units, with the exception of the lighter-than-air service which remained with the Admiralty until October, 1919. The original theory and practice of a unified air service had once more become the reality.

The RAF was only seven months old when the war ended. Its internal organization was incomplete, and it was not well enough established, either on strategic or constitutional grounds, to be accepted unquestionably as a permanent part of the British defence system. For almost five years, therefore, it was a hotly disputed question whether or not there should be a separate Air Force and Air Ministry in peace-time. The Admiralty and War Office contended, though for different reasons, that there should not. Nor was the situation made any easier by the post-war desire for retrenchment, both financial and administrative, against which all three Services fought an uphill battle.

The RAF had certain advantages, however, which were by no means negligible. The new Service was there for all to see – 'in possession' – which adds to the defendant's strength in inter-departmental struggles. It had strong supporters among military experts and parliamentarians, and could count on public sympathy for the cause of a young Service with a glamorous war record in a dispute with its more staid and elderly partners. Moreover the fascination of the air weapon was enough to promote contemporary disbelief, however irrational, in the continued need for armies and navies and a consequent distrust of the various proposals to leave aeronautical development in the hands of military and naval authorities. The future of civil flying was entrusted to the Air Ministry in 1919, and this too, added to the strength and viability of the department.

The complete abolition of the Air Force and the redistribution of its component units between the other Services was advocated in certain Army circles. The Chief of the Imperial General Staff, Sir Henry Wilson, 'strongly condemned the existence of an Air Ministry' throughout his tenure of office, which ended in February, 1922, and during his brief career as an MP between then and his assassination in the following June.[5] The Prime Minister seemed to give qualified support to this idea when he decided, in January, 1919, to appoint a single Secretary of State for War and Air (Mr Churchill).[a] In fact, while Mr Churchill held the dual office the RAF lost no ground. The Secretary of State publicly insisted throughout the two years he stayed at the Service ministries that the development of the RAF was making it impossible to re-merge it into the other Services.[6] Despite Mr Churchill's assurances, the rôle of the Air Force was being examined at length in 1921 by a sub-committee of the Committee of Imperial Defence over which Lord Balfour presided, and it was not until March, 1922, that the Government unequivocally stated their intention of retaining a separate Air Ministry and Air Force.[7] Nor was this the end of Army hopes. The whole question was reopened by

[a] Lloyd George at first gave Mr Churchill the choice of either the Admiralty and Air Ministry or the War Office and Air Ministry. Mr Churchill asked for the Admiralty, and it is interesting to read his view of the air problem in his letter to the Prime Minister of December 28, 1918:

'There wd be good reasons for connecting the air with the Admiralty; for aeroplanes will never be a substitute for armies & can only be a valuable accessory whereas they will almost certainly be an economical substitute for many classes of warships. The technical development of the air falls naturally into the same sphere as the mechanical development of the Navy – & this becomes increasingly true the larger the aeroplanes grow.'
(Lord Beaverbrook: *Men and Power, 1917–1918*, pp. 141, 361.)

But before Mr Churchill's choice had been made, trouble had arisen over the problem of demobilization, and the Premier insisted that Mr Churchill take the War Office. (W. S. Churchill: *The World Crisis: The Aftermath*, pp. 52–53.) The CIGS was unhappy about the arrangement (C. E. Callwell: *Field Marshal Sir Henry Wilson*, Vol. II, pp. 156, 162) and the Parliamentary Under Secretary to the Air Ministry, Major-General Seely, resigned in protest in November, 1919. When Lord Riddell warned Lloyd George of Seely's impending resignation, the Prime Minister remarked that 'he would be sorry but there was no alternative. The creation of a new department would no doubt mean more expenditure which could not be faced.' (Lord Riddell: *Intimate Diaries of the Peace Conference and After*, pp. 139–140.)

a Sub-Committee of the Committee of Imperial Defence (the Salisbury Committee) in 1923, when the General Staff again submitted a proposal that operational and administrative control of military air units should be transferred back to the Admiralty and War Office, while the Air Ministry should retain responsibility for 'civil aviation, research, experiment and supply'. This was turned down by the Cabinet in July, 1923.[8]

The War Office claims failed largely because of a lack of moderation which reacted in favour of the Air Ministry. A supplementary cause of the success of the Air Force case was the contemporary proof that air units had a useful peace-time function apart from the other Services. As early as 1919 Sir Hugh (later Lord) Trenchard, in his *Report on the Permanent Organization of the Royal Air Force*, remarked that:

'Recent events have shown the value of aircraft in dealing with frontier troubles, and it is not perhaps too much to hope that before long it may prove possible to regard the Royal Air Force units not as an addition to the military garrison but as a substitute for part of it.'[9]

We have seen in the previous chapter that the international settlement which followed the war included the creation of mandated territories in the Middle East for which Britain was made responsible. A new department of the Colonial Office was entrusted with the administration of these territories and at a Conference held in Cairo in March, 1921, it was decided to charge the RAF with the military control of Iraq. This was put into effect in October, 1922, and the experiment was later extended to Palestine.[b] It was found that the security of these sparsely populated areas could be maintained as well if not better by comparatively small air units as by much larger army garrisons, and at much less cost.

The arguments of the years 1919–23 were the last serious differences about distribution of operational functions between Army and Air Force. The Cabinet decision of July, 1923, settled the question, and thereafter relations between the two Services were uncon-

[b] Military control of Palestine reverted to the Army in August, 1929. The security of Aden, which had been a matter for the Indian Army until 1917, and of the War Office from then onwards, was taken over by the RAF in April, 1928. Mr Churchill, who had gone to the Colonial Office early in 1921, was the leading figure at the Cairo Conference: the Conference's recognition of the use of air power might be regarded as a pointer to the way in which his appreciation of the potentialities of the air weapon had developed while he played a dual rôle at the War Office and Air Ministry.

troversial. A more difficult issue was raised in the early conflict between the Admiralty and the RAF. The Admiralty did not support
the Army in its claim that the new Service should be abolished. The
naval authorities were concerned simply with the question of control
of air units acting in close support of the Navy.

Between 1918 and 1924 all air units working with the Navy came
under the Air Ministry's Coastal Area, which was responsible for the
administration of shore-based coastal aircraft and Fleet Air Arm
units when ashore. The Air Officer Commanding, Coastal Area, was
responsible to the Air Ministry for the training, supply and maintenance of the units and acted as adviser to the Admiralty on naval
aerial policy, but all units of the Fleet Air Arm when aboard ship
came under naval discipline. The personnel of the Fleet Air Arm was
mainly drawn from the RAF with a few 'seconded' naval officers.

The naval air service at the end of the war and in the years immediately following was largely shore-based, and the aircraft carrier was
in its infancy. This absence of a large carrier-based Fleet Air Arm was
one reason why the Air Force in 1918 was formed by amalgamating
two air services whose techniques were substantially similar. The
Admiralty argued strongly after 1918, however, that 'an air wing of
the Navy was more consistent with maritime requirements than a
naval wing of the Air Force'.[10] The Navy needed aircraft to co-operate with ships in the defence of the coast and of shipping, and for
reconnaissance, spotting and torpedo work in purely sea operations.
The Admiralty felt that it was desirable to develop an air branch of
an air-minded Fleet, wholly manned by naval personnel. They also
wanted a predominant voice in the design and supply of naval aircraft. In sum, the Admiralty's attitude was based on the argument
that 'there is no *essential* tactical connection between the operational
work of the Fleet Air Arm as a weapon and the Royal Air Force,
except that they both fly'.[11]

It is possible that the Admiralty's case for taking over control of
the Fleet Air Arm, both ashore and afloat, would have been carried
on its merits in the discussions of the early 1920s, had not other
considerations prevailed. The naval air arm constituted no less than
a seventh part of the whole strength of the already much reduced
RAF in 1923. To have severed it from the new Service would have
greatly weakened the latter's case for continued existence apart from
the Army. The fears of the Air Ministry and its supporters, and the
general dismay at the attitude of the War Office, together combined
to defeat the Admiralty's claim. Even though all the Sea Lords
threatened to resign, only minor changes in the relative positions of
the Navy and Air Force were made on the recommendations of

Lords Balfour, Peel and Weir, who reported to the Salisbury Committee in July, 1923. The new relations were embodied in what became known as the Trenchard-Keyes Agreement, which took effect in July, 1924.[12] [bb]

The Trenchard-Keyes Agreement ensured that no air units would be withdrawn by the Air Ministry from naval service without either naval consent or Cabinet approval. Operational control of the Fleet Air Arm afloat remained with the Admiralty, but disembarked units came under RAF jurisdiction. The personnel of the Fleet Air Arm was mixed: of the air crews, the Pilots held RAF ranks even if they were in fact 'seconded' naval officers, but the Observers and Telegraphist/Air Gunners were naval men. Aircraft carriers had RAF technical officers and tradesmen on board. The initial training of all flying personnel was the responsibility of the Air Ministry.

The Admiralty was never fully satisfied with the terms laid down in 1924. The case was reopened on several occasions, and eventually, in 1937, the Government decided that administrative control of the Fleet Air Arm should become the responsibility of the Admiralty, but that the Air Ministry should continue to provide initial flying training: supply, research and development were also to remain an Air Ministry responsibility.[c] It took a further two years, however, to work out the arrangements for the transfer. Administrative control of the Fleet Air Arm was not assumed by the Admiralty, therefore, until 1939. As a result of this change all the personnel of the Fleet Air Arm became fully naval. A few airfields were transferred to the Admiralty, but this did not involve any control over shore-based RAF aircraft. The airfields were merely

'required for the housing . . . of aircraft belonging to the Fleet, but not embarked, in the same way that shore establishments and dockyards are required for other naval personnel and for the ships.'[13]

[bb] While this book was going through the press, Viscount Templewood's *Empire of the Air* was published. Lord Templewood (Sir Samuel Hoare) was Secretary of State for Air for the first time in the Government formed by Bonar Law in October, 1922. He gives a detailed account of the struggle for the retention of a separate Air Force, and reveals that Bonar Law confidently expected that Force to be divided between the two older Services, and the Air Ministry closed down, within a few weeks of his taking office. Viscount Templewood paints a harsher picture of the attacks on the separate Air Force than is given in the above narrative: he stresses the widespread objections made to the expense of a third Service, and argues that only the unanimous Report of the Salisbury Committee saved that Service and the Air Ministry from partition between their older partners.

[c] 326 HC Deb. 3512–6. Responsibility for the supply of aircraft passed to the new Ministry of Aircraft Production in May, 1940.

There were good reasons for holding that the balance of advantage had moved since 1924. The Fleet Air Arm had grown and its work had become more and more specialized. It was, in fact, an integral part of the Fleet and it was thought that it would be most efficient if placed under full Admiralty control. The interchanging of personnel between RAF and Navy had hindered the development of a high morale in the Fleet Air Arm, and the interchangeability was itself fast becoming impracticable because of the special nature of naval air operations. Moreover, some of the other considerations valid at the time when Lord Balfour's sub-committee reported were no longer applicable. The RAF had firmly established itself as an independent Service: the transfer of the Fleet Air Arm would not seriously dismember the metropolitan air force and could not, therefore, be regarded as a threat to its separate existence.[14]

The Admiralty had wanted not only control of the ship-based aircraft, but also the control of those shore-based 'planes which co-operated with the Fleet – i.e., with what is known as Coastal Command. The Navy's case for having administrative responsibility for Coastal Command was not accepted in 1937, but in April, 1941, the operational control of Coastal aircraft by the Admiralty, which had in fact been the existing practice since the outbreak of war, was given formal recognition.[15] It strengthened and underlined the naval aspect of the protection of shipping but left Coastal Command administratively an integral part of the RAF. After the war a joint Admiralty/Air Ministry Committee was set up to examine the relations between the two Services in the light of war experience, and this resulted in an Agreement of October, 1946, about the allocation and direction of shore-based forces acting in conjunction with naval forces in war at sea. No drastic changes were recommended. Very briefly, the formulation of joint policy in peace is recognized by the Agreement as being (under the overriding authority of the Chiefs of Staff) the joint responsibility of the Admiralty and the Air Ministry or of the Commanders-in-Chief abroad. The Agreement also recognized that the successful conduct of joint operations can only be ensured by the proper co-ordination of the staffs concerned. The planning and conduct of joint naval/air operations is effected in Joint Headquarters and it is recognized in maritime operations that the predominant partner is usually the Naval Commander concerned.

SUPPLYING THE ARMED FORCES

The term 'supply' is used here to describe collectively all the processes involved in 'obtaining or producing the material needs of the

Fighting Services, from the requisitioning stage to the delivery of those needs to the Service Store Depots or distribution authority'.[16] It is obvious, however, that from an administrative standpoint the range of such a subject is stupendous. The ramifications of supply in 20th century conditions, especially in wartime, affect the whole of the national economy and are the concern of a very large part of the machinery of government. In order to reduce the area to manageable proportions, it is necessary to exclude all the marginal activities which cluster round the hard core of the problems of supply.

In the first place, therefore, supply does not cover the production or import of raw materials. The commodities used by the Forces fall into three main groups – food and fuel, general stores, and warlike stores. Of these, only certain types of food and fuel are unprocessed: military supply is mainly concerned with the provision and manufacture of finished articles. Secondly, the organization of supply in this context means only the organization of the Service departments themselves and of such civil agencies as have been primarily created to serve those departments. Thus the arrangements whereby certain general stores for the Armed Forces are provided by civil departments other than the special military supply departments – e.g., telecommunications equipment from the Post Office, some furniture from the Ministry of Works, and medical stores from the Ministry of Health – are not considered here. Nor is the non-military supply work of the special supply departments – e.g., the provision of vehicles to civil departments by the present Ministry of Supply – touched on. Thirdly, supply in this context does not include the organization of building construction and maintenance. The Service departments have in fact usually retained their own units or relied on their own contractors for the provision of special buildings, and the degree to which the Office (later Ministry) of Works – primarily a civil agency – has performed constructional tasks for the military authorities is not considered here.

A proper understanding of the developments and controversies which have attended the arrangement of military supply since 1914 is only possible if the complexity of the operations involved is appreciated. A sense of that complexity can perhaps best be conveyed by outlining the various processes in the supply of manufactured articles. The supply of food and fuel, of course, does not involve all the processes, nor does the supply of many of the articles included under the heading 'general' stores, which covers such items as clothing, camp and barrack equipment, medical supplies, etc. Most of the processes and the major problems arise in the provision of 'warlike' stores – arms, ammunition, warships, tanks, aeroplanes, vehicles and all the ancillary equipment connected with them. On the other hand, because the equipment of the Armed Forces has become so highly technical, it is impossible to draw a firm line between general and warlike stores. Certain items, such as clothing and guns, for instance, fall clearly enough apart, but at the margin there is much chance of confusion. It is worth making an imperfect distinction, however, as the major controversies have centred round the supply of what are loosely known as warlike stores, mainly because many of the most critically important of those stores have been special to particular Services.

A simplified statement of the processes involved in the supply of military stores begins with what may be called the process of *requirement*: the need for a particular item must be recognized – i.e., specification – and the extent of the demand – i.e., numbers – formulated. Then comes the process of *development*, a composite activity covering design – the initiatory idea – and experiment, which may be a long process of trial and error and modification. Somewhere between requirement and development we may place *research*, a continuous process which both stimulates demand and is stimulated by demand. Research in its 'pure' aspects may well precede demand, and in its 'applied' aspects may be difficult to distinguish from design and experiment. When requirement and development are completed, having drawn on the findings of research, we pass to *production*. Production in this context covers both direct manufacture by State organizations such as Ordnance Factories, and the placing of contracts with private manufacturers. It also includes the programming of production, the organization of industry for war purposes and to some extent to meet peace-time requirements, and watching the progress of manufacture and delivery. Both during and after production comes *inspection*: the examination of finished products or of complicated equipment in course of manufacture in order to ascertain that they are of the proper quality and description. Neither the storage, distribution, repair and maintenance of military material, nor the function of deciding on the allocation of industrial output among the Services are considered here as elements of supply.

Although it is possible to divide supply roughly into five component processes – requirement, research, development, production and inspection – such a division is largely theoretical. At every stage the processes overlap, with the consequent risk of friction among the people concerned. It is the inherent technical complexity and the resulting need for smooth liaison between the various authorities, coupled with the development whereby modern war involves large and vital parts of the economic and industrial capacity of the nation, which has made the organization of military supply so controversial since 1914. The main issue has been whether the supply of special warlike stores should be left to the Service departments, or whether some or all of them should be supplied by one or more separate supply departments. This in turn raises the question – which becomes acute if separate supply departments are actually set up – of whether it is possible to find a workable and acceptable division of responsibilities between the supply departments and the Service department concerned.

It is important to emphasise at the outset, however, that in any supply arrangement there is inevitably a clash between user and producer, between strategy and production. User departments tend to believe that they could do the supply job better themselves, and may be led by manufacturers to think that deliveries can be made sooner than is in fact the case. The production experts of either a Service department or a Supply department tend to be equally impatient of military opinion: they are often in a better position to estimate delivery dates than are either the manufacturers or their military counterparts. Similarly the ordering of production is very much a matter of deciding arguments between the advocates of high quality with delayed delivery, or existing quality with immediate delivery. Here again there is opportunity for friction between the strategists and the supply authority. This mutual suspicion is inherent in any military supply organization, whether unified or divided, and is only overcome by close liaison and by building up a general sense of confidence and give-and-take.

Against this brief exposition of the range of the subject and the nature of its problems we may set the narrative of events since the outbreak of the First World War.

1914–1921

In 1914, apart from one or two minor arrangements such as that whereby the Admiralty drew its small arms ammunition from War Office sources, the two Service departments were practically independent of each other and had their own supply organizations. During the First World War it is broadly true that the supply of general stores remained the responsibility of the Service departments: the main administrative changes concerned the supply of warlike stores.[d]

---

[d] Insofar as the supply of food and fuel is concerned, the independence of the Service departments has to a large extent continued ever since 1914. During our period joint contracts have on occasion been arranged or the larger consumer has purchased stocks and the smaller consumer has then indented for the amount

The War Office remained fully responsible for such stores for only nine months after the outbreak of hostilities in 1914. The Ministry of Munitions was created in June, 1915, and soon took over from the War Office the whole range of processes involved in supplying war-like stores. On the other hand, the Admiralty remained responsible for meeting almost all its supply needs: only steel, explosives and propellant, and later aircraft, were obtained through the Ministry of Munitions. The primary interest of the supply arrangements during the First World War centres, therefore, on the activities of the War Office and the Ministry of Munitions, and on developments at the two Air Boards and Air Ministry.

The obvious and inescapable explanation of why the Ministry of Munitions was set up is that the task of supplying munitions became too big for the War Office, whose machinery (which was in fact merely a purchasing organization) well nigh broke down under the strain. The scale of the conflict and the tremendous demand for guns and ammunition – particularly shells – was unprecedented: it came as a numbing shock to almost all the military experts and politicians, and it is scarcely surprising that several months passed before the problem was seen in its proper perspective and tackled accordingly. The shortage of munitions was a contributory factor in the formation of the Coalition Government in May, 1915, and the full story of the creation of the Ministry of Munitions, which can be pieced together from the numerous memoirs and commentaries which have been published, belongs perhaps as much to the field of political as of

---

it required. These arrangements have often been on a local basis, particularly with regard to foodstuffs. At home the Air Ministry buys its basic foodstuffs through the Army, and all three Services utilize the catering facilities offered by the NAAFI, of which more below. The Admiralty gets aviation fuel from the Air Ministry. These are notable exceptions to the general rule, however, and the main reason for the continued independence of the Service departments is possibly, in the case of food and domestic fuel, the predominant need for local purchases, and in the case of other fuel, is the highly specialized types used, particularly by the Navy and Air Force.

The Navy, Army and Air Force Institutes (NAAFI) were incorporated on December 6, 1920. The Corporation is a non-profit making company limited by guarantee: it consists of twelve nominal shareholders who form the Council. Four members of the Council are appointed by each Service. The NAAFI had its origin in the Board of Control of Regimental Institutes set up in December, 1914, by the War Office, which was superseded by the Navy and Army Canteen Board in 1917. The assets of the Board, which took over the Expeditionary Force Canteens, were vested in NAAFI on January 1, 1921. For more details of the history and constitution, functions, etc., see *Fifth Report from Select Committee on National Expenditure*, 1942 (HC 58).

administrative history.[e] Here all that is attempted is a brief record of the administrative developments which immediately preceded, and helped to establish, the separate supply department, and a short appraisal of the other forces which were at work.

The seriousness of the munitions problem was first widely realized in the early months of 1915, and by the end of May the Ministry of Munitions was being formed. The speed of this development reflected its political urgency, but neither the formulation nor the acceptance of the idea that a separate department was needed came at the beginning of the period of acute anxiety. Lloyd George's brilliant recognition of the importance of the supply question and his persistent attempts to galvanize the War Office and industry into livelier and more comprehensive efforts, did not at first, at any rate, include any call for a separate authority. Nor could it be expected that the War Office, under Lord Kitchener's over-secretive guidance, should give any lead in consciously promoting its own dismemberment.[f] A Cabinet Committee on Munitions had been set up in October, 1914, but lapsed in January, 1915, without achieving any great status. Lloyd George, then Chancellor of the Exchequer, demanded the appointment of a more effectual committee early in March, 1915, and two weeks later the Prime Minister thought of appointing him to a special post of Director of War Contracts – a scheme which came to nothing but was probably the first serious hint of a separate supply department.[18]

[e] Lord Beaverbrook, in *Politicians and the War*, Vol. I., Ch. 8, claims that the munitions crisis was not in any way responsible for the fall of the Liberal Government, which he attributes wholly to the dispute at the Admiralty between Mr Churchill and Lord Fisher. While that dispute was doubtless the immediate cause, the atmosphere in high political circles had previously been strongly 'conditioned' by the anxiety of the Press over the shell shortage, by the difficult relations between Lord Kitchener at the War Office, Sir John French at the Front, and Lloyd George in Cabinet, and, even before the outcry became public, by demands on the part of the engineering industry for changes in the supply policy of the War Office.[17]

[f] No one has written so vividly of the impact of Lloyd George on the munitions problem as Viscount Grey of Falloden in *Twenty Five Years*, Vol. II, pp. 242–243:

'When munitions ran short and he (i.e., Lloyd George) had realized what the needs were and how they would grow, he made the question his own, though it then belonged entirely to the War Office. Kitchener's principle and practice was to leave the work of other people alone, and to tolerate no interference from others with what he regarded as his job. When he found the activity of Lloyd George entering his department he barred the way. The torrent of Lloyd George's activity foamed against the obstruction, and for a time was delayed; but it ended by sweeping before it that part of the War Office that dealt with munitions and depositing it elsewhere. . . .'

When institutional change did come, it came fast. Kitchener appointed an Armaments Output Committee within the War Office at the end of March. It was given the 'extremely narrow' job of taking 'the necessary steps to provide such additional labour as may be required to secure that the supply of munitions of war shall be sufficient to meet all requirements'. A week later a Munitions of War Committee was set up by the Cabinet, with Lloyd George as Chairman. This body had much wider terms of reference: it was

'to ensure the promptest and most efficient application of all the available productive resources of the country to the manufacture and supply of munitions of war for the Navy and Army'

and was to have 'full power to take all steps necessary for that purpose'. In the course of the next month the 'Armaments Output Committee became informally, though not technically, subordinate to the Munitions of War Committee'.[19] Thus the War Office began to lose responsibility: the new committee structure was an admission that the Service departments 'could not be expected to carry out in addition to their other duties a task so vast as the supply of munitions in wartime had become'.[20] But the Munitions of War Committee was to lead quickly to a bigger change. While the public clamour about the lack of high explosive shells grew, while the political world was disturbed by the row at the Admiralty, and while the Liberal Government tottered and fell, the work and organization of supply under the auspices of the Munitions of War Committee was assuming a departmental character.[21] It was realized that the committee structure was

'appropriate and fairly effective so long as the sole purpose was to tide over an emergency by stimulating the rapid production of certain natures of shell which were most urgently needed. But the prospects now opening out were of a much larger scope, and involved . . . the general control both of industry and labour. This was manifestly a task beyond the powers of any committee.'[22]

It is probable, therefore, that when, on May 19 – the same day that the decision to form a Coalition Government was announced – Lloyd George wrote to the Prime Minister stating his unwillingness to remain Chairman of the Munitions of War Committee because it had in fact no real executive authority, events had already dictated the creation of a Ministry of Munitions.[23]

The unprecedented nature of the demand, the early failure to diagnose the new situation, the consequent near breakdown of the War Office supply machine, the suspicions of Kitchener, the attitude of Sir John French, the campaign of the Northcliffe Press, the dynamism of Lloyd George, all brought into focus by the sudden change of Government – these may be cited as the reasons why the Ministry of Munitions was set up.[g] The department – a statutory creation – was, at first, essentially an Army supply authority, and it never became seriously concerned with Admiralty requirements. Once it was created, however, problems of the limits of its jurisdiction soon appeared.

One of the most significant facts about the new Ministry of Munitions was its power with regard to what we have defined as the process of requirement. At first sight, the natural view of what should be the function of a supply department in this respect may be expressed in Balfour's words (written in the context of a later controversy): 'The department which supplies should do nothing but supply; it should neither determine the amount and character of the things supplied, nor the uses to which they should be put.'[24] This view was accepted when the Ministry of Munitions was first created, and

'. . . it was laid down that the duties of the new department would begin when the requirements of the War Office had been made known to it, and that the new department should be guided by the "general requirements and specific requisitions" of the Army Council.'

When the Order-in-Council defining the functions of the new department was published, however, it stated that the duty of the Minister of Munitions was to be 'to ensure such supply of munitions for the present war as may be required by the Army Council or the Admiralty, or may otherwise be found to be necessary'.[25] The last phrase fundamentally altered the position, and its inclusion was a reflection

---

[g] The Ministry of Munitions is often thought of as Lloyd George's creation and there is obviously a strong case for claiming this. The parent, however, was not keen to look after his child: 'Whatever I had done directly or indirectly to hasten or assist in the creation of this department,' wrote Lloyd George (*War Memoirs*, Ch. 9) 'the last thing I desired was to have to assume control of it. I had no wish to give up the Chancellorship of the Exchequer for something of an unknown nature.' His appointment was to some extent a political manoeuvre in the midst of frenzied jockeying for places among the senior members of the Coalition. But outside influences were also strong. The King saw Asquith on May 22 and urged that a separate munitions department be created with Lloyd George in charge (H. Nicolson: *George V*, p. 264). Northcliffe, according to one of his editors (Tom Clarke, *My Northcliffe Diary*, p. 81) 'avowedly wanted . . . a Ministry of Munitions with Lloyd George at the head of it'. In his recent book, *Men and Power, 1917–1918* (p. 60), Lord Beaverbrook claims that 'it was Lord Northcliffe's agitation over the Shell Shortage that had ensured the creation of a Ministry of Munitions with Lloyd George at its head'.

of the strong parliamentary demand that the new Minister should not
be dependent on the military authorities but should himself assess the
needs of the Armed Forces and order production accordingly. Lloyd
George certainly took advantage of this power, and in his first
months in office

'. . . made plans not only to satisfy all the demands of the Army that
were known to him, but to arrange for the production of certain
munitions . . . in excess of War Office requirements, anticipating an
increased demand later on.'[26]

The Ministry of Munitions was at first entrusted with a large share
in the wide powers of requirement discussed in the previous paragraph, and with the processes of production and inspection. The
work of design and research was retained by the War Office for about
six months, but 'serious delays . . . occurred in the supply of essential
munitions owing to the divorce between design and manufacture',
and the branches concerned were handed over to the Ministry of
Munitions in November, 1915.[27] This concentration of functions
continued throughout the war, so far as Army material was concerned, except for the period May–October, 1917, when the design
and specification of mechanical warfare supplies was handed over to
a War Office Committee. The arrangement was deemed a failure and
the work was returned to the Ministry of Munitions.[28] Responsibility
for the supply of mechanical transport, railway material and all
types of petrol engines was added to the tasks of the Ministry in
September, 1916, and January, 1917.

Controversy about the proper location of production and design,
etc., also touched the Ministry of Munitions with regard to the supply
of aircraft. Both Admiralty and War Office had their own methods
of aircraft supply during the first part of the war – the Admiralty
relying almost entirely on contracts with private firms and the War
Office producing some of their aircraft and many spares, etc., at the
Royal Aircraft Factory, Farnborough. Various efforts to co-ordinate
supply were hampered by the unwillingness of the Service departments to relinquish control and by severe inter-departmental differences. A Joint War Air Committee (February to May, 1916) and the
first Air Board (May to December, 1916) had no executive authority.
The Board 'was charged with the duty of organizing the supply of
material and preventing competition', but its 'inherent weakness was
to bring about a deadlock. . . .'[29] The quarrel between the Board and
the Admiralty in the later months of 1916 at least produced some
memorable and magnificent polemics from the pens of Lord Curzon
and Mr Balfour! The first suggestions that aircraft production and

design should pass to the Ministry of Munitions were put forward during 1916 by Mr (later Lord) Weir and Lloyd George, but the Admiralty, War Office and Air Board turned them down.[30]

In December, 1916, the War Cabinet decided that the design and production of aircraft should be transferred from the Service departments to the Ministry of Munitions, but this decision was later modified, no doubt in order to reach a compromise between the various factions. In January, 1917, production and inspection passed to the Ministry of Munitions but design was retained by a strengthened Air Board which was also empowered to decide the number of aircraft to be ordered and to allocate them between the two Services.[h] Thus responsibility lay not merely, as in the case of Army supplies, between the user and the producer, but between two user departments, a special requirement and design department, and the producer. The second Air Board, with a ministerial head, was 'a broker between Army and Navy'.[31] This diffusion of functions augured ill, but the situation was saved by the mundane though vital practical decision to house all the branches concerned with aircraft supply in one building. Thus the Air Board, the Aeronautical Supply Department of the Ministry of Munitions and the air executives of the War Office and Admiralty, came together in the Hotel Cecil. Liaison was smooth and complete: the Air Board, whatever its theoretical deficiencies, 'became, in effect, a Ministry of Supply, and as such it was eminently successful'.[32] When the Board was converted into the Air Ministry in January, 1918, however, the design functions were handed over to the Ministry of Munitions.

At the end of the war, therefore, only the Admiralty was both an operational department and a department for supplying warlike stores. Its independence in supply matters was almost complete and it retained full responsibility for the provision of lighter-than-air machines. The War Office and Air Ministry were only concerned with what we have defined as requirement, and even that was shared with the ubiquitous Ministry of Munitions, which performed all the other processes of supply. It is true that the independence of the Admiralty in the field of supply led to acute competition between it and the Ministry of Munitions, but it is misleading to argue from this that a

[h] W. Raleigh and H. A. Jones: *The War in the Air*, Vol. III, pp. 282–283. According to this authority (VI, p. 30) the main reason why the constitution of the Air Board was altered and why production was handed over to the Ministry of Munitions was Lord Curzon's opinion that an increased output of engines was impossible without 'reorganization and some form of centralized control'. The Admiralty, however, retained control of the supply of lighter-than-air machines – see a letter from Lord Cowdray, January 19, 1917, quoted in Lloyd George, *War Memoirs*, Ch. 57.

solution could have been found merely by combining the two supply organizations. The real cause of conflict lay in the larger failure to establish a full and workable control of the whole national economy until very late in the war. The departmental disputes were, largely, disputes as to the allocation of labour and raw materials. During his tenure as Minister of Munitions (July, 1917–January, 1919) Mr Churchill, while he pressed for the transfer of the Controller's Department at the Admiralty and the remaining production branches of the War Office (concerned mainly with general stores) to his Ministry, also made the much more comprehensive suggestions that the Labour branches of both departments should go to the Ministry of National Service and that the Works branches of the War Office, Air Ministry and Ministry of Munitions should be centralized in the Office of Works.[33]

Had the war lasted a little longer it is possible that the whole subsequent history of the departmental arrangements for military supply would have been very different. During 1918 Mr Churchill's ideas on supply were supported on various grounds by a Treasury Committee presided over by Lord Inchcape and by the Haldane Committee on the Machinery of Government. The suggestion that the Ministry of Munitions should become a central Ministry of Supply which would undertake all purchasing for government departments gained ground in the last months of the war, and three days before the Armistice was signed the Cabinet approved it in principle. Sixteen months later that decision was reversed: in March, 1921, the Ministry of Munitions was disbanded. The details of the re-transfer of responsibilities may well precede a recital of its causes.

The War Office broke away first: design and research were transferred from the Ministry of Munitions in March, 1919. In the following January the Air Ministry assumed responsibility for all the processes of the supply of aircraft. The remaining Army supply functions passed to the War Office in June, 1920.[j] The crucial date in the post-1918 negotiations about the future of military supply was March 23, 1920, when the Cabinet decided to abandon earlier plans for the permanent establishment of a Ministry of Supply.

A major reason for the failure of the case for a Ministry of Supply was the division of opinion among its adherents as to the proper scope of the proposed department. One school of thought held that maximum advantage could only be gained by as complete a concentration

---

[j] This account, of course, excludes the transfers of function from the Ministry of Munitions to civil departments. An inter-Service adjustment which may conveniently be recorded here was the transfer of responsibility for lighter-than-air machines from the Admiralty to the Air Ministry in October, 1919.

H

of supply as possible: the other school believed that the new department should only provide standard stores for all three Services, leaving highly differentiated technical stores to the Service departments. The problem, therefore, concerned technical warlike stores, which might be roughly covered by the three items ships, aircraft and tanks. While the Service departments were agreeable, if lukewarm, about a central supply of standard stores, in the matter of technical items the Admiralty and Air Ministry were strongly opposed to any divorce between user and producer, while the War Office was at least unhappy about the possible loss of design, research and inspection. Even though the Ministry of Munitions proposed to leave ships to the Admiralty, the latter department was unwilling to concede that another authority could efficiently supply any items other than those of a general stock nature. Deadlock ensued. The Air Ministry, newly charged with the responsibility for promoting civil flying, insisted that the technical progress of aeronautics would be seriously hampered by any division between designer, producer and user.

To these differences must be added a factor which weighed heavily against the proponents of a Ministry of Supply. Fundamentally, their case rested on the proposition that 'buying is an expert operation, and the extent and importance of government purchases justify the setting up of an expert establishment to deal with them'.[34] But the sudden end of the war left the Services with a vast amount of surplus stores on which they could probably draw for the next five years. There was, therefore, little if any need to set up a department to specialize in buying, at any rate immediately.

As a result of this opposition the Bill drafted early in 1919 to establish a permanent Ministry of Supply was drawn in very weak terms. It left the new Ministry at the mercy of the Service departments, because no power could be transferred to it without the consent of the latter. The Cabinet Home Affairs Committee felt that such an innocuous measure would not survive parliamentary attack, and the Bill was postponed – for ever, as it turned out.

To these tangible factors of interdepartmental and ministerial disagreement and the inescapable presence of vast surpluses of war materials may be added more general influences. Nobody wanted to think seriously of the possibility of further wars: there was a popular revulsion against anything which savoured of warlike preparation. There was a desire to get rid of the governmental paraphernalia of war, to reduce the cost, the controls and the vast administrative empire which had been acceptable in crisis but which had outstayed its welcome by 1919. Finally, it may be that the breakdown of the plans for a Ministry of Supply was hastened by the preoccupation of the Cabinet with more pressing matters, by the prolonged absence of the Prime Minister from the area of domestic affairs – which increased the delay in coming to a decision and allowed time for the opposition to strengthen its case – and perhaps by the transfer of Mr Churchill from the Ministry of Munitions to the dual post of Secretary of State for War and Air in January, 1919.[k]

1921–1939

Though the Ministry of Munitions disappeared, the organization of supply never returned to the position as it had been in 1914. The presence of a third Service, the lessons of the First World War and the increasing technicality of war material all forced on the supply system some degree of interdepartmental co-ordination. The whole question was thrashed out by a Committee on the Amalgamation of Services Common to the Navy, Army and Air Force in 1922. That Committee turned down the idea of amalgamating supply services but recommended inter-Service co-operation through an extended structure of co-ordinating committees and an increased use of the agency system of purchase.[35] Special warlike stores were left to the Service departments, and the peace-time extension of common supply arrangements was based on the principle that the major user of a commodity should purchase sufficient quantities of that commodity to meet the needs of the other Services as well as their own. This system was applied most fully in the relations between the War Office and the Air Ministry. The former provided the latter with foodstuffs and a wide range of general stores. Other inter-Service arrangements were very limited in scope. The War Office supplied

---

[k] Between the end of the war and the disbanding of the Ministry of Munitions the financial arrangements between that department and its clients were very rigid: the result was a 'sea of paper'. While this aspect of the experience of the post-war Ministry of Munitions apparently had no direct bearing on the decision to abandon the idea of a permanent separate supply department, it no doubt strengthened the prejudices of those already opposed to that idea on other grounds. One useful outcome of this particular financial experience was that the memory of the fiasco in 1920 led to the practice in force during the Second World War whereby detailed financial adjustment between supply and Service departments was avoided. Such a beneficial 'carry over' of experience from 1915–21 to 1939 was not, however, repeated in other contexts because not enough was recorded of the procedures adopted by the Ministry of Munitions. The official *History* was not completed and is a patchy work whose inadequacies became very clear when the Ministry of Supply was set up in 1939 and when action was necessary to close down war production in 1945. Those responsible often had to depend on the vague recollections of a few isolated individuals for guidance about much of what had been done in 1915–19. For details about the *History* see note 9 to Chapter II (p. 367).

the Admiralty with small arms and ammunition, with Marine equipment of Army type, and with a very small range of general stores. In return, as it were, the Admiralty supplied the War Office with some textiles, soap and odd local supplies of coal and oxygen. The Admiralty also supplied the Air Ministry with certain marine and navigational equipment such as motor boats, compasses and torpedoes, etc. The Air Ministry supplied the Navy with its aircraft and air stores. In short, despite the examples cited and a few joint contracts for certain stores, the Admiralty remained almost entirely its own master in supply matters, the War Office had some claim to being a supply department for the other Services, and the Air Ministry relied on its senior partners for a large proportion of its more general stores.[36]

The development of these actual peace-time inter-Service arrangements was, however, far less important than the planning of supply for war needs which went on, slowly in the 1920s but with increasing speed and comprehensiveness in the 1930s. With the real achievements of this planning we are not concerned, but the administrative arrangements and discussion of future arrangements are very relevant to a study of developments in the structure of central government. At the same time the full history of the various devices used to ensure inter-departmental co-ordination has been told elsewhere, and is far too detailed a story to repeat here except in its essentials.[37]

We have already seen in Chapter II that supply planning for a future war began with an idea which was retained until 1939 – the idea of establishing a Ministry of Material Resources to control and allocate the production and import of industrial raw materials. In the late 1920s it was considered that the co-ordination of what we are calling 'supply' should be handled by inter-departmental bodies working under the aegis of the Committee of Imperial Defence. This idea was in fact put into practice until the early months of 1939. At the top, as one of the sub-committees of the CID, was the Principal Supply Officers' Committee, originally set up in 1924

'To co-ordinate the war supply arrangements of the three Defence Services, to avoid the competition and delays that occurred in 1914, and to ensure that the most advantageous use should be made of British industry in an emergency.'[38]

This was a 'high policy' committee, with the President of the Board of Trade in the Chair, which at least before the days of rearmament and the appointment of the Minister for the Co-ordination of Defence only met at long intervals.[39] Below the Principal Supply Officers' Committee the system was split into two sections, one dealing with 'supply' in our sense, and the other dealing with raw materials. On the supply side there was a Supply Board, an inter-departmental body with numerous sub-committees which 'investigated service requirements of finished stores and the capacity to manufacture them'.[40] The numerous sub-committees of the Supply Board included the Contracts Co-ordinating Committee and technical committees dealing with various commodities such as foodstuffs, clothing, mechanical transport, medical stores, etc. All these authorities were designed to deal with war potential, i.e., the 'means of expanding production which could be put into effect after the outbreak of war'.[41] To them in 1935 was added an organization 'to prepare a programme for meeting our worst deficiencies'[42] headed by a Defence Policy Requirements Committee and its Defence Requirements Sub-Committee – which had had a previous separate existence. After 1936 the whole structure of committees fell within the purview of the new Minister for the Co-ordination of Defence.

But despite the gradual construction of this extensive system of co-ordination by committee, there was considerable public and some official misgiving about the adequacy of such a system in the event of war. In the 1930s there set in a notable parliamentary controversy over the establishment of a Ministry of Supply. Such a ministry assumed in fact 'a symbolic quality – to its advocates a symbol of Britain's readiness to meet the strident challenge of Hitler's Germany, to its opponents a symbol of what has since become known as "warmongering" '.[43] In official circles the controversy was no less bitter, reflecting as it did some severe clashes of Service interests. Proposals and counter-proposals multiplied, but all centred on three main possible alternatives – the continuance of the inter-departmental committee system plus a Ministry of Material Resources, the establishment of a combined Ministry of Supply and Material Resources, or the creation of separate Ministries of Material Resources and of Supply. Meanwhile there were two very significant intra-departmental developments. At the War Office the whole responsibility for supply was gradually concentrated on a Director General of Munitions Production – the first basic reorganization taking place in 1936. Henceforward Army supply administration could easily be separated from the operational side of the War Office. A somewhat similar concentration of supply authority was effected at the Air Ministry in 1938 when research, development and production became the responsibility of a new Member of the Air Council—the Air Member for Development and Production.

Notwithstanding the various pressures on the Government to set up a supply department in peace-time, it is highly unlikely that this would have been done had not there been an imminent danger of war. The Munich crisis was the occasion of a first-class rehearsal of mobilization which disclosed certain organizational deficiencies in supply procedure, but even this was not enough to force acceptance of a peace-time supply department. The scales were tipped by the decision to introduce conscription and thereby to launch a vast expansion of the Army. The passage of the Militia Bill drove the Secretary of State for War, who was concerned lest the War Office could not cope with the new equipment problems, to ask that responsibility for supply be transferred to a separate department. This forced the issue of a Ministry of Supply to a head and immediately brought forward the problem of how to achieve a workable division of the supply processes between user and producer departments. For their part the Admiralty and Air Ministry were opposed to any such division of responsibility. An official historian has described what followed.

'To begin with, the Admiralty "dug its toes in" against all attempts to take away from it the control of naval construction. The building of ships, it argued, was so intimately bound up with design, and the latter was so much part and parcel of the strategic planning and tactical experience of the Naval Staff, that the Admiralty could not possibly part with responsibility for naval construction. Moreover, the naval programmes in peace-time were sufficient to enable the Admiralty to maintain a fully staffed production department, a corps of naval constructors and a network of naval dockyards: in fact all the organization, all the men and all the experience necessary for naval construction in wartime.

'Their Lordships' arguments were put with customary force and apparently struck the Cabinet as cogent; so that from the very beginning it became clear that a Ministry of Supply, if set up, would not be in charge of naval construction. But once that was admitted, the way was open for a similar argument by the Air Ministry. In principle the Air Ministry was not prepared to allow its authority to be narrowed down in comparison with the authority which the Board of Admiralty enjoyed in naval matters. And in fact the arguments which held good on naval construction also applied to aircraft production – the intimate connection between production, design, tactical lessons and strategic planning, the accumulating technical competence within the Ministry, the close contact with firms. The Air Ministry therefore had to be allowed to "contract out", and in the end the authority of the new department in the production of weapons came to be largely confined to the army programme. It was at that stage that the Cabinet decided that the Ministry of Supply was so truncated that it could without overburdening itself also take over the responsibility for raw materials, and thus make it unnecessary to establish a separate Ministry of Material Resources. In this shape the blueprint of the "mule" Ministry of Supply finally took shape. . . .'[44]

1939–1945

The new Ministry of Supply which came into being in July, 1939, was, therefore, primarily an Army supply department and secondarily a Raw Materials department. The Act which authorized its existence, however, provided that it could supply munitions, stores and equipment to the Admiralty and Air Ministry, and such 'common user' articles to the Admiralty, Air Ministry, Ministry of Home Security and Office of Works as might be agreed between those departments and the Ministry of Supply. Later on, in 1942, a regulation made under the Emergency Powers (Defence) Act authorized the Ministry of Supply to provide articles to any government department. One of the most striking differences between the Ministry of Munitions and the Ministry of Supply was that the latter became responsible from the date of its origin for the provision not merely of warlike stores but also for a wide range of general stores including clothing. Moreover there does not appear to have been any confusion comparable to that in 1915 over the proper location of the various processes of supply: the new department was from the start concerned with research, development, production and inspection. This was facilitated by the existence of a combined supply organization within the War Office under a Director General of Munitions Production. The Ministry of Supply was formed mainly from the Production, Contracts and Inspectorate branches of the War Office.

The advent of the Ministry of Supply left untouched the Air Ministry's responsibility for the supply of aircraft for the RAF and for the Navy. As we have seen, the functions of research, development and production had been combined in a single Air Ministry Department of Development and Production, which was 'to all intents and purposes . . . fully self-contained', and which during the first winter of the war grew 'to rival in both size and authority the Ministry of Supply'.[45] When the disasters of 1940 led to the fall of the Chamberlain Government, the first great administrative decision of the new Administration was to take the Air Ministry's supply organization and raise it to the status of a separate department – the Ministry of Aircraft Production. 'I had resolved,' wrote Mr Churchill, 'as the result of my experiences in the previous war, to remove the supply and design of aircraft from the Air Ministry.'[46] This decision 'symbolized the urgency which was now attached to the output of aircraft'. The Ministry of Aircraft Production was 'a new expedient, as dramatic as an administrative expedient can be'.[47] Such an expedient might well have been adopted, in the circumstances, whatever the personal and political factors involved, but it is obvious from the Prime Minister's memoirs that the timing of the change, if not the change itself, was affected by the availability of Lord Beaverbrook, who had a reputation for ruthless and dynamic leadership, and on whom Mr Churchill counted to ensure that first priority was given to the production of fighter aircraft.

As had happened with the War Office and Ministry of Supply in 1939, all the supply processes regarding aircraft, except requirement, were handed over by the Air Ministry to the new department in May, 1940. By the middle of that year, therefore, the organization for supplying the Armed Forces had reached a position which with one important exception was to be retained for the rest of the war. The Admiralty administered a fighting Service and provided the great bulk of its own supply. The War Office and Air Ministry administered the Army and RAF and were only concerned with the supply of food, fuel, and a small range of general stores. The Ministry of Supply had a primary responsibility to the Army, but also acted as provider on a large scale to the Air Ministry and on a much smaller scale to the Admiralty, besides containing within itself a Raw Materials Department whose work was not so much directly relevant to the Armed Forces as to the whole field of the nation's industry. The Ministries of Supply and Aircraft Production were responsible for all the processes of supply other than requirement.

Professor Postan has pointed out that the separate supply departments, one for each fighting Service, were expected to perform more functions within their fields than a comprehensive ministry might have done. It so happened that the branches which existed within the Service departments on the eve of the war combined control of production with responsibility for development of weapons, and there were strong arguments for this.

'Again and again in Parliament and in official papers warnings were made against a "divorce" between design and production. There was the suspicion that left to themselves the technicians in the Service departments might design weapons difficult to produce or might insist on modifications and improvements which would disrupt production. . . .

'Between the authority which the supply departments were now given over design, and their existence as separate ministries there was an obvious connection. Once it was decided to entrust the design of weapons to the Ministry of Supply a single Munitions Ministry became impossible. For a ministry supervising the design, development and production of weapons for the three Services would have been too large to be run by the most efficient of ministers or civil servants. It would probably have in fact functioned as a federation of three largely independent sub-ministries; and the same problems of co-ordination which faced the three supply departments in the war would have had to be faced within the ministry itself. In short, the true alternative to the organization which emerged in the war was not a mammoth ministry of munitions engulfing the three supply departments, but a supply ministry conceived purely as a ministry of production, i.e., concerned with production alone.'[48]

On the other hand the existence of supply departments created a problem of co-ordinating the whole administration of war production. This led to the addition of the final piece of administrative machinery in the field of supply. In February, 1942, a Minister of Production was appointed, and in July of that year he was equipped with a Ministry. The functions of the new department may be broadly defined as helping to co-ordinate the execution of production programmes, providing a link between strategy and production, and representing this country in supply negotiations with the Allies, especially with regard to raw materials.

The conception of a supervising or co-ordinating Minister with powers which are likely to derogate from the responsibilities of individual departmental Ministers has always been regarded with suspicion on constitutional grounds, and few appointments of this type have been made.[m] During the war, however, in the absence of a Minister of Production the responsibility for co-ordinating the work of the supply departments was liable to fall on the Prime Minister – now also Minister of Defence – whose other burdens were very great. The idea of concentrating authority for the supervision of war industry in one Minister therefore became increasingly attractive, and it was argued – not least in Parliament – that the Prime Minister should delegate some of his arbitral and co-ordinative functions in the field of war production to a Cabinet colleague. At first Mr Churchill refused to consider this suggestion, and it has been claimed that the problems of domestic war production alone would not have needed the extra attention of a separate authority. But the need emerged to have a single channel for negotiating with America and Russia about the allocation of materials and weapons, and to have British representatives on the Anglo-American Combined Boards with a knowledge and authority equal to those of the United States. In these circumstances the Prime Minister eventually decided to

[m] This question is discussed in Chapter IX.

appoint a Minister of Production, a step which proved to be complicated by politics and personalities.

As early as October, 1940, Mr Churchill had 'hoped to secure a higher integration of war production' by placing the Ministries of Supply and Aircraft Production in the hands of a single Minister, but Lord Beaverbrook, who was chosen for this rôle, was unable for health reasons to undertake it, and the plan was dropped.[49] A year later the Prime Minister, drawing on his memories of the First World War, and with Lord Beaverbrook still in mind, again moved towards a larger jurisdiction in supply matters:

'In the Ministry of Munitions in 1917 and 1918 I had presided over the sphere now covered by the Ministry of Supply and the Ministry of Aircraft Production. These departments were so closely interwoven in the fields of raw materials and skilled labour that a single directing authority would have great advantages. As everything became more gigantic this applied with increasing force. Beaverbrook had the confidence both of the Russians and of the Americans, and no one seemed more fitted to head so great a combination than he.

'Since he had left the Ministry of Aircraft Production for that of Supply there had been much friction, some of it inevitable, on the frontiers of these two departments, and I hoped not only to restore harmony but to improve results by joining these two great branches of our armament production under a Minister of Production of War Cabinet rank. . . .'[50]

The new Minister was not, however, to displace the existing heads of the Ministries of Supply and Aircraft Production, who would each have 'his wide sphere of initiative and judgment'.

The appointment of Lord Beaverbrook as Minister of Production was announced on February 4, 1942. In the course of the next week, however, criticisms of Lord Beaverbrook, the 'very strong personal antagonisms' between him and Mr Bevin, and much inter-departmental wrangling, caused the original conception of the scope of the new office to be modified. On February 10 a White Paper was published, laying out in detail the responsibilities which Lord Beaverbrook was to assume. Within a fortnight, however, the new Minister had resigned, partly on account of health, but also because of difficult personal relationships and of his 'own doubts about the functions and powers of the new office'. Mr Oliver Lyttelton was appointed in his place, but the functions which he was to perform were less precisely defined than those set out in the White Paper.[51]

The immediate outcome of this readjustment, which took place during a crucial period of the war, was an office of a largely personal nature. 'There was no intention of establishing a new government department or of encroaching upon the existing departments.' The co-ordinating functions which had hitherto been performed by a committee structure were simply to be entrusted to a single Minister. Neither Mr Lyttelton nor the advocates of a new department were content with this conception, however, and the former 'made no secret of his intention of giving his office greater substance and defini-tion than it appeared to possess at the outset'. After weeks of argu-ment a Ministry of Production was set up on July 13, 1942, and for some months after that attempts were made to extend its jurisdiction into the spheres occupied by the supply departments. But the Mini-stry of Production had perhaps arrived on the scene too late to be able to overcome an inevitable suspicion and hostility. Compara-tively little of the work of the existing supply departments was trans-ferred to the new authority. Among the few functions which the Ministry of Production took over the most important were the allo-cation of raw materials and the machine tools control, though production responsibility remained with the Ministry of Supply. Nonetheless the new department gradually grew in importance until it reached a 'predominant position in the conduct of war industry'. That position was achieved through taking on work not hitherto assigned to other departments: by the Minister's membership of the War Cabinet and his chairmanship of vital committees: by the suc-cessful working of a Joint War Production Staff which, under the Minister's auspices, kept him 'in the total strategical picture on the one hand and the Chiefs of Staff well informed of production possi-bilities on the other', and controlled and centralized 'the demands of British production departments on American and other overseas sources of supply': by the Minister's rôle as the liaison authority with the American supply organization: by his power over imports and allocations of materials: and by his responsibility for an exten-sive system of regional industrial organization.[52]

By the middle of 1943 war production was reaching its peak, and the administrative organization which had been constantly modified to keep pace with increasing production simultaneously achieved a relative stability which was not shaken during the remainder of the war. Before leaving the history of supply organization for war purposes, however, it is worth pointing out another contrast to the experience of 1914–18. It will be recalled that in 1915 the Minister of Munitions had power to assess the needs of the armed forces and to order production accordingly, and that he made considerable use of that power. Similar responsibility for requirement was assumed only sparingly by the supply departments of the Second World War, whose functions were mainly executive:

'They worked to programmes which were settled for them by the Government as a whole and were particularized for them, item by item, under the Treasury's close supervision. In a few isolated moments in the later stages of the war, departments might take it upon themselves to form independent judgments of strategic and tactical requirements and act accordingly. Yet even in the most crucial periods of the war these instances were exceptional and did not affect the general trends of munitions production.'[53]

The explanation of this contrast is perhaps to be found in the peculiar political circumstances of 1915 and the widespread hostility towards, and lack of confidence in, the War Office on the one hand; and in the comparatively well prepared administrative arrangements of the rearmament era and the pre-war creation of a Ministry of Supply on the other hand.

Since 1945

The readjustment of the machinery of supply to post-war conditions took place between the end of fighting in Europe in May, 1945, and the creation of the Ministry of Defence in December, 1946. The sequence of events began on the formation of the Caretaker Government when the offices of Minister of Production and President of the Board of Trade were entrusted to one man. The incoming Labour Government made no appointment to the post of Minister of Production and in August, 1945, Mr Attlee appointed one man as Minister of Supply and Minister of Aircraft Production. The decision to form a single Ministry of Supply was taken in October, 1945, and came into effect on April 1, 1946, when the wartime Ministries of Supply and Aircraft Production were merged. The Board of Trade took over most of the residual functions of the Ministry of Production with the exception of the co-ordination of military supply programmes. The Raw Materials Branch of the Ministry of Supply had been transferred to the Board of Trade some months before. Finally, in December, 1946, a Minister of Defence was appointed with power to take charge of 'the formulation and general application of a unified policy relating to the armed forces of the Crown as a whole and their requirements'.

It was inevitable that the wartime organization of supply would be modified when hostilities ended. Serious discussion of such modification began in 1944 when some military people, perhaps disturbed by their experience of highly centralized supply in Washington, persuaded the Secretary of State for War to propose that the War Office should take back responsibility for technical equipment, leaving a civil department to provide common general stores. This latter point linked up with a proposal made during the war by Sir Cecil Weir that there should be a central purchasing body for general stores for the whole of the government service. The suggestions, which also covered the Air Force, were put to the Machinery of Government Committee with the backing of the War Office and Air Ministry. The Machinery of Government Committee was divided, though not entirely on party lines – some notable Labour people being in favour of centralized supply, most of the Conservatives wanting supply to go back to the Service departments. No firm decision was reached before the Caretaker Government fell, but there did seem some likelihood of restoring technical stores to the Service departments and making a civil department – most likely the Ministry of Works, which was keen to extend its activities – responsible for general common stores.

The final decision was partly influenced by the general economic outlook of the new Labour Government. We have seen in Chapter II that the Labour Party wanted departments generally to become more closely concerned with industry than ever before in peacetime. The Ministry of Supply was in a strong position to be converted into much more than a military supply department, and it was in fact entrusted with the sponsorship of the engineering and heavy metal industries and with responsibility for the development of atomic energy. By the middle of 1946, therefore, the Army and the RAF looked for the great bulk of their material needs to a Ministry of Supply which, in addition to its military responsibilities, was also much concerned with civil industry and trade.

The two World Wars had thrust home the close inter-relation, at the highest level, of strategy and supply. This was formally recognized when the separate Minister of Defence was appointed in December, 1946, and explains why that Minister inherited some part of the mantle of the wartime Minister of Production. One of his most important functions was to be

'The apportionment, in broad outline, of available resources between the three Services in accordance with the strategic policy laid down by the Defence Committee' [of the Cabinet]

and this was to include 'the framing of general policy to govern research and development, and the correlation of production programmes'.[54]

Since the end of 1946 there has been no fundamental alteration in supply arrangements. Below the Defence Committee of the Cabinet and the Ministry of Defence, which have together replaced the old

Committee of Imperial Defence and Principal Supply Officers' Committee, etc., the organization of supply for the Armed Forces at the present time is the responsibility of four departments. Of those four, the Admiralty is unique in that it is responsible not only for the operational control of the Navy but also for the provision of approximately 75 per cent. of all its material requirements, and for the research and development involved in the evolution of most items for naval use. The remaining quarter comes mainly from the Ministry of Supply, whose chief work for the Admiralty is concerned with aircraft, guided weapons and associated equipment, guns (excluding mountings) and ammunition, and the Ministry does all the research, development and production in this context. The War Office buys a few items for the Admiralty, which also gets aviation fuel and miscellaneous air stores from the Air Ministry. The War Office and Air Ministry, by contrast, are dependent on the Ministry of Supply for the bulk of their needs. For the rest they buy for themselves or through another Service department food, fuel and a small group of general commodities. Many of these purchases are made locally. The inspection of some items produced for the Navy by the Ministry of Supply is performed by the Admiralty, and of others by the Ministry itself.

In order to minimize the difficulties inherent in any division of responsibility between user and supplier, various administrative devices have been adopted. Thus officers of all three Services are lent to the Ministry of Supply for periods of service, particularly on research and development work, while consultation between the Service departments and the Ministry of Supply is continuous and far-reaching. Departmental responsibilities are clearly defined under the present system. Any problems are usually settled by direct

---

TABLE XVIII

DEFENCE DEPARTMENTS
(Showing numbers of non-industrial staffs)

	1914	1935	1956
Admiralty	4,500*	8,120	33,765
War Office	5,500*	9,440	38,870
Air Ministry		5,480	27,150
Ministry of Supply			34,650
Ministry of Defence			835
	10,000*	23,040	135,270

* Approximate figures.

discussion between the departments concerned, or may conceivably involve the Ministry of Defence. In the parliamentary context each department is responsible for its own processes.

The Ministry of Supply has since 1950 become much less concerned with matters which are not an integral part of military supply. Most of its raw materials responsibilities were transferred to the Ministry of Materials in 1951: the development of atomic energy passed to the Lord President and to a non-departmental Atomic Energy Authority in 1954, though the Ministry of Supply remains responsible for the provision of complete atomic weapons: and finally iron and steel, engineering and non-ferrous metals were handed over to the Board of Trade in July, 1955.[n] The department has been left, therefore, to concentrate on its supply work principally for the Army and Air Force, and to a much smaller extent for the Navy, while remaining responsible for the Government's relations with the whole aircraft industry and with the electronics and light metal industries. In the words of the Prime Minister's statement to the House of Commons on October 25, 1955, the Ministry of Supply 'has become mainly a fourth Defence Department within the co-ordinating powers of the Minister of Defence'.[55] [o]

The controversies which have dogged the whole problem of military supply have often been hard fought, and the subject has certainly received more parliamentary and public attention than most matters of administrative organization. Criticism of the present arrangements still breaks out from time to time, notably in the field of the development of aircraft, when the claim is made that closer integration of military, scientific and engineering thought would be an advantage. It would, therefore, be unwise to assume that the scope of the Ministry of Supply has been finally determined.

CIVIL DEFENCE

The 20th century has taught us that modern war is total war and that it almost inevitably involves aerial attack on the homeland – either, as always up to June, 1944, carried out by piloted aircraft or, as in the last stages of the Second World War and as seems highly likely in any future conflict, by guided missiles launched from hostile territory. There are three aspects of defence against this form of

[n] The responsibility for neither raw materials not iron and steel has remained where it was after it left the Ministry of Supply. For subsequent changes see Chapter II, pp. 113–16, 117[o].

[o] The jurisdiction of the Minister of Defence was extended in January, 1957. For details see footnote ([uu]) to Chapter IX, p. 320.

attack. In the first place it is necessary to attempt to destroy the air-craft and/or missiles which the enemy sends over, and this can be extended to include efforts to repulse invasion by parachutists and glider-borne forces. All such defensive tasks are primarily military in character and have been and are regarded as the responsibility of the military authorities, though some civilian organizations like the Observer Corps are also involved. The second aspect of the defence of the homeland is the need to keep the vital domestic services such as gas, water and electricity supply, sewage disposal, and internal com-munications, etc., working – i.e., an extension of normal peace-time services in the special conditions of war. Thirdly there are ser-vices peculiar to war – evacuation of people from danger areas, provision of shelters, care of the injured and homeless, etc. It is the second and third aspects of home defence which are covered by the term civil defence.

Civil defence is not a job which is done only in Whitehall. It in-volves practically every public authority in the country, and calls for the co-operation and participation of many private organizations and of the general public. In this chapter, however, we are only concerned with the way in which responsibility for civil defence has been dis-tributed within the central government. No account is therefore given here of the work of Local Authorities, extra-departmental bodies, and private organizations, and it is only intended to mention briefly one of the most interesting aspects of civil defence in the context of the central departments – the development of a regional organization.[56] That organization was planned in the years from 1935 to 1939 and in its mature wartime form comprised twelve regions. In each region there was a Regional Commissioner appointed by the Crown. The Regional Commissioner was intended to act as an autonomous authority, wielding all the powers of the central government in his area should that area be cut off from London as a result either of invasion or of the devastation of the capital, and was also responsible for co-ordinating the civil defence activities of all departments at regional level. As the feared breakdown of central government never came about, the second aspect of the system was the more important. The Commissioners acted as regional representatives of their Mini-ster – the Minister of Home Security (of whom more later) – and were 'concerned with supplementing, co-ordinating and assisting the services provided by local authorities in civil defence and the After-Raids scheme'[57] as well as co-ordinating the similar work of the regional offices of other departments. The system was only tolerated because of the emergency. In peace-time conditions the con-stitutional position of the Commissioners would have been equivocal, and their non-emergency work was not considered valuable enough to be continued. The appointments therefore lapsed at the end of the war. While the post-1945 civil defence arrangements include a regional organization in England and Wales answerable to the Home Office, and though the remaining regional offices of other departments are to varying degrees involved in civil defence work, there has been no attempt to re-establish Regional Commissioners.

So far as Whitehall is concerned, civil defence as we have defined it poses two main problems. The maintenance of vital domestic services such as power supply, railways, etc., must inevitably remain in wartime a responsibility of the authorities normally concerned with them in peace-time. Thus the Ministry of Transport's interest in roads, and the Post Office's concern for telecommunications, for example, cannot suddenly become the business of quite separate departments which would deal with 'emergency' maintenance. But such services as are peculiar to war – evacuation, provision of shelters, organization of special ambulance services, etc. – are a different matter. They have a good deal in common. Should they, therefore, be the responsibility of a single Minister and department, or should that responsibility be divided among various Ministers and departments? Moreover, both aspects of civil defence need no small degree of co-ordination. How, then, should the co-ordination of the relevant departments be achieved? It is the answers which have been found to these questions which form the main subject matter of this section.

The history of civil defence falls into four periods. The relatively slight experience of the First World War can be largely discounted: it focused attention on the subject and provided a none too reliable basis for future planning, but it had little or no influence on departmental arrangements after 1918. The first of the periods lasted from 1921 to 1935: the second from 1935 to 1938: and the third from 1938 to 1945. From 1945 to 1948 the civil defence services were suspended, but in the latter year, following from the research and planning which had gone on since the end of the Second World War, a new pattern of civil defence organization began to be built up. The fourth of our periods therefore runs from 1948 to the present day.

1921–1935

The Committee of Imperial Defence began to discuss how to deal with air attack on civil population and property in November, 1921, and for the next fourteen years argument and planning went on discreetly in Whitehall: neither the state of public opinion nor the state of international affairs encouraged any more public expression of interest. None the less it was during this period that the basic lines on which civil defence administration has developed were made clear. The idea of having a special department which would deal with all aspects of civil defence was examined and, so far as peace-time planning was concerned, was firmly discarded. Instead it was decided that civil defence was a matter for many departments. Indeed, 'from the earliest days . . . the first principle has been to allocate wartime functions to those organizations or authorities which have analogous functions in peace'.[58] Between 1924 and 1935 the departments were encouraged to make plans and their work was co-ordinated by an official sub-committee of the Committee of Imperial Defence which, after 1929, was made responsible to a ministerial committee of the same parent body. None the less, while no department was envisaged as having complete responsibility for all civil defence, the Home Office did begin to assume an important position as the department most concerned with those special services peculiar to war and as the department most suitable for exercising any form of control which might have to be imposed on the whole population.

In the early 1930s, therefore, civil defence was still confined to Whitehall files. Inquiry and planning were carried out, subject to the approval of the CID, by two of its committees – one ministerial, one official – and by various departments. Each department had an officer or section as a focal point for the discharge of its responsibility for civil defence matters. The Home Office was recognized as being more important in this context than any other department.

1935–1938

In 1935 the decision to rearm brought to an end the first period of civil defence history. The Government decided to publicize the importance of and their ideas about what were then most commonly known as Air Raid Precautions, and to seek the co-operation of the public and of Local Authorities. Investigation and initial planning in secret were to give way to intensive executive action at both the centre and in the localities. The main administrative development which this change of policy provoked at the centre was the creation in the Home Office of an ARP Department 'to act on behalf of the various Government Departments concerned' under the direction of the two CID committees, and to give greater attention to those aspects of civil defence which were the peculiar concern of the Home Office itself. 'Tradition and convenience, rather than theoretical considerations, dictated choice of the Home Department ("the recognized guardian of the public safety") as the seat of the new agency'.[59]

While there was no conscious intention that the new policy should make any change in the well-established idea of grafting ARP functions on to the normal activities of many departments, in practice there was for two or three years after 1935 a strong tendency to move away from it. The new Home Office ARP Department

'had been created mainly to be a channel between the Government and local authorities and the public on all ARP matters, and to supervise preparation of local schemes. This shift of emphasis towards the whole country, the preoccupation of other Departments with their peace-time functions, the unpopularity of ARP and apparent remoteness of the threat it was to counter and the factor of personality combined to transform the Department from a channel into a virtual fountain head. During 1935–37 and beyond it developed in practice a close resemblance to that *ad hoc* authority which, at least as a peace-time measure, had been discarded.'[60]

The principle of 'spreading the burden of ARP duties among all relevant Departments' was thus 'largely ignored' though 'never in theory abandoned'.[61] Preparations went on largely under Home Office auspices, and what the Home Secretary once called 'a complete new public service' received its first statutory recognition in 1937 when an Air Raid Precautions Act placed on County and County Borough Councils in England and Wales and on the Councils of Counties and Large Burghs in Scotland responsibility for preparing schemes which had to be approved by the Home Secretary. The organization which was being built up was given an extended rehearsal of emergency conditions during the summer of 1938, beginning with the Sudetenland crisis in May and ending with the Munich negotiations in September. Civil defence arrangements were not found satisfactory, and new plans were made for the handling of responsibility at the centre. These changes brought to an end the second of our periods.

1938–1945

The major significance of the 1938 rearrangements was the fact that they reversed the tendency of the last few years, initiated a redistribution of functions among the departments which would have to exercise them, and at the same time strengthened the organization for securing co-ordination. It is a measure of the change which had taken place in the scale of civil defence preparations that by 1938 the reapplication of the principle of distributing responsibility among the relevant departments 'was of such magnitude as to seem almost new'.[62]

The new order which came into being in 1938 included for the first time the appointment of a Cabinet Minister who was to be responsible for the whole service of civil defence. Sir John Anderson (Lord Waverley), a former Permanent Under Secretary of State at the Home Office, had recently joined the Government as Lord Privy Seal. He was made responsible for the work of the ARP Department of the Home Office and was appointed chairman of a committee of the Ministers most closely concerned with civil defence matters. The ARP Department had by that time become responsible for a very wide range of those emergency services which would come into operation on the outbreak of war, and some of the services which were in fact closely related to the normal work of the health departments were transferred to those departments during the following two years. Sir John Anderson kept the executive ARP Department in the Home Office separate from the organization which he built up to co-ordinate the whole service of civil defence. That service was provided not only by the ARP Department, but also by, among others, the Food (Defence Plans) Department of the Board of Trade, the Ministry of Transport, the Ministry of Labour, the Board of Education and Scottish Department of Education, and by the Ministry of Health and Department of Health for Scotland. For the co-ordination of the civil defence activities of all these departments the Lord Privy Seal depended on a personal secretariat or 'civil general staff' and on his own widespread and informal contacts with the Ministers concerned.

It is worth mentioning at this point a development primarily concerned with peace-time administration which none the less had an interesting bearing on the civil defence organization. With the passing of the Fire Brigades Act, 1938, the central government became directly concerned for the first time on any notable scale with Local Authority administration of fire services. The preparation of the 1938 legislation and the civil defence planning in connection with fire fighting had in fact been concentrated in a new division of the Home Office and in the Scottish Office at the end of 1936, and subsequently all the emergency fire brigade measures continued to be dealt with by that division and by its opposite number in the Scottish Office and not by the ARP Department – a reflection of the traditionally close relationship of the fire services with the police forces, whose relations with the central government formed one of the 'normal' functions of the Home Office and Scottish Office. As we shall shortly see, the new connection was to be maintained and extended during the war.

It had been urged within Whitehall during the crisis of 1938 that in the event of war a Minister of Home Security should be appointed who should take over the existing executive ARP services of the Home Office and should also be responsible for co-ordinating the civil defence services of all the other civil departments. The appointment of Sir John Anderson was a close approximation to this suggestion. It was apparently made clear when the new arrangements were planned that in the event of war the Home Secretary would act as Minister of Home Security, and by the middle of 1939 the 'decision had been made to appoint Sir John Anderson immediately war broke out to the double office'.[p]

The shape of wartime central administration of civil defence was thus clearly settled before the autumn of 1939. On the outbreak of war the Ministry of Home Security was duly set up, with Sir John Anderson as Minister and at the same time as Home Secretary. His small general staff was combined with the very much expanded Home Office ARP Department to form the new Ministry which, while separate from the Home Office, did employ the same common service organization. The Minister of Home Security had a United Kingdom jurisdiction. The distribution of departmental responsibility for civil defence did not undergo any considerable change throughout the war, and the only wartime development which needs mention here is that of the fire services.

Until 1941 the central departments concerned – the Home Office and the Scottish Home Department (the latter had taken over from the Scottish Office in the reorganization of 1939) – were in the same relationship to the Local Authority fire brigades as they were to other local government services. This particular relationship, however, did not withstand the shocks of war. As the blitz developed, it became increasingly clear that

'air raid fire-fighting was often on a scale quite out of proportion to the scale of even the larger local government units, not to mention the many small units in the fire services, and fires paid no attention to the niceties of local government boundaries. Despite the various steps taken during the months of heavy attack to integrate and improve the emergency fire brigade organization, nothing had been achieved that really went to the heart of the matter. The principal sources of

p T. O'Brien: *Civil Defence*, pp. 167, 175. Sir John Anderson's influence on the whole development of civil defence was very considerable. As Permanent Under Secretary of State at the Home Office from 1922 to 1932 he was the principal official concerned – both at the Home Office and as Chairman of the CID subcommittee – with the initial preparations. He returned to devote his full attention to civil defence as Lord Privy Seal in 1938, and as Home Secretary and Minister of Home Security he saw the organization take the first strains of actual war experience from September, 1939, until October, 1940.

weakness were the piecemeal character of a system operated at the level of local government through hundreds of separate units, the smallness of most of the units and the unevenness of their organization.'[63]

The 'nationalization' of the fire brigades was announced in May, 1941, and in the following August the National Fire Service was placed directly under the control of the Home Secretary in England and Wales and of the Secretary of State in Scotland. The Service never became a responsibility of the Ministry of Home Security. Under the new arrangements the previously 'loose-coupled fire brigade services' became 'a close knit organization of between thirty and forty Fire Services, each constructed on similar lines'.[64]

We have already noted that at the end of the war the civil defence services were suspended. The Ministry of Home Security was abolished and the civil defence powers of the 1937 Air Raid Precautions Act and of the later Civil Defence Act, 1939, reverted to the Home Secretary. In 1948 the National Fire Service was disbanded. Fire brigades became the responsibility of the larger local government units. Research and planning, however, went on under the supervision of a Home Defence Committee, and three years after the end of the war a new stage of civil defence began.

Since 1948

The present pattern of civil defence is based on the already mentioned Acts of 1937 and 1939, and on a new Civil Defence Act which was passed in 1948. This latter statute defined the component functions of civil defence as:

'(a) The organization, formation, maintenance, equipment and training of civil defence forces and services.

(b) The organization, equipment and training for civil defence purposes of police forces, fire brigades and employees of local or police authorities employed primarily for purposes other than civil defence purposes.

(c) The instruction of members of the public in civil defence and their equipment for the purposes of civil defence.

(d) The provision, storage and maintenance of commodities and things required for civil defence, and

(e) The provision, construction, maintenance or alteration of premises, structures or excavations required for civil defence and the doing of any other work required for civil defence.'

Under the 1948 Act these matters are made the responsibility of Ministers designated by Orders-in-Council, who in turn prescribe, by regulations, which functions should be entrusted to Local Authorities. The regulations may require that Local Authorities 'shall be bound to comply with any directions given to them by the designated Minister' concerning the exercise of functions conferred on them. Where no Order-in-Council is applicable, the designated Minister is the Secretary of State.

The principle of allocation of wartime functions and the responsibility for peace-time planning for the discharge of these functions to those organizations or authorities which have analogous functions in peace-time has been maintained. The Ministers with the chief concern for civil defence as a whole are the Home Secretary and the Secretary of State for Scotland. Within the Home Office there is a Civil Defence Department whose functions include the issuing of regulations, measures of defence against aerial bombardment, including atomic, bacteriological and chemical attack; instructions and advice on civil defence (the department runs Technical Training Schools and a Civil Defence Staff College); the air-raid warning organization; shelters; and the formation and training of the Civil Defence Corps. The Scottish Home Department performs these functions (other than the maintenance of central training establishments and research) in Scotland.

For other sections of civil defence work various Ministers have been designated under the 1948 Act, though 'formal designation orders are not, in practice, made until planning has been carried to a point where designation is required to facilitate executive action'.[65] Thus the Minister of Housing and Local Government and the Secretary of State for Scotland, acting through his Department of Health, are concerned with evacuation, billeting and rehousing: services in connection with demolition and clearance of damaged property: repair of houses, shops and premises required for essential services: water supplies, except for fire-fighting: and sewerage and sewage disposal. The Minister of Health and the Secretary of State for Scotland, the latter again acting through his Department of Health, deal with preparations for treating casualties and disease, and for temporary accommodation of the homeless, evacuees, repatriates, and refugees. The Minister of Agriculture, Fisheries and Food (and in Scotland the Secretary of State) is concerned with the provision, preparation, processing, storage, salvage or destruction, decontamination and distribution of food, animal feeding stuffs and soap, and with the provision of emergency feeding services including equipment. Emergency feeding arrangements in Scotland are to be organized locally by the Department of Health for that country. The Minister of Transport and Civil Aviation and the Minister of Fuel and Power have also been given specific duties, the first in connection with roads and transport services, the second in connection with the maintenance of supplies of coal, gas and petroleum, etc. Duties concerning electricity supply in England and Wales are the responsibility of the Minister of Fuel and Power, and in Scotland of the Secretary of State.[q]

All these Ministers look to the Home Secretary for the technical guidance on which their work is based, and for the central direction of those civil defence activities, such as the care of the civil population after attack, which involve joint planning by several departments. A small staff has been established in the Cabinet Office to provide the secretariat (and in the case of certain official committees the chairmen of those committees), and to assist the co-ordination of these activities generally.

One development in the post-war structure of civil defence is closer contact with the Armed Forces. It is part of the civil defence plans that, subject to their prior obligations to meet any direct enemy attack on this country, those forces should be ready to provide reinforcements to help hard-hit Local Authorities on a much greater scale than was ever contemplated in the Second World War. This increasing inter-dependence of civil and military authorities has been made even more necessary by the advent of thermo-nuclear weapons, and the need to ensure the closest administrative liaison at the highest levels was the cause of the appointment of a retired Army officer of high rank as Director General of Civil Defence at the Home Office in 1954. The appointment also no doubt helped to meet the need to focus attention on and to stimulate and maintain public interest in and recruitment for a distasteful peace-time service.[66] The Minister of Defence, as Deputy Chairman of the Defence Committee of the Cabinet, has been charged with planning the part which the Armed Forces would play in home defence in war, and with co-ordinating the plans of the military authorities with those of the civil authorities.[67]

---

[q] This paragraph states the position in 1956. There have been some detailed changes in departmental responsibility for civil defence since the new development of that service began in 1948, as a result of greater inter-departmental re-arrangements. The most important changes were those which followed the division of the Ministry of Health and the creation of the Ministry of Local Government and Planning (now Housing and Local Government) in 1951. The progress of civil defence services was subjected to detailed scrutiny by the Select Committee on Estimates in 1953 – see the Committee's *1st Report*, 1953–54, HC 19.

VII

SCIENTIFIC RESEARCH

RAPID scientific and technological advance is the hallmark of a modern industrial community. Throughout our period the impact of science on society has been growing. Government has not been responsible for this relatively new factor in human affairs, but government has been increasingly responsive to it. Before the 20th century, government had been very little concerned with scientific inquiry. In 1956 government is a leading practitioner in and patron of scientific research. The bulk of public expenditure in this field is and always has been devoted to defence research, understandably so in all the circumstances, but there has also developed since 1914 a very large governmental interest in research for civil purposes, and at the present time more than £23 million is spent on it annually. Moreover it is impossible to seal off scientific inquiry for military purposes from scientific inquiry which has civil applications, as can be seen clearly, for example, in the field of aeronautics.

In this chapter we are mainly concerned to trace the history of those governmental institutions which have been specially established to conduct, and to encourage private institutions to conduct, scientific research primarily for civil purposes. But that history can best be read against a brief general discussion of some of the problems which have been raised by the assumption of a new governmental responsibility and which, though not always recognized at the times when particular innovations or changes were made, are clear enough in retrospect.

In the first place, there is the question of what type of interest government should take in scientific research, and if it be assumed that government should actually undertake some such research, what kind should it do? In practice, as we have already implied, government has entered the field of scientific research both as practitioner and patron. Financial aid has been extended to a wide variety of private institutions – universities, research associations, etc. – and to individual scientists and post-graduate students. The financially assisted research done in universities and certain independent institutions is usually 'pure' or 'fundamental' scientific inquiry directed to the advancement of knowledge, and is likely to be undertaken even if the results appear to have no direct relevance to contemporary problems as seen in the short run. On the other hand, the research carried out with government financial aid in the laboratories of re-search associations, for example, is usually 'applied' research – i.e., research into the application of the knowledge gained by pure re-search to the practical problems of particular industrial processes. So far as research undertaken directly by government is concerned, the broad tradition has developed that such research should be applied research – i.e., it should in the main be 'confined to the attacking of problems which have a more or less direct bearing on the field of Government responsibility'.[1] But while this is a useful wide generalization, there has in practice been no attempt to bar government scientists from working in the field of pure research, and indeed a great deal of such research is done in some governmental scientific establishments. Moreover a lot of governmental research is not intended for the use of government itself, but is intended to increase the general store of knowledge available for agriculture, medicine, industry, etc., by supplementing the work of private re-search organizations. In sum, therefore, government during the last forty years has itself conducted and has aided many private institutions and persons to conduct both pure and applied scientific research, but most of the research which is carried out in governmental establish-ments has been of the applied variety.

If government is to conduct scientific research itself, where within the organization of government should responsibility for that research lie? There are two extreme alternatives. Scientific research could be regarded as a function in itself and could be made the responsibility of one or more authorities solely concerned to conduct inquiries. Thus there could be either a single, comprehensive Ministry of Research, or several authorities each exclusively concerned with research in a particular field, such as a Department of Agricultural Research, a Department of Building Research, and a Department of Geological Research, etc. At the other extreme, scientific research could be regarded merely as one aspect of each activity in which government is interested, and could therefore be regarded as an integral function of each administrative department. Thus all research into mining problems would be carried out by the Ministry of Fuel and Power, all research into forestry by the Forestry Commission, and so on.

The idea of having one comprehensive Ministry of Research, responsible for every piece of scientific research done by government, has never been tried or even mooted.[a] In practice a combination of

[a] The Haldane Committee was particularly interested in the organization of what it called Research and Information. While the Committee thought that this

the other approaches outlined in the previous paragraph has been adopted. In general, where it is largely true that the findings of scientific inquiry into a particular field are to be used by government itself, then such inquiry has tended to be the responsibility of the department which is concerned to use the findings in the course of its own work. The outstanding example of this is research for defence purposes, which has been the practical monopoly of the defence departments – Admiralty, War Office, Air Ministry and, nowadays, the Ministry of Supply. When, on the other hand, research has been undertaken not necessarily for the use of government alone, but also – or even mainly – for the benefit of particular interests such as agriculture, there has been a notable tendency to establish special research organizations. This is particularly true in the civil field, where the major feature of our period has been the establishment of three authorities whose whole *raison d'être* is research – the Department of Scientific and Industrial Research, the Medical Research Council and the Agricultural Research Council – and two bodies, the Nature Conservancy and the Atomic Energy Authority, which have primarily scientific though not wholly research functions. These special authorities are not, however, completely cut off from the administrative departments, nor does their existence mean that no civil department can have its own research section. A few departments – those concerned with agriculture and the Ministry of Fuel and Power being the most prominent – have developed their own scientific divisions, while several others have scientific advisers. In fact in the civil field there has grown up a special relationship between the departments and the research authorities which is governed by two general principles:

'(i) The executive department should be responsible for identifying problems requiring research, settling their order of priority, deciding when the various investigations should be carried out and applying their results.

(ii) The Research [authorities] . . . should . . . be free to initiate background research when they [think] fit, free from administrative control of the executive departments and consequently

---

subject formed a definitely separate function of government, and looked forward to the eventual appointment of a Minister who would preside over a Department of Intelligence and Research, they also recognized that such a department would not have a monopoly, and they considered that each department would have its own 'distinctive organization for the prosecution of specific forms of research'. The special Research Department would in fact concentrate on inquiries not connected with the problems of particular other departments, and its general aim would be the advancement of knowledge.

from considerations of day-to-day expediency. They should also undertake research at the request of the executive departments.'[2]

Responsibility for giving financial aid to private research institutions has been laid mainly on the special research authorities, although the Treasury, through the University Grants Committee and the Development Commissioners, has throughout most of our period made direct contributions to universities and independent research establishments mostly concerned with fundamental research, while grants have also been made to learned societies, etc. Some departments, in particular those concerned with agriculture, have been responsible for disbursing grants and grants-in-aid to independent institutions.

The major concern of government with scientific research, both in terms of money spent (over £150 million annually at present) and of scientists employed, is in connection with defence.[b] But while defence research looms so large, the administrative problems involved in it are peculiar to the defence departments, and form part of the wider question of defence supply which has been discussed in the previous chapter. We do not, therefore, intend to deal with it here, nor do we intend to say any more about the development of research in the civil departments. Rearrangement of work between those departments and the special research authorities is mentioned in passing. We also postpone until Chapter IX an account of the development of various mechanisms of co-ordination and of overall ministerial responsibility for research which have particularly involved the Lord President of the Council, and which reflect the increasing recognition of the importance of scientific research and of the need to have a general governmental policy towards it.

None of the special authorities whose development is described in the rest of this chapter is a wholly orthodox government department, but the five comprise a group on the fringe of central government as we have defined it whose exceptional importance makes it desirable to deal with them at some length. The youngest of the five – the Atomic Energy Authority – has a more easily understood constitutional position than the other four, and its story can safely be left to stand alone in the final section of the chapter. The Department of Scientific and Industrial Research, the Medical Research Council, the Agricultural Research Council and the Nature Conservancy, on the other hand, are all constitutionally related. Their constitutional structure is, moreover, complex, and the nomenclature involved

[b] Table XIX opposite gives a rough indication of the distribution of scientific effort over the whole of the central government in 1956.

TABLE XIX: DISTRIBUTION OF THE SCIENTIFIC CIVIL SERVICE AT APRIL 1, 1956

	Scientific Officer Class	Experimental Officer Class	Assistant (Scientific)	TOTAL
Defence Departments				
Admiralty	562	883	814	2,259
Air Ministry	213	736	1,276	2,225
Ministry of Defence	38	2	–	40
Ministry of Supply	1,432	2,589	1,542	5,563
War Office	30	27	75	132
	2,275	4,237	3,707	10,219
Civil Departments				
Ministry of Agriculture, Fisheries and Food	117	192	456	765
British Museum (Natural History)	65	69	79	213
Colonial Office	36	31	3	70
Ministry of Fuel and Power	64	102	62	228
Government Chemist	55	110	105	270
Home Office	37	24	18	79
Post Office	47	95	75	217
Department of Agriculture for Scotland	13	21	34	68
Scottish Home Department	30	20	24	74
Others	22	55	188	265
	486	719	1,044	2,249
Department of Scientific and Industrial Research	626	1,129	482	2,237
	3,387	6,085	5,233	14,705

makes any description of their development somewhat difficult reading. In order to help the reader – especially if he is unfamiliar with the general background of British constitutional forms – we preface the individual accounts of these four research authorities with a brief statement about the Privy Council, and we also refer the reader to the diagrams on pages 268–69.

The Privy Council was originally the King's body of advisers. It is no longer a Council of the Crown in that sense, its place in the realm of policy having been taken by the Cabinet. Today the main business of the Council is the transaction of certain formal acts of State. The Council has now a large membership comprising Cabinet and other Ministers, past and present, and other persons of distinction not necessarily politicians. It is the custom for the Sovereign to preside over its meetings to which are summoned a few selected members, usually Cabinet Ministers concerned with the business before the Council. The leading ministerial member is the Lord President of the Council, who is almost invariably a member of the Cabinet. While there remain a number of functions which are carried out in the name of the Privy Council, through a small Privy Council Office for which the Lord President is responsible, much of the work associated with the Council is now performed by a number of Committees. Privy Council Committees have, in fact, on occasion been put at the head of departments. Thus the Board of Trade is still, in form, the Committee of Council for the Consideration of Matters relating to Trade and Foreign Plantations, though in practice the Board has long since been recognized as an independent department headed by its President, who is solely responsible to Parliament. In the 19th century there were Privy Council Committees for Education and for Agriculture which were later replaced by statutory Boards which, in turn, were converted into Ministries.[c] It is Committees of this type which have been charged with the oversight of the four special research organizations now to be described, and those Committees are referred to throughout as Committees of Council. The significance of these Committees of Council in the context of scientific research is discussed in the penultimate section of the chapter.

DEVELOPMENT OF THE RESEARCH AUTHORITIES

In 1914 there were a number of small governmental bodies with specialized scientific interests such as some of the Museums, the

[c] Perhaps the best known Committee of Council is the Judicial Committee, whose main function is to act as the Supreme Court of Appeal for the whole of the Commonwealth except the United Kingdom and those countries which have abolished the right of appeal to it.

Geological Survey and the Government Chemist, but there was 'little organized effort towards the application of the discoveries made by scientists engaged on fundamental research'.[3] In the years just prior to 1914, however, two governmental bodies had been established which to some extent were imbued with this latter ideal, though their resources were small and they had scarcely had time to make their presence felt. The Development Commission had been set up in 1909 to advise the Treasury on the administration of a Development Fund from which grants could be made for, among other things, the promotion of research in agriculture, rural industries and fisheries. Much more directly engaged in the conduct of scientific inquiries was the Medical Research Committee, a body which had been appointed in 1913 to organize medical research with the aid of funds provided under the National Insurance Act, 1911. The Committee was answerable to the Minister responsible for National Health Insurance through the Joint Committee of the four Insurance Commissions. An Advisory Council was attached to the Medical Research Committee.

Scientific and Industrial Research

While the beginnings of direct governmental action in agricultural and medical research were thus already present before 1914, there was no organization similar to the Development Commission or the Medical Research Committee concerned with the application of science to industry. Since the Exhibition of 1851 there had been a slow but steady growth of provision for technical education, and informed circles not only wanted this provision greatly extended, but were also conscious of the lack of interest which industry itself took in the development of new techniques and of its disinclination to promote relevant scientific inquiry. Government took no active interest until after the outbreak of war, when the country suddenly became aware that it lacked the means and the skills to produce such vital commodities as dyes, drugs and optical glass. By the middle of 1915 strong official interest had been roused, and the following published statement summarized the position:

'There is a strong consensus of opinion among persons engaged both in science and in industry that a special need exists at the present time for new machinery and for additional State assistance in order to promote and organize scientific research with a view especially to its application to trade and industry. It is well known that many of our industries have since the outbreak of war suffered through our inability to produce at home certain articles and materials required in trade processes, the manufacture of which has become localized abroad, and particularly in Germany, because science has there been more thoroughly and effectively applied to the solution of scientific problems bearing on trade and industry and to the elaboration of economical and improved processes of manufacture. It is impossible to contemplate without considerable apprehension the situation which will arise at the end of the war unless our scientific resources have previously been enlarged and organized to meet it. It appears incontrovertible that if we are to advance or even maintain our industrial position we must as a nation aim at such a development of scientific and industrial research as will place us in a position to expand and strengthen our industries and to compete successfully with the most highly organized of our rivals. The difficulties of advancing on these lines during the war are obvious and are not underestimated, but we cannot hope to improvise an effective system at the moment when hostilities cease, and unless during the present period we are able to make a substantial advance we shall certainly be unable to do what is necessary in the equally difficult period of reconstruction which will follow the war.'[4]

Within the Government itself the initiative was taken by the Board of Education. The Board saw that governmental action should take two forms – to promote research and to extend the existing provision for scientific and technological education in order to make good as quickly as possible the deficiency in the national supply of trained personnel. In May, 1915, the President of the Board announced plans for advanced instruction in science and technology and for the making of grants for research projects to various institutions and individuals, and at the same time put forward a scheme for the appointment of a Council of Scientific and Industrial Research to award and supervise post-graduate and research scholarships and to advise and assist in the organization and execution of research projects. This Council was to be responsible to the President of the Board of Education.[5]

The idea of a Council was accepted, but further thought had to be given to its precise position and it did not mature in exactly the same way as originally expressed. The Board of Education only dealt with England and Wales : it was apparently felt that a Council of the type outlined should have a United Kingdom jurisdiction. The Government therefore turned to that ancient but extremely flexible body – the Privy Council – and set up a Committee of Council for Scientific and Industrial Research in July, 1915, to be 'responsible for the expenditure of any new moneys provided by Parliament for scientific and industrial research'.[6] The new Committee of Council was to be advised by a small Advisory Council of eminent scientists and people engaged in industries whose processes benefited from the findings of scientific research. The Advisory Council was to consider and report to the Committee of Council on proposals (which the Advisory Council itself could initiate):

(i)   For instituting specific researches;

(ii)   For establishing or developing special institutions or departments of existing institutions for the scientific study of problems affecting particular industries and trades; and

(iii) For the establishment and award of Research Studentships and Fellowships.

Because of the close connection between education and research, and because of the fact that in the immediate future most of the research would be done in universities, the President of the Board of Education was nominated as Vice-President of the Committee of Council and was to answer for the Vote for Scientific Investigation in the House of Commons, though the Treasury was the accounting authority. The Board of Education was also to provide office accommodation and staff.

The first members of the Committee of Council for Scientific and Industrial Research were the Lord President, the Chancellor of the Exchequer, the Secretary for Scotland, the Chief Secretary for Ireland, the President of the Board of Trade and the President of the Board of Education, all *ex officio*, together with three Privy Councillors not holding ministerial office who were named in the Order-in-Council – Lord Haldane, A. H. D. Acland and J. A. Pease. Pease had been President of the Board of Education when the original proposals were put forward. In May, 1916, the Secretary of State for the Colonies was added *ex officio*; in September, 1916, Arthur Henderson was appointed a member by name; and in February, 1917, the Marquess of Crewe joined the Committee, also in a personal capacity. The first members of the Advisory Council were named in the original Order-in-Council, which also provided that the Council should consist of 'such persons holding office for such term as the Committee [of Council] shall from time to time determine'.

The new organization did not remain closely associated with the Board of Education for very long. During the eighteen months following the appointment of the Committee of Council the character of the Government's new concern for industrial research became clearer. The Advisory Council put forward a scheme whereby the Government should encourage groups of industrial firms to set up Research Associations which would qualify for financial assistance from the State. A sum of a million pounds – the 'Million Fund' – was ear-

I

marked for the purpose and an Imperial Trust for the Encouragement of Scientific and Industrial Research was incorporated by Royal Charter in November, 1916, to administer it.[7] The members of the Trust were the Ministers who held *ex officio* places on the Committee of Council. At the same time the Committee of Council set up standing committees to deal with various fields of research, and made grants, etc., to aid researches already in progress and to initiate new researches. The increased activity led to an early break with the Board of Education:

'As the work of the Advisory Council developed and the industrial side of research grew in bulk and importance, it became clear that a separate organization having its own estimates in charge of a minister responsible to Parliament was a necessity.'[8]

The Department of Scientific and Industrial Research (DSIR), answerable ultimately to the Committee of Council but accountable for its own Vote and responsible to Parliament through the Lord President of the Council, was established in December, 1916, and its staff were, from the outset, civil servants.

Once the full organization – Committee of Council, Advisory Council, Imperial Trust and DSIR – was established, governmental concern for industrial research developed quickly along lines which have become familiar. By 1921 some twenty one private research associations had been formed and were aided by grants. Schemes of maintenance allowances for post-graduate students and senior research awards were introduced and extended. In addition, a number of research institutions were either taken over or newly established as integral parts of DSIR.

The first institution to be taken over was the National Physical Laboratory, for whose maintenance the Department assumed responsibility in April, 1918. The Laboratory's scientific work continued – and continues – to be supervised by an Executive Committee appointed by the Royal Society which is recognized by the Lord President as a Committee of DSIR. The Laboratory took over the custody and maintenance of electrical standards from the Board of Trade in 1919. In November of that year the Geological Survey and Museum of Practical Geology were transferred to DSIR from the Board of Education. Investigations into atmospheric pollution previously conducted by the Air Ministry were taken over by DSIR in 1927. Responsibility for road research was transferred from the Ministry of Transport to DSIR in April, 1933. In 1950 the programme of research on sociological and economic aspects of building, undertaken hitherto by the Ministry of Works, was made the responsibility of DSIR, and the Ministry's Scientific Advisory Division was taken over by the Department.

There have been only a few transfers in the other direction. The laboratory dealing with scientific problems affecting the collections of the British Museum was transferred to the Museum in 1930. Work on nuclear fission, which was directed by DSIR during the Second World War under the name of 'Tube Alloys', was taken over by the Ministry of Supply in 1946 and later became the responsibility of the Lord President and the Atomic Energy Authority.

DSIR itself has set up several new research establishments. Some rearrangement of them and of institutions taken over by the Department has taken place from time to time, but the scope of the Department may best be shown by listing all those existing at present. There are now fourteen laboratories or groups of laboratories. Each laboratory or group of laboratories works with the advice of a Research Board or Committee, comprising independent people from the universities, from industry, and from the professions, etc. Government departments concerned appoint Assessors to these Committees or Boards to facilitate liaison with their departments' work and problems. The fourteen laboratories or groups of laboratories are shown below, in approximate order of their first association with DSIR or of their creation by DSIR.

1918   National Physical Laboratory
1919   Geological Survey and Museum
1919   Fuel Research Station
1921   Building Research Station
1922   Food Investigation (three laboratories)
1925   Chemical Research Laboratory
1927   Forest Products Research Laboratory
1933   Road Research Laboratory
1939   Water Pollution Research Laboratory
1940   Pest Infestation Laboratory
1946   Fire Research Station
1946   Hydraulics Research Organization
1946   Mechanical Engineering Research Laboratory
1947   Radio Research Station

The mixed ministerial and non-ministerial membership of the Committee of Council for Scientific and Industrial Research came to an end in February, 1928, when by an Order-in-Council the Committee was reconstituted. Henceforward it comprised only Ministers

– the Lord President, the Secretaries of State for the Home Department, for the Colonies, for Dominion Affairs (since 1947 Commonwealth Relations), and for Scotland; the Chancellor of the Exchequer; the President of the Board of Trade; and the President of the Board (since 1944 Minister) of Education. Other changes were made simultaneously. The provision whereby the President of the Board of Education was to preside in the absence of the Lord President was replaced by a section permitting the Lord President to appoint a member of the Committee to take his place when necessary. The original provision under which the members of the Advisory Council were to be appointed by the Committee of Council gave place to a section authorizing the Lord President to appoint such members after consulting the President of the Royal Society. Another Order-in-Council issued in April, 1928, granted a Supplemental Charter for the Imperial Trust which made the personnel of the Trust the same as that of the Committee of Council. As the Million Fund was exhausted in 1932 and as assistance to industrial research associations has since that time been provided out of the annual Votes of DSIR, the Imperial Trust became of little or no significance, and it was abolished in 1956.

The modifications of 1928 produced a constitutional framework within which scientific and industrial research was to develop for nearly thirty years. Supreme responsibility lay with the Committee of Council for Scientific and Industrial Research. The Committee of Council was advised by an Advisory Council, and the actual research and aid to research was administered by DSIR, staffed by civil servants and responsible to Parliament through the Lord President. There was thus a three-tier structure, and the body of eminent scientists who formed the Advisory Council had only indirect – though considerable – executive influence. It is worth quoting an official description of the exact constitutional position as it was in 1928.

'The Council is described in the Order-in-Council as Advisory, but it enjoys powers not usually possessed by advisory bodies. No proposal for the initiation of research is accepted by the Lord President without a report from his Council. The whole programme of the work of the Department is reviewed once a year by the Council, who approve the estimates for submission to the Lord President and the Treasury. Grants from the Million Fund to Research Associations . . . are made solely on the recommendation of the Council, provided that no grants are made in excess of funds raised by the Research Association in question from industry. If the Council recommend a larger proportion of grant, Treasury sanction has to be obtained. The Lord

President has also delegated to the Council direct executive powers, within the limits of a scheme he has approved on their recommendation, over the appropriation of funds provided annually by Parliament for grants to research workers and students in training. Broadly speaking, it may be said that the Department is the administrative machine for carrying out the recommendations of the Council when approved by the Lord President. Actual supervision of particular branches of work is entrusted to special boards or committees, the membership of which, with one exception, is approved by the Council. The exception to this rule is the Executive Committee of the National Physical Laboratory, the members of which are appointed by the Royal Society . . .'[9]

The position just described survived with only detailed changes which need not concern us here until 1956. In April, 1955, the Lord President appointed a Committee of Inquiry into the organization and functioning of DSIR. The Committee reported in October, 1955. Its major finding was that the existing central direction of the scientific effort at the Department's research stations, taken as a whole, was 'inevitably inadequate to secure the most effective use of the resources in the national interest' and that many of the research programmes had become 'too diffuse or too uneven in quality'.[10] The Report suggested – and the Government accepted the suggestion – that the remedy was to convert the existing Advisory Council into an executive body to be known as the Council for Scientific and Industrial Research. In the words of the Lord President, the change was made in order 'to ensure that the supervision of the programmes is adequate to ensure that the right research is being done'.[11]

The proposals of the Jephcott Committee (as the Inquiry Committee was called) were embodied in the Department of Scientific and Industrial Research Act, 1956, which came into force in November of that year. Overriding responsibility remains with the Committee of Council for Scientific and Industrial Research whose membership is unchanged. Subject to that ultimate responsibility, however, DSIR is now in the charge of the executive Council for Scientific and Industrial Research: the Advisory Council has been abolished.

Medical Research

When the Ministry of Health and the Scottish Board of Health were set up in 1919 and took over the work of the Insurance Commissions, it was decided – after the possibility of concentrating responsibility for all medical research on the new Minister of Health had been considered – that the Medical Research Committee established under the Health Insurance Scheme should be replaced by an organization somewhat similar to that already established for scientific and industrial research. The reasons for this decision reflected in part the reasons for the use of the Privy Council Committee for Scientific and Industrial Research in 1915 – the fact that a United Kingdom authority was preferable to a department whose concern was only with England and Wales. In addition it was felt that the promotion of research should not be restricted to subjects falling within the purview of only one department, and that freedom from close ministerial control was in itself very desirable.[12]

The transfer of responsibility for medical research to a Committee of the Privy Council was provided for in the Ministry of Health Act, 1919. The Committee of Council for Medical Research was first appointed in March, 1920. Its members, all of whom held their positions on the Committee *ex officio*, were the Lord President, the Minister of Health (presiding in the absence of the Lord President), the Secretary for Scotland and the Chief Secretary for Ireland. In the following month the former members of the Medical Research Committee were incorporated by Royal Charter as the Medical Research Council.[d] The terms of office of the first appointees were laid down in the Charter, which gave the Committee of Council the power to fill vacancies and to make further appointments, after consultation with the President of the Royal Society and with the Medical Research Council itself. The Medical Research Council is a non-departmental authority, empowered to appoint its own staff; and the latter have never been classed as civil servants. The Council is financed by an annual Grant-in-Aid, and the money is carried on a Treasury Vote, the Treasury being accountable to the Public Accounts Committee.

In 1926 the membership of the Committee of Council for Medical Research was increased by the addition of the Secretaries of State for the Home Department and for the Colonies and Dominion Affairs. The Minister of Labour and National Service was added in 1955. As the office of Chief Secretary for Ireland was not filled after 1922, the present membership of the Committee of Council comprises the Lord President, the Secretaries of State for the Home Department, the Colonies, Commonwealth Relations, and Scotland, the Minister of Health and the Minister of Labour and National

---

[d] The Advisory Council which had been attached to the Medical Research Committee had in recent years played a progressively less important part, and no provision was made to continue it under the new arrangement.

Service. The Charter of the Medical Research Council has been amended – a procedure which can be initiated by the Council under a special procedure – three times since its inception, in order to increase membership and regulate the tenure of members, and to extend the Council's powers of acquisition of land and buildings.

Thus whereas industrial research was organized and conducted for thirty years by a department responsible to the Committee of Council for Scientific and Industrial Research with an Advisory Council, medical research has been organized and conducted since 1920 by an executive Medical Research Council composed mainly of medical men but with some lay members, responsible to the Committee of Council for Medical Research. The members of the Medical Research Council control the work undertaken in its name and possess full executive responsibility. Since 1920 there has not been, in medical research, any counterpart to the Advisory Council for Scientific and Industrial Research. In addition, the Medical Research Council is permitted, under its Charter, to accept bequests of money and land from private sources, and so much of the Council's resources as are not derived from Parliament are not subject to the control of the Committee of Council. Nor are the Medical Research Council's staff members of the Civil Service.

The work of the Medical Research Council is broadly similar in character to that of DSIR, though it is more homogeneous and more frequently concerned in fundamental scientific inquiry. The Council maintains central laboratories in London – the National Institute for Medical Research – and a number of research units and groups, most of them situated in universities or hospitals. It employs a permanent scientific staff at the National Institute and in some fifty research units and groups or in some cases as individually attached workers, in universities and hospitals. The Council also makes temporary grants to independent workers in universities, hospitals and elsewhere, both for personal remuneration and for research expenses, and awards postgraduate fellowships and scholarships.

Agricultural Research 1911–1949

The Medical Research Council had its roots in the Medical Research Committee which had been set up in 1913: DSIR was established within two years of the beginning of the period of this study. Both bodies had early developed a pattern of governmental participation in their respective fields which has not been substantially altered in principle since their inception. Neither was ever so closely concerned with the field of particular departments that its relations with those departments were a dominant factor: scientific and industrial research covered an enormous field of inquiry, and even after the creation of the Ministry of Health and Scottish Board of Health, the Medical Research Council was dealing with many problems outside the range of those departments. By contrast the whole of agriculture in Great Britain has throughout our period been the responsibility of two government departments – one for England and Wales and one for Scotland – and agricultural research developed, therefore, within the purview of a single set of departments with the Development Fund providing the money and the Development Commissioners enforcing a degree of co-ordination.

As early as 1911 the Development Commissioners put forward a fourfold scheme for the extension of agricultural research which formed the basis of the organization which grew up thereafter. Three of the four main lines of approach were similar to those adopted in the fields of industrial and medical research – the creation of a group of Research Institutes each devoted to a specific branch of agricultural science: the provision of grants to workers outside those Institutes: and the award of scholarships to research students. The fourth line of approach was peculiar to agriculture – the formation of an Advisory Service to bring scientists and farmers closer together and to ensure the speedy and expert application of the findings of the research workers.

Between 1911 and 1931 the two agricultural departments and the Development Commission – the latter advising the Treasury on the provision of the necessary money – recognized and gave increasing financial aid to several existing private Research Institutes and officially sponsored the establishment of new Institutes. Each Institute – and there are now twenty-one of them, fourteen in England and Wales and seven in Scotland – has an independent Governing Body which draws the bulk of its income from governmental sources. They may conveniently be called the State-aided Institutes. While those Institutes were the main instruments of agricultural research, the two agricultural departments undertook research into certain subjects in their own laboratories, and such research was financed by the departments themselves. All other expenditure, whether on the Institutes or on grants to university scientists, etc., was met from the Development Fund.

In 1929, in order to make one authority responsible for the co-ordination and supervision of agricultural research, it was decided to set up an organization similar and complementary to the existing organizations for industrial and medical research. An Order-in-Council of July, 1930, authorized the appointment of a Committee of the Privy Council for Agricultural Research, comprising the Lord President, the Minister of Agriculture and Fisheries, the Secretaries of State for the Home Department and for Scotland, and the President of the Board of Education. The Secretary of State for the Colonies was added in 1943. In July, 1931, an Agricultural Research Council was incorporated by a Royal Charter which has been slightly amended since. The Council is appointed by the Committee of Council, and some of the members are appointed after consultation with the President of the Royal Society.

Like the Medical Research Council and DSIR, but unlike the Advisory Council for Scientific and Industrial Research, the new Agricultural Research Council was given certain executive responsibilities for which it was answerable to the Committee of Council on Agricultural Research, and it had power to appoint its own staff, who with a few exceptions have never been civil servants. And again like the Medical Research Council, the Agricultural Research Council was financed by grant-in-aid and not, as was DSIR, by a normal departmental Vote. The Agricultural Research Council's grant was carried on the Treasury Vote. For the first ten years of its existence, however, the Agricultural Research Council's functions were limited by special provisions relating to the agricultural departments and the Development Commission. The Council could advise the departments only on the programmes and estimates of the existing State-aided Institutes, and could only act as scientific advisers and co-ordinators with regard to schemes of the Development Commissioners. The Council was only free to initiate research in fields not covered by the agricultural departments and the Development Commission, and then only after consultation with those authorities. An additional restraint was the fact that most of the money voted for the use of the Council came from the Development Fund. None the less the Council was able to set up new stations and units under its direct control, and there are now fourteen of these, all working in close association with the universities.

It was not until 1941 that the restrictions on the scope of the Agricultural Research Council's functions were in part lifted: henceforward the Council had full control over its grant-in-aid. A further step was taken in 1946, when the Development Commissioners withdrew altogether from the field of agricultural research, leaving the Council and the agricultural departments to share the ground. The departments maintained direct control over Veterinary and Plant Pathology Laboratories in England and over the Seed Testing and Plant Registration and Plant Pathology Service in Scotland. The Agricultural Research Council had direct control of its own research stations and units. The State-aided Research Institutes were largely maintained by the agricultural departments and received advice on research programmes, staffs and budgets from the Agricultural Research Council. The Council also aided fundamental and applied research in the universities and elsewhere, and trained recruits to the agricultural research services. Agricultural Improvement Councils, one for England and Wales and one for Scotland, were set up in 1941 and maintained close liaison with the Council. Later a joint committee of the three Councils was appointed to deal with matters of common interest.

Agricultural Research and Nature Conservancy 1949–1956

In March, 1949, the scope of the Committee of Council for Agricultural Research was widened to cover Nature Conservancy, and the Committee was renamed the Committee of Council for Agricultural Research and Nature Conservation. The Minister of Town and Country Planning (since 1951 of Housing and Local Government) was added to the Committee. A Nature Conservancy was set up oy Royal Charter:

'To provide scientific advice on the conservation and control of the natural flora and fauna of Great Britain; to establish, maintain and manage nature reserves in Great Britain, including the maintenance of physical features of scientific interest; and to organize and develop the scientific services related thereto.'

In its constitution the Conservancy is similar to the Agricultural Research Council – it is an expert body which appoints its own staff, who are not classed as civil servants. The Conservancy is, however, quite separate from the Agricultural Research Council, thus forming the fourth 'executive' scientific organization to be established under the aegis of the Privy Council.

The new arrangement lasted until 1st April, 1956. On that date two Orders-in-Council took effect. One Order relieved the existing Committee of Council for Agricultural Research and Nature Conservation of all responsibility for the organization and development of agricultural research. It therefore became a separate Committee of Council for Nature Conservation, and its members are the Lord President, the Secretaries of State for the Home Department, the Colonies, and Scotland, the Minister of Education and the Minister of Housing and Local Government. The second Order-in-Council appointed the Lord President, the Minister of Agriculture, Fisheries and Food, and the Secretary of State for Scotland a Committee of

the Privy Council for the organization and development of Agricultural Research.

These constitutional changes were not the only or the most
significant changes which occurred in the organization of agricultural
research during 1956. The Agricultural Research Act of that year
gave the Agricultural Research Council statutory responsibility for
the organization and development of agricultural research. It also
transferred responsibility for the financial and general administration
of all the State-aided Agricultural Research Institutes in England and
Wales from the Ministry of Agriculture, Fisheries and Food to the
Council, which was already responsible for the supervision and
co-ordination of their scientific inquiries. This involved raising the
expenditure of the Council from about £1¼ million to about £3½
million. It will be remembered that hitherto the Council's expenditure had been carried on a Treasury Vote with Treasury officials
answering to the Public Accounts Committee. In the future the
Secretary of the Agricultural Research Council will be Accounting
Officer. The Council has thus been placed in much the same position
financially as DSIR, but the staff of the Council will not become
civil servants. The changes were made partly as a result of a *Report
from the Select Committee on Estimates* in 1954,[13] but the new
arrangement will not apply to Scotland, in accordance with the views
of the Royal Commission on Scottish Affairs, 1952–1954.[14] Money
paid to the State-aided Research Institutes in Scotland will continue
to be charged to the Vote of the Department of Agriculture for
Scotland.

The Lord President and the Research Authorities under the Privy Council

The developments which have been described in the four previous
sections are, at first sight, apparently indicative of very complicated
constitutional evolution and relationships. To begin at the top of the
hierarchy, the four Committees of the Privy Council – for Scientific
and Industrial Research, for Medical Research, for Agricultural
Research and for Nature Conservation – are elaborate but trans-
parent screens which have never concealed the individual responsibility of the Lord President of the Council for the organizations
formally answerable to those Committees. The various combinations
of Ministers and laymen – or of Ministers alone – whereby the Lord
President has had associated with him the heads of departments
representing England and Wales, Scotland, Northern Ireland, the
Dominions and Colonies, and of departments most interested in a

ORGANISATION OF RESEARCH UNDER THE PRIVY COUNCIL

JANUARY 1956

Responsible to Parliament →

COMMITTEE OF COUNCIL FOR SCIENTIFIC AND INDUSTRIAL RESEARCH
Chairman: The Lord President

COMMITTEE OF COUNCIL FOR MEDICAL RESEARCH
Chairman: The Lord President

COMMITTEE OF COUNCIL FOR AGRICULTURAL RESEARCH AND NATURE CONSERVATION
Chairman: The Lord President

ADVISORY COUNCIL FOR SCIENTIFIC AND INDUSTRIAL RESEARCH

DEPARTMENT OF SCIENTIFIC AND INDUSTRIAL RESEARCH

Direct Control

Advice and Financial Assistance

14 Research Boards etc., each responsible for one or more laboratories

Private Research Associations. Research in universities etc

MEDICAL RESEARCH COUNCIL

Direct Control

Financial Assistance

National Institute of Medical Research. Teams and individual research workers in hospitals and universities etc.

Independent research in universities etc

Agricultural Departments

Financial Assistance

Financial Advice and Programmes

Financial Assistance

AGRICULTURAL RESEARCH COUNCIL

Agricultural Research Institutes: 14 in England and Wales; 8 in Scotland.

Direct Control

14 Agricultural Research Stations

Financial Assistance

Independent research in universities, etc

NATURE CONSERVANCY

Direct Control

Financial Assistance

Nature Reserves and Research Stations

Independent research in universities, etc

ORGANISATION OF RESEARCH UNDER THE PRIVY COUNCIL

DECEMBER 1956

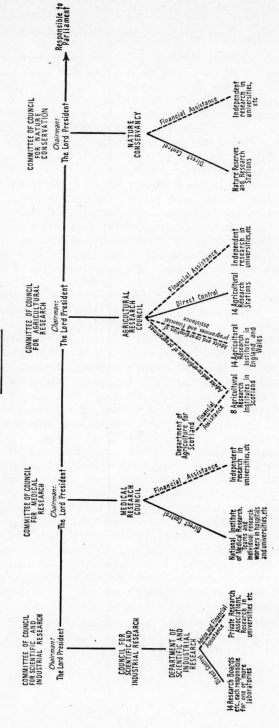

particular field of research, are of no real significance. Like those earlier Committees of Council for Trade, Education and Agriculture, and like the Boards which were so often constituted in the 19th century to preside over executive departments, the Privy Council's Research Committees have rarely if ever met *qua* Committees, though no doubt the members of them have often discussed informally with the Lord President any relevant matters concerning their administrative departments. But the operative member of all these Committees is the Lord President himself. This has been frequently admitted: and indeed the Lord President is formally responsible to Parliament for the research authorities and their establishments.

The difference, however, between the Lord President's relationship to the research organizations, on the one hand, and the relationship of the Minister who was President of, say, the Board of Education, to his department, is real and important. The President of the Board of Education had several colleagues on the Board who rarely or never met. He himself was the real working head of his department and was recognized as and expected to be such by Parliament. The Lord President, on the other hand, while he is similarly in practice the operative member of the Research Committees of Council, has never been the working head of the research authorities in any way comparable to the position of a Minister at the head of a department. And not only has he not been a working head, but he has not been expected to be one and has been generally lauded for not being one. In short, the real significance of all the complex constitutional arrangements set out above is simply that it has always been considered right for the research authorities to have a high degree of autonomy and to be regarded as institutions with entirely non-political functions, with the necessary minimum of control being exercised on behalf of Government and Parliament by a Minister without any particular departmental axe to grind – namely, the Lord President of the Council.

The loose rein which was given to the research authorities, at least in their early years, can be characterized by retailing some delightful incidents in the career of Lord Balfour. Balfour was himself greatly interested in scientific studies. He was Lord President from October, 1919, until October, 1922, and during the latter year he paid a visit to the office of the Medical Research Council, to the astonishment of the then Secretary of the Council, Sir W. M. Fletcher. Fletcher wrote about this some years later:

'The Council had worked previously under some six or seven Ministers, variously eminent, but none, I think, had ever made himself aware of the geographical position of the Office.'[15]

While out of office during the Labour Administration of 1924, Balfour was appointed Chairman of the Medical Research Council. In May, 1925, he joined the new Conservative Government as Lord President. He was thus

'Chairman of a body constitutionally advisory to himself as Lord President of the Council. He continued to occupy this anomalous dual position until the end of his public career, for, as he informed his medical colleagues, he so much enjoyed his first-hand insight into their work that he would connive at his own presence among them unless objection were raised by others.'[16]

Some Councils, however, were on a looser rein than others. The programmes of each of the main organizations have been largely under the control of the scientists themselves and freedom from undue political or official interference has been substantially achieved. DSIR is, however, clearly the least autonomous. It is financed and staffed as a Civil Service department, its Secretary is accountable to the Public Accounts Committee, and the members of its directing body – the Council for Scientific and Industrial Research – are appointed by the Lord President. To some extent this relatively strong control is due to the historical accident of the department's early association with the Board of Education. If the Department had been set up somewhat later, it might well have been non-departmental in character. But the relatively strong control also reflects the range of the Department's subject matter and the comparatively high annual expenditure – some £8 million in 1955–56. Parliament is unlikely to be willing to relax its supervision of so large a sum, and as we have seen, the variety and diffuse character of the Department's scientific inquiries have been deemed to call for the firm co-ordination and direction of an executive Council.

In contrast to DSIR, the other three research authorities are less closely supervised. The Medical Research Council probably enjoys the most freedom, for in addition to being financed by grant-in-aid it has full control of certain endowments and can initiate amendments to its own constitution. The Agricultural Research Council, while it has been, like the Medical Research Council, a grant-aided body, is now responsible to Parliament through its own Accounting Officer for its expenditure, whereas grants to the Medical Research Council and to the Nature Conservancy are still carried on the Treasury Vote. The members of the Agricultural Research Council, the Medical Research Council and the Nature Conservancy are appointed by their own respective Committees of Council, and not by the Lord President as is the case with the Council for Scientific and Industrial Research. The staffs of the Medical and Agricultural Research Councils and of the Nature Conservancy are not civil servants.

Despite these differences in detail, however, the primary constitutional characteristic of the arrangements of these major research organizations stands out clearly: it is the relative freedom from close departmental control, but at the same time general responsibility to Parliament through a Minister – the Lord President – who is not the head of a large and specialized administrative department and who is therefore not likely to approach the supervision of research organizations with any particular departmental bias.

Atomic Energy

At various points in Chapters II and VI and in an earlier section of this Chapter[e] the changes of departmental responsibility for the development of atomic energy have been mentioned, but the facts will bear repetition in greater detail. DSIR was first made responsible, under the Lord President, for research into the problems of producing an atomic bomb during the Second World War, and the work was carried on by a secret 'Directorate of Tube Alloys'. At the end of the war no method of exploiting nuclear power for peaceful purposes was yet known: atomic energy was still primarily a matter of defence, and the Government entrusted further research and development to a predominantly military department, the Ministry of Supply. Statutory powers were vested in the Minister by the Atomic Energy Act, 1946, and the Radioactive Substances Act, 1948. As rapid progress was made in finding means of applying atomic energy to civil and industrial uses it became doubtful whether the Ministry of Supply or any orthodox department was best suited for the management of the project. The Conservative Government decided to take that management out of the ordinary departments, and appointed a Committee in April, 1953, to advise on the whole question. The Report by Lord Waverley and his colleagues[17] suggested the establishment of a non-departmental authority which 'would combine the freedom and flexibility of an industrial enterprise with operation under strict Government control'.[18]

The suggestion was accepted and the transition took place in two stages. On January 1, 1954, the statutory powers of the Minister of Supply were transferred to the Lord President of the Council. On August 1 of the same year the Atomic Energy Authority Act, 1954, came into force. The new Authority took from the Lord President

[e] Ante, pp. 115, 239, 259.

most of the powers which had been entrusted to him in the previous January. The Lord President retained the rest and was himself endowed by the 1954 Act with a very considerable jurisdiction. Certain powers were also given by that Act to the Minister of Supply, the Minister of Agriculture and Fisheries (and Food since 1955), the Minister of Housing and Local Government, and the Treasury.

'The principal business of the Authority is research, the production of fissile material and the study of its industrial applications. They are also the contractors to the Ministry of Supply for the production of atomic weapons.'[19] Fundamental research into all aspects of atomic energy is carried on by a Research Group whose main stations are the Atomic Energy Research Establishment and the Radiochemical Centre. Defence research is the business of a Weapons Research Group, but except to a very limited extent the Authority cannot undertake the development or production of weapons unless ordered to do so by the Minister of Supply.

It would be out of place here to enter into all the details of the relationship between the Lord President and the Atomic Energy Authority. Broadly speaking, the Lord President has a very great general power of supervision and intervention, which is justified on grounds of security, of finance (the whole project is dependent on public funds), and of the overwhelming national and international political and economic importance of the rapid development of nuclear power. He appoints the members of the Authority, passes to them the orders of the Government, and is fully answerable to Parliament for their activities. The choice of the Lord President as the responsible Minister was due to his existing position *vis-à-vis* the other research organizations and scientific matters generally, and to the need for a senior member of the Cabinet who would be impartial between the various departments with claims for atomic material.[f]

[f] Lord Salisbury, who had been Lord President of the Council since 1952, resigned from the Government in March, 1957. On April 2, 1957, the functions of the Lord President with regard to atomic energy were transferred to the Prime Minister and First Lord of the Treasury by SI 561/1957, made under the authority of the Ministers of the Crown (Transfer of Functions) Act, 1946.

VIII

COMMON SERVICES

THERE are ancillary services of varying importance which departments require in order to carry out their functions. Some of them, such as typing and messenger services, are provided within each department, and we are not therefore concerned with them in this study. Others, however, are provided wholly or partly by separate departments, known generally as 'common service departments'. Already in 1914 accommodation, furniture, etc., for the civil departments (abroad as well as at home) was provided by the Office of Works; postage and telecommunications by the Post Office; stationery and printing by the Stationery Office; legal services for many departments by the Treasury Solicitor; audit by the Exchequer and Audit Department; payment of rates on government property by a sub-department of the Treasury; a number of financial services by the Paymaster General's Office; and analytical services by the Government Chemist. Such services have been and are often provided at the expense of the common service unit itself – i.e., the charge does not appear on the Vote of the receiving department.[a]

The proper organization of common services is a matter of considerable importance for the efficiency of government. In a record of changes in the distribution of functions, however, there is little to be said about the common service units. Treasury Ministers were and still are responsible to Parliament for most of them. All the units existing in 1914 have survived our period and all have expanded greatly – a natural corollary of the general increase in the work of government. What changes there have been in the distribution of common service functions were so relatively minor as not to be worth mention here. The Office of Works underwent a considerable administrative and constitutional metamorphosis during the Second World War: it became a Ministry of Works and its scope was widened to include a general oversight of the nation's building industry and, for a brief period, responsibility for town and country planning.[b] But despite these changes, the department has throughout

[a] In government accounting parlance such services are called 'allied services'.

[b] The building and planning side of the department's work has been dealt with in Chapters II and IV – see pages 97–8, 162–8. Although the Office of Works

retained as its principal duty the provision of the common service of accommodating government departments. Several new common service units have been established since 1914. In 1917, for instance, the actuary who had been appointed to deal with problems of National Health Insurance was raised in status to become the Government Actuary, and has since performed actuarial work for all departments needing it. Mention should also be made of the Central Statistical Office, which was set up in 1941: its establishment is treated in more detail in the next chapter. The most important innovation, however, in the present context, has been the Central Office of Information, which was set up in 1946. Its evolution has attracted much public attention, and must be dealt with in some detail.

INFORMATION SERVICES

In the context of British central government, information services may be divided into two broad categories – overseas and domestic. Overseas information is concerned to publicize and expound the policies of British Governments and the achievements, ideas and values of British society to foreign and Commonwealth countries and to colonial peoples. Domestic information services have three main objectives – to maintain an informed public opinion on a whole range of subjects and problems which come within the purview of government: to instruct the citizen in the carrying out of particular administrative procedures, such as those involved in applying for social welfare benefits, for example: and to exhort the citizen to participate in such government-sponsored activities as improving road safety, having children vaccinated, and buying National Savings Certificates.

The growth of governmental information services was, like the growth of governmental scientific research, merely a response to a widespread social movement. And again like scientific research, the rise of this new governmental function brought with it a problem of organization – whether all information services should be the responsibility of a single authority, or whether each department should make its own provision. Historically, overseas information or propaganda was probably the first governmental information service,

---

became the Ministry of Works in October, 1940, the Commissioners of Works remain in being and the Minister of Works is still, *ex officio*, First Commissioner. This is so because certain properties abroad are registered in the names of the Commissioners of Works.

in so far as diplomatic representation means putting forward the views and policies of the Government. It was in the field of overseas propaganda that the first separate information department – the Ministry of Information of March to November, 1918 – operated. While that department was quickly and completely disbanded at the end of the First World War, it was again in the field of overseas publicity that special provision outside the conventional departments, such as the founding of the BBC's Empire Service and the establishment of the British Council, was made in the early 1930s. But apart from these isolated exceptions, the development of information services both external and domestic was until 1939 left to individual departments, each making its own arrangements. The tempo of that development quickened considerably in the 1930s as the techniques of mass communication were further improved and exploited. Some home departments – notably the Post Office, the Ministry of Health and the Home Office – established Public Relations Divisions in the years before the Second World War, and we have seen in Chapter V that a number of Press Attachés were appointed to the more important diplomatic missions abroad.

It was the Second World War, however, which provided the greatest impetus to the development of governmental information services and brought into prominence the problem of how governmental publicity should be organized. In September, 1939, a Ministry of Information was set up in accordance with plans made before the outbreak of war. The new Minister was made responsible primarily for press censorship and for facilitating the collection and transmission of war news. In addition, he was charged with the policy and conduct of all overseas publicity except to enemy and enemy-occupied territories, and he was responsible for the provision of publicity services, including the production of publicity material, for most of the domestic departments. But whereas the Minister was responsible for both the policy and the execution of overseas publicity, he was not responsible for the policy of home information services. The work of his department in connection with the latter was, in fact, the work of a common service unit. Home departments had their own Public Relations Divisions which planned their publicity programmes and dealt directly with the press and the BBC. A few departments – the most prominent being the Ministry of Food and the National Savings Committees – had their own large-scale publicity production staffs, but the other departments turned to the Ministry of Information for advice on and for the execution of their information programmes.

At first the Ministry of Information was the target for a great deal of criticism, from both within and without the central administration. The new Ministry antagonized some of the home departments by tending to assume that it had some kind of special responsibility for the maintenance of morale and for the conduct of such governmental publicity as flowed from the policy of the Government as a whole rather than from the policy of any one department. The interdepartmental argument was eventually settled, decisively, against the Ministry of Information, and it was accepted henceforward that there was no subject for publicity which was not also a subject for the general handling of which some individual Minister, or group of Ministers, was responsible.

Much of the public criticism was due to a healthy public dislike of any governmental authority concerned with the handling and censorship of news, and much to the early confusion which prevailed in the organization of information facilities.[1] This phase of discontent soon passed, however, and after 1941 the department incurred very little hostile criticism. None the less, the whole idea of governmental publicity inevitably raised argument about how far such publicity can possibly go without becoming an instrument employed by the Government of the day to influence public opinion in favour of its policies for party political purposes. The latter point remained contentious throughout and for many years after the war, and indeed the whole conception of centrally organized governmental publicity in peacetime was only accepted as necessary and constitutionally respectable by the Conservatives after they had themselves become responsible for it in and after 1951. It is not surprising, therefore, that the whole question was deeply probed in a series of inquiries after 1945. All those inquiries, however, did not lead to any basic alteration of the system introduced by the Labour Government in April, 1946.

At the end of the war the duties of the Ministry of Information in connection with censorship and the press came to an abrupt end. The Labour Government decided to accept the recommendations of an official inquiry on the future of information services which had been held under the auspices of the Coalition Administration in 1944. On December 17, 1945, Mr Attlee announced the Government's decisions, which, he said, were based on the belief that:

'It is essential to good administration under a democratic system that the public shall be adequately informed about the many matters in which Government action directly impinges on their daily lives, and it is in particular important that a true and adequate picture of

British policy, British institutions and the British way of life should be presented overseas.'[2]

The Labour Government felt that while in peace time it was not desirable to concentrate policy responsibility for information services on a separate Minister, it was desirable to retain those parts of the Ministry of Information which performed common technical and production publicity services. The detailed changes were subsequently worked out at the official level, and on March 31, 1946, the Ministry of Information was abolished. On the next day the previous responsibility of the Ministry of Information for overseas publicity reverted to the Foreign, Colonial and Dominions Offices. At the same time the common service, or production, sections of the Ministry of Information became the nucleus of a new Central Office of Information.[3]

The Central Office of Information was thus conceived as, and remains, a common service department. It has no responsibility for the information policy of other departments, but merely advises on and produces publicity material for those departments which ask for its help. The responsibility for any particular piece of publicity rests with the Minister who asked that it be prepared. The common service is available to the departments which deal with external affairs as well as to domestic departments.[4]

The constitutional position of the COI is in many ways akin to that of the Stationery Office – headed and staffed by civil servants, and financed by the Exchequer with a separate Vote for which Treasury Ministers are responsible in Parliament. But in 1946, partly because of 'the theoretical apprehension that the public information services might be used for party purposes', and partly because the Government had made the Lord President responsible generally for co-ordinating all information services, the 'higher policy' of the Central Office of Information was brought within the purview of the Lord President, who to that extent became the new department's Minister.[5] The Labour Government had Cabinet Committees concerned with information services, and the Lord President remained generally responsible until he was replaced by the Secretary of State for Commonwealth Relations in May, 1951. The Conservatives, who came into office in October, 1951, did not appoint any Minister with a similar rôle until May, 1952, when Lord Swinton, then Chancellor of the Duchy of Lancaster, was given certain responsibilities for helping his colleagues with departmental publicity.[6] Lord Swinton became Secretary of State for Commonwealth Relations in December, 1952, but he continued to exercise responsibility for information matters until he relinquished office in April, 1955. For the next eighteen months there was again no Minister specifically charged with responsibility for information services.[c] In November, 1956, Sir Walter (now Lord) Monckton, as Paymaster General, undertook the co-ordination of information from the Service departments during the Suez crisis. In the following month it was announced that the Postmaster General was, 'under the authority of . . . the Prime Minister . . . co-ordinating Government information'. [7d]

AGENCY ARRANGEMENTS

The use of the common service department, as we roughly defined it at the beginning of this chapter, is an important device in British central government. To complete our general survey, it is necessary to draw attention to another method by which departments take in one another's work – namely the use of agency arrangements. It has sometimes been considered that duplication of effort can be avoided if departments whose primary duties involve the use of special administrative facilities and techniques undertake work demanding the same facilities and techniques on behalf of departments with different primary purposes. Thus a department may be able to avoid setting up a special network of local offices, or other special machinery, by arranging that another department which already has those facilities shall do a large part of the routine work on its behalf. For instance, the actual payment of many pensions and social welfare allowances is handled by the Post Office because the latter has numerous local offices designed to deal with constant cash transactions. The investigation of the personal circumstances of citizens, which may be necessary for one of a variety of purposes

c While matters of general information policy are thus from time to time the responsibility of a particular Minister, routine questions about the COI are normally answered in Parliament by the Financial Secretary to the Treasury. The COI is, therefore, listed in Table III (p. 34) as one of the departments for which the Chancellor of the Exchequer is ultimately responsible.

d In January, 1957, Dr Charles Hill, who had been Postmaster General in the previous Administration, was appointed Chancellor of the Duchy of Lancaster, with a seat in the Cabinet, by the new Prime Minister, Mr Macmillan. Dr Hill's duties were to include 'the co-ordination of Government information services at home and abroad'. (*The Times*, January 14, 1957.) It was later stated in the House of Commons that this appointment did not alter the existing responsibility of departmental Ministers for their own information services.

other than that of receiving national assistance, has often been undertaken for the department primarily concerned by the National Assistance Board because the latter has a staff which is expert in such work. And so on.[e] A department may act as agent for many other departments, though the work which an agent department does under such arrangements is normally different in each case. The Board of Customs and Excise is a good example: its officials undertake or have undertaken in the past such varied duties as collecting fees in connection with probate on behalf of the Inland Revenue and Probate Registry: preventing – on behalf of the Home Office – the importation of obscene literature: enrolling and paying members of the Royal Naval Reserve for the Admiralty: acting as Registrars of Shipping and Superintendents of Mercantile Marine on behalf of the Ministry of Transport and Civil Aviation: and collecting fees for Trinity House, etc. There is even one instance in modern British administration where a major department exists primarily to provide the equipment and materials needed by only three other departments: but the Ministry of Supply's relations with the Services are unique and can scarcely be compared with more usual agency arrangements in the civil sphere or with what we have called common services.

[e] Inter-departmental working of this type is usually carried out on a 'repayment' basis – i.e., the user department pays the agent department and the payment is shown as an 'appropriation-in-aid' on the agent department's Vote.

IX

THE CENTRAL CO-ORDINATION
OF GOVERNMENT

IN the previous chapters we have been concerned with changes in structure and distribution of functions. We now turn to the arrangements which have been made to co-ordinate the working of the central administration. We have not tried, however, to assess the part played by inter-departmental committees, many of which are ephemeral: nor have we dealt with the vital but elusive subject of informal contact between departments. What is attempted in this chapter is a description of the evolution of the more continuing features, such as the Cabinet Committee system, the arrangements for dealing with defence, economic and scientific questions at the highest level, and certain other central services in most of which the Treasury plays an important part. The development of each of these features or institutions has often been bound up with the development of one or all of the others. Separate treatment would not only lead to much repetition, but might well distort the whole picture of particular periods of development. The various subjects are therefore treated together when their development has been closely associated, and the whole chapter is as far as possible arranged chronologically. It must be emphasized, however, that in treating some of the institutions together there is no wish to imply that those institutions comprise some sort of disguised 'super' department or organization which presides over the rest of British central administration. Such an implication would be quite unjustifiable. The institutions discussed are loosely related by the basic nature of their task – co-ordination – but only the Cabinet has a general and undisputed authority over the whole apparatus of British government.

1914: CABINET, COMMITTEE OF IMPERIAL DEFENCE, TREASURY

We have insisted many times in the previous pages on the relatively limited character of governmental work in and before 1914 as compared with the position today. The point must be repeated, however, in explanation of the equally limited importance of co-ordina devices. The administrative duties of the central government in 1914 were, in fact, sufficiently circumscribed to be carried out by small departments whose jurisdictions seldom overlapped or needed to overlap. There may not, therefore, have been much inter-departmental co-ordination by later standards, for the good reason that little was needed. There were, however, three institutions concerned in large degree with co-ordination. The first, obviously enough, was the Cabinet, whose primary functions were deemed by the Haldane Committee in 1918 to include the control of the national executive and the continuous co-ordination and delimitation of the activities of the central departments. The second was in form an advisory body attached to the Cabinet – the Committee of Imperial Defence (CID) – in which most of the later institutional developments in Cabinet organization and high-level inter-departmental co-opera- tion have had their origin. The third was the Treasury, whose unique position *vis-à-vis* the other departments had evolved mainly in response to parliamentary demands for tighter control of expenditure.

Cabinet and C.I.D.

Since the turn of the century the Cabinet had comprised about nineteen or twenty Ministers, usually including all those with de- partmental responsibilities, though on occasion either the Postmaster General or the First Commissioner of Works was left outside. By present-day standards the Cabinet of 1914 was a rudimentary body. No secretary set foot within the Cabinet room, and no minutes were kept, though the Prime Minister wrote a 'private and personal' letter to the King after each meeting, giving an account of the proceedings. With the exception of the CID the only committees of the Cabinet were of an occasional and *ad hoc* character. And if the Cabinet itself was able to control and co-ordinate the central administration with- out the aid of any special secretarial organization, so too its most important member and co-ordinator-in-chief – the Prime Minister – asked no more than one or two private secretaries.

By 1914 the beginnings of departmental inter-dependence were apparent but had been recognized only in the field of defence. There were two aspects of top-level defence organization – the con- trol of the two Services on the one hand, and the relationship of the Services to the civil administration on the other hand. Both aspects were dealt with by the Committee of Imperial Defence. Its function was to co-ordinate:

(*a*) The preparations for war made by all the military and civil branches of government.

(*b*) The rapid conversion from peace-time to wartime organization on the outbreak of hostilities.

(*c*) The overall strategic direction of military operations.

The history of what is nowadays often called the Central Organization for Defence might be summed up in the phrase 'Committee into Ministry' – the Committee being the CID and its predecessors, the Ministry being the present Ministry of Defence. As early as the 1850s Benjamin Disraeli put forward a plan to place the Admiralty and War Office under one Minister[1] and he was followed in the late 1880s by Lord Randolph Churchill.[2] Apart from these two highly unorthodox suggestions, however, the development of a method of co-ordinating defence administration was until 1914 thought of – and put into practice – as the job of a special structure of inter-departmental committees. This committee activity grew up in the latter part of the 19th century and the early years of the 20th century as the result of the reaction of British opinion to radical changes in foreign and colonial affairs.

'The growing rivalry of continental groups after the Franco-Prussian War led slowly in this country to a realization of the need for increased naval and military strength even while "splendid isolation" remained the political ideal. That realization coincided with a period of increasing colonial rivalry, particularly in Africa and the Far East, which underlined the need for strength because of the danger that war against major European Powers might grow out of colonial quarrels. And, finally, the disasters of the first months of the Boer War, accompanied as they were by the evident hostility to Great Britain of nearly every major European Power, brought to a head agitation for careful and detailed planning in national and imperial defence which had been growing steadily for the past twenty years.'[3]

The beginnings of this defensive planning has recently been traced from the appearance of a Colonial Defence Committee, first to conduct an inquiry in 1878, and then as a standing committee from 1885 onwards, through the creation of a Joint Naval and Military Committee on Defence in 1891, and the setting up of the first Cabinet Defence Committee in 1895, to the evolution, at first as a Prime Minister's Committee in 1902, of the CID, and the appointment of a permanent Secretariat to that Committee in 1904.[4] In the ten years that followed, the CID became thoroughly established as an advisory, consultative and planning organization. The Prime Minister was its Chairman, but otherwise the membership was elastic: Cabinet Ministers, representatives of Dominion Governments, elder statesmen, prominent members of the Opposition, and military and Civil Service experts attended from time to time, and a network of sub-committees was created to consider a wide range of topics.[5]

The main task of the CID was to prepare a co-ordinated plan to be put into effect immediately on the outbreak of war. The 'War Book' was compiled by the Secretariat and kept up to date by a Co-ordination Sub-Committee presided over by the Permanent Under Secretary of State for Foreign Affairs. While the CID was strongly supported by the Prime Ministers, in this most important period of its development most of the initiative in defence preparations came from the Secretariat, which gradually established contacts in all the relevant departments, allayed suspicion and overcame the unwillingness of authorities to have their weaknesses discussed. All the posts in the Secretariat were held by Service officers, and this probably helped its acceptance by the military departments. The network of sub-committees was only gradually created, however, and the fact that nothing was done about supply and manpower was due partly to the small resources of the Secretariat and partly to departmental reluctance. Moreover up to the outbreak of war Government policy did not envisage a huge expansion of the army such as suddenly became necessary in 1914.

The Treasury

We have already quoted the opinion of Lord Bridges that the Treasury is 'in some sense the Department which is the headquarters of civil government or perhaps of all the government'. The Treasury is, however, itself only a department, and it is in the last resort only as strong as the desire of the Government as a whole to put financial considerations first, or the man who holds the office of Chancellor of the Exchequer. But the Treasury is responsible, under the Cabinet, for controlling expenditure, and it is on this that its influence and its position as a 'central' department is primarily based. Most actions of government have financial aspects which automatically bring them into the Treasury's orbit, and in 1914 the supervision of departmental expenditure by the Treasury was already complete. Whatever the full reasons may be, the Treasury was – and has remained throughout our period – at least *primus inter pares* in Whitehall. This status, impossible to define precisely, had long enabled the Treasury to take an interest in matters of general administrative structure and organization. It will be recalled, for instance, that the Northcote/Trevelyan Report of 1854, which laid down so persuasively and yet so compactly the principles on which the Civil Service should henceforward be recruited, was only one special extension of a series of reviews of administrative structure which had been undertaken very largely under Treasury auspices. And throughout the second half of the 19th century the Treasury was often involved in inquiries which might well be considered today as 'Machinery of Government' matters. Even so, it was not the Treasury's responsibility in 1914 – nor anybody's formal responsibility – to keep the distribution of governmental functions under review. Indeed at that time any such responsibility would have seemed neither desirable nor practicable nor necessary. Departments were comparatively small and fewer in number, their work was largely self-contained, and it would have been difficult to reconcile any central responsibility for allocating work with the essential autonomy of departments and the individual responsibility of their Ministers to Parliament.

CABINET, C.I.D. AND SECRETARIATS 1914–1923

Before 1914 the Committee of Imperial Defence was concerned to formulate general principles on which national defence policy should be based, and to plan the transition from peace to war within the framework of the existing machinery of government and in accordance with contemporary ideas of the probable scope of future armed conflict. When the First World War broke out the Committee was at first left to deal, in the main, with questions of Home Defence, and remained quite separate from the Cabinet. Between August, 1914, and December, 1916, this division gradually disappeared – or rather it was broken down by a series of institutional experiments which reflected the search for a supreme directing body small enough to be flexible but still retaining full constitutional authority. The experience gained from these experiments pointed the way to the small War Cabinet which Lloyd George established at the end of 1916.

The first attempt to find a better agency of supreme direction than the full peace-time type of Cabinet was the appointment of a War Council in November, 1914. It originally consisted of eight members – five Ministers, the Leader of the Opposition and the two Chiefs of Staff – and was an adaptation to war conditions of the procedure of the CID. There was in fact much less difference between the CID and the War Council than is generally admitted. In practice, except on big policy questions, the departments had acted on the recommendations of the CID unless objection was taken: the War Council was a little more advanced in this respect owing to the frequent need of very rapid execution, but the difference was one of degree and not of principle. The second experiment began in the early summer of 1915, when the Coalition Government was formed. The War Council was replaced by the Dardanelles Committee, which because of the insistence of the Unionist Ministers began as a Cabinet Committee without military advisers or even a secretary. Very soon, however, it became similar in composition, procedure and machinery to the War Council. The attempt to limit its scope to the Dardanelles Campaign broke down, and the Committee only lasted until November, 1915, when it was succeeded by a War Committee, originally with six, but later with thirteen, members.

Each of these changes brought some improvement in the top administration of the war machine as the practice of constant inter-Service co-operation became familiar. But even though the permanent Secretariat, which had been taken over from the CID by each of the new authorities in turn, provided the continuity of experience on which even more efficient supreme direction could be built, the major weakness lay in the relationship of the War Committee to the full Cabinet. It was important that the Cabinet should be kept informed of the work done by the War Committee and thereby allay any suspicions of those members of the Cabinet who were not also members of the Committee. When this liaison was lacking, as happened when the evacuation of the forces from Gallipoli began, the whole process of argument and decision-making had to be repeated by the Cabinet. Asquith, in order to facilitate good liaison, authorized the Secretary of the War Committee to circulate its conclusions to the Cabinet.

The solution was found in December, 1916, when Lloyd George became Prime Minister. He discarded both the traditional Cabinet and the War Committee and set up instead a War Cabinet of five Ministers. Only one of those Ministers – Bonar Law – had departmental responsibilities, and his membership of the War Cabinet was due less to his holding the Chancellorship of the Exchequer than to his position as leader of the House of Commons and as leader of the Conservative Party. Lloyd George also attached to the War Cabinet the Secretariat which had previously served the CID, the War Council, the Dardanelles Committee and the War Committee. The War Cabinet system lasted from December, 1916, until November, 1919. It was certainly one of the most radical innovations of the present century in British governmental institutions, and it set a pattern of Cabinet organization which was to reappear in slightly amended form in the economic crisis of 1931 and in the Second World War, while the idea of leaving several Ministers outside the

Cabinet was to become a feature of the post-1945 period. It was under Lloyd George, too, that there first appeared ministerial standing committees, though only one such committee – that on Home Affairs – survived after the end of the war. The members of the War Cabinet presided, as Chairmen, over the most important of those committees.

The retention of the War Cabinet for a year after the Armistice has been described as 'the casual outcome of a compromise adopted largely on personal grounds to meet a particular political situation'. At the end of 1918 Lloyd George considered that because he and some of his most senior colleagues were likely to be in Paris for long periods dealing with foreign affairs which it would be impossible to continuously refer back to London for consideration, there should for the time being not be a Cabinet at all. This proposal was, however, particularly unacceptable to Austen Chamberlain, who had been invited to be Chancellor of the Exchequer.

'Chamberlain was adamant that he would never be Chancellor without a seat in the Cabinet, while Lloyd George was equally adamant against having the full Cabinet which, he averred, would be forced on him if the Chancellor was included—because of the claims that would then be made by other Ministers. At this stage Bonar Law who agreed with Chamberlain made a compromise proposal. Why not simply preserve the old War Cabinet? Chamberlain was already a member and could continue, although not appointed specifically as Chancellor of the Exchequer. In this way the claims of other Ministers to membership could be postponed, and Chamberlain would be satisfied. The arrangement could prevail until the Paris negotiations had come to an end.'[6]

Bonar Law's plan was put into effect, and the War Cabinet continued until November, 1919, when Lloyd George reverted to a full peacetime Cabinet of twenty Ministers.

The other major innovation of December, 1916 – the establishment of the War Cabinet Secretariat – was to be retained and was to develop continuously after the war. The Secretariat which had originally been created to serve the CID in 1904 lost its exclusively military character for the first time in 1916 when a group of civilian members was added, composed mainly of people from outside the regular Civil Service. The Secretariat owed much of its success to the organizing genius of its chief – Lt-Col Sir Maurice (now Lord) Hankey. It became indispensable to the War Cabinet and greatly enhanced its reputation by its services to the Imperial War Cabinet, to the Supreme Allied War Council and to the international conferences at Versailles which followed the end of the war. Its procedure was in large measure taken as a model when the League of Nations Secretariat was established.

When the War Cabinet was disbanded in November, 1919, it was decided that the CID should be re-established and that the War Cabinet Secretariat should divide its attention between the Cabinet and the CID. Sir Maurice Hankey remained as Secretary to both bodies. The civil side of the Secretariat was much reduced: henceforward both the civil and the military members formed one staff, and on many occasions in the future both military and civil secretaries were sent to committees dealing with marginal topics. The Cabinet Secretariat, in so far as it was separate from the Secretariat of the CID, was from the start based on the traditions established by the latter. It has no 'policy' and has developed as a strictly secretarial organization, charged with the duty of assisting the Cabinet by the recording of decisions and the collection and distribution of papers. The way in which the Secretariat performs its duties necessarily varies with the policies pursued, with the change of events and moods, and with the personal methods of work of Ministers – especially of the Prime Minister. As we shall see, there have at different periods been special sections of the Secretariat to deal with economic subjects and with scientific matters, as well as with defence. The Secretariat's organization has in fact been sufficiently flexible and adaptable to meet special needs as they have arisen.

The immediately post-1919 history of the Cabinet Secretariat cannot, however, be separated from the history of a much less permanent institution which grew up around Lloyd George himself from 1916 onwards. Prime Ministers before 1914 were, as we have already said, served by one or two private secretaries. Those secretaries and their clerical staffs have grown in numbers as the central government has grown, and they have continued to deal with much of the business of the Prime Minister. The latter has always had the Permanent Secretary to the Treasury to turn to for advice on Civil Service matters, and since the establishment of the Cabinet Secretariat he has tended to rely on the Secretary of the Cabinet as a personal staff officer. Indeed, official co-ordination at the centre of matters likely to be handled by the Prime Minister depends on close day-to-day working between the Permanent Secretary to the Treasury, the Secretary of the Cabinet, and the Prime Minister's Principal Private Secretary.[a] This trio of senior officials, backed up

[a] This statement does not take account of the change made in the autumn of 1956, whereby Sir Norman Brook was appointed Joint Permanent Secretary to

by the staffs at their disposal has, however, not always seemed enough to some Prime Ministers, who have wanted additional advisers. The arrangements for providing this additional advice which have been made during the last forty years have been essentially personal and have no lasting effect on the structure of the central administration. Stanley Baldwin and Neville Chamberlain, for instance, both made use of Sir Horace Wilson as a personal adviser. Mr Churchill called on Lord Cherwell and, as will be described later, the latter built up a small staff of his own. But the personal instrument which we must mention here, in order to tell the later story of the Cabinet Secretariat, was that fashioned by Lloyd George.

Lloyd George was not content to introduce the Cabinet Secretariat alone: he also gathered around himself a small personal Secretariat detached from and with far more extensive functions than the normal Prime Minister's Private Secretaries. This new group was composed of various experts from outside the Civil Service who formed a sort of political and economic intelligence bureau quite unconnected with the orthodox hierarchy of Whitehall. The original idea, put forward by David Davies, M.P. (later Lord Davies), was to have 'a department for examining and tabulating data relating to war activities' for the Prime Minister, 'providing in condensed form the essential facts on matters demanding his personal attention, enabling him to decide the line of action with a minimum of labour'. This scheme gave place to Thomas Jones's suggestion that what the Prime Minister needed was 'something wider than a statistical bureau . . . a Prime Minister's Secretariat, composed of members of varied training and experience, on whom he could depend in any matters requiring his personal attention and interposition'.[7] Officially the group's job was 'to assist the Prime Minister in the discharge of the heavy responsibilities which fall upon him under the War Cabinet system'.[8] The head of the statistical branch indicated the wide scope of the Secretariat's activity when he stated that

'In military and naval action we have no part . . . Our work embraces all other divisions of the nation's war effort. These include finance, food, coal, munitions, manpower, shipping, shipbuilding, railways and docks. . . .'[9]

The new organization was housed in temporary buildings in the

---

the Treasury while continuing to be Secretary of the Cabinet. That change is dealt with in the concluding section of this chapter.

K

garden of No. 10 Downing Street, and from its earliest days was known as the 'Garden Suburb'.

While the war lasted neither the Cabinet Secretariat nor the Garden Suburb, though both highly unorthodox by pre-1914 standards, attracted any serious criticism, but it is hardly surprising that when the war ended they should have aroused some suspicion and hostility. The Cabinet Secretariat was to many people suspect as a body which had broken into the sacred privacy of the Cabinet, while the Garden Suburb became increasingly controversial in the stormy post-war years as it appeared to interfere, especially in foreign affairs, with the prerogatives of the regular departments. Within Whitehall itself there was hostility towards both the Cabinet Secretariat and the Garden Suburb because both were largely composed of people from outside the Civil Service whose comparative lack of knowledge of the internal working of the central administration did not help their relations with career Civil Servants. The Cabinet Secretariat suffered in the estimation of many people because it was often confused with the Garden Suburb, so that doubts were cast both on the value of its real work and on its genuine political impartiality. This confusion was to some extent understandable, especially after the Cabinet Secretariat was made responsible for dealing with correspondence concerning the League of Nations, as well as providing secretarial services to the Peace Conference. In addition, for the years 1921–1923 it was given a separate annual Vote.[b] On top of all this, Sir Maurice Hankey's position as Secretary of both the Cabinet and of the CID, and his constant presence with the Prime Minister at the international conferences of the time, laid him open to the quite unfounded charge of being Lloyd George's 'minion' and of promoting the latter's 'interference' with departmental policy, especially on foreign affairs.

The mischief for which the existence of the Garden Suburb was mainly responsible came to a head in 1922. There was a debate about the Cabinet Secretariat in the House of Commons on June 13.[10] While some weighty constitutional arguments were voiced it was obvious that the real hostility to the Secretariat was based on the belief that it interfered in foreign affairs and that its existence re-

---

[b] Except during those years the Cabinet Secretariat has always been considered as a 'subordinate department' of the Treasury for purposes of the annual Estimates. The same procedure is followed in the case of the salaries and staffs of various non-departmental Ministers. This is done merely for financial and administrative convenience, and does not make these offices branches of the departmental Treasury.

flected a tendency to personal government by Lloyd George.[c] When
the Coalition broke up in the following October, Bonar Law made
it a point of his election promises that the Cabinet Secretariat should
be reorganized and that the Foreign Office should be unequivocally
responsible for foreign affairs.[11] Moreover, while Bonar Law
recognized the value of Sir Maurice Hankey and his staff and had
no intention of disbanding the Cabinet Secretariat, he wanted to get
rid of the Garden Suburb and also had doubts about the wisdom of
sending Sir Maurice Hankey to any more international conferences.

With the fall of Lloyd George and the advent of Bonar Law as
Prime Minister the Garden Suburb came to an end, and the Cabinet
Secretariat was left to carry on its work in an atmosphere cleared of
suspicion. But one more threat remained. Sir Warren Fisher, the
Permanent Secretary to the Treasury, sought to make the Secretariat
an integral part of the Treasury establishment, and suggested that
the Secretary of the Cabinet should become a Fourth Controller in
the Treasury. Sir Maurice Hankey fought this proposal to the point
of offering his resignation, and the attempt to bring the Secretariat
into the Treasury's orbit was dropped. Sir Maurice Hankey's official
status was enhanced in 1923 by his appointment as Clerk to the
Privy Council, an office which he held in addition to his joint
Secretaryship of the Cabinet and CID. His organizing skill and experience were in such demand by British delegations that any doubts
about the desirability of his presence at international conferences
were put aside, and in fact he continued to attend almost all such
conferences outside the League of Nations in a secretarial capacity
during the inter-war years.

THE TREASURY AS THE 'CENTRAL' DEPARTMENT 1914–20

During and immediately after the First World War considerable
awareness was shown of the desirability of achieving a closer integration of the Civil Service and of making a consequent change
in the position of the Treasury *vis-à-vis* other departments. The

[c] An interesting light is thrown on this debate and on the confusion of thought in
the House of Commons by the entry in Field Marshal Sir Henry Wilson's diary
for the same day (Wilson was then an MP): 'I could have knocked Lloyd George
and his quibbles with ease, but not without using my inside knowledge, which I
did not think was fair. The truth, of course, being that Hankey and his Secretariat are essential, whereas Philip Kerr, Ned Grigg, etc., are poisonous.' (C. E.
Callwell: *Field Marshal Sir Henry Wilson*, Vol. II, pp. 343–344.) Philip Kerr
(later Marquess of Lothian) had been the chief foreign affairs man in the Garden
Suburb since its inception, and in the middle of 1922 was just handing over his
duties to Sir Edward Grigg (Lord Altrincham).

Royal Commission on the Civil Service which had been sitting before 1914 felt that 'the Treasury should be strengthened for the purpose of establishing a more effective control over the organization of the Civil Service', and even went so far as to recommend that a special branch of the Treasury be created 'to carry out inquiries and investigations into any matters connected with Departmental administration or methods of working'.[12] The relaxation of Treasury supervision during the war led the Select Committee on National Expenditure in 1917 to demand a strengthening of the Treasury 'for the purpose of establishing a more effective control over the organization of the Civil Service'.[13] To these suggestions was added the advocacy, by the Haldane Committee and the Bradbury Committee on the Organization and Staffs of Government Offices, in 1918 and 1919 respectively, of more comprehensive arrangements in both the Treasury and all the other departments for dealing with establishment matters.[14] The meticulous and unimaginative control for which the Treasury was renowned in Edwardian days was deplored by the Haldane Committee, which suggested that

'the traditional attitude of antagonism between the Treasury and other Departments which so often manifests itself might be substantially modified if the officers of the Treasury could establish closer personal relations with the several Departments with which they deal, and acquire a fuller knowledge of their work and their difficulties.'

The outcome of all this discussion was a big reorganization of the Treasury and of its relations with the other departments in 1919–20. A Controller of Establishments was appointed in the Treasury and control of expenditure on staff was no longer dealt with as an incidental part of the work of the supply divisions. Principal Establishment Officers were appointed in departments. Greater emphasis was thus placed on 'establishments' and in the Treasury itself the first move towards the employment of 'efficiency experts' was made when a few persons with special knowledge of the use of office machines and appliances were appointed 'to control the supply of such equipment to Government Departments'. These Treasury Investigating Officers, as they were called, were the forerunners of the present 'O & M' staffs.[15] It was also recognized that there was a need for greater delegation of financial responsibility by the Treasury to departments. This was a special objective of the new Permanent Secretary to the Treasury, Sir Warren Fisher, and one of the steps taken was to make each Permanent Secretary the Accounting Officer for his department in order to ensure that finance and policy should go hand in hand. The practice did not become invariable until several years after 1920. In the latter year it was laid down that the Prime Minister's consent was required for the appointment of Permanent Secretaries, Deputy Secretaries, Principal Finance Officers and Principal Establishment Officers. A Treasury Minute of September, 1919, declared that henceforward the Permanent Secretary to the Treasury would 'act as permanent Head of the Civil Service and advise the First Lord in regard to civil service appointments and decorations'. In 1920 an Order-in-Council which superseded and extended similar previous Orders was issued stating that

'The Treasury may make regulations for controlling the conduct of His Majesty's Civil Establishments, and providing for the classification, remuneration, and other conditions of service of all persons employed therein, whether permanently or temporarily.'

The early post-war years also saw the beginnings of the Whitley Council system for negotiating about salaries and conditions of employment.

During the First World War it was found necessary to appoint an informal committee of Treasury officials to consider what would now be called Machinery of Government questions. Little is known of the work of this Committee, which was set up in 1916, but it is understood to have made *prima facie* recommendations, subject to later discussion with the interested departments, about the need to retain a separate Ministry of Labour after the war in order to avoid an excessive load on the President of the Board of Trade and his Permanent Secretary, the need for a Ministry of Health and for increased co-ordination of medical research, the need for an investigation into the various responsibilities for railways, the concentration of actuarial work, and for a standing Statistical Committee to review departmental statistical work and prevent duplication. It is evident that most of these recommendations were accepted.

In July, 1917, the Haldane Committee on the Machinery of Government was appointed. Originally it was a sub-committee of the Reconstruction Committee, and was reconstituted when the Ministry of Reconstruction was established. Its Report appeared in December, 1918. The method of this Committee was to define general principles which should govern the distribution of responsibilities and then to illustrate the application of those principles in 'sufficient outline'. The Report has been reprinted from time to time and is something of a classic, partly because it is still the only published document on the Machinery of Government apart from personal or academic expressions of opinion. The Bradbury Com-

294 The Organization of Central Government 1914–1956

mittee also drew attention to serious overlapping of functions between some of the temporary wartime departments and the older departments.

None of these committees recommended that there should be any special standing body for the consideration of Machinery of Government problems. The wide-ranging Report of the Haldane Committee had only slight direct and immediate influence on the shape of the central administration, but perhaps the greatest value of that Report was that it provoked thought about a problem of government which was to become more pressing as the area of state activity widened.

TOWARDS A CENTRAL SERVICE OF
ECONOMIC INTELLIGENCE

It is only in recent years that we have come to take for granted the need for and existence of special organs of economic intelligence and advice at the very centre of government. Before 1914 what thinking was done on economic matters in government circles was confined almost entirely to the Treasury and the Board of Trade. Little if any sustained thought was involved at Cabinet level on such matters, and the people mainly concerned were departmental officials. The academic study of economics was not very widespread, and there were no professional economists as such in the Civil Service. Nor were the great powers taken by the State to control the economic life of the community during the First World War to lead to the establishment of any noteworthy central machinery for the widespread collection of economic data and for study of general economic problems. Despite the creation of several new trade and industry departments there was no sustained attempt to form a staff organization to co-ordinate and advise all the authorities concerned with the national economy.

None the less an attempt was made to establish some sort of economic intelligence unit at the Board of Trade. The idea may well have come from Sir Hubert Llewellyn Smith, the Permanent Secretary of the Board. A big reorganization of the department was carried out at the end of 1917 on the recommendation of the Clarendon Hyde Committee. When this reorganization was discussed by the Haldane Committee, Llewellyn Smith described the functions of a new General Economic Department which was being set up within the Board. He thought it should

'anticipate, watch and suggest means of dealing with, important questions and movements likely to arise in commerce and industry,

and which from their generality or novelty did not fall within the
scope of any specialized Department. It would therefore be in essence
an Intelligence Department. While such a Department would, in the
main, consider questions within the scope of the Board of Trade, it
would be necessary for it to establish relations with other Government Departments; some at least of the staff of the Department
would hold their appointments on a temporary basis, and he hoped
to encourage students who had taken Degrees in Economics at the
Universities to pass through this Department, and also to give
members of the permanent staff of the Board of Trade an opportunity of serving in it temporarily.'[16]

This passage bears a close resemblance to the official statement
of the duties of the General Economic Department dated the same
month. The Department was to assist the Permanent Secretary

'in relation to questions involving economic policy, especially those
which, owing to their generality or novelty, extend beyond the sphere
of any special department. . . . The section will have no executive
functions but will be charged with the duty of systematically studying
the general economic position of the country and the problems arising therefrom.'[17]

The subsequent history of the General Economic Department is
not exactly clear from the available evidence, but the scope of the
Department was obviously too ambitious for it to withstand the
tremendous post-war reaction against government concern with the
economy, and the drive to reduce administrative expenditure. For
some time after the Department appeared Llewellyn Smith seems to
have pressed its claims, and Lord Waverley has recorded that he was
consulted, after the war, on a proposal to establish an Economic
General Staff in the Board of Trade alongside the normal departmental organization.[18] In 1919, however, the General Economic
Department ceased to have a separate existence. It was combined
with the Industrial Power and Transport Department of the Board
of Trade which had also been set up in the reorganization of 1917.
This merger was probably entirely due to the creation of a separate
Ministry of Transport which took over not only railway matters but
also electricity administration, thus leaving the Industrial Power and
Transport Department with few of its previous functions. The new
joint organization was called the Power, Transport and Economic
Department.

In the following years the Power, Transport and Economic
Department came under fire from the Hilton Young Committee on
the Staffing and Methods of Work of the Board of Trade[19] and

from the Geddes Committee on National Expenditure. The former could see no need for the continuance of the economic section of the Power, Transport and Economic Department, which it claimed was largely occupied in special inquiries for the heads of the office, and thought it should be combined with other intelligence organs of the Board in a Private Secretariat to the President. The Board admitted that the Power, Transport and Economic Department had in fact become something of an 'odd job' section, but insisted that the economic side was still valuable:

'. . . it has been found . . . necessary to have a small staff whose whole time is available for furnishing information on important matters dealt with by the Board of Trade in order to prevent misconceptions arising as to the action taken by the Board and the grounds of such action.'

This defence was a far cry from the earlier confident justification of the need for a comprehensive General Economic Department! In January, 1922, the Geddes Committee, concerned with reducing expenditure, added their condemnation of the Power, Transport and Economic Department.[20] This was, perhaps, the last straw. The Department seems to have been finally disbanded later in the year. When a Board of Trade witness was questioned about it in April, 1924, he declared that 'substantially the Department has gone entirely' and that its functions had ceased.[21] The only long-term practical result of this early experiment in organizing economic intelligence and advice was the appointment in 1919 of a Chief Economic Adviser to His Majesty's Government. The post was attached to the Board of Trade and filled by Llewellyn Smith when he retired from the office of Permanent Secretary. When the Power, Transport and Economic Department of the Board of Trade was disbanded in 1922 the Chief Economic Adviser remained as the sole embodiment of the idea that government could benefit from the services of the economist.

THE CABINET BETWEEN THE WARS

Between November, 1919, and September, 1939, the Cabinet reverted very largely to its pre-1914 pattern of membership in so far as it normally included all but two or three of the Ministers. This meant that the average size of the Cabinet was about twenty: the Paymaster-General, the Postmaster General, the First Commissioner of Works, the Minister of Pensions and the Minister of Transport seldom found places. Only for a few weeks in 1931 was there a serious departure from this pattern, when Ramsay MacDonald formed his first 'National' Government. His Cabinet then had ten members, the great majority of them being departmental Ministers. Nor did the existence of the Cabinet Secretariat encourage the establishment of a system of standing Cabinet committees. The Home Affairs Committee which had been established in 1918 was retained by each Cabinet in turn during the inter-war period but was apparently only concerned with the drafting of Government Bills and the arrangement of the legislative programme. The CID returned to its formally advisory rôle, and was the model for the only real innovations of the period in internal Cabinet organization—the Committee of Civil Research set up in 1925, and its successor the Economic Advisory Council which appeared in 1930. These advisory bodies are treated separately. Their careers formed a sketchy prelude to the more extensive developments in economic intelligence and advice from 1939 onwards, and an account of them is included in a later part of the chapter which traces the history of the central machinery of economic intelligence and advice from the early 1920s to the present time.

THE CO-ORDINATION OF DEFENCE IN THE INTER-WAR YEARS

When the War Cabinet was abolished in November, 1919, the Committee of Imperial Defence reappeared and again took up its advisory and consultative rôle. The experience of total war and the establishment of a third Service emphasized the need for co-ordinated planning in defence matters, and the realization of this led to notable additions to the pre-1914 organization. During the First World War all departments made records of their experiences of the working of the War Book, in order to provide material from which a future Book could be prepared. When these records were collected the resurrected Co-ordination Sub-Committee of the CID found that manpower and supply had been the weakest points of the pre-1914 organization. The new sub-committee structure which was built up in the early 1920s included, therefore, not only all the pre-war sub-committees but also a Manpower Committee and a Principal Supply Officers Committee. Among other new committees was one concerned with Air Raid Precautions.

The most important innovation in defence arrangements in the inter-war period was the establishment of the Chiefs of Staff Committee early in 1924. The system had been given a 'trial run' during the Chanak crisis in the autumn of 1922, and its adoption as part of the permanent defence organization was recommended by a sub committee which reviewed the provision for National and Imperial Defence under the Chairmanship of Lord Salisbury in 1923.[d] The scope of this vitally important instrument was thus defined by Lord Salisbury and his colleagues:

'In addition to the functions of the Chiefs of Staff as advisers on questions of sea, land or air policy respectively, to their own Board or Council, each of the three Chiefs of Staff will have an individual and collective responsibility for advising on defence policy as a whole, the three constituting, as it were, a Super-Chief of a War Staff in Commission. In carrying out this function they will meet together for the discussion of questions which affect their joint responsibilities.'[22]

It was soon found that the Chiefs of Staff, concerned as they were with the whole field of defence policy, could not make their joint responsibility fully effective without an organization additional to that of the CID. In 1927 the Directors of Plans of the three Service departments were brought together in a Joint Planning Committee – i.e., the immediate subordinates of the Chiefs of Staff were put 'in commission' just as the Chiefs themselves had been four years earlier. In practice the Directors were at first very much only the representatives of their Services, but no doubt through constant working together on common problems they developed some of the characteristics of a team. In 1936 steps were taken – by the establishment of a Joint Planning Staff – to ensure that the Joint Planning Committee really was an inter-Service organization, and at the same time a Joint Intelligence Sub-Committee was set up alongside it. The Joint Intelligence Sub-Committee was at first composed of the Deputy Directors of the Service Intelligence Departments, but as the whole structure of joint planning and intelligence grew stronger the Directors of Intelligence themselves took over membership and a representative of the Foreign Office was added. At or about the time of the outbreak of war in 1939 the Foreign Office representative began to take the Chair, and a Joint Intelligence Staff was appointed.

[d] In August, 1926, a warrant was issued to the Chiefs of Staff Committee laying down its duties. Similar warrants were henceforward issued whenever the Committee was reconstituted, until the outbreak of war in 1939. The original warrant is printed as an Appendix to W. S. Chalmers: *Life and Letters of David, Earl Beatty*, pp. 474–475, but the implication contained in the title there given to the warrant and in a statement in the text (p. 380) that it marked the inauguration of the Committee, is incorrect. L. S. Amery's reference, in *My Political Life*, Vol. II, p. 265, to the 'more formal constitution' of the Chiefs of Staff 'as a permanent committee in 1926' is also misleading. The Committee was completely and formally inaugurated in 1924.

The personnel for much of these new joint organizations was recruited on the Service side from high-ranking officers who graduated from the Imperial Defence College after its foundation in 1927. The Joint Staff system was thus grafted on to the older machinery of the CID between the two World Wars, and one result of this was a markedly increased Secretariat.[e]

The experience of the First World War and the establishment of a third Service stimulated the first serious discussions of the idea of having a single Minister of Defence in place of or in addition to existing Service Ministers. The debate on this subject was to continue for many years and helped to initiate several notable constitutional experiments.

The first official statement on the subject of a Ministry of Defence which was made after the war came from the Geddes Committee on National Expenditure in 1921.[f] The Committee, primarily concerned to stress the need for economy, believed that there was 'overlapping and duplication' throughout the three Fighting Services, and argued that optimum economy, through the complete co-ordination of common services, could only be ensured by the creation of 'a Co-ordinating Authority or a Ministry of Defence responsible for seeing that each Force plays its part and is allotted appropriate responsibility for carrying out various functions'. It was the Committee's view that 'the theory of such a Ministry in embryo appears already to exist in the Committee of Imperial Defence', and that a Minister of Defence together with his staff 'could all be drawn from existing organizations'.[23]

Here, then, was a very narrow approach to a complex subject: the suggestions of the Geddes Committee were quite unrelated to the problems of the strategic direction of fighting units in three very different media. None the less the case was submitted immediately to a Committee on the Amalgamation of Services common to the Navy, Army and Air Force, which sat throughout 1922.[24] This Mond/Weir Committee, as it was called after its successive Chairmen, asserted that

'the amalgamation of the common services would only be practicable if it formed part of a comprehensive scheme of reorganization which provided for the establishment of a Ministry to control a defence

[e] The membership of the CID itself remained flexible. The 'panel' of Ministers and officials who could attend any meeting without special invitation included in 1939 the Prime Minister, eleven other Ministers, the three Chiefs of Staff, the Permanent Secretary to the Treasury and the Secretary of the Cabinet.

[f] But see footnote *h*, p. 301 for earlier 'high level' ideas.

force in which the identity of the Navy, Army and Air Force had been merged.'

The Report claimed, however, that 'such a revolutionary idea as the merging of the identity of the three Services' had never been contemplated, and that short of such a decisive step it was impossible

'. . . to devise means by which responsibility can be allocated as between the authority charged with the administration of an amalgamated common service and the Ministers who are severally responsible to Parliament for the administration of the Navy, Army and Air Force.'

It is worth noting that the Geddes Committee was a group of five eminent representatives of the commercial – especially the railway and shipping – world, who had been engaged on government work during the war, but that the Mond/Weir Committee, while it contained an important 'civil' element, was much more governmental in character and worked through sub-committees whose members were predominantly drawn from the Services and the three Service departments. It was not until the Salisbury Committee on National and Imperial Defence was appointed in March, 1923, that the idea of a Ministry of Defence was fully treated, from military, economic and administrative standpoints.

From the evidence submitted to the Salisbury Committee it became clear that the majority of experts favoured a compromise between the extreme course foreshadowed by the Geddes Committee and a return to pre-1914 arrangements. The most extreme proposal – a full blooded amalgamation of the existing Service departments – came from Sir Frederick Sykes and was, and has remained until the present day, quite unacceptable.[9] The scheme put forward by Sir Eric Geddes, on the other hand, while still beyond the bounds of possibility in the 1920s, was sufficiently prophetic, in the light of later developments, to deserve quotation here. Geddes wanted a single Minister responsible for all three Services but would have retained the separate Service departments, putting at the head of each a Parliamentary Secretary who would preside over the Board of

[9] It is a measure of the effect of the Second World War on military thinking that the idea of one combined defence force, deemed 'revolutionary' in 1922, was treated with much greater respect in 1946 when it was stated that the Government did not 'wholly reject it', and conceded that 'at some stage in the future amalgamation might be found desirable'. (*Central Organization for Defence.* Cmd. 6923.)

Admiralty, the Army Council and the Air Council respectively.[h] The germ of the Ministry of Defence eventually set up in December, 1946, may be discovered in the suggestion that the Minister should have

'. . . a very small office, containing a Statistical Accountant and a Council consisting of the sub-Ministers of the Navy, Army and Air Force, with two members each from the Board of Admiralty, the Army Council and the Air Council.'

From the other expert advice tendered to the Committee, Lord Salisbury and his colleagues concluded that a Ministry of Defence was impracticable and that the best arrangement would be to establish permanently the Chiefs of Staff Committee and to strengthen the whole structure by appointing a Chairman of the Committee of Imperial Defence to act as deputy to the Prime Minister. It was felt that as the Prime Minister could 'only devote a small part of his time and attention to defence questions', a separate Chairman should be responsible, 'under the general direction of the Committee of Imperial Defence and with the assistance of the three Chiefs of Staff', for

'. . . the initiation of a consistent line of policy directing the common action of the three or any two of the three Services, taking account of the reactions of the three Services upon one another.'

Again with future developments in mind, it is of interest to reproduce the Salisbury Committee's definition of the functions of what may be called this Minister of Defence in embryo. Those functions were to be:

'(i) To preside over the Committee of Imperial Defence in the absence of the Prime Minister.

(ii) To report to the Prime Minister (when he himself has not presided) and to the Cabinet the recommendations of the Committee of Imperial Defence.

[h] A similar scheme was discussed informally by the Prime Minister, Mr Churchill (then Secretary of State for War and Air) and the Chief of the Imperial General Staff, Field Marshal Sir Henry Wilson, at Criccieth in July, 1919. According to Wilson, he and Mr Churchill were in favour, but Lloyd George 'put up all the objections he could think of'. (C. E. Callwell: *Field Marshal Sir Henry Wilson*, Vol. II, p. 203.) Only a few months later, however, Lloyd George told Lord Riddell that he 'was strongly in favour of a Ministry of Defence to be responsible for the Army, Navy and Air Force' to ensure that 'the efforts of the three services would be co-ordinated and they would not be competing against each other'. See entry in Lord Riddell's *Intimate Diaries of the Peace Conference and After*, for November 9, 1919, pp. 139–140.

(iii) In matters of detail, to interpret the decisions of the Prime Minister and the Cabinet thereupon to the Departments concerned.

(iv) Assisted by the three Chiefs of Staff, as laid down . . . above, to keep the defence situation as a whole constantly under review so as to ensure that defence preparations and plans and the expenditure thereupon are co-ordinated and framed to meet policy, that full information as to the changing naval, military and air situation may always be available to the Committee of Imperial Defence and that resolutions as to the requisite action thereupon may be submitted for its consideration.'

The first Government of Stanley Baldwin approved the Salisbury Report. L. S. Amery, who was First Lord of the Admiralty at that time, suggested the appointment of a Minister of Defence Policy, but this was regarded as 'too theoretical'. In his memoirs, Amery expressed the view that the idea of a Ministry of Defence was un-acceptable 'mainly because it was discussed as an administrative problem'.[25]

The subsequent development of the central organization for defence until 1939, and in particular the work of the Chiefs of Staff Committee, was based on the Salisbury Report, but the plan for a Chairman of the Committee of Imperial Defence other than the Prime Minister was not fully accepted until the mid-1930s. Lord Salisbury himself, as Lord President of the Council, filled the place during the remaining months of the first Baldwin Government, and Lord Haldane combined the duty of presiding over the Committee with his office of Lord Chancellor during the Labour Administration of 1924. Lord Curzon, who was appointed Lord President in Baldwin's Second Administration, was Chairman until his death early in 1925. For the next eleven years, however, no separate Chairman of the Committee was appointed.

The discontinuance of this practice was a confession of failure. There were four reasons why the scheme failed. In the first place, the Chiefs of Staff were never happy in meetings with the Chairman. His presence inhibited frank interchange of views and any genuine wish to compromise: each Chief of Staff 'fought his corner'. All three Chairmen recognized that their presence did more harm than good, and each in turn decided to leave the Chiefs of Staff to meet alone. Even so, if the Chiefs failed to agree among themselves, which was normally only on big questions of principle, they were not prepared to accept the arbitration of anyone except the Prime Minister. The latter alone was able to secure agreement. Secondly, this lack of status on the part of the Chairmen weakened the position of the CID. When the Chairmen presided instead of the Prime Minister, the quality of attendance declined: Ministers, Chiefs of Staff and senior civil servants tended to send their deputies or even their sub-deputies. The recommendations which came from meetings so weakly attended carried little weight, and often the whole business would have to be taken again in Cabinet. In the third place, the Prime Minister and his deputy often disagreed about the handling of the CID and/or the Chiefs of Staff Committee, and this often led to the Prime Minister's taking over himself. All these factors combined to put the Chairmen into an embarrassing and minor position. In addition, a fourth reason for the failure of the system was the double work which it threw on the Secretariat, whose members – and particularly Sir Maurice Hankey, who was Secretary of the Cabinet, the CID and the Chiefs of Staff Committee – had to consult both the Prime Minister and his deputy and had to keep an unnecessarily clumsy and unpredictable machinery running smoothly. Once the separate post of Chairman of the CID was left unfilled the Prime Minister himself presided, as had always been the practice before 1923. One of the Chiefs of Staff – the first being Earl Beatty – henceforward took the chair at their Committee. Under these arrangements the whole machine worked much more easily.

In official circles, therefore, the idea of a Minister of Defence was firmly shelved by the mid-1920s. The Chiefs of Staff Committee had successfully established itself and had apparently vindicated the majority decision of 1923.[j] In July, 1931, the May Committee on National Expenditure took a view of the matter exactly opposite to that expressed by the Geddes Committee a decade before. They claimed that 'no substantial reduction of cost would follow from the creation of a Ministry of National Defence', and feared that 'there would be a serious risk that the efficiency of the Services might be impaired by the alteration of system involved'.[26] Parliamentary and public interest in the question was, however, kept alive by a group of

[j] Sir Maurice Hankey considered that Earl Beatty's Chairmanship 'meant everything in starting the Chiefs of Staff Committee'. When Beatty retired from the office of First Sea Lord in 1927 Sir Maurice wrote that 'Without a really first class Chairman we might have failed, and that would have been disastrous. It might have brought a Ministry of Defence even'.

It is interesting to note in this context that early in 1926 Beatty had privately stated that he personally was 'all for a Minister of Defence in certain conditions'. The conditions were rather drastic, however – the Minister of Defence was to replace the three Service Ministers, whose offices would be abolished, thus leaving 'the Naval, Military and Air Officers chiefs in their own Departments without another Civilian over them'. (Chalmers: *op. cit.*, pp. 380–382, 411.)

MPs among whom the most prominent was, perhaps, Rear-Admiral Sueter, who had introduced a Ministry of Defence (Creation) Bill in 1922, under the ten-minute rule.[27] There were many questions and occasional debates in both Houses after 1925, and the middle way trodden by most of the experts before the Salisbury Committee was rather lost in the discussions, which tended to reflect a complete division of opinion between those who supported a comprehensive Ministry of Defence with functions similar to those outlined by Sir Frederick Sykes or Sir Eric Geddes, and those who denied the practicability of any proposal for a co-ordinating Minister or department. The desirability of having a Ministry of Defence with limited co-ordinating functions was not strongly canvassed, though Lord Haldane pleaded for the reappointment of a Chairman for the Committee of Imperial Defence in 1926, and the same idea was expressed by Mr (now Earl) Attlee in 1929.[28] Much of the public debate revealed an apparent lack of distinction in the minds of the speakers between the possible rôles of a Ministry of Defence as an organ for planning high-level policy and strategy on the one hand, and as an authority for co-ordinating supply and common service administration at a much lower level on the other hand. This theoretical confusion was not to be avoided in official practice, as will be seen.

A second stage in the evolution of a Minister of Defence began with the decision to re-arm in the mid-1930s. It would be out of place in a study of administrative organization to attempt a description and an appraisal of the complex and crowded political history of that decision and its immediate aftermath. It is sufficient to mention here some of the official occurrences which marked the progress from disarmament to rearmament. They included the relaxation of the Ten Year Rule – which assumed that no major war was likely within ten years – in 1933 : the establishment of the official Defence Requirements Committee in the winter of 1933–1934 and of its ministerial counterpart in March, 1934 : the report of the latter Committee in the following August and Sir Maurice Hankey's journey with it to the Dominions at the end of the year : the work of the Royal Commission on the Private Manufacture and Export of War Material in 1935–1936 : and the issue of the first of an annual series of *Statements on Defence* in 1935.

In March, 1936, Sir Thomas Inskip (later Lord Caldecote) was appointed Minister for Co-ordination of Defence. The new appointment was part of a general strengthening of defence organization which also included the firm establishment of the Joint Planning Staff and the beginnings of the Joint Intelligence Sub-Committee.

It has been claimed that the appearance of a 'co-ordinating' Minister was 'impelled' by Neville Chamberlain on administrative grounds after prolonged study of 'the whole structure of Defence':[29] an official historian, however, believes that

'. . . one of the political functions of the office of the Minister for Co-ordination of Defence . . . was to make some concession to the parliamentary demand for a co-ordinated effort in re-armament.'[k]

It is perhaps unnecessary to try to allot precise shares of influence to these and other factors, but there can be little doubt that one of the primary reasons for the experiment was the overriding need to relieve the pressure on the Premier. In Baldwin's words, as there appeared to be 'no likelihood of any diminution in the other demands upon the time and attention of the Prime Minister', it was obvious that 'he must have some special assistance in regard to defence matters'.

The White Paper describing the rôle of the Minister for Co-ordination of Defence 'harked back' in a striking way, in some respects, to the Salisbury Report of 1923.[30] The new Minister was to undertake 'the day-to-day supervision and control . . . of the whole organization and activity of the Committee of Imperial Defence' on the Prime Minister's behalf, and was to preside at meetings of the Committee in the absence of the Premier. Instead of being 'assisted' by the Chiefs of Staff 'to keep the defence situation . . . constantly under review', etc., as was laid down by the Salisbury Committee,[m] the new Minister, who was to be Deputy Chairman of the Committee of Imperial Defence, was to have

'Personal consultation with the Chiefs of Staff together, including a right to convene under his Chairmanship the Chiefs of Staffs Committee whenever he or they thought desirable.'

He was not expected, however, to preside at every meeting of the Chiefs of Staff Committee.

As Lord Salisbury himself was quick to point out, the new Minister was only to be Deputy Chairman rather than Chairman of

---

[k] M. M. Postan: *British War Production*, p. 77. Just before the new appointment was announced, Rear-Admiral Sir Murray Sueter brought in another Ministry of Defence (Creation) Bill which proposed a scheme somewhat similar to that of Sir Eric Geddes in 1923. The Bill was discussed at length and the debate may have helped to hasten the Government's 'concession'. (308 HC Deb. 1295–1378. February 14, 1936.)

[m] Ante, p. 302.

the Committee of Imperial Defence, and he was not, as was provided in 1923, expressly charged with the initiation of defence policy.[31] So far as the making of strategic policy was concerned, the Minister for Co-ordination of Defence was, theoretically, in a weaker position than the Chairmen appointed in 1923 and 1924. The only real innovation in 1936 was that the new Minister was to act as Chairman of the Principal Supply Officers' Committee. This reflected the current preoccupation with the rearmament programme, and in some measure was also a product of that confusion between the strategic and administrative aspects of a Minister of Defence already noted in the parliamentary discussions of the previous decade. The views of Neville Chamberlain (who was then Chancellor of the Exchequer and became Prime Minister in May, 1937) and Mr Churchill are revealing on these matters.

Mr Churchill – who was at that time a back-bench MP – expressed his opinion in a Note on Supply Organization written in June, 1936. The most relevant passage stated that:

'The existing Office of the Minister for Co-ordination of Defence comprises unrelated and wrongly grouped functions. The work of the Minister charged with strategic co-ordination is different, though not in the higher ranges disconnected, from the work of the Minister charged with (a) securing the execution of the existing programmes, and (b) planning British industry to spring quickly into wartime conditions and creating a high control effective for both this and the present purpose.

'The first step therefore is to separate the functions of strategic thought from those of material supply in peace and war, and form the organization to direct this latter process. An harmonious arrangement would be four separate departments – Navy, Army, Air Force and Supply – with the Co-ordinating Minister at the summit of the four having the final voice upon priorities.'[32]

Chamberlain, while admitting the possibility that the Minister for Co-ordination of Defence might be 'so occupied with supply that he has not time to attend to strategy', did not believe that the Minister 'should himself be a strategist' but should 'see that strategical problems are fairly and thoroughly worked out by the strategists'. Chamberlain considered that the most important of those problems was 'the best distribution at the outbreak of a major war of our manpower between the Services and the supply of munitions'. The chief task of the Minister for Co-ordination of Defence was, in short, regarded by the Cabinet as being 'to smooth out priorities' and to 'co-ordinate strategy'.[33]

In the event the fear which Neville Chamberlain recognized but repressed in 1936 was justified. During the years 1936, 1937 and 1938 the Minister for Co-ordination of Defence became more and more engrossed in questions of supply and particularly in the finance and administration of production.[34] To what extent this development was due to the conditions under which the Minister had to work, or to the personality of Sir Thomas Inskip, is a matter which has often been debated.[35] When Lord Chatfield took over early in 1939 he was already convinced that it was 'unsound, even if it was not impracticable, for one Minister to control in detail both the supply of arms and the planning for war', and he decided to apply himself, as far as possible, to the side of his duties 'other than supply'. He was, however, unable to carry this resolution into practice, as he was immediately engaged in the problems of equipping a suddenly enlarged army.[36]

It has been officially conceded that this first peace-time experiment of one Minister co-ordinating the work of others only contributed to the evolution of the idea of a Minister of Defence in a negative sense, in that it showed the inherent weakness of a Minister who had 'no power to take executive action', who was 'not given responsibility to Parliament', and who had no 'jurisdiction over the apportionment of the available resources between the three Services'.[37] Perhaps the two most important factors which denied the Minister for Co-ordination of Defence any chance of putting forward a substantial claim to be the leading representative of defence, however, were his lack of constitutional authority over the Chiefs of Staff and the continued presence of the Service Ministers in the Cabinet.

The Minister for Co-ordination of Defence had no department, and he worked through the Secretariat of the CID. The last development of the inter-war period concerned that Secretariat which, as we have seen, formed one staff with the Cabinet Secretariat. In 1938 Sir Maurice Hankey retired.[n] He had for twenty years been the key 'co-ordinator' at the official level, and the organization over which he presided had as a result of his widespread interests become an office for co-ordinating a very large area of State activity. In addition to being Secretary of the Cabinet, of the CID and of the Chiefs of Staff Committee, he was Clerk to the Privy Council, Joint Secretary of all the Imperial Conferences held in London from 1921 to 1937, and as was mentioned earlier, he was present at most of the major international conferences of the same period. On his retirement the

[n] Sir Maurice Hankey was raised to the peerage in 1939. He served as Minister without Portfolio, then as Chancellor of the Duchy of Lancaster and finally as Paymaster General from September, 1939, until March, 1942.

posts of Secretary of the Cabinet, Secretary of the CID, and Clerk to the Privy Council were separated and filled by different people. Mr Edward (now Lord) Bridges became Secretary of the Cabinet and Colonel (now General Lord) Ismay took over as Secretary of the CID.[o] While this division of responsibility symbolized the weight of work which the Secretariat was now handling it also marked the beginning of a new era in the staffing of the organization. Prior to 1938 the Secretariat had been predominantly military in character and personnel, the military officers being seconded to Whitehall from their respective Services for set periods. Henceforward the civil side of the Secretariat increased and was staffed on the same principle as applied to the military personnel – officials were seconded from departments for periods of service. The introduction of this policy of using career civil servants and thus tapping a wide departmental experience helped to break down any barriers which remained in Whitehall against the Secretariat. The latter came to be regarded within the Civil Service, in fact, as part of the professional team.

If we pause to look back on developments in the central organization for defence between the wars there is an opportunity to make two general points. In the first place, throughout our period the influence of public and parliamentary opinion has been considerable in this context. This is not due only to the inherent importance of defence, but also to the fact that a considerable number of senior ex-Service officers sit in Parliament and keep defence topics to the fore. In an earlier chapter we saw how parliamentary pressure was brought to bear on the Government to establish a Ministry of Supply and in this chapter we have noted the strong advocacy of the idea of a Ministry of Defence. But there are limits to the effectiveness of public and parliamentary opinion on administrative arrangements, however enlightened and far-seeing some aspects of that opinion may be, and this brings up the second general point. It is a fair criticism that prior to 1939 the Services were excessively concerned with their individual status in combined defence programmes, and that this made it difficult to achieve a co-ordinated view. But no organization is efficient unless the people involved believe in it, and until the Second World War the Services did not believe that a Ministry of Defence was needed. The Army and Navy did not impinge on one another very much in their First World War operations and there was no technique of co-ordination between them: and though the appearance of the RAF increased the need for co-ordination, any chance of a really effective Ministry of Defence foundered on the rock of Service independence and on the Service dislike of

[o] The Clerkship to the Privy Council has always been held separately since 1938.

having a 'super' Minister who might interfere with the work of the Chiefs of Staff. How the structure of Cabinet, Minister for Co-ordination of Defence, CID, Chiefs of Staff and Joint Staffs was to be shaped for the conduct of the Second World War must be dealt with in a later section.

THE TREASURY AND THE MACHINERY OF GOVERNMENT 1920–1939

The changes at the Treasury and in the departments concerning establishment matters which were begun in 1920 and completed in the following years were the only changes which have to be recorded in this context between 1918 and 1939. We have made no attempt to appraise the effects of those changes on the relations between the Treasury and the other departments. Nor was there any move during the inter-war period to establish within or without the Treasury any unit to review the whole organization of the central administration. A greater continuity of treatment of 'machinery' questions may well have been brought about by twenty years of continuous service as Permanent Secretary to the Treasury and as Secretary of the Cabinet of two outstanding public servants, Sir Warren Fisher and Sir Maurice Hankey, whose interests ranged widely over the whole field of government and whose concern for efficiency and for fostering team work was intense. But after the radical structural rearrangements of 1916–22 there were only a few major additions to the central administration and not many big transfers of functions between departments until 1939: it was a time of relative structural quiescence. There was, however, a gradual stirring of interest in study of the problems of administration, in part no doubt because of the general increase in the size of governmental administrative units and because of the parallel movement towards large-scale organization in commerce and industry. This interest stimulated a feeling that there were new techniques of large-scale organization and management which should be applied to governmental administration, and one manifestation of such a feeling was a suggestion made to the Royal Commission on the Civil Service in 1931 by Sir Josiah (later Lord) Stamp, a former civil servant and a noted economist who became Chairman of the LMS Railway. Stamp felt that provision should be made for a small section of highly trained staff whose duties should comprise independent criticism and co-ordination of the Machinery of Government. The Commission took up this idea and proposed that such a staff recruited from the Service generally and borne on the Treasury Vote, should undertake a continuous overhaul of the Machinery of Government.[38] Even though it seems clear from the context that the Commission was using 'Machinery of Government' mainly to refer to major questions of the internal organization of departments, the whole episode is significant in the light of much later developments.

THE CABINET: MEMBERSHIP AND COMMITTEES SINCE 1939

Since September, 1939, both the form and method of working of the Cabinet have been very different from what they were prior to that date, and the difference can best be discussed in terms of membership and of the use of committees. So far as membership is concerned the period falls into two parts: from September, 1939, until May, 1945—i.e., the extent of the war in Europe – and from May, 1945, until the present day. In the first of the periods both Prime Ministers – Mr Neville Chamberlain and Mr Winston Churchill – used small Cabinets. The Chamberlain War Cabinet had nine members. For a few months after he became Prime Minister Mr Churchill relied on a five-man Cabinet, but this was increased to six in August, 1940, and to eight in the following October, membership thereafter varying from eight to ten. These last figures need to be used carefully, however, because they include the British Ambassador in Washington (Viscount Halifax) and a Minister Resident in the Middle East. Those two members could only attend meetings when their duties called them—none too frequently – to London. Except for the first six months of Mr Churchill's premiership, when only the Foreign Secretary and (for a shorter part of the period) the Minister of Aircraft Production were departmental members, the members of the War Cabinet were almost equally divided between departmental and non-departmental Ministers.

From May, 1945, onwards Cabinets have been much nearer to the inter-war size, though not as large. The 'Caretaker' Cabinet (May–July, 1945) had sixteen members and its post-war successors have usually had about seventeen or eighteen members. This has meant that no less than fourteen Ministers, apart from the Law Officers and Ministers of State, were left outside the Cabinet in 1950, and no less than ten Ministers, again excluding those mentioned, were left out at the end of 1956 when there were nineteen Ministers in the Cabinet. In fact the modern Cabinet normally includes some fourteen departmental Ministers, most of whom it would be difficult to omit because of the nature of their departments. One or two departmental Ministers may be in the Cabinet at particular periods because of personal political claims, or because the current work of their departments includes something of exceptional political importance such as the introduction of extensive and controversial legislation. As we shall see later, the three Service Ministers have since 1946 been excluded because of the presence of a separate Minister of Defence. Any Minister who is not a member of the Cabinet nonetheless sees its papers and is entitled to attend whenever subjects in which his department is closely concerned are to be discussed. Attendance of this type is frequent, and the Ministers concerned are more likely to be invited than to have to ask permission to attend.

The wartime pattern of Cabinet membership was the response to the same question which had faced the Government in 1914–16: what size of supreme body could best be given the responsibility of taking vital wartime decisions quickly? The 'ideal' size for a 'small' Cabinet of this type had come to be regarded as five to seven, and though for most of the Second World War the membership tended to exceed this slightly, the emphasis was on keeping as close as possible to that desirable nucleus of Ministers. The question to be asked was 'Who should be added to that nucleus?' The post-1945 Cabinet has, however, been the result of applying a very different test. It has been recognized that the great growth of the central administration makes an 'inclusive' Cabinet with all the departmental Ministers far too cumbersome an instrument even for the slower tempo of peace-time government.[p] Consequently the main preoccupation since 1945 has been 'How many and which Ministers can be left out?'

Neither the small wartime Cabinets nor the post-war Cabinets which exclude a number of Ministers would have been possible without the development of the widespread use of standing Cabinet committees backed by the continued and extended services of the Cabinet Secretariat. There is already a substantial literature on the growth and use of standing committees in the Cabinet during and after the Second World War.[39] It is therefore not intended to give a detailed account, but certain general comments may be made. The consideration of practically all governmental action has been divided up among committees of the Cabinet, but it would be wrong to suggest that the distribution of work has followed any permanent, strict or precise pattern based on closely defined 'fields' of activity. It is very unlikely, for instance, that there has ever been a ministerial committee on the whole of external affairs, though there have been

[p] Apart from other arguments against a Cabinet including every Minister, there is the practical point that such a large group could not be conveniently accommodated in the Cabinet Room of 10 Downing Street.

committees on India and Burma, on Commonwealth Affairs, and on the Middle East. There have certainly been committees whose business was with wide but fairly clearly defined fields of action, such as those on Civil Defence, on Economic Policy, on the Socialization of Industry, and on the Social Services. And there have been many committees with rather narrower interests, such as the Service Ministers' Committee and the Committee on Atomic Energy. On the other hand some committees have ranged over an immense area like the Lord President's Committee during the war, which was practically a sub-Cabinet on home affairs: or like the Future Legislation Committee of the Labour Government: or like the Machinery of Government Committee, of which more will be said in a later section of this chapter. What emerges most strongly from examination of the experience of the last fifteen years is that there is no rigidity about the number or scope of standing committees of the Cabinet, but that the committee structure varies with each Government and with the policies being followed or the exigencies of the times.

It is sometimes the case that a high-level official committee of senior civil servants is appointed to work closely with a ministerial committee, both types being loosely referred to as Cabinet committees. The whole system could not work without the expert help of the Cabinet Secretariat. The Secretariat's purely secretarial work for the Cabinet and its committees has not, however, changed in character (though it has naturally greatly changed in amount) since 1939, nor has the constitutional position of the Secretariat been modified: it remains a completely neutral organization. The main interest in the Secretariat in the present context lies in the changes in the arrangement of secretarial work which have followed from developments in the central organization for defence and in the attachment to the Secretariat of certain units of economic intelligence and advice. Those developments are dealt with in later sections, but before turning to them we must consider another aspect of recent developments at Cabinet level – the question of 'co-ordinating' Ministers.

The Prime Minister and three or four of his most important ministerial colleagues, some of whom may have non-departmental or only relatively light departmental duties, like the Lord President, act as Chairmen of the most important standing committees and do a considerable amount of informal co-ordination. There is, however, no formal constitutional authority vested in those Chairmen which makes the departmental Ministers who sit as members of the committees in any way subordinate to them. Whatever practical co-ordinative influence they exercise comes primarily from their personal and political stature, and only secondarily from their position as Chairmen. While it is common knowledge that standing Cabinet committees exist, and while it is sometimes known that a particular committee exists, the composition of current committees and the names of their Chairmen are kept secret. If they were revealed, there would be a danger that MPs would tend to ask questions about policy of the Chairmen of committees rather than of the departmental Ministers who must, constitutionally, bear responsibility. That responsibility might as a result be blurred and the status of the departmental Ministers might be depressed.

The co-ordination of work in large fields of governmental activity has in the main been achieved at the highest levels by this discreet and anonymous machinery of standing Cabinet committees and their Chairmen. Since the late 1930s, however, there have been other attempts to ensure co-ordination by giving to a Minister (either an existing Minister or a Minister specially appointed with a specific title) certain duties of a co-ordinative character which may be laid down in a published document, or at any rate may be announced in Parliament, or even – as in the one case of the present Minister of Defence, whose office dates from 1946 – may be broadly defined in a statute. In general terms it is true that with the single exception of the statutory Minister of Defence, the experiments with this sort of 'co-ordinating' Minister have either been outright failures (as was the Minister for Co-ordination of Defence 1936–40) or have been confined to very special war conditions (the Minister of Production 1942–45) or have been highly controversial and short-lived (as were the appointments of a Secretary of State for the Co-ordination of Transport, Fuel and Power and of the Lord President as co-ordinator of food and agricultural policy in 1951–53). All have certainly roused considerable suspicion because of the difficulty of affixing responsibility for action. If a departmental Minister likes to accept the verdict of an anonymous Cabinet committee with an anonymous Chairman on some question concerning his department, he knows that he personally must take full responsibility before Parliament for what is done by his department in his name. But if a Minister is appointed with a publicly declared responsibility for the Co-ordination of Transport, Fuel and Power, then the positions of that Minister and of the Minister of Transport and the Minister of Fuel and Power are immediately equivocal, unless their respective spheres of action are explicitly laid out in a document. If the departmental Ministers take orders from the 'co-ordinator', are they not still constitutionally responsible for the actions of their departments? And so on. This sort of question was hotly debated during the most recent experiments in 1951–53, and since those experiments were dropped only the Minister of Defence remains in the position of a publicly recognized 'co-ordinating' Minister. The continued existence of the post of Minister of Defence is in part a reflection of the unique character of defence administration, in which a fairly clear line can be drawn between strategical direction, etc., and the administration of fighting forces, but it is also in part due to the fact that the functions of the Minister of Defence – which are defined in broad terms in an Act and which have been defined in more detail in official statements – are clearly different functions from those of the three Service Ministers. Constitutional authority is therefore not confused: the Service Ministers are not subordinate to the Minister of Defence, though the latter sits in the Cabinet and accordingly ranks as a more senior Minister.[q]

THE CENTRAL ORGANIZATION FOR DEFENCE 1939–1956

When war began in September, 1939, the Cabinet and the CID became one body, the War Cabinet. It was served throughout the war by a Secretariat which despite the appointment of separate Secretaries of the Cabinet and of the CID in 1938 remained a single organization. The main development in defence administration during the war was the part played by the Prime Minister after May, 1940. Lord Chatfield, as Minister for Co-ordination of Defence, was from the outset a member of the Chamberlain War Cabinet, but it was soon clear that his presence was an anomaly.

'He could not control the mobilization and direction of the whole resources of the nation for total war, a task which of necessity falls to the Prime Minister, nor had he any specific responsibility for knitting together the activities of the three Services.'

Shortly before the fall of the Chamberlain Government the post was abolished.[40]

When Mr Churchill became Prime Minister in May, 1940, he took the additional title of Minister of Defence, and quickly achieved the necessary concentration of authority and a real unification of policy-making. The tremendous change which took place in the whole character of the supreme direction of the war from that time forward can be attributed to four factors; the unprecedented concentration of power in a single man who had a great knowledge of

q More details about the position of the Minister of Defence are given in the next section.

warfare: the impact of land/sea/air operations on military thinking and the consequent development of a working philosophy of co-operation: the speed and pressure of events which forced inter-Service co-operation: and the growing power of the Chiefs of Staff Committee which met every morning and was served by an extremely efficient secretariat – the Chiefs of Staff organization was, in fact, a dynamic machine which collected power as it went along. The idea of inter-Service co-operation was also stimulated, as the war went on, by the appearance of Supreme Commanders – in the Second World War originally an American technique.[r]

Sir Winston Churchill has given a full account of his conception of the dual office of Prime Minister and Minister of Defence:

'In calling myself, with the King's approval, Minister of Defence I had made no legal or constitutional change. I had been careful not to define my rights and duties. I asked for no special powers either from the Crown or Parliament. It was however understood that I should assume the general direction of the war, subject to the support of the War Cabinet and of the House of Commons. The key change which occurred on my taking over was of course the supervision and direction of the Chiefs of Staffs Committee by a Minister of Defence with undefined powers. As this Minister was also the Prime Minister, he had all the rights inherent in that office, including very wide powers of selection and removal of all professional and political personages. Thus for the first time the Chiefs of Staffs Committee assumed its due and proper place in direct daily contact with the executive head of the Government, and in accord with him had full control over the conduct of the war and the armed forces.'[41]

At Cabinet level Mr Churchill presided over a Cabinet Defence Committee (Operations) which 'examined the military plans prepared by the Chiefs of Staff and the Joint Staffs and took decisions on behalf of the War Cabinet'. The Prime Minister

'... used as his staff the small military Secretariat of the War Cabinet. ... The military head of the Secretariat became his chief Staff Officer and a member of the Chiefs of Staff Committee. The task of the Secretariat was to draft reports and telegrams on behalf of the Chiefs of Staff, to ensure co-ordination and continuity in the activities of the various committees and sub-committees dealing with military questions, and generally to facilitate the smooth running of the inter-Service machine. It was not their duty to act as military advisers to

[r] The joint Allied Staff organization which developed made the British more conscious of the value of their own co-ordinating machinery but did not substantially influence its structure.

the Minister of Defence. It was their duty to procure for him advice from those who would be responsible for action.'[42]

It was not only the Chiefs of Staff Committee which found its status enhanced under the new régime.[s] The Joint Planning Organization grew to large proportions and became very effective. In August, 1940, the Joint Planning Committee, which since its formation in 1927 had worked under and for the Chiefs of Staff, was placed under the personal control of the Prime Minister and Minister of Defence, but this was merely a formal transfer: in fact the Committee continued to work under the Chiefs of Staff, and after the war was again placed under the formal control of the Chiefs.[43] By 1942 the Joint Planning Staff was in three sections dealing respectively with Strategical Planning, Executive Planning and Future Operational Planning: it included among its members not only Service officers, but liaison officers from civil departments such as the Ministry of War Transport, the Ministry of Economic Warfare and the Ministry of Home Security. The Joint Intelligence Staff had expanded similarly.[44]

One result of all these developments was that the Service departments 'rapidly and almost imperceptibly ceased to be responsible for the formulation of strategic plans and the day-to-day conduct of operations'. This happened without any formal change in the position and powers of the three Service Ministers, except that the latter were not members of the War Cabinet.[45]

The story of supply arrangements during the Second World War has already been told, but it is of some interest here to comment on those arrangements as they appear in the context of a discussion about the rôle of a Minister of Defence. Mr Churchill's plan in 1936[t] was to have a Minister of Supply as the fourth member of a quartet of defence Ministers over which the co-ordinating Minister of Defence should preside and have 'the final vote upon priorities'. This plan assumed, however, that one supply department would be set up with comprehensive jurisdiction over the whole field of supply, excepting the construction of warships and the provision of special naval stores. As we know, no such department was ever created: the

---

[s] The Chiefs of Staff Committee was enlarged by the presence as members during the war of General Ismay as the representative of the Prime Minister and Minister of Defence and as the head of the military secretariat of the War Cabinet, and of the Chief of Combined Operations when his special interests were being discussed. A Vice-Chiefs of Staff Committee was also set up to deal with such matters as were delegated to them.

[t] Ante, p. 306.

Admiralty retained the greater part of its supply organization, while the Ministry of Supply and the Ministry of Aircraft Production were primarily concerned with the needs of the Army and Air Force respectively. It was not until 1942 that a Minister of Production appeared, and though he was the nearest approach to the Minister of Supply envisaged by Mr Churchill in 1936, his rôle was essentially co-ordinative rather than executive, and he ranged over an extremely wide economic field.

By the end of the war, therefore, the supreme strategic direction lay firmly in the hands of the Prime Minister and Minister of Defence, working through the Defence (Operations) Committee of the War Cabinet and the Chiefs of Staff Committee which were served by the military section of the War Cabinet Secretariat and by the Joint Planning Organization, while the three Service Ministers played a secondary part. The supply side was equally subject to the Prime Minister and Minister of Defence, but there was in addition a co-ordinating Minister of Production who dealt with three supply departments, one Service and two civil.

The immediate problem after 1945 was how to adapt this highly effective organization to peace-time conditions. For over a year after the end of the war in Europe the Service Ministers were again members of the Cabinet while the Prime Minister exercised overall responsibility for defence. Throughout the first months of the Labour Government Mr Attlee presided over a small committee which studied the future pattern of the central organization. During this interim period the Ministry of Production disappeared and the Ministries of Supply and Aircraft Production were combined. Finally, at the end of 1946 a new scheme was announced, whose basic feature was the establishment of a statutory Ministry of Defence.[u] While some modifications have been made to the scheme since its inception, it remains basically the same at the present time.

It has been accepted since the Second World War that it is possible to separate the sphere of strategic policy from the administration of the Services. Even so it is recognized that strategy cannot be separated from the major decisions to be made in the field of supply—long-term allocation of materials and the choice of weapons

[u] The three Service Ministers came back into the Cabinet when the 'Caretaker' Government took office in May, 1945. They left the Cabinet in October, 1946, when it was announced that Mr A. V. Alexander (now Viscount Alexander of Hillsborough) was to be the first Minister of Defence. Two months were to elapse, however, before the proposals received statutory authority. Until then Mr Alexander was appointed Minister without Portfolio. He became Minister of Defence when the Ministry of Defence Act was passed on December 19, 1946. Until then Mr Attlee retained the title of Prime Minister and Minister of Defence.

are to a large degree inherently strategic. It is, in fact, necessary to have a Ministry of Defence even if there is no Ministry of Supply, and in the latter case the work of the Ministry of Defence would be much greater than it is at present. It is in the acceptance by the Services of the need of a Ministry of Defence that the strength of the present structure lies. That acceptance has been not only the result of a realization of the nature of modern warfare and of the needs of the British defence system alone, but has also been due to the appearance in the years since 1945 of the North Atlantic Treaty Organization and the Brussels Treaty which make it essential to have one department which can speak for all the Services in the international field. Moreover, as we shall see, the rôle of the Ministry of Defence as it has developed hitherto has been sufficiently specialized, and the constitutional position of the Minister has been sufficiently fluid, to make their arrival palatable to the long-entrenched Service departments.

In considering the possibilities of defence organization after 1945 the first idea to be firmly discarded was that of having a combined 'Ministry of Defence and Armed Forces'. Such a department was – and still is – ruled out because of the size of the job which it would have to do. A more realistic controversy at the end of the Second World War was over the question of whether the Ministry of Defence should concern itself with common services as well as with overall strategy. The decision to confine the Ministry to matters of overall strategy avoided the possibility of the department becoming unwieldy and at the same time avoided arousing the hostility of the Services.

The three Service Ministries are prerogative departments, but the Minister of Defence and his department were given a statutory basis in the Ministry of Defence Act, 1946. The Act did not contain any detailed specification of the Minister's duties, but stated that

'It shall be lawful for His Majesty to appoint a Minister of Defence ... who shall be in charge of the formulation and general application of a unified policy relating to the armed forces of the Crown as a whole and their requirements.'

The full extent of the Minister's jurisdiction was made clear in a White Paper – *Central Organization for Defence* – issued in December, 1946. The Minister's functions as laid out in that paper included 'the apportionment, in broad outline, of available resources between the three Services in accordance with the strategic policy laid down by the Defence Committee' (of the Cabinet) and 'the framing of general policy to govern research and development, and the correlation of production programmes'. He was also made responsible for the settlement of 'questions of general administration on which a common policy for the three Services is desirable' and for the supervision of certain inter-Service organs such as the Combined Operations Headquarters, the Joint Intelligence Bureau and the Imperial Defence College.[46] In 1955 the authority and influence of the Minister of Defence were strengthened when arrangements were made for him to co-ordinate 'planning and training for the joint action of civil and military forces in home defence', and when his most important responsibility for the apportionment of available resources between the three Services was extended 'to a responsibility for seeing that the composition and balance of forces within individual services meets the strategic policy laid down by the Defence Committee'.[47] This extension of the Minister's jurisdiction did not need statutory implementation.

The post of Minister of Defence attracts a top-ranking political figure because it carries with it a seat in the Cabinet, whereas the Service Ministers are not in the Cabinet. A new body has in fact evolved since 1946 – the Service Ministers' Committee – of which the Minister of Defence is Chairman. The Committee meets two or three times a month, and is recognized as an integral part of the central organization for defence. In addition to this institutionalized liaison with each other and with the Minister of Defence, the Service Ministers – like any other departmental Ministers who are not Cabinet members – may be invited to attend meetings of the Cabinet when matters directly concerning their departments are being discussed. Constitutionally the Minister of Defence cannot direct a Service Minister, but there is now an expectation that disputes should be referred to the Minister of Defence and there is some presumption in view of his status that his decisions should be accepted. He acts as Deputy Chairman of the Defence Committee of the Cabinet, which was continued after the war when the very big decision was taken not to revive the CID – the Prime Minister is Chairman of the Committee and has the supreme responsibility for defence.

The collective responsibility of the Chiefs of Staff before the war was to the CID. After the Minister of Defence was appointed that responsibility was made to the Government through the Minister. The latter would not suppress the collective advice of the Chiefs of Staff if he disagreed with it, and the Chiefs could therefore appeal to the Government against his decisions. Until 1955 the Chiefs of Staff retained the practice of having one of their own members take the Chair at meetings, but in that year there appeared on the scene a permanent Chairman additional to the three Chiefs, who has taken up on the professional plane a position which would appear to be the counterpart of the Minister of Defence at ministerial level. The first Chairman to be appointed was the senior Chief of Staff, Marshal of the Royal Air Force Sir William Dixon. The new arrangement does not prevent an individual Chief of Staff from tendering his personal advice should he differ from his colleagues. The reason for the new appointment was the 'indisputable' need to have someone with high military authority to speak for all three Services at international organizations and meetings and who would be free to do the extensive travelling necessary to fulfil this increasingly pressing international job.[48] [uu]

The decision to have a separate Ministry of Defence in 1946 involved splitting the organization built up under the CID and continued throughout the war as part of the Secretariat of the War Cabinet. The CID had covered both military and civil matters, and the potential loss of this close link caused the greatest hesitation as to whether the Committee should not be revived. Once the die was cast, however, there was the greatest concern to see what could be done to avoid any separation of military and civil planning for defence.

The Ministry of Defence was designed as a complete but small

[uu] On the formation of a new Government by Mr Macmillan in January, 1957, the powers of the Minister of Defence were extended. The Prime Minister made the following statement in the House of Commons in reply to Questions on January 24:

'The Service Departments and the Ministry of Supply will continue as separate Departments of State. I have, however, taken steps to define more precisely the functions of the Minister of Defence in relation to them.

'Under the Ministry of Defence Act, 1946, the Minister of Defence is responsible for the formulation and general application of a unified policy relating to the Armed Forces of the Crown as a whole and their requirements. I have entrusted the Minister of Defence with the task of formulating, in the light of present strategic needs, a defence policy which will secure a substantial reduction in expenditure and in manpower, and to prepare a plan for reshaping and reorganizing the Armed Forces in accordance therewith.

'Subject as necessary to consultation with the Cabinet and Defence Committee, and with the Treasury on matters of finance, the Minister will have authority to give decisions on all matters of policy affecting the size, shape, organization and disposition of the Armed Forces, their equipment and supply (including defence research and development) and their pay and conditions of service. He will similarly have power of decision on any matters of Service administration or appointments which, in his opinion, are of special importance.

'The Minister of Defence will henceforward have a Chief of Staff, responsible to him in that capacity, who will be the Chairman of the Chiefs of Staff Committee. Marshal of the Royal Air Force Sir William Dickson has been appointed to be the Minister's Chief of Staff.

'The corporate responsibility of the Chiefs of Staff as the professional military advisers of the Government will remain unchanged.'

department – some might call it a large Private Office – organized functionally to assist the Minister in carrying out his detailed responsibilities, which include dealing with the increasing number of problems associated with this country's participation in international defence organizations. The Ministry took over all the purely military aspects of war organization, but the Defence Committee continued to handle those matters which 'engage the collective responsibility of the Government as a whole', namely

'the organization for national defence in its broader aspect, including both current questions of high policy in the sphere of defence, and also the preparation of plans over the whole field of Government activity, both civil and military, for mobilizing the entire resources of the nation in a major war.'[49]

The committees and sub-committees concerned, under the aegis of the Defence Committee, with those broad issues of defence planning are still, therefore, served by a small military section of the Cabinet Secretariat. Most of the military side of what used to be the War Cabinet Secretariat has, however, become part of the Ministry of Defence. So too have the Secretariats of the Joint Planning Staff and of the Joint Intelligence Committee.

Both force of events and the determination of those concerned have ensured that there has been no dangerous separation between the military and civil aspects of defence planning. The probable nature of future war – especially the use of nuclear weapons and the problems of civil defence – have forced an increasingly close interlocking between military and civil administration. Close liaison and understanding between military and civil departments are encouraged by having the Secretary of the Cabinet act as Secretary of the Defence Committee: by making the Chief Staff Officer of the Ministry of Defence the Deputy Secretary of the Cabinet: by the tendency of the Chiefs of Staff to invite to their meetings representatives of the civil departments concerned: and by the constant interchange at the Ministry of Defence of both military and Civil Service staff with the Service departments and occasionally with other departments, which helps to ensure a common outlook on defence questions.

CENTRAL MACHINERY FOR ECONOMIC INTELLIGENCE AND ADVICE 1922–1955

We must now turn back to the early 1920s and trace the development since then of a service of economic intelligence and advice. We saw

L

a little earlier how the first attempt to establish such a service at the Board of Trade had petered out by the end of 1922, leaving only the Chief Economic Adviser to H.M. Government attached to the Board as an indication that the idea of looking at the economy as a whole with an expert eye was not entirely abandoned. Within two years the idea was reinforced by no less a Minister than the Lord Chancellor in the first Labour Government – Lord Haldane. Haldane had been keen in 1918 to see a special department created to be responsible for undertaking research, but he had since modified his views and now sought a more flexible method of co-ordinating all 'civil' research – economic and scientific. He wanted to introduce a system of committees akin to that which already existed for defence planning, with a high-level committee at the apex parallel to the CID. His plans were not put into effect during his period of office, partly because of Ramsay MacDonald's lack of interest, but on the return of the Conservatives Lord Balfour championed the scheme, which had Civil Service support, and in June, 1925, it came into operation.[50] A Treasury Minute authorized the appointment of a standing committee of the Cabinet to be known as the Committee of Civil Research,

'. . . charged with the duty of giving connected forethought from a central standpoint to the development of economic, scientific and statistical research in relation to civil policy and administration. . . .'[51]

It was intended that the economic side of the work of the Committee should be linked with the action of the Board of Trade through the medium of the Chief Economic Adviser.[52] In 1930 the Committee was replaced by an Economic Advisory Council whose Chairman was the Prime Minister and whose functions were:

'(i) To advise His Majesty's Government in economic matters.

(ii) To make continuous study of developments in trade and industry and in the use of national and imperial resources, of the effect of legislation and fiscal policy at home and abroad, and of all aspects of national, imperial and international economy with a bearing on the prosperity of the country.'[53]

Both the Committee and the Council were similar to the CID in that they were standing bodies attached to the Cabinet with a membership which included not only Ministers but officials and experts as well: in that their work was advisory, not administrative or executive: and in that they both used sub-committees. A few reports on economic and scientific subjects made by sub-committees were published, but the bulk of the work of the Committee and

Council was confidential. The Council never met in full session after the summer of 1931 and was wound up on the outbreak of war in 1939.[54] Its work was in fact carried on by two standing committees – one on Economic Information and the other on Scientific Research. The Committee on Economic Information, which was served by the Cabinet Secretariat and by a small group of professional economists, had as its Chairman Sir Josiah Stamp, who was raised to the peerage in 1938. It was designed 'to supervise the preparation of periodic reports on the economic situation and to advise as to the continuous study of economic development'. The committee continued its work up to the beginning of the war, and was notable as 'the first body at the centre of Government consisting preponderantly of economists and concerned exclusively with economic advice'.[55]

Though these experiments in organizing a service of economic intelligence at the centre of government did have some influence on administrative thought and action, and though the experience gained was by no means wasted, as the developments after 1939 were to prove, it is now generally conceded that progress in the inter-war years was disappointing. It has been suggested that the main reasons for the comparative ineffectiveness of the Committee of Civil Research and the Economic Advisory Council were the separation of economic advisers from those engaged in day-to-day administration, the lack of agreement among economists 'on any course of action which could materially diminish the burden of unemployment', and the belief that Britain's economic troubles were 'largely due to international conditions over which we had little control'.[56]

The post of Chief Economic Adviser to H.M. Government and the Committee on Economic Information of the Economic Advisory Council were the only special institutions providing high-level economic intelligence and advice to the Government in the early part of 1939, and both disappeared during that year. It was another venture associated with the name of Stamp, however, which formed the immediate starting point for the development of new organs of economic advice. That venture was the Survey of Financial and Economic Plans (the 'Stamp Survey') undertaken at the invitation of the Government by Stamp and two other eminent economists in the summer of 1939. A month after the outbreak of war an interdepartmental committee on economic co-ordination was appointed to continue under Stamp the work of the Survey, and a few weeks later a ministerial Economic Policy Committee was superimposed on it.

We are not concerned to trace the complex history of the standing committees of the Cabinet which have dealt with economic policy since 1939. Only the briefest outline is given here in order to provide a proper perspective for the developments which concerned individual Ministers and the establishment of new official units. From the appointment of the ministerial Economic Policy Committee in the first months of the war the Cabinet has never been without some such committee with a vital and far-reaching jurisdiction in economic matters, while lesser committees on narrower economic topics have been numerous. Until May, 1940, however, the committees operated very much under the eye of the Treasury, whose prior interest in economic policy was at that time generally conceded. The political upheaval which resulted in the fall of the Chamberlain Government, and the realization of the full economic implications of the war, upset the sense of values hitherto accepted about the rôle of the Treasury in economic matters. The shift in emphasis away from money to real resources as a basis for major decisions, the arrival in the Cabinet of Labour Ministers, and to some extent the reaction which set in against the men and measures of the previous Administration, weakened the Treasury's position and afforded an opportunity for the initiative and influence in economic affairs to pass to the committees of the Cabinet.[v] After several months of rather uncertain adjustments, the Lord President's Committee emerged as the major authority, and it remained so not merely throughout the war but continued under the Labour Government until 1947, when the Lord President (at that time Mr Herbert Morrison) relinquished his economic responsibilities.[w] Henceforward, as will be seen later, after a short interlude the Chancellor of the Exchequer became the dominant Minister in the economic field and except when the Prime Minister himself has presided, he has presumably taken the Chair at the most important standing committee on economic policy.

We must now return to 1939 and trace the development of a service of professional economic intelligence and advice. A small number of professional economists had served the Economic Advisory Council, but in November, 1939, the first step in the establishment of a comprehensive expert staff was taken with the creation of a Central Economic Information Service – a body of

[v] The Chancellor of the Exchequer was left out of the Cabinet between May and October, 1940, and between February, 1942, and September, 1943.

[w] The great prestige of the Lord President's Committee was built up while Sir John Anderson was Lord President, from October, 1940, until September, 1943. The Committee dealt not only with economic questions but ranged widely over the whole of domestic administration. In September, 1943, Sir John Anderson went to the Treasury: he was succeeded as Lord President by Mr Attlee (September, 1943, to May, 1945). Lord Woolton (May, 1945, to July, 1945) gave place in turn to Mr Herbert Morrison.

statisticians and economists recruited temporarily from the universities to work under the directions of the official 'Stamp' Committee. It was by then becoming clear that the scope of the Economic Policy Committee was going to be much wider than the interests of the Treasury, and Sir Horace Wilson's informal suggestion that the Central Economic Information Service would be better placed in the Cabinet Office than in the Treasury was readily taken. As it turned out, a move which brought the Cabinet Office and the Treasury into the same building, thereby facilitating intimate and informal contact between the economists and the Treasury officials, proved to be most important.

The rise of the Lord President's Committee to the first place in economic matters was marked by the dissolution of the 'Stamp' Committee in January, 1941, and the simultaneous division of the Central Economic Information Service into two parts. One part became the Central Statistical Office and the other the Economic Section: like their parent body, they were attached to the Cabinet Secretariat. The Central Statistical Office was from the start a 'common service' unit, but the Economic Section, while its advice was formally available to all Ministers, in practice became an advisory body to the Lord President and his Committee.

In addition to these new units which at any rate formally served the Cabinet as a whole, there also grew up a small Prime Minister's Statistical Section which Mr Churchill had brought with him from the Admiralty. A large part of the Section's work was to assist the Prime Minister's personal adviser, Professor Lindemann, who was raised to the peerage and took the title of Lord Cherwell in July, 1941, and was appointed Paymaster-General in December, 1942. The section 'was concerned not merely with the collection and presentation of statistics but with the conclusions to be drawn from them, and it also made frequent recommendations on general economic policy'. . . . 'There is no doubt that the Section did develop views – or prejudices.'[57] As we shall see, this Statistical Section was to reappear in Mr Churchill's second Administration, but it is worth noting here that it had little in common with the Garden Suburb of Lloyd George. Lord Cherwell was a single adviser who had a staff of his own and who later became a Minister: but the Garden Suburb was a group of people all acting as advisers to the Prime Minister.

By 1942 there had thus evolved an effective system of providing high-level intelligence and advice on which decisions about economic policy could be taken by an equally effective structure of Cabinet committees. The war had, in fact, led to the employment of economists and statisticians on a notable scale and had encouraged the application of economic theory and expertise to the solution of problems of government. All this had been achieved in order to facilitate the waging of war, but in fact it included sufficient institutional innovations to cope with the post-war economic order which the Government endorsed and envisaged in their statement on *Employment Policy* in 1944.[58] In accepting the Keynesian theses, the main political parties shared a willingness to try a new course, though not without some sensible misgivings.

'In submitting proposals for an extension of State control over the volume of employment, the Government recognize that they are entering a field where theory can be applied to practical issues with confidence and certainty only as experience accumulates and experiment extends over untried ground. Not long ago, the ideas embodied in the present proposals were unfamiliar to the general public and the subject of controversy among economists. Today the conception of an expansionist economy and the broad principles governing its growth are widely accepted by men of affairs as well as by technical experts in all the great industrial countries. But the whole of the measures here proposed have never yet been systematically applied as part of the official economic policy of any Government. In these matters we shall be pioneers. We must determine, therefore, to learn from experience; to invent and improve the instruments of our new policy as we move forward to its goal. And it would be no less foolish to ignore, than to be dismayed by, the certainty that unsuspected obstacles will emerge in practice.'

The administrative implications of the new policy can be divided simply into two sections – the short and long term. Over the short term it was obvious that the immediate post-war years would be a time of continued shortages, and that to cope successfully with them a large part of the existing wartime control machinery would have to stay. The long-term aspects of ensuring full employment demanded a statistical organization at least as, if not more extensive than, the wartime machinery: a service of high-level economic advice: and a system of regulating capital investment. Most if not all of the machinery was in fact already in existence. So long as physical controls such as direction of labour and rationing of commodities were needed, they had to be exercised by executive departments. The Central Statistical Office was already a comprehensive unit. The Economic Section offered expert high-level advice: the Treasury, the Capital Issues Committee, and the controls over building, machinery, etc., dealt with investment. The White Paper of 1944 said very little about 'the instruments of our new policy'. Its only reference in this connection was to the Government's intention 'to establish on a permanent basis a small central staff qualified to measure and analyse economic trends and submit appreciations of them to the Ministers concerned'. It is mainly with the location of that 'small central staff' that the rest of this section is concerned. The Central Statistical Office has never posed any problem from this point of view, and in fact it has remained in the Cabinet Office.

As we have seen, the Labour Government at first kept the Lord President's Committee as the main organ of economic co-ordination. Mr Attlee was perhaps persuaded to retain the same organization (over which he had himself presided as Lord President from September, 1943, until May, 1945) in part because of the wide range of the Lord President's functions and perhaps to some extent because of personal considerations. There was some doubt in Whitehall as to the advisability of dividing responsibility in peace-time for economic affairs between the Chancellor of the Exchequer, who was inevitably deeply involved, and another Minister.* Given the existence of that other Minister – the Lord President – however, there was a strong case for keeping the Economic Section mainly for his use in the Cabinet Office, where it could also serve other non-departmental Ministers who otherwise might have demanded their own economic advisory staffs. The only major alterations in 1945 occurred when the Labour Government took office in July–August. The Prime Minister's Statistical Section was disbanded and a group of important inter-departmental committees were established at the official level to deal with various aspects of economic policy under the general guidance of a Steering Committee of which the Permanent Secretary to the Treasury was Chairman.

The tasks which faced the organization of economic intelligence and advice immediately after the end of the war were tasks of economic reconversion, and they were not complicated by problems of heavy unemployment. No changes were made in the organization until two violent setbacks revealed inadequacies in the control of the economy and focused attention on the need for a new approach. The immediate post-war era came to an end in 1947, first with the fuel crisis of the early months and then with the crisis over sterling convertibility in July-August. In September, Mr Herbert Morrison, while remaining Lord President, was succeeded as the Minister generally responsible for economic policy by Sir Stafford Cripps,

x The Treasury had begun to regain its old position from the day in September, 1943, when Sir John Anderson became Chancellor of the Exchequer, and its progress back to pre-war status was made easier towards the end of the war as more orthodox financial and economic considerations re-asserted themselves.

who moved from the Board of Trade to a new post of Minister for Economic Affairs. At Cabinet level the Lord President's Committee was replaced as the main economic committee by an Economic Policy Committee over which the Prime Minister presided, while Sir Stafford Cripps became Chairman of a new Production Committee.

The forthcoming establishment of new official machinery was announced in March, 1947, and in June–July an Economic Planning Board – a high-level advisory body – an Economic Planning Staff under a Chief Planning Officer, and an Economic Information Unit were established.[y] They were at first attached to the Lord President, but when Sir Stafford Cripps was appointed Minister for Economic Affairs he took them over, and worked through them and through the Economic Section and the Central Statistical Office. He also took from the Board of Trade responsibility for the Regional Boards for Industry. These Boards were the successors to those set up during the war which had executive functions to stimulate production in the engineering trades. They had passed from the Ministry of Supply to the Ministry of Labour and then to the Ministry of Production: in 1945 they had been placed under the Board of Trade, their jurisdiction had been extended to all industry, and they had been converted into advisory bodies.

Thus in September, 1947, Sir Stafford Cripps was made explicitly responsible for 'Economic Affairs' and while only having a very small personal staff, he had at his disposal a rather diffuse group of highly specialized units of economic intelligence and advice. It was obvious that the relations between Sir Stafford and the Treasury would be crucial. In the control of the national economy the weapons of financial manipulation are vital, but they form only one method of control, and a method which must be administered by a specialized unit. A Minister who was responsible for the whole of the economy might with some justice claim the right to direct all methods of control, including those of a purely financial character. If the Minister for Economic Affairs was not to be in a position to tell the Chancellor of the Exchequer how to use his financial powers, it was essential that the two Ministers should work in the closest harmony.

The experiment of having a Minister for Economic Affairs and a Minister of Finance was never put to the test. The new arrangements had scarcely been inaugurated when the Chancellor of the Exchequer, Mr Dalton, resigned. Sir Stafford Cripps became Chancellor of the Exchequer and the duties and responsibilities of the post of Minister

---

[y] The Economic Planning Staff was not a body of economists, but a group of officials whose job was to co-ordinate the economic plans of the executive departments.

for Economic Affairs were taken by Sir Stafford to the Treasury. In November, 1947, therefore, the Chancellor of the Exchequer became, in fact, Minister of Finance and Economic Affairs, and succeeding holders of the office have inherited the dual mantle. Sir Stafford Cripps brought to the Treasury the Economic Planning Staff, the Regional Boards and the Economic Information Unit. The latter soon took over part of the Overseas Information Division of the Board of Trade and was later renamed the Treasury Information Division. But the central unit of expert economic advice – the Economic Section – remained separate from the Treasury at the Cabinet Office for another six years. That it was not immediately placed in the Treasury was in part due to some doubt as to whether a single Minister would be able to carry the tremendous load involved in assuming responsibility for economic co-ordination as well as for Treasury business at a time when physical economic controls were still being widely used. At the same time there was some fear that if the Economic Section was taken into the Treasury its independent judgment and advice would be lost to other departments and its staff would have to be fitted into the normal Treasury hierarchy.

When the rearranged and extended organization settled down in the winter of 1947–1948, it was not long before the Economic Section was working closely – ever more closely – with the Chief Planning Officer and his Economic Planning Staff. The Economic Section gradually lost its character as a separate advisory body serving the Cabinet as a whole, and became for all practical purposes part of the establishment of the Chancellor of the Exchequer. Meanwhile the chance of having another Minister for Economic Affairs faded and disappeared altogether after the Conservatives came into power at the end of 1951 and proceeded to discard most of the physical economic controls which remained. The load on the Chancellor of the Exchequer, though still great, had shrunk substantially. One result of the relaxation of physical controls was the retransfer of responsibility for the Regional Boards for Industry from the Treasury to the Board of Trade. The Boards do not unequivocally fit into the work of any department: the arrangement whereby the Treasury had responsibility for them after 1947 was never very satisfactory, and the Board of Trade, which took them over in 1952, had perhaps the best claim because it already had a regional organization and could therefore conveniently take on the staffing of the Boards. The most important outcome of the two developments outlined earlier in this paragraph, however, was the decision to move the Economic Section into the Treasury. This took place in the autumn of 1953. The Economic Planning Staff and the Economic Section came within the purview of a newly appointed Deputy to the Permanent Secretary to the Treasury, who also became Chairman of the Economic Planning Board. The Chief Planning Officer resigned and his post was abolished, but the head of the Economic Section, a one-time professional economist, became Chief Economic Adviser to H.M. Government and in fact the Chancellor of the Exchequer's intimate adviser on economic matters. These changes completed the process of bringing all the machinery for helping in the making of economic policy under the hand of one Minister which had begun with Sir Stafford Cripps's appointment as Chancellor of the Exchequer in 1947.

When Mr Churchill became Prime Minister for the second time in November, 1951, he appointed Lord Cherwell to his old post of Paymaster-General and re-established the Statistical Section. Lord Cherwell, who was on temporary leave of absence from his Chair at Oxford, resigned and the Section broke up two years later, but the episode is significant in so far as it was the first time, except when the country has been at war, that a Prime Minister has provided himself with an advisory body (as opposed to a single adviser) quite separate from the Treasury, from the Cabinet Secretariat and from any of his departmental colleagues.

THE LORD PRESIDENT AND SCIENTIFIC POLICY

The growth of governmental participation in scientific research and the special position of the Lord President *vis-à-vis* the five special scientific authorities have been described in Chapter VII. As those authorities developed, and as the research interests of administrative departments grew, the need to prevent overlapping of effort became more pressing and, together with the wider importance of scientific affairs, led eventually to the concept of a definite governmental policy towards scientific research. Until the Second World War, however, those developments were very limited, and the Lord President, despite his special responsibility for the Research Councils, was only slightly in evidence as a scientific co-ordinator. There were informal working contacts between and among the Research Councils and the administrative departments from the earliest days. The first formal co-ordinating machinery dated from 1921, when the Cabinet set up a quarterly conference consisting of representatives of the various governmental and some outside research organizations, to whom representatives of the Dominions and Colonies were added later. We have already seen how in 1925 a Standing

Committee of the Cabinet – the Committee of Civil Research—was established 'to provide in the most flexible manner for the timely discussion of problems that may be common to more than one field of applied science, common to more than one administrative Department, or common again to more than one part of the Kingdom or Empire'.[59] When the Committee was replaced by the Economic Advisory Council in 1930 the scientific side of the Council's work was in practice supervised by a Standing Committee on Scientific Research which apparently met regularly as late as 1938. In the main, the actual scientific work of both the Committee of Civil Research and the Economic Advisory Council was promoted through *ad hoc* sub-committees, several of whose reports were published. There is, however, no published account of the co-ordination of scientific work by the Committee of Civil Research and the Economic Advisory Council: it is probably reasonable to suppose that such co-ordination was unassuming, by no means extensive, and basically similar in character to normal inter-departmental consultation.

As the First World War had stimulated the development of scientific research under governmental auspices, the Second World War saw both a great extension of the range of governmental concern with scientific inquiry and the real beginnings of high-level co-ordination of that inquiry. A Scientific Advisory Committee of the Cabinet was set up in 1940 with the Lord President as Chairman 'with the object of providing the Government with the best scientific advice available, and of co-ordinating defence and civil research for the successful prosecution of the war'.[60] In the following year the Lord President was made personally responsible for the development of research into the problems of nuclear fission, though he relinquished it – temporarily as it turned out – to the Ministry of Supply at the end of 1945. By the end of the war the whole status of the scientist in government had been very notably raised, the range of governmental participation in research was greater than ever before, the Lord President was recognized as the Minister with the major responsibility for scientific policy, and the need for continuing and extending the machinery of supervision and co-ordination was obvious. In September, 1945, scientists in government establishments were given improved conditions of employment and were brought together into a Scientific Civil Service with centralized recruitment through the Civil Service Commission. At the beginning of 1947 two new advisory bodies took the place of the wartime Scientific Advisory Committee of the Cabinet, and the basic framework of the post-war system was complete.

The new bodies set up in 1947 were the Advisory Council on

Scientific Policy and the Defence Research Policy Committee. The Council, whose members have been drawn from the universities, industry and government, has as its terms of reference 'To advise the Lord President of the Council in the exercise of his responsibility for the formulation of Government scientific policy'. The Committee is associated with the Ministry of Defence and links the scientific organization of the three Service Departments. One man served as Chairman of both bodies until March, 1952, but thereafter there have been separate Chairmen. The Defence Research Policy Committee's work must obviously be largely secret in nature, and the Committee publishes no report, but the Advisory Council reports annually to the Lord President and the reports are issued as Command papers. The Council ranges widely over the whole field of scientific inquiry, and has dealt – sometimes through sub-committees – with such matters as the broad organization of government research, the problems of scientific manpower, overseas scientific relations, higher technological education, how to narrow the gap between scientific discovery and industrial output, libraries and information services, and so on. On its recommendation Scientific Advisers were appointed in some of the departments which undertake research.

Thus the Lord President, in addition to his responsibilities for the five major scientific organizations, is well advised generally on scientific matters. Since he again became the Minister primarily responsible for work on atomic energy in January, 1954, he also 'presides over the Cabinet Committee on Atomic Energy'. This Committee

'consists of those Ministers who have a share of responsibility in the activities of the [Atomic Energy] Authority and it probably includes the Chancellor of the Exchequer, the Foreign Secretary, the Secretary of State for Commonwealth Relations, and the Ministers of Fuel and Power and of Defence. They are assisted by an Official Committee composed of high civil servants drawn from their departments. These two committees, at their different levels, discuss what shall be required of the Authority, the policy of the various departments concerned, and the co-ordination of their work.'[61]

To provide the Lord President with the official assistance which he needs in dealing with this wide range of scientific activity there is an Office of the Lord President, comprising a small personal scientific secretariat, and an Atomic Energy Office. These establishments are quite separate from the Privy Council Office, which deals with the general and non-scientific work of the Privy Council.[yy]

yy On April 2, 1957, the Lord President's powers re atomic energy were transferred to the Prime Minister. See footnote *f*, p.273.

THE TREASURY AND THE MACHINERY OF GOVERNMENT
1939–1955

The Second World War, like the First, stimulated a good deal of official and unofficial discussion about the organization of the Civil Service and about how it should be improved in the future. So far as the Treasury was concerned, the ferment of ideas led to three major innovations. The first was the beginning of organized training for civil servants after their first appointment. The Assheton Committee on the Training of Civil Servants reported in 1944,[62] and in the following year a Training and Education Division was set up in the Treasury with a central supervisory responsibility for all post-entry training and education. At the same time, departmental Training Branches were instituted under their own training officers. More spectacular has been the growth of 'Organization and Methods'. The handful of Treasury Investigating Officers who had been originally appointed in 1919 blossomed into a sizeable O & M Division during the Second World War. This was no doubt the result of the stimulus given by the great increase of work and by realization of the possibilities of ensuring, by careful inquiry into questions of organization, a higher and more economic standard of governmental administration. Similar staffs were appointed in other departments, and O & M is now a recognized part of the government service. As in the case of training, the Treasury Division, whilst not having any specific power to direct the activities of departmental O & M Divisions, has none the less developed a *primus inter pares* status.

The third innovation is the one which has the greatest relevance to this study. We have seen that up to 1939 no Minister, official or institution had any formal responsibility for keeping the distribution of functions among departments under constant review, and that the only inquiries into such distribution had been made on an *ad hoc* basis by an official Treasury committee in 1916 and by the Haldane Committee on the Machinery of Government in 1917–1918. The first public sign of a renewal of interest in what we may call henceforward 'review of the Machinery of Government' after 1939 was a Report from the Select Committee on National Expenditure in October, 1942, on the *Organization and Control of the Civil Service*,[63] which developed the suggestion made by the Royal Commission on the Civil Service in 1931[z] and proposed that in future 'continuous attention should be directed to the problem of detecting and preventing overlapping, duplication and lack of co-ordination either

[z] Ante, pp. 309–10.

within a single Department or between two or more Departments'. The Committee was convinced that the time was near when 'the problem of the distribution of Government services will have to be comprehensively tackled'. While the Committee's Report no doubt reflected a significant and widespread feeling, not unusual in time of war, that things could have been done better in the past and ought to be done better in the future, it is unlikely that the Report itself was in any way directly responsible for what the Government actually did in this context. The rapid growth of the central administration after the outbreak of war soon brought up the question of what reorganization would be needed when the war was over. Sir Stafford Cripps was keen to see another 'Haldane' inquiry launched. The Cabinet agreed with the need for such an inquiry but felt that the necessary work could be more profitably entrusted to an entirely internal body. A strong ministerial Cabinet Committee on the Machinery of Government was therefore appointed in 1942, and it had the help of a high-powered official committee.

The appointment of the Machinery of Government Committee marked the beginning of a period which, in retrospect, can be divided into four phases. The first phase lasted from 1942 until the end of the war. During those years the ministerial Committee met frequently and was mainly concerned with finding solutions to the problems which would arise during the reconstruction period at the end of the war, such as the organization of the post-war Cabinet. The reports of the Committee were not published, but it is generally believed that the 1946 Romanes Lecture on *The Machinery of Government*, given by Sir John Anderson, was a tacit report of the Committee's main findings on Cabinet organization and on other related subjects.[64] Among other topics considered by the Committee were the future of wartime departments, the organization of the post-war Civil Service, training and education policy, the use of economists and statisticians, scientific and research work, the use of non-departmental organizations, the organization of transport, defence supply, government information services, regional organization, responsibility for the factory inspectorate, forestry, culture and fine arts, homeless children, and the functions of the Treasury.

It was from the last named of these inquiries that there came a change which inaugurated the second phase of development. The Committee came to the conclusion that the Treasury should assume a continuing responsibility for Machinery of Government questions. This would involve continuous study of the Machinery of Government and the duty of devising solutions rapidly to problems brought to the attention of the Treasury either by the Cabinet Secretariat (who are often in a position to know where difficulties are arising) or by other departments. To enable the Treasury to deal effectively with this new responsibility a small Machinery of Government Branch was established in 1946. Among its early concerns were the Ministers of the Crown (Transfer of Functions) Bill, the Statutory Instruments Bill, and various questions of departmental responsibility which called for early decision, some of which had already been considered by the Machinery of Government Committee. In the long term, perhaps the most important outcome of this period was the Ministers of the Crown (Transfer of Functions) Act, 1946. By Orders-in-Council under the Act subject to negative resolution in Parliament, statutory functions may be transferred between departments. By Orders subject to affirmative resolution a department may be dissolved and its functions allocated to other departments. It has always been possible to modify prerogative functions and departments by administrative action: the new procedure has brought nearly as high a degree of flexibility to the rearrangement of statutory departments and functions.

The second phase lasted only about two years: from the end of the war until the middle of 1947. It was a time of readjustment in all walks of life, and a time when there was inevitably a reaction against the intense pressure of the war years. The relaxation of that pressure was felt all round, and in our immediate context, despite the setting up of the Machinery of Government Branch and the valuable work which was done, it was manifest in the less frequent meetings of the ministerial committee. A further period of intense activity was, however, not far off, but to understand the next step it is necessary to introduce a different, though related, topic.

We have already mentioned the great expansion of Organization and Methods work during the war. After the end of the war a Working Party on Business Efficiency in Government Departments recommended that an official Business Efficiency Committee be set up to stimulate and supervise the development of O & M. Such a committee, composed mainly of Permanent Secretaries, with the Permanent Secretary to the Treasury in the Chair, was formed at about the same time that the Machinery of Government Branch was established, though the two were entirely separate. In 1947 the Select Committee on Estimates examined the position of the O & M service in government departments and made proposals for further developing its functions and improving its status.[65] They went beyond the question of O & M within particular departments and suggested that as the activities of government were altering rapidly, the whole pattern of administration should be adjusted to meet the new requirements. In short, they recommended an application of O & M techniques to the distribution of the functions of government, and proposed a speedy general review at the highest level.

During his evidence to the Select Committee the Permanent Secretary to the Treasury announced some impending changes which went part of the way to meet the Committee's ideas. The Business Efficiency Committee was to be reconstituted as a Government Organization Committee, the Machinery of Government Branch was to be placed in the O & M Division, and a Third Secretary was to become responsible within the Treasury for establishment questions in the widest sense in which they covered organization and people. The Government Organization Committee's terms of reference were to include Machinery of Government questions. The Committee was not itself to carry out high-level inquiries (which would call for specialized experience in particular fields), but was to make sure that the questions which ought to be studied were being studied. Both in the Treasury officials' evidence to the Select Committee, and in a later official Government reply,[66] it was made clear that the Government doubted whether an attempt to overhaul the whole pattern of central administration in one operation was either practicable or would meet the needs of the situation. It was agreed, however, that there was a need for intensive review in the economic field, and that in any such review or similar reviews the Government would 'seek every possible help from persons outside the Service, who will be associated with particular investigations'.

The review of the Machinery of Government thus entered a third phase in 1947—a phase of intensive review which lasted until 1950–1951. The most important venture of those years was a general economic organization inquiry, together with a review of controls, a review of production authorities, a review of the relationship between government departments and boards of nationalized industries, a review of functions in connection with housing, building and land, and other questions of departmental responsibility which demanded attention – e.g., in the sphere of mining (other than coal mining) and quarrying, and in the co-ordination of government activities for the promotion of industrial productivity. The specific subjects chosen in this economic field were those in which there had been most changes since before the war: it was in this sphere, naturally, that the pressure was greatest and the need for review most obvious. In the majority of cases concrete recommendations were made which (so far as they were not overtaken by the rapid march of events) were subsequently carried into effect. The results of the general economic organization inquiry, however, were less impressive, mainly because the position was changing so rapidly that the nature of the functions of the departments concerned with economic matters was altering from year to year. It became evident before long that many of the functions of departments in this field were not at that time sufficiently clear or firmly defined to form the basis of such a wide-ranging and comprehensive review as had been launched. Thus the main inquiry did not come to any very definite conclusion. Nevertheless, a number of specific problems were identified which were remitted for further investigation, and most of them were in fact dealt with during the next few years.

Apart from inquiries in the economic field, there were during this third phase investigations of such matters as the medical staffs of government departments, local offices, the departmental responsibility for health, housing, local government and town and country planning, for archaeological work, and for the former Italian colonies. The work of the Local Government Manpower Committee and the setting up of the Ministry of Materials also came within the purview of the organization for reviewing the Machinery of Government. That organization was still headed by the ministerial Machinery of Government Committee, but that Committee met infrequently. The main authority was the official Government Organization Committee, while the detailed work was performed by a strengthened Machinery of Government Branch.

In 1950–51 a fourth phase began as a somewhat different technique than that of formal inquiry through the Government Organization Committee was gradually introduced. It became the practice that the Ministers concerned should be advised on the more important problems coming within their own fields by informal committees of Permanent Secretaries under Treasury chairmanship. This was the procedure followed, for instance, in considering the future responsibility for raw materials as soon as there ceased to be a need for a separate Ministry of Materials, the future of the Ministry of Food when rationing ended, and the future allocation of responsibility for iron and steel and the engineering industry, and for distribution of industry questions. Some major problems have been referred to outside committees for advice. Thus the future responsibility for atomic energy was referred to a small Committee under the Chairmanship of Lord Waverley: Sir P. J. Grigg took the Chair at a committee which inquired into the responsibility for Departmental Records: and the organization for the management of Crown Lands was examined by a committee over which Sir Malcolm Trustram Eve presided.[67] Some minor problems of organization have been dealt with informally by departmental officials in consultation with the Machinery of Government Branch.

In addition to its work in connection with the problems involving the distribution of work between two or more departments, the Government Organization Committee has taken the initiative in having review committees set up in a substantial number of the major departments. On a strict definition, questions of the internal organization of departments do not perhaps rank as Machinery of Government questions. Nevertheless, the broad organization of particular departments is often important for the working of the whole central administration, and may sometimes involve significant questions about relations with other departments or about the distribution of functions. These top-level reviews have been conducted by committees containing in all cases members from outside the Civil Service, sometimes with one of the outsiders as Chairman. In this way the Government has fulfilled its pledge that outside experts would be brought in to help in the review of the Whitehall machine, and the practice is still regularly adopted.[68]

Since 1950–51, therefore, normal practice has come to mean informal inquiry by Permanent Secretaries or eminent men of affairs working part-time in small groups. The Government Organization Committee remains in being, but like the Machinery of Government Committee from 1946 to 1950, it has not met frequently in recent years. As part of the change of method the Machinery of Government Branch was reduced in size. Continuity is now provided by two or three very senior Treasury officials and by one whole-time Principal in the Machinery of Government Branch, who assists the more senior officials as required, serves as Secretary to successive review committees, and is a focal point for knowledge about general and miscellaneous questions of organization and procedure. From time to time extra staff have been added to the Machinery of Government Branch as necessary, to deal with specific problems.

CHANGES AT THE TREASURY IN 1956

Certain changes concerning the Treasury and the Cabinet Secretariat were made in the autumn of 1956 which add an important postscript to several of the earlier sections of this chapter. It is perhaps as well to summarize the position as it was immediately before those changes took effect. The Treasury and the Cabinet Secretariat were quite separate. The Permanent Secretary to the Treasury, who since 1919 had been officially known as the Head of the Civil Service, was the Prime Minister's main official adviser on all matters concerning the organization of the Civil Service and the Machinery of Government, and at the same time, as the head of the Treasury, was responsible to the Chancellor of the Exchequer for the financial and economic work of that department. The Secretary of the Cabinet had no departmental responsibilities other than those relating to the organization and working of the Cabinet Secretariat, which had no 'policy', but he was inevitably in a very close relationship with the Prime Minister and acted as his personal staff officer. The Treasury had since 1953 been the home of the Economic Planning Staff and the Economic Section. The Chancellor of the Exchequer was helped by a Chief Economic Adviser to H.M. Government, and the economic and financial side of the department's business was the special responsibility, at the official level, of a Deputy to the Permanent Secretary to the Treasury who was also Chairman of the Economic Planning Board.

It was announced in July, 1956, that on the retirement in the autumn of Sir Edward Bridges and Sir Bernard Gilbert, respectively Permanent Secretary and Deputy to the Permanent Secretary to the Treasury, the post of Deputy would lapse and henceforward there would be two joint Permanent Secretaries. One of these Permanent Secretaries was to be Sir Roger Makins, then H.M. Ambassador at Washington and a career Foreign Service official, who was to 'have charge of the financial and economic work of the Treasury', was to be 'responsible wholly to the Chancellor of the Exchequer', and was to be Chairman of the Economic Planning Board. The other Permanent Secretary was to be Sir Norman Brook, then Secretary of the Cabinet. He was to remain Secretary of the Cabinet, but in addition was to take charge of all the other work of the Treasury not dealt with by Sir Roger Makins 'including that which falls within the responsibility of the Prime Minister in his capacity as First Lord of the Treasury'. Sir Norman Brook was to become official Head of the Home Civil Service.[69] These arrangements came into operation in October, 1956.

Whatever the immediate reasons for the new appointments, it is clear that the pressure on the single Permanent Secretary to the Treasury had become so great that some method of relieving the holder of the post was bound to be tried. The Prime Minister explained that it was desirable for the Chancellor of the Exchequer to have a 'full-time Permanent Secretary' to help him with his responsibility for directing and co-ordinating economic policy,[70] and Sir Roger Makins is now, in fact, in full charge of financial and economic affairs at the official level. Sir Norman Brook, on the other hand, advises the Prime Minister on the organization of the Civil

Service and on the machinery of government generally. For these matters, and for the work of the Cabinet Secretariat, he is responsible to the Prime Minister. He is answerable to the Chancellor of the Exchequer only for matters relating to the pay, conditions, pensions and numbers of civil servants.[zz]

[zz] For a discussion of the implications of these rearrangements see an article by D. N. Chester on 'The Treasury, 1956' in *Public Administration*, Spring, 1957.

X

THE HANDLING OF
ADMINISTRATIVE CHANGE

THE historical narrative is now complete. In conclusion, we propose to discuss some of the factors which influence the distribution of functions among departments, and to consider the present arrangements for securing the continuous review and study of the Machinery of Government.

THE DISTRIBUTION OF FUNCTIONS

If any Minister or senior civil servant were asked why the work of the central administration is arranged in its present form – why there are about thirty major and a host of minor departments, and why function X is the responsibility of department Y rather than of department Z – he would probably have no ready reply. If he were asked what principles governed these arrangements he would almost certainly suspect that the questioner had in mind two or three rules or laws whose application would make it possible to decide at any moment, clearly and without room for controversy, how many departments there should be and which department should undertake this or that new function, or which would reveal whether any particular arrangement of work was 'right'. Can there be, he might ask in turn, a set of rules so clear, so mechanical and so certain, applicable to a structure of government which is the result of centuries of growth and which is so liable to be affected by the needs and the public opinion of the moment?

Our study of the experience of the last forty years has convinced us that scepticism of this kind is thoroughly justified. There is no simple or single formula by whose application all the problems of administrative arrangement can be solved. The structure of central government and the distribution of functions among departments is the result in any one case of the interplay of several of a number of possible factors, all of which must be taken into account by anyone who attempts to find the best solution to any problem of administrative structure. At the same time it would be equally wrong to swing to the other extreme and to assume that there are no rules or guides to action. Indeed, as will appear from the subsequent analysis of the factors involved, there is a good deal of knowledge and experience available for those who have to make decisions in this field.

It is not possible to infer from a study of the period 1914–56 alone the factors underlying the present distribution of functions. In the first place, the main framework of departments already existed in 1914 – the result of a long period of development. Secondly, the historical narrative does not record all the factors which were taken into account in each administrative change: in most cases it only gives the immediate and particular causes. Nor is the narrative much concerned with functions which were added to existing duties without involving any structural change. Finally there must be brought into the reckoning certain general considerations, particularly of a basic constitutional character. The subsequent analysis is not based exclusively, therefore, on our study of the last forty years, though where possible examples from the narrative are given to illustrate the analysis.

The main factors influencing the distribution of functions will be analysed under two headings.

(*a*) The Number of Ministers;

(*b*) The Grouping of Functions.

THE NUMBER OF MINISTERS

In the British system the performance of any function of the central government must always be the responsibility of some Minister who is individually answerable to Parliament. The functions of government must, in fact, be distributed among a group of Ministers. A Minister may be responsible for several departments other than his main department – called hereafter his ministry – but this does not materially affect the constitutional position. A dominant consideration bearing on the distribution of functions is, therefore, the number of Ministers among whom functions can be distributed.

A variety of factors influences the upper and lower limits to the number of departmental Ministers at any one time. In British experience the most powerful pressure forcing an increase in the number has been the relentless growth in the functions and responsibilities of the central government, which in turn has resulted in some ministries becoming too large for their Ministers to control effectively.

Size, however, is not a simple concept. The size of a ministry cannot be measured by numbers employed, for this may not by any means indicate the pressure of work and responsibility on the Minister and his senior civil servants. If it did, the Post Office would be at least 200 times more difficult for a Minister to control than is the Treasury and some 30 times more than is the Board of Trade. The number of Under and Assistant Secretaries is perhaps a better guide, particularly if those holding positions of corresponding administrative responsibility in the Services and in certain scientific and professional fields are added in the case of the Service ministries and the Ministry of Supply. Nor is it only a question of the number of powers and statutory responsibilities, though this is a surer guide than number of employees. For some functions may involve almost entirely routine and non-controversial action and seldom raise questions requiring the attention of the Minister or his senior advisers. The ideal size for a ministry is the size that throws up no more business than can flow smoothly across the desks of the Minister and his Permanent Secretary.[a] It is also worth noticing that the same ministry with broadly the same functions may be a heavier responsibility and therefore from this point of view 'bigger' at one

[a] Various expedients have been used when the load on either the Minister or the Permanent Secretary would be too heavy. The first is the device of the Minister of State. There are now five such Ministers – two in the Foreign Office and one each in the Colonial Office, Board of Trade and Scottish Office. They may relieve the Minister of a certain amount of work, particularly where the department has to be represented abroad a good deal or where, as in the case of the Secretary of State for Scotland, the Minister often has to be away from the scene of his main administrative responsibilities. An extra Parliamentary Secretary may also help in this direction. It is not suggested that in the absence of a Minister of State the ministry would have to be divided: but his presence should make a departmental Minister's life and responsibilities more tolerable. Another device of special value when the load on the Permanent Secretary would be too great is the use of two or more departments, each with its own permanent head, under the Minister. Thus the Chancellor of the Exchequer has responsibility for the Treasury, for the two large Revenue Departments (Customs and Excise and Inland Revenue) and for a large number of other bodies – some sizeable like the Stationery Office, others small like the Public Works Loan Board and the National Debt Office. Here again the alternative may not be additional Ministers – indeed the satellite departments of this kind are usually engaged in work which raises few issues of policy. If that work was carried out by a special branch or branches of a ministry, it would add to the responsibilities of the ministry's senior officials. On the other hand, a separate Board or Office with its own senior staff, dealing directly with the Minister on such issues of policy as may arise, leaves the senior officers of the ministry free to concentrate on the main stream of the Minister's responsibilities. The motive for setting up such satellite departments is thus not to secure a measure of independence of the Minister, but the effect of creating them may in some instances be not unlike the effect of establishing the public boards and corporations mentioned later in this chapter.

time than at another. Thus during a year of coal shortage and of overburdened electricity plant the task of the Minister of Fuel and Power is obviously much greater than in other years, even though his legal powers may not have changed.

It is also probably true to say that the more diverse the range of matters to be dealt with, the more difficult a department becomes and the larger the number of higher staff needed. The Foreign Office, which deals with almost every country in the world, and the Board of Trade, which deals with industries as diverse as cotton, films and furniture, present special problems to those at the top. Something of course depends on whether the internal organization of the department is good enough to prevent an undue load on the Minister and on whether the Minister and Permanent Secretary are prepared to delegate.

In passing it should be noted that any growth in the functions of government is likely to throw up problems of maintaining internal unity for some of the ministries. Not merely will each ministry become larger, but its functions are likely to become more diverse. On the other hand an increase in the number of departmental Ministers is likely to provide an opportunity to regroup functions with more regard for their affinities and homogeneity.

It is difficult to say at what point one should draw the line about the size of a ministry. It might be argued that the Treasury under Sir Stafford Cripps was too large – i.e., that at that time too many major and urgent decisions arose out of its functions – and that this hastened his death. It would probably be difficult to argue that the Ministry of Pensions and National Insurance has too much to do now that the teething troubles of the arrangements introduced by the legislation of 1946 have been solved. But was the Ministry of Health too large in 1950? Or are the Foreign Office, the Board of Trade and the Ministry of Supply too large now? Perhaps the only thing that can be said with any certainty is that sometimes in the life of a ministry there comes an increasing recognition that it has become so large that either it is no longer a candidate for new functions, or that it is time it lost some to another ministry. At this stage it may lose its appetite for adding any new function to its empire, particularly a really new function and not one which is just an extension of the powers available for carrying out an existing function. At a somewhat later stage the ministry may even contemplate without too much distress the prospect of losing part of its present empire.

On the whole, in view of the great increase in governmental activity during the last forty years, it is remarkable that the number of

Ministers has been kept so low. In 1914 there were seventeen of them. The number had risen to twenty-five by the end of 1918 but fell to twenty during most of the inter-war period, after the Government's wartime powers and functions were abandoned or became unnecessary. The number rose again during the Second World War and again there was a decline afterwards. Since 1945 there has undoubtedly been a definite governmental policy to reduce the number. There are now twenty-four departmental Ministers, including for this purpose the Lord Chancellor and the Lord President of the Council – only seven more than in 1914, though the total number of non-industrial civil servants has increased from about 270,000 to 635,000; or more strikingly from about 40,000 to 320,000 if three big employing departments which have been in existence throughout (the Post Office and the Boards of Inland Revenue and of Customs and Excise) are excluded.

There must, therefore, be factors which offset the pressure for more Ministers. One such factor is that the greater the number of Ministers the greater the difficulty of securing inter-departmental co-ordination, notwithstanding the greater need for such co-ordination. The most important general factor, however, which limits the increase in the number of departmental Ministers, arises from the working of the Cabinet. Whether or not there can be said to be an optimum size of Cabinet, there is undoubtedly a size beyond which Prime Ministers will go only with considerable reluctance. When the number of Ministers reaches this point any increase may cause difficulties in the working of the Cabinet.

The largest Cabinets in British history were Mr Asquith's in 1915–16 and Mr Neville Chamberlain's in 1937–39: at times during those years the Cabinet had twenty-three members. Twenty to twenty-two was more usual in the inter-war period and since the end of the Second World War there have rarely been more than eighteen. If, in addition to the Prime Minister, the inclusion of the Lord President and possibly one so-called 'non-departmental' Minister is accepted as common form, there can only be twenty departmental Ministers at the maximum – and only fifteen if post-war experience counts – if they are all to have seats in the Cabinet. As Britain had fifteen departmental Ministers as long ago as 1889, clearly there must have been an increasing need to balance the advantages of creating new Ministers against the disadvantages of leaving more Ministers out of the Cabinet.

The use of Cabinet Committees and the work of the Cabinet Secretariat have made it easier to leave some Ministers out of the Cabinet, but there remain notable disadvantages in such a practice.

Regular attendance at the Cabinet makes for greater administrative, political and personal cohesion. Ministers who are not members must inevitably feel of a lower status, the departments they manage may on occasion not get the decisions and attention they need from the Government as a whole, and the unity of the Administration may suffer. The fewer Ministers there are outside the Cabinet, therefore, the better. Other considerations point in the same direction. Politicians of ministerial calibre and experience are not unlimited, and the more powerful and able party leaders prefer departments with plenty of scope. The House of Commons dislikes having a very large number of 'placemen' among its Members, and it is politically and constitutionally impossible to have more than a small handful of Ministers in the House of Lords. Convention and considerations of expense also play some part.

There is, in short, a reluctance to establish new ministerial posts, and whenever the central government is charged with a new function there is a presumption in favour of adding it to the responsibilities of an existing Minister. In normal circumstances this accords with the manner in which the functions of government develop. Each year Parliament adds to the powers and responsibilities of the central government. But the great bulk of these additions consists of a multitude of smaller items, small at least in terms of the additional staff required to carry them out. The tasks which the Ministry of Housing and Local Government or the Board of Trade have to perform arise from literally hundreds of Acts extending for over a century. Probably no one of those powers or Acts would constitute in itself anything like sufficient reason for the establishment of a new ministry. Usually only the mass creation of new powers and functions in preparation for or during a war is sufficient to warrant this step, e.g., the establishment of the Ministries of Information and of Economic Warfare in 1939. In peace-time a new ministry is usually produced by a rearrangement of functions involving the transfer of powers from one or more existing ministries. This in itself constitutes a further important limit on any increase in the number of Ministers. For the powers that Ministers have they tend to hold and in any case the disruption caused to a ministry which loses part of its work and staff invites caution. If the transfer of a major function is suggested the effect on the remaining parts of the ministry must be seriously considered. Moreover, whether the function is major or minor it will have developed a network of links many of which will be broken if it is transferred. Transfers, like surgical operations, are only worth while if they achieve some important advantage.

It is also worth noticing two devices usually introduced for other reasons, which have, however, enabled public powers and functions to be increased without the equivalent pressure for further Ministers with claims to seats in the Cabinet. They are:

(i) The use of Boards, such as the National Coal Board, to manage the affairs of a large enterprise and be a large employer, leaving the Minister to concern himself with a much more limited range of matters concerning the industry. Had coal, electricity and gas been nationalized by transferring them not to public corporations but to a Minister, their everyday management might have been in total too great for a single Minister of Fuel and Power.

(ii) The practice of placing politicians in charge of small departments but not giving them normal ministerial status. The Secretary for Mines and the Secretary for Overseas Trade were in this position.[b]

Notwithstanding the pressure to restrict the number of departmental Ministers, a number of quite small ministries have been established. At the moment, for example, there are three – the Lord Chancellor's Department, the Ministry of Defence and the Commonwealth Relations Office. Until recently there were three other relatively small ministries – of Civil Aviation, of Pensions and of Materials. There was also a Ministry of Town and Country Planning between 1943 and 1951. In all these cases, therefore, there must have been exceptional forces pulling in the other direction. There was no need to have a separate Dominions Office in 1925 because of the burden of work on the Colonial Secretary – indeed the Dominions Office and the Colonial Office continued to have the same Minister until 1930. The Dominions (now Commonwealth Relations) Office was set up in order to take account of the independent status of the

---

[b] A device which has the effect of decreasing the number of Ministers with claims to seats in the Cabinet, but which involves an increase in the total number of Ministers, is that of appointing a Co-ordinating Minister with a seat in the Cabinet, leaving two or more ordinary departmental Ministers out of the Cabinet. Thus the existence of the Minister of Defence has affected the status of the Ministers at the heads of the three Service departments. The appointment of a Secretary of State for the Co-ordination of Transport, Fuel and Power – one of the so-called 'Overlords' – by Mr Winston Churchill in 1951 had a similar effect on the position of the Minister of Fuel and Power and the Minister of Transport.

The limit to this kind of arrangement is set by the fact that the departmental Minister still remains responsible to Parliament for the performance of the many duties conferred on him. Unless a clear distinction can be drawn between the responsibilities of the Co-ordinating Minister and of the other Ministers concerned – as is done in the case of the Minister of Defence and the Service Ministers – there is a serious danger of confusion both in Parliament and within Whitehall.

senior Commonwealth countries and to provide a channel of communication with them at once less paternal than that associated
with the Colonial Office and more intimate than that associated with
the Foreign 'Office. The Office has been continued under its new
name as the Commonwealth's membership has extended because it
appears to meet the peculiar needs of what, to a foreigner, is a
strange and intangible community of nations. The Ministry of
Materials was set up in 1951 when international economic conditions
made the procurement of raw materials very difficult and when it
appeared that those conditions would last for a considerable time.
In fact an improvement set in almost as soon as the department was
established and within three years it was abolished.

The Ministries of Civil Aviation and of Town and Country Planning represent a different idea. The initial stages of developing
rapidly a new or enlarged function are capable of occupying the full
time of a Minister and his senior advisers, but when the initial
impetus has been given and the administrative machine is running
smoothly the new ministry can be merged into some other
ministry. Thus the Ministry of Civil Aviation, set up in 1945, had
to deal with the relatively new and peculiarly difficult problem of
putting Britain's civil aviation services on a sound and greatly extended basis immediately after a war in which civil flying had been
almost completely subordinated to military needs. Not only did the
domestic aspects of civil aviation demand close attention but its
international aspects were equally important. As the new structure
of Air Corporations and the machinery of international services
settled down, the need for a separate ministry declined, and in 1953
it was deemed practicable to make one Minister responsible for all
transport matters, including civil aviation.

If, therefore, we look at the administrative history of Britain since
1914 simply in terms of the number of departmental Ministers, the
dominant theme is a struggle between two powerful forces. On the
one hand, the continual increase in functions has created problems
of size and heterogeneity which have generated pressure for the
appointment of more Ministers. On the other hand, the needs of
co-ordination and the advantages of government by a small and
well-knit body of Ministers have been strong arguments against increasing the number of Ministers. The main pressure for an increase
has been supplemented by the need, on occasion, to establish new
ministries to handle functions which, in the view of the Cabinet,
demanded special attention, or which well-organized interests or
interests with a strong public appeal felt would not receive adequate
attention unless they became the sole responsibility of particular

Ministers. The main pressure against an increase was supplemented by such factors as the recurring shortage of politicians of front-rank ministerial calibre, the preference of prominent politicians for administrative responsibilities which gave them plenty of scope, parliamentary dislike of too many 'placemen', and the use of public boards and corporations instead of ministerial departments.

The precise number of departmental Ministers suitable at any particular time cannot be calculated from a consideration of the factors discussed – there is always room for difference of opinion. But such consideration would at least narrow the limits. It would not enable one to decide whether at the end of 1956 there should be twenty-two or twenty-six departmental Ministers rather than twenty-four. It would, however, incline one to doubt whether fifteen or thirty departmental Ministers would be equally desirable. The balance of these opposed factors decides the number of Ministers among whom the functions of government have to be distributed. We may now turn, therefore, to examine the factors which influence the grouping of functions under these Ministers.

THE GROUPING OF FUNCTIONS

General Criteria

It is clear from simple inspection that some functions are closely related whereas others have little or nothing in common. Housing, for example, has close affinities with sewerage and street cleansing, less with agriculture and fisheries, and little or none with foreign affairs. As one writer has put it, a first approximate answer to the question of which functions should be grouped together in one department can undoubtedly be found by seeking the closest affinity or the greatest measure of homogeneity.

'Each Government Department should have a reasonably homogeneous block of work, or one or two homogeneous blocks of work amounting *in toto* to enough, and not more than enough, to keep fully occupied the normal departmental hierarchy consisting of Minister, Permanent Secretary, Deputy Secretary (or Secretaries), etc. . . . one should avoid (always provided there are not overwhelming common sense reasons to the contrary) creating unnecessary heterogeneity either in assigning new functions or in switching existing ones.'[1]

It is easy for those familiar with the names of the British central departments to think of the total functions of government as distributing themselves naturally among a number of readily recognizable departments or boxes: agriculture, education, foreign affairs, health, home affairs, labour, trade, war and so on. That departments with similar names are to be found in other countries shows that thinking in these terms is at least a reasonable starting point. Yet these titles are not due to any one basis of classification. Foreign affairs and home affairs obviously are mutually exclusive, but agriculture is an industry and labour is a section of the population, and it is therefore by no means self-evident what should go into each of the boxes so labelled. Does agriculture exclude any activities concerned with agricultural labour, or does labour cover all workers except agricultural workers? Are there any alternative labels, i.e., any alternative methods of grouping functions? In other words, what criterion or criteria will result in the greatest measure of homogeneity?

Before dealing with these questions one overriding consideration needs to be stressed. In the British system of Cabinet Government ministerial responsibility is a fundamental constitutional principle. Some individual Minister is responsible to Parliament for the performance or non-performance of every power conferred on the central government. Therefore the distribution of functions between different Ministers must as far as possible be such as to make it clear who is responsible for any major issue of governmental policy. Any distribution which blurred the responsibility for any important field of governmental policy over two or three Ministers would be most unlikely to work satisfactorily as regards Parliament and the public and even as regards the working of the Cabinet system as a whole. It also follows that where a departmental Minister is responsible for an important field of policy he has a *prima facie* case for having within his department any minor or ancillary functions of government essential to the successful performance of that policy.

Four Alternative Methods

General experience indicates that there are four main ways in which governmental powers and activities may be grouped for administrative purposes:

(i)   By class of persons dealt with or clientele—e.g., children, pensioners, a particular industry, Local Authorities.

(ii) By major purpose—e.g., education, health, defence.

(iii) By area served—e.g., Scotland.

(iv) By kind of work or administrative process—e.g., legal, research, printing.

The distinction between 'clientele' and 'major purpose' goes back to Aristotle who, in his discussion of the distribution of functions in a Greek city state, said

'we have also to consider whether to allocate duties on the basis of the subject to be handled, or on that of the class of persons concerned: e.g., should we have one officer for the whole subject of the maintenance of order, or a separate officer for the class of children and another for that of women?'[2]

The Haldane Committee spelt this out in a much-quoted passage. They defined the alternatives as

'distribution according to the persons or classes to be dealt with, and distribution according to the services to be performed. Under the former method each Minister who presides over a Department would be responsible to Parliament for those activities of the Government which affect the sectional interests of particular classes of persons, and there might be, for example, a Ministry for Paupers, a Ministry for Children, a Ministry for Insured Persons, or a Ministry for the Unemployed. Now the inevitable outcome of this method of organization is a tendency to Lilliputian administration. It is impossible that the specialized service which each Department has to render to the community can be of as high a standard when its work is at the same time limited to a particular class of persons and extended to every variety of provision for them, as when the Department concentrates itself on the provision of the particular service only, by whomsoever required, and looks beyond the interests of comparatively small classes.

'The other method, and the one which we recommend for adoption, is that of defining the field of activity in the case of each Department according to the particular service which it renders to the community as a whole. Thus a Ministry of Education would be concerned predominantly with the provision of education wherever, and by whomsoever, needed. Such a Ministry would have to deal with persons in so far only as they were to be educated, and not with particular classes of persons defined on other principles.'[3]

Let us now look at these and the other two alternative methods of distributing functions.

Class of Person

It is difficult to see how any government could be organized wholly or even to any major extent on the basis of class of person dealt with: for in its extreme form it would mean having separate police forces and fire brigades, and separate educational and health services, etc., for each category of persons. And if the classes of people were not mutually exclusive the difficulties would be even greater. The classic British example found in Local Government of the use of this basis – viz., the Boards of Guardians which existed between 1834 and 1929 for the relief and care of the poor – did not go very far. The local Poor Law was overwhelmingly a system of cash payments to and workhouses for the poor, and the medical and hospital attention provided specially for paupers was limited.

The criterion is worth discussing, however, for it underlines the contrast between services seen in terms of law and administration and services seen in terms of groups of citizens. In other words the same function can be viewed either as a job to be undertaken by officials, or as work of special concern to a particular section of the community. However much the stress is placed on distribution by service provided, the department concerned will find itself dealing regularly with certain individuals. This departmental clientele is likely to include not only the recipients of the service but also Local Authorities and associations concerned in the administration, their staffs, and a variety of other interested bodies. Experience shows that there is a tendency for this clientele to look to the department with whom it is in regular contact to provide other governmental services for it, and the department is also tempted in this direction. Thus a new function is sometimes added to a department because it already has the closest contact of any existing department with the groups or bodies that are the concern of, or are concerned with, the new function. During the recent period when new building, raw materials and other matters were subject to governmental control and allocation, links of this kind led to the development of the idea that each department should act as the sponsor of, or as the advocate for, the interests of its particular clientele in securing the necessary supplies.

The danger in certain circumstances is that a department, because of the direct pressure on its Minister or because of its desire for a quiet life, may so become the mouthpiece of its clientele as to find it increasingly difficult to take a general view of the public interest. It was sometimes alleged, for example, that the Minister of Agriculture was the mouthpiece of the farmers, and the amalgamation of his Ministry with the former Ministry of Food may in part have been due to the desire to secure that the different demands of the consumers and the producers of food are reconciled in the one department. Even if functions are distributed without reference to clientele there will probably be a tendency in practice for each department dealing with a particular section of the public, whether as

individuals or as associations, to try to satisfy that public. Sometimes, however, a department may be able to show that it cannot
please one part of its clientele without offending another part –
e.g., the Ministry of Housing and Local Government in relation to
the boundaries of Counties and County Boroughs.

Purpose

The purposes of government may be defined at differing levels of
generality. At the most general level they would include defence
against external aggression, preservation of law and order, promotion of trade and industry, education of the population, promoting the well-being of the Commonwealth, safeguarding the
public health, and providing security against want. At a lower level
of generality they would include the provision and proper utilization
of fuel and power supplies, development of agriculture, provision of
adequate housing and roads, and the planning of town and country.

   Distribution of functions by purpose at the most general level
might lead to the establishment of some ten or twelve ministries. As
some of these would be too large, the functions in respect of certain
major objectives would have to be divided among two or more
ministries. A less general approach might avoid this difficulty but run
into another, because some of the purposes at this level might not
justify the exclusive attention of separate departments. Apart from
these limitations, however, British experience has shown distribution according to purpose to be an important criterion. It gives, on
the whole, a greater unity of work at the policy level than any of the
other criteria, and this is very important, as Parliament is mainly
interested in policy and in seeing that ministerial responsibility is
unequivocal.

   The promotion of trade and industry provides a good example of
the manner in which the component functions of a major purpose
can be distributed if they are too numerous for one Minister. In and
for some time before 1914 the powers of government with regard to
trade and industry (excluding agriculture and fisheries, which were
treated separately) were in the hands of one department – the Board
of Trade. When those powers became too wide in range or too
heavy for a single department, subdivision by industry was considered to be the solution. The different forms of transport and the
fuel and power industries, by virtue of their size and their need for
special consideration, have been separated. The building industry
has also been made the responsibility of another department; in this
case it was found convenient to use the department responsible for

M

government building. For a time the Ministry of Supply, established primarily to provide the arms and equipment required by the Army, was responsible for government policy and control in respect of the engineering and metal industries because its work brought it into close contact with those industries. There has indeed been a tendency to place governmental responsibilities for any particular industry in the hands of the ministry which, as part of its other activities, already has close links with that industry. The Board of Trade has tended, therefore, to be left with those industries which are not large or complex enough to warrant a separate ministry, or for which no other Minister can be made conveniently responsible.

There are some functions within the field of trade and industry not peculiar to a particular industry but common to all industries. To what extent should distribution by industry apply only to the former and totally exclude the latter? In Britain such general matters as control over the location of industry, registration and supervision of patents, promotion of exports, supervision of monopolies and restrictive practices, are the responsibility of the Board of Trade even though they concern industries which are the responsibility of other departments. If these general matters were split among the several departments the formulation and carrying out of a general governmental policy would be more difficult. Indeed it would probably need almost constant inter-departmental consultation, certainly more consultation than is caused by the present distinction between general and particular industrial responsibilities.

Let us take the field of labour or employment. How far should the distribution by industry apply here? Should all matters connected with agricultural labour, with transport workers, or with coal miners, be the responsibility of the ministries concerned with those industries, leaving either no need for a Ministry of Labour or only for a smaller ministry confined to functions not easily sub-divided according to industry? In Britain it has increasingly been assumed that unless there are strong reasons to the contrary all the Government's powers in respect of labour should reside in the Ministry of Labour. This ministry is thus able to specialize in what is a difficult field for governmental action, and to be responsible for a general governmental policy. It is also put in a position to develop close relations with an important and well-organized section of the community – the Trade Unions. Moreover the arrangement gives that section a single Minister to whom representations can be made on all matters affecting the unions, wages and conditions, and employment generally.

Area

A distribution on the basis of area[c] has obvious limitations in the case of a country or countries with a common Parliament and Government and a unified economic system. This has not, however, ruled out the possibility of recognizing, in the sphere of administration, the differing conditions, partly political, partly legal, partly historical, that prevail in the countries making up Great Britain and Ireland. Arrangements of this kind are of course still operating in Northern Ireland, Scotland and to a much smaller extent in Wales.

As regards the general principles as to which functions may properly be handled by an area Minister, it is clear that certain activities, e.g., defence, external affairs, finance and economic affairs, call for a unified approach, not least by reference to their international aspects; shipping and civil aviation are also international in scope. Moreover, as was recently pointed out by the Committee on Scottish Finance and Trade Statistics,[4] Scotland and England have a unified economic system with complete freedom of intercourse by rail, road, sea and air and this is equally true of Wales. Consequently it has been the practice for government to deal with trade and industry primarily on the basis of Great Britain as a whole, though this principle is not now followed in the case of electricity. The Ministry of Labour has also remained a Great Britain department with headquarters in London where are also to be found the headquarters of many organizations such as Trade Unions which operate throughout Great Britain and with which the Ministry requires to keep in close touch. On the other hand in this case and in the case of other Great Britain departments with important Scottish and Welsh interests, e.g., the Board of Trade, it is customary to maintain strong organizations in Scotland and Wales under senior officers in order that those interests shall be duly safeguarded.

So far as Scotland is concerned, it has been possible to go further towards recognizing what the recent Royal Commission on Scottish Affairs[5] called 'a separate Scottish ethos, history and tradition'. Thus in such matters as education, health, housing and police, both policy and administration have been placed by legislation or otherwise in the hands of a Scottish Minister and Scottish departments. The same has also happened to Scottish agriculture and fisheries.

It would be useless to attempt to make a strictly logical distinction between those activities which are properly capable of being dis-

---

[c] We are not concerned with the regional organization of central departments or with the distribution of functions between central and local government.

tributed according to the area in which they are administered and those which are not. It can, however, be said that subject to the over-riding authority of a common Parliament and Cabinet, and the exclusion from separate treatment of activities on which it is essential or highly convenient to have a common front, there have been continuing efforts over many years to recognize in administration the existence of special Scottish conditions as well as the insistent urge of the Scottish people to manage their own business. Administrative measures with similar aims have also been taken from time to time as regards Welsh affairs.

Kind of Work

There are two main interpretations of this criterion. First, there is what is known as the common service, which applies to services needed by all or most departments, e.g., provision of offices, stationery and equipment, printing, or legal advice. Should each department cater for its own needs or should the service be concentrated in a single department, or should there be some mixture of these two extremes? Examples of all three possibilities can be found in British Government, though usually some degree of concentration is favoured. The Stationery Office (for printing), the Ministry of Works (for Government buildings, offices, furniture and a wide range of office needs and equipment) and the Central Office of Information (for general governmental publicity) are three examples of concentration which have resulted in separate departments, though only Works has a Minister all to itself. The Ministry of Supply provides arms, equipment and other supplies for the fighting Services, though it only provides a relatively small proportion of the Admiralty's requirements.

The advantages of the common service department are the pooling of expert knowledge, of which there may not be enough to go round, the concentration of a particular kind of work and, in some cases, the gains from large-scale purchases. The disadvantages are that the other departments lose control over what to them may be an important ingredient in the successful performance of their functions; that they may have to accept something which suits all departments on average rather than something designed or provided for their peculiar needs; and that another department is added to the number to be dealt with and co-ordinated.

The conduct of scientific research by the government raises issues only partly of the common service kind for it is also a matter of providing the right environment. Instead of such research being treated as a normal governmental function efforts have been made to give it a special status by creating special research authorities under the Privy Council. Where, however, research is vital to a department, e.g., as is research on weapons to the Ministry of Supply, it is kept within the department. In other cases the department has some liaison with the main research body in the field, e.g., the Ministry of Works with the Building Research Board.

The second interpretation of this criterion concerns the suitability of a department for carrying out a function either because it has the relevant experience and expertise, or because the attitude or tradition required to operate the new function successfully is found in this particular department, or because the new service needs some administrative management – regional or local – already possessed by this department. In a sense this is no more than underlining the advantage of affinity whether it be by clientele, purpose or area. But it can be a more specific pointer than that. Thus it was presumably because the Office of Works had developed some expertise in the handling of government building that this common service department became a Ministry of Works with responsibility for an important economic function – conducting the Government's relations with the building and civil engineering industries. Possession of the necessary administrative machinery has been an important factor on several occasions. A good example before the period of this study concerns the executive work of Old Age Pensions, which was entrusted to the Board of Customs and Excise because the latter had a comprehensive network of outposts. More recently the merger of the Ministries of Pensions and of National Insurance was in part defended because the combined department would be able to offer war pensioners a better local counter service than the Ministry of Pensions could provide. Running the Post Office Savings Bank is a function which can hardly be said to be part of the postal, telephone or telegraph services, but it nevertheless fits conveniently into the Post Office organization. Sometimes a department with a wide network of local offices is used on an agency basis by another department – e.g., the Ministry of Labour acts as an agent for the Foreign Office in the issue and renewal of passports. The 'principal' department still retains responsibility for policy in these cases.

Other Criteria

Though at first glance the functions of government may appear to be composed of large, homogeneous and indivisible blocks of work readily recognizable as health, education, industry, defence and so on, closer inspection shows them to be made up of a mass of smaller items. When these are looked at in detail it is by no means always clear which function should be placed in which ministry even though the broad pattern of ministries is already well known and accepted.

If military administration, for example, is scrutinized closely it will be seen to involve a wide variety of tasks, even in peace-time. Some of them are:

Recruitment, including appeals on grounds of distress or conscientious objection.
Settlement of pay and conditions.
Clothing and provisioning.
Training.
Equipment.
Research and development work on weapons.
Medical care and attention.
Housing.
Transport.
Payment of pensions to disabled soldiers or to dependents of soldiers killed in course of duty.

In 1914 all these tasks were part of the total responsibility of the Secretary of State for War. Today some are handled by other Ministers. Thus the actual job of calling men up now falls to the Minister of Labour and National Service[d]: the provision of equipment and research and development on weapons are now the province of the Minister of Supply: and disablement pensions are mainly handled by the Minister of Pensions and National Insurance. Several other departments are concerned at various other points.

The word function may thus cover anything from the direction of the armed forces to the arrangement whereby conscientious objectors may appeal against their call-up. The question of which ministry handles the call-up of conscripts is probably more typical of the vast majority of decisions affecting the distribution of work between departments than is a question which involves the creation of a new

[d] In 1914 recruitment was voluntary and small-scale. Now national service is compulsory and involves all males when of a certain age. A national network of local offices is therefore required. The Ministry of Labour has those offices. Moreover as the call-up is linked with such matters as exempted occupations and reinstatement into civilian occupations, it is administratively convenient to use the department which is concerned with placing labour in jobs, collecting and analysing employment statistics, etc. It should be noted, however, that the War Office still recruits those wishing to enter the Army other than under the compulsory call-up.

department. Though the four general criteria are important tests however small the activity of government under consideration, it is probably true that the less important a function is in itself the greater the choice of possible ministries for its home. In any case there will quite often be a choice of solutions. The hospitals for the military sick could be the responsibility of the War Office or the Ministry of Health: the grants to universities could be made either by the Treasury (as at present) or by the Ministry of Education: the Factory Inspectorate could be either in the Home Office or in the Ministry of Labour or in the Board of Trade or even split among the departments concerned with the various industries.

The Haldane Committee thought that further help on how functions should be related could be obtained from drawing a distinction between dominant and subordinate interests. They suggested that, subject to the main principle of allocation by service, all decisions to concentrate functions in particular departments should be governed by the extent to which particular functions conduce to the primary end of the department's administration.

Once the main framework of the departments has been settled, a test of this kind is sometimes of assistance. Thus having decided on other grounds that there should be Ministries of Education and of Health the question of which should be responsible for the School Medical Service can be subjected to this test. In this case, however, the answer is complicated by the fact that the service was originally established by the Board of Education and is more easily administered as part of the educational service because the inspection normally takes place on the school premises. Sometimes the dominant interest is a matter of opinion. Is control over the location of industry subordinate to the dominant purpose of securing full employment in formerly depressed areas, or to that of securing a properly planned community, i.e., part of town and country planning policy? Here again other factors may be more important – for example, the methods which the Government proposes to use to influence location. These methods may in some cases dictate the choice of a department which has the kind of relations with industrial concerns most likely to lead to successful persuasion. These are good examples of the difficulty that may arise in practice from using this test.

Some of the changes which have taken place in the distribution of functions have been due to the emergence of new primary purposes. Thus when in 1940 the Minister of Labour and National Service was charged with the difficult task of securing the best use of the nation's manpower, including the power of direction, he took the view that this aim made it necessary for him to take over the

Factory Inspectorate. If he was to be responsible for the industries and firms in which individuals must work he must be able to assure himself that factory conditions, including such matters as canteens, were up to standard. In reply it could hardly be argued that this particular function was essential to the primary purpose of the Home Office, which is law and order.

Another example of the way in which the passage of time can render an existing pattern of distribution inappropriate is in the field of National Insurance. What is now National Insurance, a unified service under the control of a single Minister, first developed as a series of services in the hands of five Ministers. Perhaps it could not be argued in each of these five cases that the particular function was in a particular department because it conduced to that department's primary purpose, but undoubtedly there were close links in each case, e.g., workmen's compensation with the Factory Inspectorate (at the Home Office), health insurance with the health services, and unemployment insurance with the employment service. As soon, however, as the emphasis came to be placed on a comprehensive uniform scheme of national insurance the existing distribution appeared indefensible, and was indeed so administratively.

So far this discussion has proceeded on the assumption that the task is to find the closest affinity for the function or functions whose proper allocation is in question. There are, however, occasions when an 'obvious' affinity is deliberately avoided, and where some measure of heterogeneity appears to give the best result. Thus the University Grants Committee answers to the Chancellor of the Exchequer and not to the Minister of Education – the main reason being the desire of the universities to avoid the kind of approach and the measure of control which characterizes the Ministry's relations with other branches of the educational system. Again, the Eve Committee on Crown Lands[6] recommended that the responsibility for Crown Lands should be that of a Minister without any special interest in land, rather than that of a Minister like the Minister of Agriculture. The classic case in our period has been the refusal of official opinion to be impressed by the Haldane arguments for a Ministry of Justice which began: 'If the principle to be adopted in distributing the business of Government is that of concentrating the various branches of each service as far as possible in the hands of a single authority, considerable changes will be requisite in the case of the administration of Justice.'[7] The orthodox view on this has been that we should be particularly chary of concentration of authority when dealing with the delicate relation between the executive and the judiciary.

It is sometimes suggested that political and personal considerations should play no part in questions of administrative organization. This view ignores the fact that government is essentially political, and that a democratic Government must take account of parliamentary and public opinion on all matters, including departmental arrangements. Long-term political considerations may rightly affect the structure of the central administration, as for instance in the setting up of Scottish departments for health, home affairs, etc. Shorter-term political considerations inevitably affect the timing of change, as they probably did when the Ministry of Health was divided into two departments in 1951. Occasionally, too, in allocating functions, regard is paid to the views on policy and to the personalities of the Minister who will become responsible for the work. Thus the allocation of planning to the Ministry of Works in the Second World War owed much to the presence there of a Minister, Lord Reith, who was known to be keenly interested in planning policy. His successor, Lord Portal, preferred to concentrate on other matters and in due course planning was taken away from the Ministry of Works and assigned to a separate department. Cases must also arise from time to time in which the political strength or persuasiveness of a particular Minister in the Cabinet may prevent or delay administrative change or secure it against some opposition.

There are some obvious dangers if considerations of this kind play anything but a minor part in decisions affecting the structure of government. There is a limited case for them in the rare instance of a difficult task depending for its success entirely on the right man being put in the position to carry it out. The main danger is that though the allocation of a function to a particular ministry may be successful whilst the particular person is in charge, once he departs, which in the case of a Minister may be quite soon, the basic inappropriateness of the allocation may cause difficulties. In the long run, therefore, in deciding on the distribution of functions, primary consideration must be given to the administrative factors discussed in the earlier paragraphs of this chapter.

Just which criterion or combination of criteria will give the best result, or just which modifying factors must be taken into account, will depend on the circumstances of any case. In many instances it will be found that the considerations set out in this chapter are most effective when turned into a series of questions which should be answered before a decision is reached. What is the precise character of the function to be performed? Where is it to be performed, and for what purpose? What kind of work is involved: is it mainly regulatory, or stimulative, or managerial, routine or discretionary, highly specialized and technical or mainly clerical? With whom will the department concerned mainly have to deal? Does the new function need to be administered locally, and if so which department has the most appropriate local arrangements? Is the function likely to grow rapidly and if so will a particular department continue to have the capacity to be responsible for it? Has the clientele to be served any strong views? Which departments already have links with the function, or already do this kind of work, or have this type of staff or experience? And so on. It is the multiplicity of argument, the difficulty of settling the issue by appeal to one or more clear and uncontestable principles, that leaves room for disputes, for the exercise of judgment, and even, on occasion, for the interplay of personalities and of politics.

Nevertheless knowledge of the possible criteria, of the questions to be asked and of how similar issues have been dealt with in the past should be of the utmost assistance. This knowledge, wisely used, should reduce the possibility of a wrong allocation of functions because it should narrow the range of effective choice. This is the significance of the development in recent years of Machinery of Government work within the Treasury. We turn, in conclusion, therefore, to consider the way in which such matters are handled at present.

THE HANDLING OF MACHINERY OF GOVERNMENT QUESTIONS

It is extremely difficult to pass any worthwhile judgment on the period and the changes surveyed in this book. Were all the changes justified, and if not, which proved to be failures? Should some of the changes have come earlier? Should other changes have been made? Nobody with a real knowledge of British government would claim that everything was for the best of all possible worlds. Nobody could possibly make that claim for any large-scale and complicated organization over forty years. To express a judgment on more particular matters is even less easy. Should a Minister for the Co-ordination of Defence have been established earlier than 1937 and should he in any case have been a Minister of Defence on the present model? Was it only the problems of war that led to a Minister of Fuel and Power being appointed, or did the need for such a Minister exist in the 1930s? Were the various changes involving the Ministries of Health, Town and Country Planning, and Housing and Local Government during the period 1943–1951 evidence of fumbling, or were they mainly inevitable and the correct responses to a changing situation? These and many other questions come to mind in reading the administrative history of the period. To answer them with any conviction would need far more evidence than is provided in this study. It would need an inquiry not merely into the reasons advanced for and against the changes but also into the consequent working of the machinery over a reasonable period. And if the judgment was to be fair it would have to take account of what was possible in the political climate of the day.

The sheer volume of change during the period must strike the reader. New departments have been created, quite a few departments have been abolished or amalgamated with others, and there have been numerous transfers of functions between departments. It can hardly be charged, therefore, that British government has proved too rigid to meet the changing needs of the period. The Ministers of the Crown (Transfer of Functions) Act, 1946, has greatly facilitated the continuous process of readjustment, especially in connection with comparatively minor changes. Over forty Orders have been made under the Act. It is probable that had this procedure been available in the inter-war years some changes – especially minor changes which were crowded out of the legislative programme by more urgent matters – would have been accomplished earlier.

There is thus less reason nowadays why the Machinery of Government should not keep pace with the changing demands on it. This, however, brings us to the arrangements available for ensuring that the decisions taken in this field are based on adequate information and advice. Decisions affecting the distribution of functions fall into three main categories according to whether they concern:

(i) Entirely new functions, e.g., conscription, food rationing, or the control of monopolies.

(ii) Existing functions which need to be considered afresh due to some major event or change of policy or because there is something wrong – e.g., shipping during a war, the Ministry of Food after the end of rationing, or the Commissioners of Crown Lands after the Crichel Down case.

(iii) Existing functions, other than (ii), which for one reason or another are not working as they should.

Every new function immediately poses the question of which department should be responsible for its administration: the question cannot be avoided. Similarly a major change of emphasis or policy usually quickly brings to light any administrative problems. Experienced advice is very necessary when decisions in either of these cases have to be made. But with the third category, finding the right solution once the issue is posed may be very much the lighter part of the task compared with discovering which problems need consideration.

The present arrangements within the Treasury for handling Machinery of Government questions and the development of these arrangements in recent years have been described in the penultimate section of the previous chapter (pages 333–38). So far as transfers of existing functions are concerned, whether falling in category (ii) or (iii) – for the two categories are not always readily separable – the present arrangements are briefly as follows. Main reliance is placed on informal committees of Permanent Secretaries under a Treasury Chairman. In some cases, however, committees composed wholly or partly of non-civil servants are appointed and asked to advise. Continuity is provided by two or three very senior Treasury officials and by one whole-time Principal in a Machinery of Government Branch. The latter assists the more senior officials, serves as Secretary to successive review committees, and is a focal point for knowledge about questions of organization and procedure.

So long as the need for paying continuous attention to the organization of government is fully recognized and responsibility for securing it rests clearly with the Treasury, there is much to be said for the present procedure. This is not to say, however, that it is necessarily the best in all possible future circumstances. Indeed, we have seen that the procedure has been changed several times in recent years. The arrangements are modest and might have to be altered if there was a major reorientation of Government policy or of pressure on departments. In such circumstances, it might be necessary to revert either to the 1942 arrangements, including a ministerial committee, or to the 1948 arrangements for intensive review.

The adaptation of the organization of government must be continuous and cannot be divorced from the normal administrative process. It is a governmental responsibility which cannot be entrusted to some form of intermittent public inquiry. At the same time, if all such matters are handled internally by the Civil Service, the public is not likely to be well informed, and the Government will not be drawing on those people outside the departments who may have worthwhile advice to offer. From this viewpoint, therefore, the public inquiry as exemplified by the Royal Commission, with its representative membership, its public hearings of evidence, and its published report, is a better device. The present procedure does not completely rule out the possibility of using these features of the open inquiry, however. There are recent examples in our field of committees con-

taining outside members and publishing their findings,[8] and rather
more examples of such committees dealing with the organization of
particular departments.[9] Nevertheless, there are two suggestions
which deserve consideration.

In the first place, more might be done to fulfil the pledge given
by the Government in 1948 to 'seek every possible help from persons
outside the Service, who will be associated with particular investigations'.[10] 'Mixed' committees might well be more frequently used
to examine problems involving relationships between departments:
men and women of affairs, and indeed academic students of public
administration, may have relevant experience of a kind complementary to that of the senior civil servants concerned. Unless there
are strong and clear reasons to the contrary, the reports of such
bodies should be published.

Secondly, there is a case to be made for the publication from
time to time – not necessarily each year – of a report surveying the
changes in the Machinery of Government in the period covered,
and giving as much information as possible about the reasons for
the changes and about any studies or inquiries conducted since the
last survey. For there will always remain many 'machinery' questions
which can best be handled by the Treasury or the departments,
either because no inquiry is needed, or because the matter is urgent,
or for general reasons of government. Moreover, periodical surveys
of this kind would be of considerable interest to the informed
public and of particular value to teachers and students of administration. In the long run they would both stimulate studies in this
rather neglected field and would provide the data for further advances in our knowledge of the administrative process.

It may be asked what the rôle of Parliament should be in this
context. In British constitutional development the central administration, by virtue perhaps of its origin as the personal instrument of
the Crown and because of the special rôle of the Cabinet in our
system of government, has usually been left to keep its own house
in order. Certainly during our period Parliament has never conceived its duty as being to handle the details of administrative
organization. Nowadays departmental arrangements are rarely of
primary political concern: 'machinery' Bills are almost sure to empty
the House of Commons. Parliament does, however, from time to
time – generally through the Public Accounts Committee or through
the Select Committee on Estimates – consider whether adequate
arrangements exist for ensuring the efficiency of the central administration. It is, of course, most important that Parliament should
satisfy itself that the Treasury and all departments are alive to the

need to keep the Machinery of Government up to date. But unless there is to be a radical change in the functioning of the House of Commons whereby it becomes involved in masses of detail, the House would presumably wish to stop there. A periodical report of the kind envisaged above might provide the basis for informed debate.

When we consider the great strain that has been thrown on the central administration during most of the period since 1914, the story of the way in which the whole machinery has developed and has been adapted is impressive. Problems remain, but the structure which has evolved over the centuries has been changed and extended with a fair degree of success to meet the conditions of the mid-20th century. The process of adaptation is more conscious than formerly, and more attention is paid to what Lord Waverley has called 'the broad organizational plan on which Ministers rely for the discharge of their executive responsibilities'.[11] We have seen that the beginning of wisdom in this context is the firm rejection of any belief in the possibility of defining a rigid and comprehensive framework of organization into which every function of government can be fitted for all time: but we are convinced that within the limits set by the essential need of flexibility the efficiency of administration can be enhanced by the constant study of the factors influencing the structure of government and by the application of such knowledge as can be distilled from that study. We hope that a little of that knowledge is contained in these pages.

APPENDIX A

NOTES

II. FINANCE, TRADE AND INDUSTRY

1. *Report of the Committee appointed to review the Working of the Agricultural Marketing Acts*, Ministry of Agriculture and Fisheries, Economic Series, No. 48, 1947, pp. 6, 11–12.
2. *Employment Policy*, Cmd. 6527/1944.
3. *Royal Commission on Scottish Affairs*, Evidence 1338. July 7, 1952.
4. See essays by A. J. Brown and R. W. Baldwin in R. V. Vernon and N. Mansergh (editors): *Advisory Bodies*, pp. 117–120, 137–138.
5. T. H. Middleton: *Food Production in War*, p. 4.
6. *Report of the War Cabinet for 1917*, Cd. 9005/1918.
7. D. Lloyd George: *War Memoirs* (2 vol. edition), Vol. I, p. 627.
8. 88 HC Deb. 1144; J. Hodge: *Workman's Cottage to Windsor Castle*, p. 177.
9. *History of the Ministry of Munitions*, Vol. VI, Part II, Ch. II, p. 19. This twelve-volume official History was never put on sale to the public. Copies of the first eight volumes were placed in a number of libraries during the inter-war years, and since the Second World War the remaining four volumes have been made available to those libraries. Copies of the complete History may now be read in the libraries of the House of Lords, House of Commons, British Museum and Imperial War Museum; in the London Library, the National Library of Scotland, the National Library of Wales, the Birmingham Public Library, the Leeds Public Library, the Newcastle upon Tyne Library and the Bodleian Library, Oxford; and in the libraries of the Universities of Aberdeen, Bristol, Cambridge, Glasgow, London, Manchester and Wales. For an interesting account of the preparation of the History see D. Hay, 'The Official History of the Ministry of Munitions 1915–1919', *Economic History Review*, Vol. XIV, No. 2, 1944.
10. H. Wolfe: *Labour Supply and Regulation*, p. 22.
11. W. H. Beveridge: *British Food Control*, pp. 85–86.
12. Ibid., p. 115.
13. *Report of a Sub-Committee of the Advisory Committee to the Board of Trade on Commercial Intelligence, with respect to measures for securing the position, after the war, of certain branches of British Industry*, p. 15. January, 1916. Cd. 8181.

14. *Report of the Machinery of Government Committee of the Ministry of Reconstruction*, Cd. 9230/1918.

15. H. Llewellyn Smith: *The Board of Trade*, p. 73.

16. Ibid., p. 75.

17. Ibid., p. 85. The Commercial Department was after 1919 called the Commercial Relations and Treaties Department.

18. *Report from the Select Committee on Estimates*, 1939, Evidence 2485. HC 145/1938–39.

19. Llewellyn Smith, op. cit., pp. 147–148.

20. In its final Report the Haldane *Committee on the Machinery of Government* thought that it would be impracticable to combine the Board of Trade and the agricultural departments, but one of the early drafts of that Report, dated February, 1918, was in favour of combining the Boards of Trade and of Agriculture and Fisheries and the Development Commission. See the Committee's Paper 18 in Mrs Webb's Reconstruction Papers in the Library of the London School of Economics and Political Science. The Acland *Forestry Sub-Committee of the Committee on Reconstruction* (Cd. 8881/1917–18) in a Note to their Report expressed certain opinions about the handling of forestry questions in the event of a combined United Kingdom Ministry of Agriculture being set up.

21. The Acland and Haldane Committees took very different views about forestry, the former being in favour of a separate administrative body while the latter felt that 'the supervision of agriculture should, under whatever scheme of geographical distribution of duties, always rest in the hands of the same authority for a given area as the supervision of forestry'. *Report*, p. 42.

22. *Committee on Civil Aerial Transport*, Cd. 9218/1918, pp. 16–18.

23. *Second Report from the Select Committee on Transport*, HC 136/1918.

24. Sir Auckland Geddes: *The Forging of a Family*, p. 244.

25. Lord Riddell: *Intimate Diary of the Peace Conference and After*, pp. 116–117, 132.

26. *Second Interim Report of the Committee on National Expenditure*, Cmd. 1582/1922, p. 26.

27. *Select Committee on Estimates* 1936, Evidence 1994–1996, HC 130/1935–36. Admiralty tankers and colliers were not included in this transfer.

28. Cd. 9218/1918, pp. 7, 21.

29. Ibid., pp. 16–18.

30. Sir Frederick Sykes: *From Many Angles*, p. 271.

31. G. D. H. Cole: *Labour in the Coal Mining Industry*, pp. 98, 119. The Sankey Commission's Reports were published as Cmd. 84, 85, 86, 210, 359–61/1919.

32. Cmd. 652/1920: Cd. 9084/1918: Cmd. 156/1919.

33. *First Annual Report of the Secretary for Mines in the year ending December 31, 1921*, p. 16. HMSO.
34. 131 HC Deb. 486.
35. 41 HL Deb. 790.
36. 41 HL Deb. 783/94.
37. *The Times*, February 26, 1920.
38. Sir Harold Butler: *Confident Morning*, p. 158.
39. *The Times*, October 18, 1920.
40. *Appropriation Accounts* 1922-23, HC 10/1924, p. 158.
41. The *Committee on National Expenditure* issued three Reports – Cmd. 1581, 1582, 1589/1922.
42. The Imperial Economic Committee was a Commonwealth body: the Empire Marketing Board was a United Kingdom organization. For an assessment of their influence see W. K. Hancock: *Survey of British Commonwealth Affairs*, Vol. II, Part 1, pp. 198-203.
43. 420 HC Deb. 1837.
44. Cmd. 3201/1928: 3252/1929.
45. Wolfe: op. cit., p. 46.
46. *History of the Ministry of Munitions*, Supplement to Part I of Vol. II, p. 9.
47. C. M. Kohan: *Works and Buildings*, p. 73.
48. 'The Co-ordination of Transport in Great Britain during the years 1935-1944,' *Journal of the Institute of Transport*, May-June, 1945.
49. *The Times*, May 3, 1941.
50. Cf. W. S. Churchill: *The Grand Alliance*, pp. 131-132.
51. *The Times*, May 2, 1941: 373 HC Deb. 1785.
52. *Public Accounts Committee*, 1941, Evidence 2963, HC 105/1940-41.
53. W. H. B. Court: *Coal*, Ch. 2 (ii).
54. Ibid., p. 45.
55. 373 HC Deb. 1785.
56. *Coal*, Cmd. 6364/1942.
57. Court, op. cit., p. 176.
58. Ibid., p. 162. Lord Beveridge, in *Power and Influence*, p. 288, has claimed that the new department was set up 'to save the face of the Board of Trade and its President'.
59. Court, op. cit., p. 177.
60. *Social Insurance and Allied Services*, Cmd. 6404, 5/1942.
61. *Social Insurance*, Part I, Cmd. 6550/1944, para. 158.
62. *Employment Policy*, p. 13. Cmd. 6527/1944.
63. Lord Swinton: *I Remember*, p. 249.
64. 517 HC Deb. 1366.
65. Ibid.

66. *The Times*, June 6, 1945, quoting the Prime Minister.

67. 413 HC Deb. 482.

68. 415 HC Deb. 1284.

69. *The Future Organization of the United Kingdom Atomic Energy Project*, Cmd. 8986/1953.

III. LAW, JUSTICE AND PUBLIC ORDER

1. Cf. Sir Frank Newsam: *The Home Office*, Ch. IV. For a full-length study of the police, see J. M. Hart: *The British Police*.

2. For a full description of the functions of the Home Office in this context see Newsam, op. cit., pp. 126–129.

3. R. M. Jackson: *The Machinery of Justice in England* (2nd edition), p. 341.

4. *Government Policy on Charitable Trusts in England and Wales*, Cmd. 9538/1955.

IV. SOCIAL SERVICES

1. Cmd. 6404, 5/1942.

2. *Report of the Committee on Scottish Administration*, p. 69. Cmd. 5563/1937.

3. *Social Insurance, Part II, Workmen's Compensation*, Cmd. 6551/1944, para. 2.

4. Lucy Masterman: *C. F. G. Masterman*, pp. 220–221, 230; Cf. 34 HC Deb. 1678; 37 HC Deb. 589–590. Masterman, first as Financial Secretary to the Treasury and then as Chancellor of the Duchy of Lancaster, was succeeded as Chairman by E. S. Montagu (Chancellor of the Duchy), Charles Roberts and Sir Edwin Cornwall (Comptrollers of the Household), and Waldorf Astor (Parliamentary Secretary to the Local Government Board) up to the creation of the Ministry of Health in July, 1919.

5. B. M. Allen: *Sir Robert Morant*, pp. 288–289; Violet Markham: 'Robert Morant – Some Personal Reminiscences', *Public Administration*, Winter, 1950.

6. *Beatrice Webb's Diaries, 1912–1924* (edited by M. Cole), p. 99.

7. Viscount Samuel: *Memoirs*, p. 84. For a somewhat similar judgment on Burns and the Local Government Board see R. C. K. Ensor: *England 1870–1914*, pp. 516–517.

8. Allen, op. cit., p. 268; Markham, loc. cit.

9. Sir Arthur Newsholme: *The Ministry of Health*, p. 103. Newsholme was Principal Medical Officer at the Local Government Board from 1908 to 1919.

10. C. Addison: *Four and a Half Years*, Vol. I, p. 23.

11. The negotiations can be traced in the works of Addison, Allen and Beatrice Webb already cited. See also Sir George Newman: *The Building of a Nation's Health.*

12. Allen, op. cit., pp. 288–289.

13. The group published a pamphlet in 1917 entitled *The Health of the People – a New National Policy.*

14. *Report of the War Pensions , etc., Statutory Committee for 1916,* Cd. 8750/1917. The voluntary response to appeals for money was negligible: in the year 1916 the receipts from public funds totalled over £1,500,000, those from private sources less than £10,000.

15. *Final Report of the Royal Commission on Unemployment Insurance,* Cmd. 4185/1932.

16. Sir A. Wilson and G. S. Mackay: *Old Age Pensions,* p. 94.

17. Cmd. 6153/1940.

18. Lord Reith's autobiography (J. C. W. Reith: *Into the Wind,* pp. 403–465) is a major documentary source for the following narrative. The other main documentary source is *Hansard,* particularly the group of debates in the House of Lords on planning and reconstruction during the years 1941 and 1942.

19. C. M. Kohan: *Works and Buildings,* p. 73.

20. Ibid., p. 77.

21. *The Report of the Committee on Land Utilisation in Rural Areas* was published as Cmd. 6378/1942: the *Final Report of the Committee on Compensation and Betterment* was published as Cmd. 6386/1942.

22. *A National Health Service,* Cmd. 6502/1944. *Social Insurance,* Parts I and II, Cmd. 6550, 6551/1944.

23. Cmd. 6550, para. 152.

24. Ibid., para. 158.

25. Ibid., para. 161.

26. *Report of the Committee on Homeless Children* (Scotland), Cmd. 6911/1946. *Report of the Care of Children Committee* (England and Wales), Cmd. 6922/1946.

27. 430 HC Deb. 763–785.

28. *The Ministry of Pensions Proposed Transfer of Functions,* Cmd. 8842/1953.

V. EXTERNAL AFFAIRS

1. For a fuller discussion of the general background and for details of internal departmental organization, see the following volumes in the *Whitehall Series* and *New Whitehall Series* – Sir John Tilley and S. Gaselee: *The Foreign Office* (1933); Lord Strang: *The Foreign Office* (1955); Sir George Fiddes: *The Dominions and Colonial Offices* (1926); Sir Charles Jeffries: *The Colonial Office* (1956); Sir Malcolm Seton: *The India Office* (1926).

2. L. S. Amery: *My Political Life*, Vol. II, p. 335.
3. *Proposals for the Reform of the Foreign Service*, Cmd. 6420/1943.
4. *Report on the System of Appointment in the Colonial Office and Colonial Services*, Cmd. 3554/1930.
5. *Organization of the Colonial Service*, Colonial Paper 197/1946.
6. *Reorganization of the Colonial Service*, Colonial Paper 306/1954.
7. *Her Majesty's Oversea Civil Service*, Cmd. 9768/1956.
8. *United Kingdom Administration and International Organizations*. A Report by a Study Group of the Institute of Public Administration. Royal Institute of International Affairs.

VI. DEFENCE

1. The origins of the air services are fully treated in W. Raleigh and H. A. Jones: *The War in the Air*, Vol. I.
2. Raleigh and Jones: op. cit., Vol. II, p. 354.
3. *Report on Air Organization*. Printed in the Volume of Appendices to Raleigh and Jones, op. cit.
4. See the speech of the Parliamentary Secretary to the Air Board on the second reading of the Air Force Bill, November 12, 1917. 99 HC Deb. 126–137. For other information about the formation of the RAF and the Air Ministry see Raleigh and Jones, op. cit., Vol. VI, Ch. 1, and also, *inter alia*, Lloyd George: *War Memoirs*, Ch. 57; Viscount Long: *Memories*, pp. 274–280; J. A. Spender: *Weetman Pearson, First Viscount Cowdray*, Ch. 20; Lord Beaverbrook: *Men and Power, 1917–1918*, Ch. VII.
5. C. E. Callwell: *Field Marshal Sir Henry Wilson*, Vol. II, pp. 312, 333.
6. See, for example, 112 HC Deb. 232–4: 113 HC Deb. 1531: 126 HC Deb. 1618–32. For an unfavourable opinion of Mr Churchill's attitude to the RAF at this time see the autobiography of the then Chief of the Air Staff, Sir Frederick Sykes: *From Many Angles*, pp. 266–267.
7. 151 HC Deb. 2477. Even the Geddes Committee on National Expenditure could see no advantage in scrapping the new Service. See its *First Interim Report*, Cmd. 1581, pp. 7–8.
8. The Report of the Salisbury Committee was published as Cmd. 2029/1924: for details of the Army proposals see p. 20. The Cabinet's decision was announced on August 2, 1923 (167 HC Deb. 1717). For an interesting account of the whole controversy about a separate Air Force, see N. Macmillan: *Sir Sefton Brancker*, Book II, Chs. 1–3.
9. Cmd. 467, para. 3.
10. W. S. Chalmers: *Life and Letters of David, Earl Beatty*, pp. 360–361.
11. Lord Chatfield: *It Might Happen Again*, p. 102. See also L. S. Amery: *My Political Life*, Vol. II, pp. 263–264.
12. *The Report of the Sub-Committee on Relations between the Navy and*

the Air Force was published together with the Report of the Salisbury Committee as Cmd. 2029/1924, pp. 28ff. See also the works of Amery, Chalmers and Chatfield cited, and Viscount Swinton: *I Remember*, Ch. XI.

13. Rear-Adm. H. G. Thursfield: 'The Transfer of the Fleet Air Arm', in *Journal of the United Service Institution*, February, 1939.

14. For the naval case, see Chatfield, op. cit., Ch. 15, and W. S. Churchill: *The Gathering Storm*, pp. 534–536. For the Air Force arguments, see Swinton, op. cit., pp. 140–142.

15. 367 HC Deb. 783; Churchill: *The Gathering Storm*, pp. 595–597: *The Grand Alliance*, p. 103.

16. *Report of the Committee on the Amalgamation of Services common to the Navy, Army and Air Force*, Cmd. 2649/1926, p. 44.

17. See, *inter alia*, Lloyd George, op. cit., Chs. 5, 6, 8, 9; *History of The Times*, Vol. IV, Part 1, pp. 271–275; Tom Clarke: *My Northcliffe Diary*, pp. 80–81; *History of the Ministry of Munitions*, Vol. I, Part I, Ch. 5; J. A. Spender and C. Asquith: *Life of Herbert Henry Asquith*, Vol. II, Ch. 40; C. Addison: *Four and a Half Years*, Vol. I, pp. 69, 73–74, 79; Viscount French: *1914*, Ch. 18.

18. Lord Beaverbrook: *Politicians and the War*, Vol. I, p. 65.

19. *History of the Ministry of Munitions*, Vol. I, Part III, Ch. 2; Lloyd George, op. cit., Vol. I, p. 111 (2 vol. edition).

20. Lloyd George, op. cit., Vol. I, p. 111.

21. *History of the Ministry of Munitions*, Vol. I, Part III, Ch. 5.

22. Ibid., Vol. II, Part I, Ch. 5.

23. Lloyd George, op. cit., Vol. I, pp. 121–122.

24. Quoted in Raleigh and Jones, op. cit., Vol. III, p. 278.

25. Quoted in *History of the Ministry of Munitions*, Vol. II, Part I, Ch. 2.

26. *History of the Ministry of Munitions*, Vol. II, Part I, Ch. 2. For his own story of these developments see Lloyd George, op. cit., Ch. 19.

27. Extract from a memorandum by the Joint Parliamentary Secretary to the Ministry of Munitions, Dr Addison, in November, 1915. See Addison, op. cit., Vol. I, pp. 148–150, 296–297. See also Lloyd George, op. cit., Ch. 19. The Ministry of Munitions set up its own research branch for new inventions and improvements some time before the rest of the work was transferred from the War Office.

28. *History of the Ministry of Munitions*, Vol. II, Part I, Ch. 5.

29. Raleigh and Jones, op. cit., Vol. III, p. 273.

30. Ibid., p. 274.

31. J. A. Spender: *Weetman Pearson, First Viscount Cowdray*, p. 229.

32. Raleigh and Jones, op. cit., Vol. III, pp. 282–283.

33. *History of the Ministry of Munitions*, Vol. II, Part I, Ch. 4, and Supplement to Part I, pp. 8–15. For Mr. Churchill's strictures on the Admiralty see *The World Crisis, 1916–18*, Part II, Ch. 12. The

remainder of this section is very largely drawn from the Supplement to Part I of Vol. II of the *History of the Ministry of Munitions.*

34. *History of the Ministry of Munitions*, Vol. II, Supplement to Part I.
35. The Report was not published until 1926. Cmd. 2649.
36. For a short survey of inter-Service supply between the wars see *11th Report from the Select Committee on National Expenditure*, 1940, Appendix 6, HC 156/1939–40.
37. For the fullest account see J. D. Scott and R. Hughes: *The Administration of War Production*, Part I. See also M. M. Postan: *British War Production*, and J. Hurstfield: *The Control of Raw Materials.*
38. Hurstfield, op. cit., pp. 33–34.
39. Ibid., p. 433.
40. Ibid., pp. 33–34.
41. Scott and Hughes, op. cit., p. 60.
42. Ibid.
43. Ibid., p. 70.
44. Postan, op. cit., p. 78.
45. Ibid., pp. 20, 137.
46. Churchill: *Their Finest Hour*, p. 12.
47. Postan, op. cit., pp. 116, 137.
48. Ibid., pp. 270–271.
49. W. K. Hancock and M. M. Gowing: *British War Economy*, p. 218n.
50. Churchill: *The Hinge of Fate*, p. 55.
51. Ibid., pp. 63–70: Postan, op. cit., p. 252: *Office of the Minister of Production*, Cmd. 6337/1942.
52. Scott and Hughes, op. cit., Part V: Postan, op. cit., pp. 252–265: Hurstfield, op. cit., p. 418. For details of American supply, which are most important in this context, see H. Duncan Hall: *North American Supply.*
53. Postan, op. cit., p. 111.
54. *Central Organization for Defence*, Cmd. 6923/1946.
55. 545 HC Deb. 34.
56. For a detailed account of all aspects of the subject, see T. H. O'Brien: *Civil Defence*, on which this chapter draws heavily.
57. J. W. Grove: *Regional Administration.* Fabian Research Series No. 147, 1951, p. 11.
58. Sir Frank Newsam: *The Home Office*, p. 58.
59. O'Brien, op. cit., p. 60.
60. Ibid., p. 63.
61. Ibid., p. 167.
62. Ibid.
63. Ibid., p. 469.

64. Ibid., p. 480.

65. 482 HC Deb. *231.*

66. *The Times,* September 28, 1954: *First Report of Advisory Committee on Publicity and Recruitment for the Civil Defence and Allied Services,* Cmd. 8708/1952.

67. 194 HL Deb. 217.

VII. SCIENTIFIC RESEARCH

1. *Third Report from the Select Committee on Estimates,* HC 132/1946–7.

2. *First Annual Report of the Advisory Council on Scientific Policy,* Cmd. 7465/1948.

3. *Government Scientific Organization in the Civilian Field,* p. 3., HMSO, 1951.

4. *Scheme for the Organization and Development of Scientific and Industrial Research,* Cd. 8005/1915.

5. For some details of the origin of the scheme see C. Addison: *Four and a Half Years,* Vol. I., Chapters 3 and 4 and Appendix I. ·

6. Order-in-Council, July 28, 1915.

7. The Charter was printed in the *Report of the Committee of the Privy Council for Scientific and Industrial Research for 1916–17,* pp. 47–48, Cd. 8718/1917.

8. Ibid., p. 3.

9. *Report of the Research Co-ordination Sub-Committee of the Committee of Civil Research,* para. 51. HMSO, 1928.

10. *Department of Scientific and Industrial Research – Report of a Committee of Enquiry.* Cmd. 9734/1956.

11. 196 HL Deb. 932. April 10, 1956.

12. *Memorandum on the Provisions of the Ministry of Health Bill as to the Work of the Medical Research Committee.* Cmd. 69/1919.

13. *Fifth Report* 1953–54, HC 218.

14. Cmd. 9212/1954, p. 92.

15. Quoted in B.E.C. Dugdale: *Arthur James Balfour,* Vol. II, p. 371. As there had been only one holder of the office of Lord President since October, 1919 – i.e., Lord Balfour – Fletcher was obviously thinking not of the career of the Medical Research Council but of the career of the earlier Medical Research Committee. For a list of the Ministers responsible for the Medical Research Committee see Note 4 to Chapter IV, ante, p. 370.

16. Ibid., p. 372.

17. *The Future Organization of the United Kingdom Atomic Energy Project.* Cmd. 8986/1953.

18. R. Darcy Best: 'The United Kingdom Atomic Energy Authority', *Public Administration,* Spring, 1956.

19. Ibid.

VIII. COMMON SERVICES

1. The biographies of the first three Ministers of Information contain sad stories of the early days of the department. See Lord Macmillan: *A Man of Law's Tale*, Ch. ix; J. C. W. Reith: *Into the Wind*, pp. 351–385; Duff Cooper: *Old Men Forget*, Ch. 17.

2. 417 HC Deb. 916–18.

3. The reports of the official inquiries mentioned were not published. The first of the 'probings' was carried out by a *Committee on the Cost of Home Information Services* under the chairmanship of Sir Henry L. French, which reported in July, 1949 (Cmd. 7836). In the early summer of 1950 the *Select Committee on Estimates* examined 'Government Information Services' in their *Fifth Report* of the 1950 Session (HC 131). The Treasury reply to the Select Committee was published in the Committee's *Second Report* for the Session 1950–51 (HC 79). Shortly after the Conservatives took office, in October, 1951, a ministerial committee reopened the question of the need for the Central Office of Information and decided that the department should continue. No report was published. Finally, in 1952, an official review of the Overseas Information Services was made, and this was immediately followed by the appointment of an independent Committee under the chairmanship of the Earl of Drogheda. Parts of the Drogheda Report were published in April, 1954, under the title *Summary of the Report of the Independent Committee of Enquiry into the Overseas Information Services* (Cmd. 9138).

4. For details of the work of the Central Office of Information see the three *Annual Reports* which the department issued for 1947–48 (Cmd. 7567), for 1948–49 (Cmd. 7830), and for 1949–50 (Cmd. 8081). The first of these contains a useful historical account of the growth of information services.

5. Herbert Morrison: *Government and Parliament*, p. 19.

6. *The Times*, May 13, 1952.

7. 561 HC Deb. 1048.

IX. THE CENTRAL CO-ORDINATION OF GOVERNMENT

1. W. F. Monypenny and G. E. Buckle: *Life of Benjamin Disraeli, Earl of Beaconsfield* (2 vol. edit.), Vol. I, Pt. IV, Ch. 2.

2. Suggestion to the *Royal Commission on Administration of Military and Naval Departments*, 1890, C.5979.

3. N. H. Gibbs: *The Origins of Imperial Defence*, p. 8.

4. Ibid., pp. 9–22.

5. The main sources for the history of the Committee from 1904 to 1939 are Lord Hankey's two books: *Government Control in War* and *Diplomacy by Conference*, and an article by Major General (now Lord) Ismay on 'The Machinery of the Committee of Imperial

Defence' in the *Journal of the Royal United Service Institution* for May, 1939.

6. Robert Blake: *The Unknown Prime Minister*, p. 397; see also Austen Chamberlain: *Down the Years*, Ch. 8.

7. Joseph Davies: *The Prime Minister's Secretariat 1916–1920*, pp. 52, 59.

8. *Report of the War Cabinet for 1917*, Ch. I. Cd. 9005/1918.

9. Davies, op. cit., p. 62.

10. 155 HC Deb. 213–276.

11. Blake, op. cit., pp. 466, 501.

12. *Fourth Report*, p. 86. Cd. 7338/1914.

13. *Second Report*, HC 125, 151/1917–18. See also *First Report*, HC 113/1919.

14. Cd. 9230/1918: Cmd. 62/1919.

15. 'O & M: How it all began,' *Public Administration*, Spring, 1949.

16. Minute of the Haldane Committee, January 11, 1918, among the Reconstruction Papers of Beatrice Webb in the Library of the London School of Economics and Political Science.

17. *Memorandum with respect to the reorganization of the Board of Trade*, Cmd. 8912/1918.

18. Sir John Anderson: *The Organization of Economic Studies in relation to the problems of Government*, p. 7.

19. Cmd. 1461/1921.

20. *Second Interim Report*, p. 8. Cmd. 1582/1922.

21. *First Report from the Select Committee on Estimates*, Evid. 750–3. HC 96/1924.

22. Cmd. 2029/1924, p. 18.

23. *First Interim Report*, signed December 14, 1921, p. 8. Cmd. 1581/1922.

24. The Committee's Report was signed on January 2, 1923, but was not published until 1926. Cmd. 2649.

25. L. S. Amery: *My Political Life*, Vol. II, p. 265.

26. Cmd. 3920/1931, pp. 64–65.

27. 153 HC Deb. 1352–6.

28. 64 HL Deb. 415–46: 232 HC Deb. 2393–2454.

29. K. Feiling: *Neville Chamberlain*, pp. 277, 314.

30. *Statement on Defence*, 1936, Cmd. 5107.

31. 100 HL Deb. 141, March 19, 1936.

32. W. S. Churchill: *The Gathering Storm*, pp. 536–537.

33. Feiling, op. cit., pp. 314–315, 318. For another similar ministerial statement see the speech of Viscount Swinton, the Secretary of State for Air, on February 27, 1936. 99 HL Deb. 833–47.

34. M. M. Postan: *British War Production*, pp. 35–36: Feiling, op. cit., p. 318.

35. For the controversy about the appointment and career of Sir Thomas Inskip as Minister for Co-ordination of Defence, and for some of the political arguments against appointing one of the other possible contenders for the office, see, *inter alia*, Churchill, op. cit., pp. 156–157; Feiling, op. cit., pp. 277–279, 312–319; G. M. Young: *Stanley Baldwin*, p. 225; Viscount Templewood: *Nine Troubled Years*, pp. 200–201.

36. Lord Chatfield: *It Might Happen Again*, pp. 166–167.

37. Cmd. 6923/1946.

38. Cmd. 3909/1931, p. 172.

39. See, *inter alia*, Sir John Anderson: 'The Machinery of Government' in *Public Administration*, Autumn, 1946; Herbert Morrison: *Government and Parliament*, Ch. 2; W. K. Hancock and M. M. Gowing: *The British War Economy*, Chs. 3, 8; chapters by D. N. Chester in *British Government Since 1918* (Institute of Public Administration, 1950), in *Lessons of the British War Economy* (edit. D. N. Chester), and in *The British Economy 1945–50* (edit. G. D. N. Worswick and P. Ady).

40. Cmd. 6923/1946. For Lord Chatfield's own account of his impossible position see *It Might Happen Again*, Ch. 23, and his pamphlet *Defence After the War* (1944), pp. 14–15.

41. Churchill: *Their Finest Hour*, pp. 15–16.

42. Cmd. 6923/1946.

43. Churchill: *Their Finest Hour*, pp. 219–221.

44. For details of the position in 1942 see *The Organization for Joint Planning*, Cmd. 6351/1942.

45. Churchill: *Their Finest Hour*, p. 16. See also P. J. Grigg: *Prejudice and Judgment*, pp. 356–357.

46. Cmd. 6923/1946.

47. 545 HC Deb. 33–37. October 25, 1955.

48. Ibid. See also an interesting article on 'Single-Minded Defence' in *The Times*, October 20, 1955.

49. Cmd. 6923/1946.

50. Haldane: *Autobiography*, pp. 331–332; F. Maurice: *Haldane 1915–28*, p. 179; E. C. Dugdale: *Arthur James Balfour*, Vol. II, p. 372; Sir John Anderson: *The Organization of Economic Studies*, pp. 9–10.

51. Cmd. 2440/1925.

52. H. Llewellyn Smith: *The Board of Trade*, pp. 239–241.

53. Cmd. 3478/1930.

54. Essay by Sir Piers Debenham in the Supplement to *Oxford Economic Papers*, 1953, on 'Sir Hubert Henderson'.

55. Sir Richard Hopkins: Introductory Note to D. N. Chester (edit.): *Lessons of the British War Economy*.

56. Sir Richard Hopkins: loc. cit.; Sir Edward Bridges: *Treasury Control,*

p. 14; Sir John Anderson: *The Organization of Economic Studies*, pp. 16–17.

57. G. D. A. MacDougall, 'The Prime Minister's Statistical Section', in D. N. Chester (edit.): *Lessons of the British War Economy*, pp. 59, 66.

58. Cmd. 6527/1944, p. 26.

59. *Report of the Research Co-ordination Sub-Committee of the Committee of Civil Research*, p. 11. HMSO, 1928.

60. *Government Scientific Organization in the Civilian Field*, p. 5. HMSO, 1951.

61. R. Darcy Best: 'The United Kingdom Atomic Energy Authority,' *Public Administration*, Spring, 1956.

62. Cmd. 6525/1944.

63. *Sixteenth Report from the Select Committee on National Expenditure*, HC 120/1941–2.

64. The Lecture was reprinted in *Public Administration*, Autumn, 1946.

65. *Fifth Report from the Select Committee on Estimates*, HC 143/1946–7.

66. *Fourth Report from the Select Committee on Estimates*, HC 100/1947–8.

67. The reports of these three inquiries have been published in full or in part. See Cmd. 8986/1953; 9163/1954; 9483/1955.

68. Two reviews by 'outside' committees which have been published are the Report of the Ryan Committee on the *Organization of the Ministry of Agriculture and Fisheries*, HMSO, 1951, and the Jephcott Report on the *Department of Scientific and Industrial Research*, Cmd. 9734/1956.

69. The full text of the announcement was published in *The Times*, July 20, 1956.

70. 557 HC Deb. 636. July 26, 1956.

X. THE HANDLING OF ADMINISTRATIVE CHANGE

1. L. Petch: 'The Study of the Structure of Government,' *O & M Bulletin*, Vol. 5, No. 6.

2. *The Politics of Aristotle*, Bk. IV, Ch. xv. (Translated by Sir Ernest Barker.)

3. Cd. 9230/1918, pp. 7–8.

4. Cmd. 8609/1952.

5. Cmd. 9212/1954.

6. Cmd. 9483/1955.

7. Cd. 9230/1918, p. 63.

8. Cf. *The Future Organization of the United Kingdom Atomic Energy Project*, Cmd. 8986/1953; *Report of the Committee on Departmental Records*, Cmd. 9163/1954; *Report of the Committee on Crown Lands*, Cmd. 9483/1955.

9. The following reports were issued by 'independent' or 'mixed' committees: *Organization of the Ministry of Agriculture and Fisheries*, HMSO, 1951: *Report of the Committee appointed to review the Provincial and Local Organization and Procedures of the Ministry of Agriculture, Fisheries and Food*, Cmd. 9732/1956; *Department of Scientific and Industrial Research, Report of a Committee of Enquiry*, Cmd. 9734/1956; *Report of the Committee of Enquiry into the Public Trustee Office*, Cmd. 9755/1956.

10. *Fourth Report from the Select Committee on Estimates*, p. 15, HC 100/1947–8.

11. Sir John Anderson: 'The Machinery of Government,' *Public Administration*, Autumn, 1946.

BIBLIOGRAPHICAL NOTE

WHILE a great deal has been written on various aspects of British government, little attention has been paid hitherto to the subjects dealt with in this survey. The number of official papers, books and articles devoted specifically to the structure of the central administration and to the distribution of functions among departments is very small. At the same time there are obviously a great many sources which are not directly concerned – or not even intended to be concerned at all – with the subject matter of our study which none the less provide highly relevant information and background material. Many such sources have been cited, and indeed the footnotes collected together in Appendix A form a select reading list. In this Note, therefore, we mention only some of the more general works of help to those interested in particular in the subject matter of this study.

Before doing this it may be useful to readers unfamiliar with the main outlines of British Government to be given a short reading list of general books. Wilfrid Harrison: *The Government of Britain* (3rd edition, 1955) is a very useful short introduction, and in rather a different way so is E. N. Gladden: *Introduction to Public Administration* (2nd edition, 1952). Two standard works are Sir Ivor Jennings: *Cabinet Government* (2nd edition 1951), and the second edition of A. B. Keith's *The British Cabinet System*, by N. H. Gibbs (1952). A sound recent full-scale survey of our system by an American scholar is H. M. Stout: *British Government* (1953). An authoritative account 'from the inside' is Herbert Morrison: *Government and Parliament* (1954). For a detailed and comprehensive study of the executive side of British government see the 1935 edition of Part II of W. R. Anson's *Law and Custom of the Constitution* – 'The Crown' – by A. B. Keith. For a short historical account of the Civil Service see E. Cohen: *The Growth of the British Civil Service* (1941). Among the numerous descriptive and critical books on the Service see H. E. Dale: *The Higher Civil Service of Great Britain* (1941); H. R. G. Greaves: *The Civil Service in the Changing State* (1946); T. A. Critchley: *The Civil Service Today* (1951); F. Dunnill: *The Civil Service – Some Human Aspects* (1956); and W. A. Robson (edit.): *The Civil Service in England and France* (1956). A great deal of interesting material on British administration is published in *Public Administration*, the Journal of the Royal Institute of Public Administration.

There have only been two attempts, in short compass, to deal critically with the special subject matter of this study. Chapters VIII, X and XI of the second edition (1950) of K. B. Smellie's *A Hundred Years of English*

Government contain a description of the main changes in the structure of central government between the years 1914 and 1949. W. J. M. Mackenzie contributed a stimulating essay on 'The Structure of Central Administration' to a volume entitled *British Government since 1918*, published by the Institute of Public Administration in 1950. Some of the other essays in that valuable collection are also highly relevant to this study. An interesting book by the first Secretary to the Cabinet – Lord Hankey's *Diplomacy by Conference* (1946) – discusses the history of the Cabinet during the early part of our period.

The annual volumes of *Public General Acts, Statutory Rules and Orders,* and *Statutory Instruments*; the verbatim reports of parliamentary debates – *Hansard*; the Reports from and evidence given to the House of Commons' Select Committees on *Public Accounts, Estimates,* and *National Expenditure*; and the columns of *The Times,* are basic sources used in the preparation of this survey. The *Index to Statutes* and the *Guide to Government Orders* are particularly helpful to students, since much of the material listed in them appears under the names of the departments. There is, of course, no Manual of British Government, issued annually, which gives complete details of the number of departments and the distribution of work among them. In recent years the Central Office of Information has published *Britain: An Official Handbook,* which contains excellent short descriptions of the departments. A picture of the central administration as a whole at any one time can be pieced together from the following annual publications: *The Imperial Calendar and Civil Service List*; *Whitaker's Almanack*; the *Estimates* of the amounts of money required each year by the Civil, Revenue and Defence departments; the Foreign, Colonial, and Commonwealth Relations Offices' *Lists* (there was also an *India Office List*); and the Navy, Army and Air Force *Lists.* Some departments issue Annual Reports which usually record any changes or transfers of functions.[a]

For a good general picture of the central departments a few years before the beginning of the First World War see A. L. Lowell's classic *Government of England* (1908), Chapters IV–VI. The best sources of detailed information about the distribution of work, etc., in or about the year 1914 are the Reports and massive volumes of evidence issued by the *Royal Commission on the Civil Service,* 1912–1915 (Cd. 6209, 6210, 6534, 6535, 6739, 6740, 7338, 7339, 7340, 7748, 7749, 7832, 8130).

A great deal of valuable material on the administrative arrangements of the First World War is contained in the two *Reports of the War Cabinet* for 1917 and 1918 (Cd. 9005, Cmd. 325) and in the volumes sponsored by the Carnegie Endowment for International Peace. The most useful of those volumes for our purposes are J. A. Fairlie: *British War Administration* (1919); E. M. H. Lloyd: *Experiments in State Control* (1924); N. B. Dearle: *Dictionary of Official War-Time Organization* (1928); W. H. Beveridge: *British Food Control* (1928); T. H. M. Middleton: *Food Production in War*

---

[a] For lists of the Annual Reports issued by departments see an article on 'Departmental Reports' by F. M. G. Willson in *Public Administration,* Summer, 1952. There have been very few changes since that article was written.

(1923); C. E. Fayle: *The War and the Shipping Industry* (1927); J. A. Salter: *Allied Shipping Control* (1921); H. Wolfe: *Labour Supply and Regulation* (1923).

For the reconstruction period after 1918 the following official papers are useful: the Report of the Haldane *Committee on the Machinery of Government*, 1918 (Cd. 9230), and Pamphlet No. 38 of a series called 'Problems of Reconstruction', issued by the Ministry of Reconstruction in 1919 – *The Business of Government*; the Reports of a *Committee on the Organization and Staffing of Government Offices*, 1918–19, Cd. 9074, 9219/20, Cmd. 61/2; and the Reports of the *Committee on National Expenditure*, 1922, Cmd. 1581/2, 1589.

The books composing the *Whitehall Series*, edited by Sir James Marchant, were published between 1925 and 1935. Taken together they give an extensive but incomplete picture of the central administration in the inter-war period, while each contains some valuable material on the earlier history of the departments concerned. The books appeared in the following order – Sir Edward Troup: *The Home Office* (1925); Sir Arthur Newsholme: *The Ministry of Health* (1925); Sir Malcolm Seton: *The India Office* (1926); Sir George Fiddes: *The Dominions and Colonial Offices* (1926); Sir L. A. Selby-Bigge: *The Board of Education* (1927, revised edition 1934); Sir G. Evelyn Murray: *The Post Office* (1927); Sir Francis Floud: *The Ministry of Agriculture and Fisheries* (1927); Sir Thomas W. Heath: *The Treasury* (1927); Sir H. Llewellyn Smith: *The Board of Trade* (1928); J. K. Moylan: *Scotland Yard* (1929, revised edition 1934); Sir J. Tilley and S. Gaselee: *The Foreign Office* (1933); H. Gordon: *The War Office* (1935).

Particularly useful for the distribution of social welfare functions are the Reports by Political and Economic Planning on *British Health Services* and *British Social Services* (1937). See also J. D. Millett: *The Unemployment Assistance Board* (1940).

Surveys of some aspects of inter-war administration, as well as great detail of the administrative developments between 1939 and 1945, are to be found in the as yet incomplete set of official volumes on the *Civil History of the Second World War* edited by Sir Keith Hancock. See especially: W. K. Hancock and M. M. Gowing: *British War Economy* (1949); M. M. Postan: *British War Production* (1952); R. J. Hammond: *Food* (1951–56); E. L. Hargreaves and M. M. Gowing: *Civil Industry and Trade* (1952); T. H. O'Brien: *Civil Defence* (1955); K. A. H. Murray: *Agriculture* (1955); W. H. B. Court: *Coal* (1951); C. M. Kohan: *Works and Buildings* (1952); J. Hurstfield: *The Control of Raw Materials* (1953); J. D. Scott and R. Hughes: *Administration of War Production* (1955). There were fewer official publications about general departmental arrangements in the Second than in the First World War. The most interesting parliamentary papers on administrative organization issued during the war and in the immediately post-war period were the *Sixteenth Report from the Select Committee on National Expenditure* (HC 120/1941–42), and the *Fifth Report from the Select Committee on Estimates* (HC 143/1946–47). Sir

John Anderson's 1946 Romanes Lecture on *The Machinery of Government* is an important statement about Cabinet organization. The lecture was published separately and was reprinted in *Public Administration*, Autumn, 1946.

For the position in the early 1950s the first three volumes of Memoranda submitted to the *Royal Commission on Scottish Affairs*, 1952–1954, lay out in considerable detail the functions of many of the central departments. The first volume of a *New Whitehall Series*, edited by Sir Robert Fraser, appeared in 1954 – *The Home Office* by Sir Frank Newsam. Later volumes so far issued are Lord Strang: *The Foreign Office* (1955); Sir Charles Jeffries: *The Colonial Office* (1956); Sir Harold Emmerson: *The Ministry of Works* (1956). *The Scottish Office and other Scottish Government Departments* by Sir David Milne, and *The Ministry of Pensions and National Insurance* by Sir Geoffrey King will both be published in 1957. A very useful recent book on the Treasury is S. H. Beer: *Treasury Control* (1956).

The structure of Scottish administration has already been well covered. *The Report on Scottish Administration* 1937 (Cmd. 5563) and the *Report of the Royal Commission on Scottish Affairs*, 1952–54 (Cmd. 9212) contain very thorough accounts of recent Scottish administrative development. The Scottish Office published a useful *Handbook on Scottish Administration* in 1950 and issued a revised version in 1956.

APPENDIX C

TABLE OF CHANGES:
AUGUST 1914 – DECEMBER 1956

THIS table is mainly composed of the following items:

1. The establishment, division, amalgamation and abolition of departments within the central administration.
2. Certain major changes concerning the Cabinet.
3. Transfers of functions between departments.

Where the changes were made by statute, the Act and any relevant Statutory Order or Statutory Instrument made under the Act are given. Where there is no such reference it may be assumed that the change was made by administrative action.

The table is not exhaustive. While practically all the statutory transfers are included, some of the transfers made by administrative action are omitted because of their relatively minor importance.

1914

August   Declaration of War.

November   War Council appointed.

1915

February   War Trade Department established.

May   Board of Trade to Board of Agriculture and Fisheries:
> Functions concerning the maintenance of small harbours principally used by the fishing industry in England and Wales.
>> (Fishery Harbours Act, 1915)

June   War Council replaced by Dardanelles Committee.

> Ministry of Munitions established. Various supply functions transferred to it from the War Office, and certain powers in future to be exercised concurrently by the Admiralty, the Army Council and the Minister of Munitions.
>> (Ministry of Munitions Act, 1915: SR & O 580/1915)

July   Committee of the Privy Council for Scientific and Industrial Research appointed.

N

November   Dardanelles Committee replaced by War Committee.

War Office to Ministry of Munitions:
Specification, design and research functions.

1916
January   Home Office to Foreign Office:
Functions concerning trading with the enemy.

February   Ministry of Blockade established.

National Organizing Committee for War Savings and Central Advisory Committee for War Savings set up by Treasury Minute. The two were amalgamated as the National War Savings Committee in April, 1916. The Scottish War Savings Committee was established at about the same time. In 1919 the word 'War' was dropped from the titles of the two Committees.

Admiralty to War Office:
Responsibility for all home air defence.

April   Board of Trade to Colonial Office:
Management of the Imperial Institute.
(Imperial Institute (Management) Act, 1916)

May   First Air Board appointed. (Advisory.)

September   War Office to Ministry of Munitions:
Supply of mechanical transport and railway material.

December   Cabinet and War Committee replaced by War Cabinet. Secretariat of the War Committee (originally of Committee of Imperial Defence) became War Cabinet Secretariat.

Ministry of Pensions established.
(Ministry of Pensions Act, 1916)

Ministries of Labour, Food and Shipping established under a Minister of Labour, a Food Controller and a Shipping Controller. President of the Air Board deemed to be a Minister, and power given to reconstitute the Air Board as an executive authority (this was done in February, 1917).
(New Ministries and Secretaries Act, 1916)

Department of National Service established under a Director General.

Department of Scientific and Industrial Research established.

1917
January   Food Production Department established, at first as an integral part of the Board of Agriculture and Fisheries and later

as a separate department responsible to the President of the Board.

Board of Trade to Ministry of Labour:
Functions under the Conciliation Act, 1896, the Labour Exchanges Act, 1909, the Trade Boards Act, 1909, the National Insurance (Unemployment) Acts, 1911–16, and Part I of the Munitions of War Act, 1915.
(New Ministries and Secretaries Act, 1916: SR & O 46/1917)

February   Admiralty to Ministry of Shipping:
Transport Department.

Admiralty, War Office and Commissioners of Chelsea Hospital to Ministry of Pensions:
Functions relating to disablement pensions and grants to servicemen and their dependants.
(Ministry of Pensions Act, 1916: SR & O 125/1917)

Food Controller given concurrent powers with Admiralty and Army Council under Defence of the Realm (Amendment) (No. 2) Act, 1915.
(New Ministries and Secretaries Act, 1916: SR & O 124/1917)

March   Department of National Service converted into a Ministry.
(Ministry of National Service Act, 1917)

Board of Trade to Ministry of Labour:
Functions under Munitions of War (Amendment) Act, 1916.
(New Ministries and Secretaries Act, 1916: SR & O 288/1917)

Board of Trade to Ministry of Food:
Powers relating to restriction of the output of beer.
(New Ministries and Secretaries Act, 1916: SR & O 287/1917)

Service departments to Ministry of Munitions:
Manufacture and inspection of aircraft other than lighter-than-air machines.

April   Board of Trade to Ministry of Shipping:
Ship Licensing Committee and Inter-Allied Chartering Executive.

May   Ministry of Munitions to War Office:
Design and specification of mechanical warfare supplies.
(Re-transferred October, 1917.)

War Office to Board of Trade:
Control of timber supplies.

Ministry of Shipping to Admiralty:
Responsibility for building and repair of merchant ships.

Government Actuary appointed. Previously this officer had been Chief Actuary to the Joint Committee of the Insurance Commissions.

July   Board of Trade to Ministry of Labour:
Department of Labour Statistics.
(New Ministries and Secretaries Act, 1916: SR & O 666/1917)

August   Ministry of Reconstruction established.
(New Ministries Act, 1917)

November   Ministry of National Service reconstructed: powers of Army Council and Secretary of State relating to recruitment, enlistment of aliens, claims for discharge, exemptions, reserve forces, etc., transferred to it. Minister of National Service henceforward to exercise certain powers under the Army Act and the Reserve Forces Act, 1882, concurrently with Army Council and Secretary of State.
(Ministry of National Service Act, 1917: New Ministries and Secretaries Act, 1916: SR & O 1095/1917)

1918
January   Air Council and Air Ministry set up.
(Air Force (Constitution) Act, 1917: SR & O 1333/1917, 11/1918)

February   Secretary for Overseas Trade appointed, responsible jointly to Foreign Secretary and President of the Board of Trade. The Department of Overseas Trade had been set up at the end of 1917. The statutory authority for the appointment of the Secretary was not effective until March, 1918.
(Overseas Trade Department (Secretary) Act, 1918)

March   Ministry of Information established.

April   Treasury to DSIR:
Responsibility for maintenance of the National Physical Laboratory. (Royal Society previously responsible with Treasury Grants.)

Royal Naval Air Service and Royal Flying Corps combined to form the Royal Air Force.
(Air Force (Constitution) Act, 1917: SR & O 424/1918)

November   Armistice.

Ministry of Information disbanded.

Ministry of Munitions to Ministry of Labour:
Labour functions.

December   Powers of Minister of National Service under Army Act and Reserve Forces Act, 1882, to be exercised concurrently by the Minister and the Army Council.

(Ministry of National Service Act, 1917: New Ministries and Secretaries Act, 1916: SR & O 1688/1918)

1919

February   Air Ministry became responsible for civil aviation. Civil flying had been banned during the war, but prior to 1914 the Home Office had been responsible for its regulation.

(Air Navigation Act, 1919)

March   Ministry of National Service and Food Production Department disbanded. War Trade Department taken over by Board of Trade.

Ministry of Munitions to War Office:
Responsibility for design, research, inventions and technical military stores.

April   Ministry of Munitions to Board of Trade:
Electrical Power Supply Department.

May   Ministry of Pensions to Ministry of Labour:
Powers relating to training and employment of disabled servicemen.

(New Ministries and Secretaries Act, 1916: SR & O 674/1919)

Ministry of Blockade disbanded.

June   Ministry of Munitions to Board of Trade:
Functions relating to industries concerned with optical glass.

Ministry of Reconstruction disbanded.

July   Treasury to Air Ministry:
Meteorological Office – amalgamated with the Meteorological Service of the Admiralty and Air Ministry and the Meteorological Section of the Royal Engineers. For accounting purposes the date of transfer was taken to be October 1, 1919. The transfer was not completed until 1922.

Ministry of Health established and assumed all the powers of the Local Government Board, the English and Welsh Insurance Commissioners, and the powers of the Privy Council and the Lord President under the Midwives Acts, 1902 and 1918. Welsh Board of Health set up.

(Ministry of Health Act, 1919: SR & O 850/1919)

Scottish Board of Health set up and assumed all the powers and duties of the Local Government Board for Scotland and the Scottish Insurance Commissioners; the powers and duties of the Scottish Education Department for medical inspection and treatment of children and young persons; the powers of the Minister of Pensions with respect to the health of disabled servicemen after they have left the service so far as these powers relate to Scotland; and any other powers in Scotland of any department as to health matters.

(Scottish Board of Health Act, 1919: SR & O 851/1919)

Government Actuary's Department set up under the Treasury.

University Grants Committee appointed.

August   Consequential transfer of property from various departments to Ministry of Health.

(Ministry of Health Act, 1919: SR & O 1283/1919)

September   Ministry of Pensions to Ministry of Labour:
Powers relating to the training and employment of dependants of deceased servicemen.

(New Ministries and Secretaries Act, 1916: SR & O 1280/1919)

Forestry Commission established. Took over functions relating to forestry and powers under the Destructive Insects and Pests Acts, 1877 and 1907, from the agricultural departments.

(Forestry Act, 1919)

Export Credits Department set up at the Board of Trade.

Powers under the Highlands and Islands (Medical Services) Grant Act, 1913, transferred to the Scottish Board of Health.

(Scottish Board of Health Act, 1919: SR & O 1285/1919)

Ministry of Transport established with all the powers of the Road Board: most of the powers of the Board of Trade relating to inland transport and certain powers concerning harbours, docks and piers: and certain transport powers of the Minister of Health.

(Ministry of Transport Act, 1919: SR & O 1440, 1441, 1442/1919)

Board of Trade to DSIR:
Custody and maintenance of electrical standards.

October   Board of Education to Ministry of Health:
Powers relating to expectant mothers and nursing mothers, and to children under five.

Home Office to Ministry of Health:
Powers of supervising the administration of Part I of the Children Act, 1908, relating to infant life protection.
(Ministry of Health Act, 1919: SR & O 1443/1919)

Admiralty to Air Ministry:
Airship Section.

November War Cabinet replaced by Cabinet of pre-December, 1916, size. Committee of Imperial Defence reconstituted. War Cabinet Secretariat divided into Cabinet Secretariat and Secretariat of CID.

Board of Education to DSIR:
Geological Survey and Museum of Practical Geology.

Paymaster General to Board of Education:
Payment of teachers' pensions.

Board of Trade to Home Office:
All powers as to appointment of members and procedure of Railway and Canal Commissioners.
(Ministry of Transport Act, 1919: SR & O 1901/1919)

December Board of Education to Ministry of Health:
Powers relating to medical inspection and treatment of young persons.
(Ministry of Health Act, 1919: SR & O 1894/1919)

Board of Agriculture and Fisheries renamed Ministry of Agriculture and Fisheries.
(Ministry of Agriculture and Fisheries Act, 1919)

1920
January Ministry of Munitions to Air Ministry:
Supply of aircraft.

Various Irish departments to Ministry of Transport:
Transport functions.
(Ministry of Transport Act, 1919: SR & Os 1939, 1940, 1941, 1942, 1943/1919)

Board of Trade to Ministry of Transport:
Certain powers relating to electricity.
(Electricity (Supply) Act, 1919: SR & O 58/1920)

Ministry of Pensions to Ministry of Labour:
Consequential transfer of power of certifying land, required for a power previously transferred.

(New Ministries and Secretaries Act, 1916: SR & O 184/1920)

March   Committee of the Privy Council for Medical Research appointed.

April   Secretary for Scotland to Scottish Education Department: Responsibility for reformatory and industrial schools.

(Education (Scotland) Act, 1918: SR & O 429/1920)

Home Office to Secretary for Scotland:
Power to appoint Inspectors of Reformatory and Industrial Schools in Scotland.

(Children Act, 1908: SR & O 374/1920)

Privy Council and Lord President to Scottish Board of Health:
Powers under the Midwives Acts.
Secretary for Scotland to Scottish Board of Health:
Powers concerning alkali works; births, deaths and marriages; burial grounds; marriage notices; rivers pollution; and vaccination.

(Scottish Board of Health Act, 1919: SR & O 1944/1920)

Medical Research Council incorporated by Royal Charter. Duties of the Medical Research Committee under the National Insurance Act, 1911, transferred to the Medical Research Committee of the Privy Council.

(Ministry of Health Act, 1919: SR & O 252/1920)

Lord Lieutenant of Ireland to Ministry of Transport:
Transport functions.

(Ministry of Transport Act, 1919: SR & O 828/1920)

May   Board of Trade to Ministry of Transport:
Property in Holyhead and Ramsgate Harbours.

(Ministry of Transport Act, 1919: SR & Os 829, 830/ 1920)

Home Office to Ministry of Health:
Powers and duties under the Anatomy Acts, 1832 and 1871, and certain powers under the Lunacy and Mental Deficiency Acts.

(Ministry of Health Act, 1919: SR & Os 808, 809/1920)

Ministry of Health to Board of Education:

Powers and duties in relation to public libraries, museums and gymnasiums.

(Ministry of Health Act, 1919: SR & O 810/1920)

June   Ministry of Munitions to War Office:
Remaining Army supply functions.

(Ministry of Munitions Act, 1915: SR & O 1308/1920)

Admiralty to Ministry of Pensions:
Certain mercantile marine pensions.

(War Pensions (Administrative Provisions) Act, 1919: SR & O 1307/1920)

July   Ministry of Munitions to Office of Works:
The Housing Department of the Ministry.

August   Ministry of Pensions to Ministry of Labour:
Powers concerning disabled officers and nurses.

(New Ministries and Secretaries Act, 1916: SR & O 1667/1920)

November   Secretary for Scotland, Scottish Board of Health and Board of Agriculture for Scotland to Ministry of Transport:
Certain transport powers and duties.

(Ministry of Transport Act, 1919: SR & Os 2122, 2123, 2124/1920)

Board of Trade to Ministry of Health:
Certain powers in relation to private water undertakings in England and Wales.

(Ministry of Health Act, 1919: SR & O 2126/1920)

Ministry of Health to Board of Trade:
Certain powers in relation to gas undertakings of Local Authorities.

(Ministry of Health Act, 1919: SR & O 2125/1920)

December   Mines Department set up under a Secretary for Mines to be responsible to the President of the Board of Trade. Powers of the Secretary of State concerning mines and quarries transferred from the Home Office.

(Mining Industry Act, 1920: SR & O 2193/1920)

Board of Trade to Ministry of Transport:
Consequential transfer of property in two colliery railways.

(Ministry of Transport Act, 1919: SR & O 2296/1920)

1921
January   Office of Works to Ministry of Transport:
Powers and property in relation to the Menai Bridge.

(Ministry of Transport Act, 1919: SR & O 2379/1920)

March	Ministry of Munitions to Board of Trade: Powers under the Petroleum (Production) Act, 1918, to be exercised by the Secretary for Mines. (Ministry of Munitions Act, 1915: SR & O 362/1921)
April	Ministry of Munitions dissolved: remaining powers to the Treasury, to be exercised by a Disposals and Liquidation Commission. Ministry of Shipping dissolved: residual functions to Board of Trade, including those carried out before 1917 by the Admiralty's Transport Department. (New Ministries and Secretaries Act, 1916: Ministries of Munitions and Shipping (Cessation) Act, 1921: SR & Os 446, 447/1921) Ministry of Food dissolved: residual functions mainly to Board of Trade. (New Ministries and Secretaries Act, 1916: Ministry of Food (Continuance) Act, 1920: SR & O 445/1921)
May	Home Office to Ministry of Health: Certain powers under the Factory and Workshops Act, 1901. (Ministry of Health Act, 1919: SR & O 958/1921) Ministry of Health to Home Office: Powers relating to the registration of electors and the conduct of elections. (Ministry of Health Act, 1919: SR & O 959/1921)
May and later months	Various powers and duties relating to Ireland were transferred to the Governments of Southern and Northern Ireland under the Government of Ireland Act, 1920, by the following SR & Os of 1921: 533, 1130, 1243, 1527, 1691, 1696, 2006.
June	Ministry of Transport to Lord Lieutenant of Ireland: Certain powers under the Special Constables (Ireland) Act, 1845. (Ministry of Transport Act, 1919: SR & O 1023/1921)
August	Home Office to Scottish Board of Health: Certain powers in Scotland under the Factories and Workshops Act, 1901. (Scottish Board of Health Act, 1919: SR & O 1011/1921)
September	Ministry of Transport to Ministry of Labour: Matters concerning labour and wages on railways. Treasury to Lord Chancellor's Department: Administration of the County Courts.

Ministry of Pensions to Service departments:
All powers previously transferred from those departments except powers relating to disablement or death resulting from service in 1914–18 war, and pensions already awarded in respect of disablement in former wars.

(War Pensions Act, 1920)

November   India Office to Foreign Office:
Relations with Afghanistan, on conclusion of Anglo-Afghan Treaty of 1921.

1922   Registrar General (Ministry of Health) to Board of Trade:
Registration of business names. (Work done for Board of Trade by Controller of Stamps, Inland Revenue.)

January   Office of Registrar General (Scotland) separated from Office of Deputy Clerk Register.

(Registrar General (Scotland) Act, 1920)

April   Board of Trade to Ministry of Transport:
Certain powers under Railway and Canal Traffic Act, 1888, and Port of London Act, 1908, as re-enacted by Port of London (Consolidation) Act, 1920.

(Ministry of Transport Act, 1919: SR & O 356/1922)

Transfer of various functions to Irish Provisional Government (Irish Free State).

(Irish Free State Agreement Act, 1922: SR & O 315/1922)

August   Ministry of Agriculture and Fisheries to Ministry of Health:
Powers under Rats and Mice (Destruction) Act, 1919, so far as they relate to the supervision of the administration and enforcement of that Act in any port sanitary district, or in regard to vessels.

(Ministry of Health Act, 1919: SR & O 948/1922)

September   Admiralty to Colonial Office:
Responsibility for Island of Ascension.

October   Post of Chief Secretary to the Lord Lieutenant of Ireland vacated: responsibility for work of Irish Office in relation to Irish Free State transferred to Colonial Secretary, and in relation to Northern Ireland to Home Secretary.

War Office to Air Ministry:
Military control of Iraq.

November   Cabinet Office to Foreign Office:
Correspondence with the League of Nations.

1923   Board of Trade to Board of Inland Revenue:
Registration of business names.

Ministry of Agriculture and Fisheries to War Office:
Administration of light horse breeding scheme.

Mines Department to Home Office:
Returns of manufacture of coke at coke ovens.

Home Office to Treasury:
Administration of the Order of the British Empire.

March   Ministry of Transport to Treasury Solicitor:
Legal work of the Ministry other than that concerning
electricity supply.

April   Admiralty to Board of Trade:
The Coastguard Service. (Later in the year the Office of
Works took over from the Admiralty the provision and
maintenance of Coastguard stations. In 1924 the Office of
Works took over from the Board of Trade similar services
of maintenance and equipment.)

(Administrative action, ratified by Coastguard Act,
1925)

Board of Education to Ministry of Labour:
Oversight of, and grant aid to, classes and centres provided
by Local Education Authorities for unemployed young
persons under the Unemployment Insurance Act, 1923.

Colonial Office to Home Office:
Work in connection with the disbanded Royal Irish Constabulary.

1924   Chiefs of Staff Committee appointed.

Post Office to Office of Works:
Responsibility for erection and maintenance of Post Office
wireless stations.

April   Irish Office abolished: residual functions to Colonial Office in
respect of Irish Free State, and to Home Office in respect of
Northern Ireland.

Commissioners of Woods, Forests and Land Revenues to
Forestry Commission:
The majority of Crown woods and forests. (In December,
1924, the Commissioners of Woods, etc., were renamed
Commissioners of Crown Lands.)

(Forestry (Transfer of Woods) Act, 1923: SR & Os 386,
1370/1924)

July   Air Ministry to Admiralty:
Certain functions concerning the Fleet Air Arm. (Trenchard-Keyes Agreement.)

1925	Public Trustee to Board of Trade: Custodian of Enemy Property work for England and Wales.
April	Board of Education to Ministry of Health: Administration of grants for the training of midwives and health visitors.
June	Committee of Civil Research appointed.
July	Dominions Office established. A Parliamentary Under-Secretary for Dominion Affairs was appointed in August, but the Office came under a single Secretary of State for the Colonies and for Dominion Affairs, along with the Colonial Office.

Colonial Office to Board of Trade:
Responsibility for the Imperial Institute.
(Imperial Institute Act, 1925)

| October | Paymaster General to Lord Chancellor:
Functions of pay office under Court of Chancery Funds Act, 1872.
(Administration of Justice Act, 1925) |
| December | Secretary of State and Secretary for Scotland (i.e., Home and Scottish Offices) to Ministry of Labour:
Regulations relating to the registry of Trade Unions.
(New Ministries and Secretaries Act, 1916: SR & O 1261/1925) |

1926	Colonial Office to Dominions Office: Relations with Irish Free State.

Board of Education to Paymaster General:
Payment of teachers' pensions.

| July | Secretary of State for Scotland appointed in place of Secretary for Scotland.
(Secretaries of State Act, 1926) |

1927	Air Ministry to DSIR: Responsibility for investigations into atmospheric pollution.
April	Political and military control of Aden taken over by British Government. Civil administration to remain the responsibility of Indian Government – i.e., certain responsibilities transferred from India Office to War and Colonial Offices.
September	Board of Education to Ministry of Labour: Supervisory and grant-aiding duties concerning Local Authority youth employment service. (Second stage of transfer March, 1928.)

(New Ministries and Secretaries Act, 1916: SR & O
677/1927)

October   Board of Inland Revenue to Board of Customs and Excise:
Registration of moneylenders.

(Moneylenders Act, 1927)

1928   Board of Trade to Mines Department:
Functions relating to petroleum.

April   War Office to Air Ministry:
Military security of Aden.

August   Office of Deputy Clerk Register abolished: powers transferred
to the Keeper of Registers and Records of Scotland.

(Reorganization of Offices (Scotland) Act, 1928)

1929
January   War Office to Air Ministry:
Control of the Observer Corps.

Department of Agriculture for Scotland set up in place of
Board of Agriculture for Scotland.
Department of Health for Scotland set up in place of Scottish
Board of Health.

(Reorganization of Offices (Scotland) Act, 1928:
SR & Os 958, 959/1928)

April   Prisons Department for Scotland set up in place of Prison
Commissioners for Scotland.

(Reorganization of Offices (Scotland) Act, 1928:
SR & O 91/1929)

1930   War Office to Air Ministry:
Acquisition, management and sale of Air Ministry lands.

Ministry of Health and Department of Health for Scotland to
Ministry of Labour:
Certain powers for sanctioning grants for relief work pro-
vided by Local Authorities.

January   Economic Advisory Council set up to take over and expand
the functions of the Committee of Civil Research.

June   A separate Secretary of State for Dominion Affairs appointed.
Henceforward the post was held separately from the Colonial
Secretaryship except for two brief periods in 1931 and 1938-39.

July   Committee of the Privy Council for Agricultural Research
appointed.

1931

July   Home Office to Ministry of Health:
                Approval of salaries of Clerks of County Councils.
                (Local Government (Clerks) Act, 1931)

                Agricultural Research Council incorporated by Royal
                Charter.

August   Formation of a Cabinet with only ten members.

November   Reversion to Cabinet with larger membership.

1932   Ministry of Labour to Ministry of Agriculture and Fisheries:
                Supervision of grant payments to Society of Friends to-
                wards provision of allotments for the unemployed.

March   Import Duties Advisory Committee appointed.
                (Import Duties Act, 1932)

October   Colonial Office to Foreign Office:
                Relations with Iraq, on termination of the Mandate.

1933

April   Ministry of Transport to DSIR:
                Road research.

1934

July   Unemployment Assistance Board established with powers
                from the Ministry of Health. The Board took over responsi-
                bility for the care of the able-bodied unemployed from the
                local Public Assistance Committees in two instalments –
                January, 1935, and April, 1937.
                (Unemployment Act, 1934)

September   Home Office to Ministry of Health:
                Powers of confirming bye-laws as to parks and open spaces
                made by Metropolitan Borough Councils and County
                Councils other than the London County Council.
                (Local Government Act, 1933: London County Council
                (General Powers) Act, 1934)

November   Home Office to Ministry of Health:
                Power of confirming bye-laws for regulating the business
                and proceedings of Metropolitan Borough Councils.
                (London County Council (General Powers) Act, 1934)

December   Two Commissioners for Special Areas appointed: one for
                England and Wales appointed by Minister of Labour, the
                other for Scotland appointed by Secretary of State.
                (Special Areas Development and Improvement Act,
                1934)

1935   Board of Inland Revenue to Post Office and HMSO:
Responsibility for the manufacture, distribution and sale of postage stamps (not insurance stamps).
Responsibility for medicine duty labels went to the Board of Customs and Excise.

April   Air Raid Precautions Department set up at the Home Office to act on behalf of the various departments concerned with civil defence.

1936   Home Office to Mines Department:
Returns of manufacture of coke at coke ovens.

March   Minister for the Co-ordination of Defence appointed.

August   Tithe Redemption Commission set up with duties from Ministry of Agriculture and Fisheries.
(Tithe Act, 1936)

1937   Air Ministry to Admiralty:
Functions of the Naval Division of the Meteorological Office.

Home Office to Ministry of Transport:
Responsibility for the preparation of annual returns of road accidents.

February   Air Registration Board incorporated under Companies Act, 1929; certain regulatory functions delegated to the Board by the Air Ministry.
(Air Navigation Act, 1936)

April   Burma Office established, with same Secretary of State, Parliamentary and Permanent Under Secretaries as the India Office.

Settlement of Aden became a Crown Colony: responsibility for it henceforward wholly with Colonial Office and not, as before, shared between Colonial and India Offices.
(Government of India Act, 1935: SR & O 1031/1936)

May   Minister of Transport and Board of Trade to Secretary of State for Scotland:
Functions relating to provisional orders for harbour, pier and ferry works.
(Harbours, Piers and Ferries (Scotland) Act, 1937)

July   Air Ministry to Admiralty:
Control of Fleet Air Arm.

Department of Agriculture for Scotland to Ministry of Agriculture and Fisheries:

Control of attested herds scheme in Scotland.
(Agriculture Act, 1937)

December   Home Office to Health departments:
Organization of base hospitals for civil defence purposes.

1938   Home Office to Treasury:
Administration of Imperial Service Order and Medal.

June   Home Office to Health departments:
Responsibility for Emergency Hospital Service.

October   Lord Privy Seal given task of co-ordinating civil defence
preparations.

December   Home Office to Health departments:
Responsibility for preparation of first-aid posts, ambulance
services and evacuation scheme for civil defence purposes.

1939   Import Duties Advisory Committee dissolved and its functions transferred to the Board of Trade.

July   Home Secretary to Lord Privy Seal:
Functions under the Air Raid Precautions Act, 1937.
(Civil Defence Act, 1939: SR & O 862/1939)

August   Ministry of Supply established. Agreed supply functions trans-
ferred from Service departments, Home Office and Office of
Works. Powers and duties as to fertilizers transferred from
Board of Trade.
(Ministry of Supply Act, 1939: SR & O 877/1939)

September   Declaration of War.

War Cabinet of nine members appointed. Committee of
Imperial Defence absorbed into the War Cabinet and its
Secretariat merged into that of the Cabinet.

Powers of the Scottish departments vested in the Secretary of
State. The departments thus ceased to exist as statutory
bodies but were reconstituted by Minute as the administrative
departments of the Secretary of State, under the titles Home,
Health, Agriculture and Education. The Scottish Home
Department succeeded the old Scottish Office and inherited
the functions of the Prisons Department and the Fishery
Board. A small Parliamentary and liaison Scottish Office was
set up in London.
(Reorganization of Offices (Scotland) Act, 1939:
SR & O 865/1939)

Ministry of Home Security established. Functions of the Lord
Privy Seal under the Air Raid Precautions Act, 1937, and the

Civil Defence Act, 1939, and of a Secretary of State under the former Act, transferred to the Minister of Home Security.

(Ministers of the Crown (Emergency Appointments) Act, 1939: SR & O 1142/1939)

Service departments and Commissioners of Chelsea Hospital to Ministry of Pensions:
Administration of pensions and grants on account of disablement or death arising out of service after September 2, 1939.

(Pensions (Navy, Army, Air Force and Mercantile Marine) Act, 1939: SR & O 1194/1939)

Ministry of Economic Warfare established.

(Ministers of the Crown (Emergency Appointments) Act, 1939: SR & O 1188/1939)

Ministry of Information established. Functions of Secretary of State concerning censorship, etc., under Defence Regulations, 1939, transferred to the new Minister.

(Ministers of the Crown (Emergency Appointments) Act, 1939: SR & O 1189/1939)

Ministry of Labour became Ministry of Labour and National Service.

(Ministers of the Crown (Emergency Appointments) Act, 1939: SR & O 1118/1939)

Ministry of Food established. Functions of holding, using and disposing of stocks transferred from the Board of Trade.

(Ministers of the Crown (Emergency Appointments) Act, 1939: SR & O 1119/1939)

Ministry of Agriculture and Fisheries and Department of Agriculture for Scotland to Ministry of Food:
Various functions concerning subsidies on sugar, milk and cattle, etc.

Capital Issues Committee appointed by Treasury Minute, succeeding the Foreign Transactions Advisory Committee appointed in July, 1936.

Board of Trade to Ministry of Supply:
Powers re petroleum and petroleum products under Essential Commodities Reserves Act, 1938.

(Ministry of Supply Act, 1939: SR & O 1298/1939)

October   Board of Trade to Ministry of Food:
Functions under listed orders made by Board of Trade before the Ministry of Food had been declared a competent authority for making Defence Regulations.

(Ministers of the Crown (Emergency Appointments) Act, 1939: SR & O 1419/1939)

Ministry of Shipping established. Functions relating to ships and seamen; navigation; wreck and salvage; assistance to the shipping industry; harbours, docks and piers, and conservancy; sea fisheries and whaling; oil in navigable waters; coastguard, foreshore and tidal lands and the protection of the coast against inroads of the sea; boiler explosions; and all functions of the Board of Trade under Part I of the War Risks Insurance Act, 1939, and the Air Navigation Acts, 1920–38; transferred from the Board of Trade.

(Ministers of the Crown (Emergency Appointments) Act, 1939: SR & Os 1425, 1470/1939)

November Central Economic Information Service set up.

1940
February Ministry of Shipping to Admiralty:
Control of merchant shipbuilding and repairs.

(Emergency Powers (Defence) Act, 1939: SR & O 142/1940)

March Unemployment Assistance Board renamed Assistance Board. The Board took over the duty of supplementing the incomes of old age pensioners from local Public Assistance Authorities, and the Minister of Health and Secretary of State for Scotland were placed in a similar relationship to the Board as the Minister of Labour had been since its inception.

(Old Age and Widows' Pensions Act, 1940)

Ministry of Information to Home Office:
Functions relating to censorship, etc., under Defence Regulations, 1939.

(Ministers of the Crown (Emergency Appointments) Act, 1939: SR & O 399/1940)

April Post of Minister for the Co-ordination of Defence abolished. In May Mr Churchill became Prime Minister and Minister of Defence.

May Ministry of Shipping to Admiralty:
Control of Coastguard Service.

(Coastguard Act, 1925: SR & O 1021/1940)

Petroleum Department of Board of Trade set up, under a Parliamentary Secretary of the Board to be known as the Secretary for Petroleum.

(Emergency Powers (Defence) Act, 1939: SR & O 749/1940)

Ministry of Aircraft Production established. Agreed functions concerning the supply of aircraft transferred from Air Ministry and Admiralty, and Minister to exercise certain powers concurrently with them and with Minister of Supply.

> (Ministers of the Crown (Emergency Appointments) Act, 1939: SR & Os 747, 762, 763/1940)

June
Home Office to Ministry of Labour and National Service: The Factory Inspectorate.

> (Emergency Powers (Defence) Act, 1939: SR & O 907/1940)

October
Ministry of Works and Buildings established in place of Office of Works. Minister also appointed First Commissioner of Works.

> (Ministers of the Crown (Emergency Appointments) Act, 1939: SR & O 1825/1940)

British Council incorporated by Royal Charter. The Council had been set up as a voluntary body in 1934.

1941

January
Central Economic Information Service divided into Economic Section of the War Cabinet Secretariat and the Central Statistical Office, both remaining part of the War Cabinet Office.

March
War Damage Commission established.

> (War Damage Act, 1941)

April
Air Ministry to Admiralty:
Operational control of RAF Coastal Command.

May
Ministries of Transport and Shipping merged to form Ministry of War Transport.

> (Ministers of the Crown (Emergency Appointments) Act, 1939: SR & O 654/1941)

September
Ministry of War Transport to Board of Trade:
Powers concerning electricity.

> (Emergency Powers (Defence) Acts, 1939–40: SR & O 1403/1941)

1942
Board of Trade to Ministry of Works and Buildings:
Responsibility for problems relating to the building industry.

February
Minister of Production appointed. The Ministry of Production was not fully established until July, 1942.

> (Ministers of the Crown (Emergency Appointments) Act, 1939: SR & O 1383/1942)

April	Board of Trade to Ministry of War Transport:

April   Board of Trade to Ministry of War Transport:
Functions concerning wreck and salvage of ships, vessels or aircraft in the Isle of Man.
(Emergency Powers (Defence) Acts, 1939–40: SR & O 808/1942)

Ministry of Agriculture and Fisheries and Sugar Commission to Ministry of Food:
Functions under the Sugar Industry (Reorganization) Act, 1936, including the general control of the British Sugar Corporation.
(Sugar Industry Act, 1942)

Ministry of Agriculture and Fisheries to Ministry of Food:
Powers relating to infestation control in England and Wales except insofar as exercisable in rural districts.
(Ministers of the Crown (Emergency Appointments) Act, 1939: SR & O 807/1942)

June   Ministry of Fuel and Power established with functions from the Board of Trade in relation to coal, gas, electricity, hydraulic power, petroleum, mines and quarries, etc. The Mines Department and the Petroleum Department were abolished.
(Ministers of the Crown (Emergency Appointments) Act, 1939: SR & O 1132/1942)

July   Ministry of Works and Buildings became the Ministry of Works and Planning and took over the planning powers of the Ministry of Health under the Town and Country Planning Act, 1932.
(Ministry of Works and Planning Act, 1942: SR & O 1313/1942)

1943   Ministry of Aircraft Production to Ministry of Works:
Responsibility for erection of aircraft factories.

Ministry of Food to Department of Agriculture for Scotland:
Responsibility for acreage payments on crops in Scotland.

January   Board of Customs and Excise to Assistance Board:
Responsibility for payment of non-contributory old age pensions to pensioners whose pensions were being supplemented by the Board.

February   Ministry of Town and Country Planning established and took over the planning functions of the Ministry of Works and Planning. The latter department was renamed the Ministry of Works.
(Ministry of Town and Country Planning Act, 1943: SR & O 206/1943)

May   Board of Customs and Excise to Ministry of Agriculture and Fisheries:
Responsibility for corn returns.
(Agriculture (Miscellaneous Provisions) Act, 1943)

October   Ministry of Health to Ministry of Food:
Power to regulate labelling and composition of food.
(Emergency Powers (Defence) Acts, 1939–40: SR & O 1553/1943)

November Minister of Reconstruction appointed.

1944

August   Board of Education reconstituted as Ministry of Education.
(Education Act, 1944)

October   Minister of Civil Aviation appointed. The Ministry of Civil Aviation was not established until April, 1945, by the Ministry of Civil Aviation Act, 1945, which transferred the powers of the Air Ministry under the Air Navigation and other Acts to the new department.

November Ministry of National Insurance established: in April, 1945, the powers and duties of the Minister of Health and the Secretary of State for Scotland relating to health insurance and pensions, of the Minister of Labour and National Service relating to unemployment insurance and assistance, and of the Home Office relating to Workmen's Compensation were transferred to the new department.
(Ministry of National Insurance Act, 1944: SR & Os 316, 317, 318/1945)

1945

April   Ministry of Fuel and Power made permanent.
(Ministry of Fuel and Power Act, 1945)

May   End of War in Europe.

Small War Cabinet replaced by Cabinet with sixteen members.

Post of Minister of Reconstruction abolished. Posts of President of the Board of Trade and Minister of Production held by one man. The Ministry of Production was merged into the Board later in the year.

Ministry of Home Security dissolved: residual functions to Home Office. Research and Experimental Department to Air Ministry, DSIR and Ministry of Works.
(Civil Defence Act, 1939: Ministers of the Crown (Emergency Appointments) Act, 1939: SR & O 612/1945)

Ministry of Economic Warfare dissolved: residual functions to Foreign Office.

(Ministers of the Crown (Emergency Appointments) Act, 1939: SR & O 613/1945)

June   Ministry of Education to Ministry of Labour and National Service:
Responsibility for the vocational training of blind and physically handicapped persons not under sixteen years of age.

(Disabled Persons (Employment) Act, 1944: SR & O 615/1945)

Foreign Office to War Office:
Responsibility for British elements of Control Commission for Germany.

Ministry of Health to Ministry of Education:
Functions under the Camps Act, 1939.

(Camps Act, 1945)

Forestry Commission reconstituted. Henceforward to comply with directions of Minister of Agriculture and Fisheries and Secretary of State for Scotland. This replaced the 1919 arrangements under which the Commission was ultimately responsible to the Treasury. The power of acquiring land for forestry was transferred from the Commissioners to the Minister of Agriculture and Fisheries and the Secretary of State for Scotland.

(Forestry Act, 1945)

Ministry of Labour and National Service to Board of Trade:
General responsibility for distribution of industry and development area policy. Certain powers to be exercised jointly with the Secretary of State for Scotland.
Ministry of Labour and National Service to Ministry of Agriculture and Fisheries:
Responsibility for the Land Settlement Association.

(Distribution of Industry Act, 1945)

August   End of Japanese War.

Ministries of Supply and Aircraft Production under one Minister, and from September under one Permanent Secretary.

Board of Trade to Ministry of Supply:
Responsibility for engineering industries.

All functions of the Commissioners of Works and of the Commissioners of Public Works for Ireland were vested in the Minister of Works. In October the Irish Commissioners were

dissolved, but the Commissioners of Works still remain and the Minister of Works is *ex officio* First Commissioner.
> (Ministry of Works Act, 1942: SR & Os 991, 992, 1277/ 1945)

October   Admiralty to Ministry of War Transport:
Control of the Coastguard Service.
> (Coastguard Act, 1925: SR & O 1239/1945)

Control Office for Germany and Austria set up as an independent department under the Chancellor of the Duchy of Lancaster, with ultimate responsibility to the Secretary of State for War.

1946   Colonial Office to Foreign Office:
Relations with Jordan, following termination of the Mandate.

March   Ministry of Food made permanent.
> (Ministers of the Crown (Transfer of Functions) Act, 1946)

April   Ministry of Information dissolved. Overseas publicity work transferred to overseas departments. Central Office of Information set up.

Department of Overseas Trade dissolved, but Secretary for Overseas Trade continued with functions relating to the Imperial Institute. Other work of the Department reverted to the Board of Trade.
> (Ministers of the Crown (Transfer of Functions) Act, 1946: SR & O 373/1946)

Ministry of Aircraft Production dissolved and functions transferred to Ministry of Supply.
> (Ministers of the Crown (Transfer of Functions) Act, 1946: Emergency Powers (Defence) Acts, 1939–40: SR & Os 367, 374/1946)

Ministry of War Transport became the Ministry of Transport.
> (Ministers of the Crown (Transfer of Functions) Act, 1946: SR & O 375/1946)

Home Office to Ministry of Labour and National Service:
Permanent transfer of administration of Factories Acts (first transferred temporarily in 1940) together with transfer of administration of Truck Acts, Anthrax Prevention Act, 1919, and Check-weighing in Various Industries Act, 1919.
> (Ministers of the Crown (Transfer of Functions) Act, 1946: SR & O 376/1946)

Ministry of Supply to Ministry of Fuel and Power:
Certain powers relating to petroleum under Essential Commodities Reserves Act, 1938.

(Ministers of the Crown (Transfer of Functions) Act, 1946: SR & O 377/1946)

Minister of Supply to Board of Trade:
Control of all raw materials other than iron and steel, non-ferrous and light metals: various controls over commodities transferred in April and later months.

(Ministers of the Crown (Transfer of Functions) Act, 1946: Supplies and Services (Transitional Powers) Act, 1945: Defence (General) Regulations, 1939: SR & Os 378, 407, 450, 489, 1306/1946)

Board of Trade to Ministry of Supply:
Various controls.

(Defence (General) Regulations, 1939: SR & O 401/1946)

Ministry of Supply to Air Ministry:
Group 43 of RAF Maintenance Command.

Development Commission to agricultural departments:
Functions relating to agricultural research, advisory and education services.

November	DSIR to Ministry of Supply: Duty of promoting and controlling the development of atomic energy. (Atomic Energy Act, 1946)
December	Ministry of Defence established. (Ministry of Defence Act, 1946)
1947	Home Office to Ministry of Town and Country Planning: Regulation of advertisements. (Town and Country Planning Act, 1947)
January	Home Office to Ministry of Health: Certain functions relating to fees for interment. Ministry of Health to Home Office: Confirmation of bye-laws under numerous Acts. (Ministers of the Crown (Transfer of Functions) Act, 1946: SR & O 1757/1946)
March	Home Office to Treasury: Certain functions under the Building Societies Acts connected with the work of the Registrar of Friendly Societies. (Ministers of the Crown (Transfer of Functions) Act, 1946: SR & O 418/1947)

Board of Customs and Excise to Assistance Board:
Responsibility for payment of non-contributory old-age pensions to pensioners not receiving national assistance. (For earlier transfer see January, 1943.)

April   War Office, Air Ministry and an interim Treasury Committee to Assistance Board, Ministries of Health, Education, and Labour and National Service:
Polish Resettlement.

(Polish Resettlement Act, 1947)

War Office to Foreign Office:
Control Office for Germany and Austria renamed Foreign Office (German Section).

Ministry of Transport to Ministry of Health and Secretary of State for Scotland:
Functions relating to the protection of the coast against erosion, etc.

(Ministers of the Crown (Transfer of Functions) Act, 1946: SR & O 609/1947)

May   Board of Trade to Minister of Agriculture and Fisheries and Secretaries of State for the Home Department and for Scotland, acting jointly:
Powers relating to home-grown wool.

(Ministers of the Crown (Transfer of Functions) Act, 1946: SR & O 984/1947)

War Office to Ministry of Supply:
Functions under the Gunbarrel Proof Act, 1868.

(Ministers of the Crown (Transfer of Functions) Act, 1946: SR & O 985/1947)

July   Board of Control to Ministry of Health:
All powers except those of a quasi-judicial nature.

(National Health Service Act, 1946: SR & O 983/1947)

Dominions Office renamed Commonwealth Relations Office.

(Ministers of the Crown (Transfer of Functions) Act, 1946: SR & O 1422/1947)

August   India Office disbanded, following Indian Independence Act, 1947. Relations with India and Pakistan transferred to Commonwealth Relations Office.

Ministry of Supply to Air Ministry:
Group 41 of RAF Maintenance Command.

September   Ministry of Agriculture and Fisheries to Ministry of Town and Country Planning:
Questions concerning access to mountains, moors, etc.

Ministry of Health to Home Office:
Functions relating to the care of children deprived of a normal home life.

(Ministers of the Crown (Transfer of Functions) Act, 1946: SR & O 1644/1947)

Ministries of Health and Food to Ministry of Agriculture and Fisheries:
Functions relating to the control of rats, mice and food pests except for the powers of the Ministry of Health in respect of vessels.

(Ministers of the Crown (Transfer of Functions) Act, 1946: SR & O 1705/1947)

Ministry of Food to Secretary of State for Scotland:
Control of food pests.

(Ministers of the Crown (Transfer of Functions) Act, 1946: SR & O 1706/1947)

Minister for Economic Affairs appointed. Chief Planning Officer and staff transferred to him from the Lord President: Regional Boards for Industry transferred to him from the Board of Trade.

November   Central Land Board established.

(Town and Country Planning Act, 1947)

Sir Stafford Cripps (who was Minister for Economic Affairs) became Chancellor of the Exchequer. He retained his economic responsibilities and took the Chief Planning Officer and the Economic Planning Staff with him to the Treasury, which thus became responsible for co-ordination over the whole field of economic policy.

Ministry of Supply to Ministry of Works:
Responsibility for provision of housing supplies, other than production of aluminium houses.

December   Ministry of Supply and Board of Trade to Ministry of Health:
Certain functions relating to medical supplies.

(Ministers of the Crown (Transfer of Functions) Act, 1946: SR & O 2472/1947)

1948   Board of Inland Revenue to Board of Trade:
Companies registration.

(Companies Act, 1948)

January   Burma Office dissolved, following Burma Independence Act, 1947: relations with Burma transferred to Foreign Office.

February   Colonial Office to Commonwealth Relations Office:
              Relations with Ceylon, following Ceylon Independence Act,
              1947. Relations with Maldive Islands also passed to CRO
              in 1948.

              Public Trustee to Board of Trade:
              Functions of the Custodian of Enemy Property.

March   Certain powers under the Food and Drugs Act, 1938, which
              hitherto had been exercised by the Ministry of Health or the
              Ministry of Agriculture and Fisheries acting alone, to be
              exercised in some cases by the Ministries of Health and Food
              jointly, and in other cases by the Ministries of Health, Food,
              and Agriculture and Fisheries jointly.
                    (Ministers of the Crown (Transfer of Functions) Act,
                    1946: SI 107/1948)

April   Ministry of Health to Ministry of Transport:
              Confirmation of compulsory purchase orders and authori-
              zation of speedy acquisition of land for certain highway
              purposes.
                    (Ministers of the Crown (Transfer of Functions) Act,
                    1946: SI 490/1948)

              War Office to Ministry of Defence:
              Joint Services Staff College.

              Home Office to Ministry of Health (Board of Control):
              Management and buildings of Broadmoor Institution, con-
              trol of admission and discharge of patients remaining with
              the Home Secretary.
                    (Criminal Justice Act, 1948)

              Ministry of Agriculture and Fisheries to University Grants
              Committee:
              Grants-in-aid to university departments of agriculture in
              England and Wales.

May   Colonial Office to Foreign Office:
              Relations with Israel, on termination of the Palestine
              Mandate.

July   Ministry of Health to Home Office:
              Functions relating to the regulation of markets and fairs.
                    (Ministers of the Crown (Transfer of Functions) Act,
                    1946: SI 865/1948)

              Assistance Board renamed National Assistance Board on
              taking over functions from local Public Assistance Authorities,
              etc.
                    (National Assistance Act, 1948)

October	Separation of the judicial and prosecuting functions of the Judge Advocate General's Office. The Judge Advocate General and the judicial functions of his office were transferred to the Lord Chancellor.
	Board of Trade to Treasury Solicitor: Legal work for the Ministry of Fuel and Power.
December	Civil Defence Act, 1948, and numerous Statutory Instruments spread over the following years, clarified the responsibilities of Ministers and other public authorities for civil defence purposes.

1949

March	Ministry of Supply to Board of Trade: Functions in relation to ethyl chloride and kitchen waste.
	(Ministers of the Crown (Transfer of Functions) Act, 1946: SI 355/1949)
	Nature Conservancy set up by Royal Charter under the Committee of the Privy Council for Agricultural Research, which was renamed the Committee for Agricultural Research and Nature Conservation.
April	Home Office to Scottish Office: Administration of civil defence in Scotland.
	War Office to Foreign Office: Responsibility for former Italian colonies in Africa.
	Board of Trade (Secretary for Overseas Trade) to Ministry of Education: Functions concerning the Imperial Institute. (The Scientific and technical work of the Institute was transferred to the Colonial Office.)
	(Ministers of the Crown (Transfer of Functions) Act, 1946: SI 588/1949)
	Separate Scottish Record Office and Department of Registers of Scotland established in place of the Department of Registers and Records of Scotland.
	(Public Registers and Records (Scotland) Act, 1948)
June	Rearrangement of functions under the Food and Drugs Act between the Secretary of State for Scotland and the Ministry of Food.
	(Ministers of the Crown (Transfer of Functions) Act, 1946: SI 1047/1949)
September	Charity Commission to Ministry of Education: Jurisdiction relating to quasi-educational trusts in England and Wales.

(Education (Miscellaneous Provisions) Act, 1948: SI 1845/1949. See also SI 520/1950)

October   Secretary of State for Scotland to University Grants Committee:
Responsibility for grant-aiding the Glasgow Veterinary College.

1950   Home Office to Ministry of Works:
Responsibility for providing technical advice to Local Authorities on structural precautions for civil defence.

January   Board of Trade to Forestry Commission:
Various functions relating to the production and supply of timber.

(Emergency Laws (Transitional Provisions) Act, 1946: Emergency Laws (Miscellaneous Provisions) Act, 1947: Ministers of the Crown (Transfer of Functions) Act, 1946: Supplies and Services (Transitional Powers) Act, 1945: SIs 2388, 2389/1949)

April   Ministry of Transport to Commissioners of Crown Lands:
Management of Crown foreshore.

(Coast Protection Act, 1949)

Ministry of Works to DSIR:
Research on sociological and economic aspects of building, with staff of Chief Scientific Adviser's Division.

Board of Trade to agricultural departments:
Certain functions relating to the salvage, sale and disposal of kitchen waste.

(Ministers of the Crown (Transfer of Functions) Act, 1946: SI 509/1950)

June   Home Secretary to Lord Chancellor:
The duty of recommending to Her Majesty the names of persons for appointment as Recorders, Chairmen and Deputy Chairmen of Quarter Sessions for the County of London, metropolitan magistrates and stipendiary magistrates. Other minor judicial appointments have since been similarly transferred.

(Justices of the Peace Act, 1949)

Ministry of Food to Board of Trade:
Certain functions concerning the labelling, etc., of food containers.

(Ministers of the Crown (Transfer of Functions) Act, 1946: SI 1044/1950)

1951

January

Ministry of Town and Country Planning became the Ministry of Local Government and Planning. In addition to the planning functions, the new department took from the Ministry of Health functions relating to local government rating and valuation, environmental health services including water supply, sewerage and sewage disposal, housing, rent control, burials and coast protection.

(Ministers of the Crown (Transfer of Functions) Act, 1946: SI 142/1951)

April

Ministry of Food to Colonial Office:
Responsibility for the Overseas Food Corporation. The Ministry of Food was given certain functions in relation to the Queensland-British Food Corporation (wound up in September, 1952).

(Overseas Resources Development Act, 1951)

Secretary of State for Scotland to University Grants Committee:
Responsibility for grant-aiding the Royal (Dick) Veterinary College.

May

Ministry of Health to Ministry of Local Government and Planning:
Functions relating to local government superannuation, local government finance, Local Authorities' land, mortuaries, and certain civil defence services.

(Ministers of the Crown (Transfer of Functions) Act, 1946: SI 753/1951)

Ministry of Local Government and Planning to Ministry of Transport:
Functions concerning authorization of compulsory purchase of land by a County Council for the improvement of highways.

(Ministers of the Crown (Transfer of Functions) Act, 1946: SI 751/1951)

July

Ministry of Materials established, with functions transferred from the Board of Trade and the Ministry of Supply.

(Ministry of Materials Act, 1951: Ministers of the Crown (Transfer of Functions) Act, 1946: SIs 1242, 1243, 1244/1951)

October

Ministry of Works to Secretary of State for Scotland and Minister of Agriculture and Fisheries:
Responsibility for control of pests in Government establishments, Royal Palaces, and grace and favour residences maintained out of Exchequer funds.

Home Secretary became Minister for Welsh Affairs.

November   Ministry of Local Government and Planning renamed Ministry of Housing and Local Government.

(Ministers of the Crown (Transfer of Functions) Act, 1946: SI 1900/1951)

Posts of Minister of Transport and Minister of Civil Aviation held by one man.

Secretary of State for the Co-ordination of Transport, Fuel and Power appointed, and the Lord President of the Council (later the Chancellor of the Duchy of Lancaster) nominated as co-ordinator of the Ministries of Food and Agriculture.

1952
April   Treasury to Board of Trade:
Regional Boards for Industry.

Ministry of Supply to Ministry of Works:
Official car service, merged with car pools of Ministry of Works and certain other departments to form a Government car service for all departments except the Post Office and the Foreign Office.

1953   Ministry of Education to Prison Commission:
Financial responsibility for education in prisons and Borstals.

January   Ministry of Housing and Local Government to Ministry of Food:
Functions concerning slaughterhouses and knackers' yards or otherwise relating to the slaughter of animals.
Home Office to Ministry of Housing and Local Government:
Power to approve charges for the use of public slaughterhouses.

(Ministers of the Crown (Transfer of Functions) Act, 1946: SI 2033/1953)

May   Treasury to Ministry of Housing and Local Government:
Responsibility for giving the consent required by municipal corporations under Acts of 1873 and 1882 for grant of land for the building of places of worship or ministers' residences.

(Ministers of the Crown (Transfer of Functions) Act, 1946: SI 734/1953)

July   Ministry of Education to Home Office:
Responsibility for financial assistance, etc., to Local Authorities for school crossing patrols.

(School Crossing Patrols Act, 1953)

August   Ministries of Pensions and National Insurance amalgamated: new department called Ministry of Pensions and National Insurance. Certain functions relating to medical and surgical treatment and the provision of appliances, vehicles, etc., transferred to health departments.
(Ministers of the Crown (Transfer of Functions) Act, 1946: SI 1198/1953)

September Chancellor of the Duchy of Lancaster no longer responsible for co-ordinating the policies for food and agriculture. The post of Secretary of State for the Co-ordination of Transport, Fuel and Power abolished.

October   Post of Secretary for Overseas Trade abolished: functions of Secretary relating to Export Credits Guarantee Department transferred to President of the Board of Trade.
(Ministers of the Crown (Transfer of Functions) Act, 1946: SI 1452/1953)

Treasury to Board of Trade:
Co-ordination of the work of departments in connection with industrial productivity.

Ministries of Transport and Civil Aviation amalgamated. New department called Ministry of Transport and Civil Aviation.
(Ministers of the Crown (Transfer of Functions) Act, 1946: SI 1204/1953)

November Cabinet Office to Treasury:
The Economic Section, whose Director became Chief Economic Adviser to HM Government.

1954   Development Commission to Secretary of State for Scotland: Responsibility for grant-aiding the Scottish Gardens and Allotments Society.

January   Ministry of Supply to Lord President:
Responsibility for atomic energy.
(Ministers of the Crown (Transfer of Functions) Act, 1946: SI 1673/1953)

April   Ministry of Transport and Civil Aviation to Ministry of Pensions and National Insurance:
Functions in relation to the award of pensions to merchant seamen and fishermen disabled in war of 1914–18 and to dependants of those men who died as a result of injuries sustained in that war.
(Ministers of the Crown (Transfer of Functions) Act, 1946: SI 1674/1953)

o

Development Commission to Ministry of Agriculture and Fisheries:
Responsibility for grant-aiding the UK sponsoring authority for the international exchange of young agriculturalists.

Home Office to Ministry of Housing and Local Government:
Certain functions relating to markets.

Board of Trade to Ministry of Housing and Local Government:
Functions under London Central Markets Act, 1875.

(Ministers of the Crown (Transfer of Functions) Act, 1946: SI 141/1954)

August   Ministry of Materials dissolved: functions transferred to Board of Trade.

(Ministers of the Crown (Transfer of Functions) Act, 1946: SI 1028/1954)

October   Posts of Minister of Agriculture and Fisheries and Minister of Food held by one man.

Civil Service Commission to Service departments:
Responsibility for interview and selection test arrangements for Service commissions and cadetships: the Commission retaining responsibility for examining candidates' educational qualifications and for conducting written examinations.

1955
April   Minister of Fuel and Power to Secretary of State for Scotland:
Functions relating to electricity in Scotland.

(Electricity Reorganization (Scotland) Act, 1954)

Lord Chancellor to Secretary of State for Scotland:
Appointment and removal from office of Justices of the Peace in Scotland.

(Ministers of the Crown (Transfer of Functions) Act, 1946: SI 240/1955)

Development Commission to Ministry of Agriculture and Fisheries and Secretary of State for Scotland:
Power to make grants and loans for fishery harbours.

(Fisheries Act, 1955)

Ministry of Agriculture and Fisheries and Ministry of Food amalgamated. New department called Ministry of Agriculture, Fisheries and Food. Primary responsibility for the main food hygiene functions in England and Wales transferred to Ministry of Health. Distribution of functions between the

Ministries of Health, Housing and Local Government, and Agriculture, Fisheries and Food re-defined in July, 1955.

>(Ministers of the Crown (Transfer of Functions) Act, 1946: SIs 554, 959/1955)

July Ministry of Supply to Board of Trade:

Responsibility for the iron and steel and non-ferrous metals industries and the engineering industry.

>(Ministers of the Crown (Transfer of Functions) Act, 1946: SI 876/1955)

August Minister of Agriculture, Fisheries and Food to Secretary of State for Scotland:

Responsibility for certain animal diseases in Scotland and joint responsibility for other animal health matters, excluding operational control of epidemic diseases.

>(Ministers of the Crown (Transfer of Functions) Act, 1946: SI 958/1955)

1956

January Permanent Chairman of Chiefs of Staff Committee appointed.

To agricultural Ministers acting jointly:

Functions relating to guaranteed prices, etc., which had hitherto been exercised by different Ministers in different countries.

>(Ministers of the Crown (Transfer of Functions) Act, 1946: SI 87/1956)

April Statutory Publications Office incorporated in the Treasury Solicitor's Department.

Minister of Transport and Civil Aviation to Secretary of State for Scotland:

Powers relating to the construction, maintenance and management of roads, bridges and ferries in Scotland. Certain traffic functions to Secretary of State and Minister jointly.

>(Ministers of the Crown (Transfer of Functions) Act, 1946: SI 1955/1955)

Ministry of Agriculture, Fisheries and Food to Agricultural Research Council:

Grant-aiding and administration of independent agricultural research institutes in England and Wales.

>(Agricultural Research Act, 1956)

New Committee of the Privy Council for Agricultural Research appointed. Previous Committee for Agricultural Research and Nature Conservation henceforward only responsible for Nature Conservation.

o*

July   Ministry of Health to Ministry of Housing and Local Government:
            Certain civil defence functions.
            (Ministers of the Crown (Transfer of Functions) Act, 1946: SIs 824, 825/1956)

October   Secretary of the Cabinet appointed Joint Permanent Secretary to the Treasury and Head of the Home Civil Service, to be mainly responsible to Prime Minister. Other Joint Permanent Secretary to be responsible to Chancellor of the Exchequer.

December   Crown Lands Commissioners replaced by Crown Estate Commissioners, responsible in English and Northern Ireland matters to Lord Privy Seal, in Scottish matters to Secretary of State, and on UK matters to both jointly.
            (Crown Estate Act, 1956: SI 1890/1956)

            Home Office to Ministry of Transport and Civil Aviation:
            Duty of receiving returns of deaths resulting from railway accidents.
            (Ministers of the Crown (Transfer of Functions) Act, 1946: SI 1699/1956)

INDEX

P

Ministry of Defence (1946–), 26, 32, 33, 36, 204, 207, 208, 236, 283, 321, 347, 409, 412
Establishment and character of, 317–321
Proposals for and development of ideas of, 299–309
Scientific policy and, 332
Scientists employed by, 1956; 253
Staff of, in 1956; 238
Supply organization and, 237–239
Ministry of Defence and Armed Forces, little possibility of, 318
Ministry of Economic Warfare (1939–1945), 31, 95, 96, 108, 316, 346, 402, 407
Ministry of Education (1944–), 33, 35, 135, 141, 175–176, 183, 204, 351, 359, 406
Transfers from:
to Home Office:
financial aid to Local Authorities re school crossing patrols, 1953; 416
to Ministry of Labour and National Service:
vocational training of blind and handicapped adults, 1945; 407
to Prison Commission:
financial responsibility for education in prisons and Borstals, 1953; 416
Transfers to:
from Board of Trade:
functions re Imperial Institute, 1949; 413
from Charity Commission:
jurisdiction over quasi-educational trusts, 1949; 143, 413
from Ministry of Health:
functions under Camps Act, 1939, 1945; 407
from War Office, Air Ministry and Treasury:
Polish Resettlement (with other departments), 1947; 410
Ministry of Food (1916–1921), 24, 59, 62, 65, 71, 86, 386
Transfers from:
to Board of Trade:
residual functions and remaining staff, 1921; 86, 394
Transfers to:
from Board of Agriculture and Fisheries:
food preservation, c. 1917; 65

Ministry of Food—*cont.*
from Board of Trade:
responsibility for cheese and frozen fish, c. 1917; 65
powers re production of beer, 1917; 387
from Ministry of Munitions:
control of oils and fats, c. 1917; 65
from War Office:
supply of oats, c. 1917; 65
from War Savings Committee:
Food Economy Campaign, c. 1917; 65
Ministry of Food (1939–1955), 31, 32, 93, 95, 104, 111, 112, 276, 337, 352, 363, 408
Food and Drugs administration, rearrangements with other departments, 1948–1949; 412, 413
Transfers from:
to Board of Trade:
functions re labelling of food containers, 1950; 414
to Colonial Office:
responsibility for Overseas Food Corporation, 1951; 415
to Department of Agriculture for Scotland:
acreage payments on crops in Scotland, 1943; 405
to Ministry of Agriculture and Fisheries:
powers re infestation, 1947; 411
to Ministry of Agriculture, Fisheries and Food and Secretary of State for Scotland:
continuing functions, 1955; 113–114, 116, 418
to Secretary of State for Scotland:
control of food pests, 1947; 411
Transfers to:
from Board of Trade:
Food (Defence Plans) Department, etc., 1939; 96, 402
from Ministry of Agriculture and Fisheries:
control of infestation in urban areas in England and Wales, 1942; 405
from Ministry of Agriculture and Fisheries and Department of Agriculture for Scotland:
various functions re subsidies, 1939; 402
from Ministry of Agriculture and Fisheries and Sugar Commission:

GEORGE ALLEN & UNWIN LTD
London: 40 Museum Street, W.C.1

Auckland: 24 Wyndham Street
Sydney, N.S.W.: Bradbury House, 55 York Street
Cape Town: 109 Long Street
Bombay: 15 Graham Road, Ballard Estate, Bombay 1
Calcutta: 17 Chittaranjan Avenue, Calcutta 13
New Delhi: 13-14 Ajmeri Gate Extension, New Delhi 1
Karachi: 254 Ingle Road
Toronto: 91 Wellington Street West
São Paulo: Avenida 9 de Julho 1138-Ap. 51

THE HOME OFFICE

SIR FRANK NEWSAM

The reader will find here a fascinating account of the many and varied functions which constitute the work of the oldest Department of State. The intimate concern of the Home Office with the preservation of the liberty of the subject and with many other features of the British way of life gives this book a particular interest. The Home Office, moreover, is the main channel of communication between the subject and the Crown, it advises on the exercise of the prerogative of mercy and is responsible for many aspects of the administration of justice. This book deals with these subjects and also describes the Department's duties in connection with the police and fire services, civil defence, explosives, dangerous drugs, children's welfare, prisons, the control of aliens, naturalization, the licensing laws and the management of the public houses which were nationalized during the first World War.

'The book preserves a nice balance between official accuracy and human interest, and is written as if it were meant to be read. There are few pages which do not contain something to enlarge one's knowledge or stir one's imagination.' *The Times*.

Demy 8vo   *Second Impression*   15s *net*

THE FOREIGN OFFICE

LORD STRANG

'Admirably written, with clarity and wit; . . . all who take interest in foreign affairs will gain by learning how a skilled and devoted service defines its aims and methods.' *The Economist*.

'If the efficiency of the Foreign Service is a more vital national interest than ever before, it is a duty for every serious citizen to read carefully this comprehensive and deeply informative book.' *The Sunday Times*.

'Lord Strang and his collaborators have been eminently successful in producing, not without some dry humour, a human story and record, and not a dehydrated treatise.' *Quarterly Review*.

'. . . the Foreign Office, its methods of work, the methods of work of its various representatives abroad . . . for information on all those points there could be no better book. It is clear and accurate and yet remains very readable.' *The Glasgow Herald*.

Demy 8vo   *Second Impression*   18s *net*

THE NEW WHITEHALL SERIES

THE COLONIAL OFFICE
SIR CHARLES JEFFRIES

Recent decades have witnessed far-reaching changes in the work the Colonial Office has to perform and the ways in which its tasks are carried out. No longer is it mainly concerned with supervising the working of the dependent governments. It is today the headquarters of an all-out effort to develop the resources of the overseas territories and to free them from poverty, ignorance and other obstacles to their progress and welfare. Sir Charles Jeffries shows how this development has come about and how the Colonial Office is equipped to meet the changing needs of the territories; and describes the organization and work of the Office.

The book opens with a brief introduction describing in broad outline the work and tradition of the Office. It then proceeds to consider the nature of the responsibilities of the Secretary of State and of the Office and follows this description with a survey of the various territories for whose good government they are concerned. After showing how the Office has expanded and adapted its organization to meet the changing demands made on it, the book describes the main aspects of its work today. A concluding chapter takes stock of developments over the last thirty years and suggests some possible lines of future evolution.

'This accomplished sketch . . . is likely to be a useful guide for some time to come.' *Times Literary Supplement*.

'. . . detailed and factual yet extremely warm-hearted . . . Sir Charles's account, both historical and descriptive, is a most valuable survey.' *The Evening News*.

Demy 8vo   *Second Impression*   18s *net*

THE MINISTRY OF WORKS
SIR HAROLD EMMERSON

Under the most prosaic of titles the Ministry of Works hides a range and variety of functions of extraordinary fascination. The provision of official accommodation and furniture, the construction of buildings for scientific research, the organization of State ceremonies, the upkeep of the Royal Parks, and the care of ancient monuments all fall within its duties. The Ministry includes in its staff a great variety of professions and occupations.

Demy 8vo   15s *net*

GEORGE ALLEN & UNWIN LTD